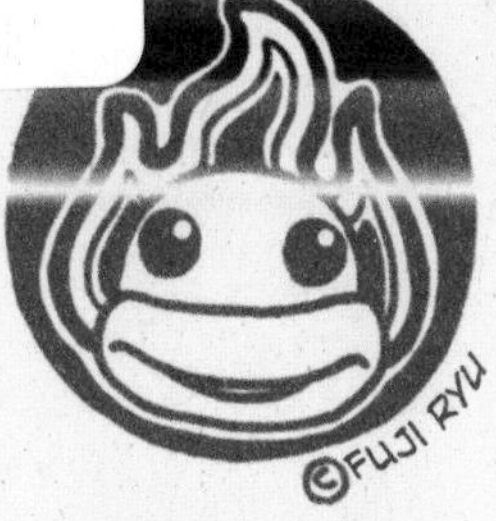
©FUJI RYU

藤崎　竜

Ryu Fujisaki

I do the coloring of the cover with my computer, but I lost the data and had to do it over again. Redoing it wore me out so much. I had used my New Year's vacation to work on it and got nothing for my troubles.

Ryu Fujisaki's *Worlds* came in second place for the prestigious 40th Tezuka Award. His *Psycho +*, *Wāqwāq* and *Hoshin Engi* have all run in *Weekly Shonen Jump* magazine, and the *Hoshin Engi* anime is available on DVD in Japan. A lover of science fiction, literature and history, Fujisaki has made his manga a mix of genres that truly showcases his amazing art and imagination.

Wāqwāq vol. 2
SHONEN JUMP Manga Edition

Story and Art by Ryu Fujisaki

Translation/Alexis Kirsch
Touch-up Art & Lettering/James Gaubatz
Design/Sean Lee
Editor/Joel Enos

VP, Production/Alvin Lu
VP, Publishing Licensing/Rika Inouye
VP, Sales & Product Marketing/Gonzalo Ferreyra
VP, Creative/Linda Espinosa
Publisher/Hyoe Narita

Printed in the U.S.A.

Published by VIZ Media, LLC
P.O. Box 77010
San Francisco, CA 94107

10 9 8 7 6 5 4 3 2 1
First printing, November 2009

www.viz.com

THE WORLD'S
MOST POPULAR MANGA

www.shonenjump.com

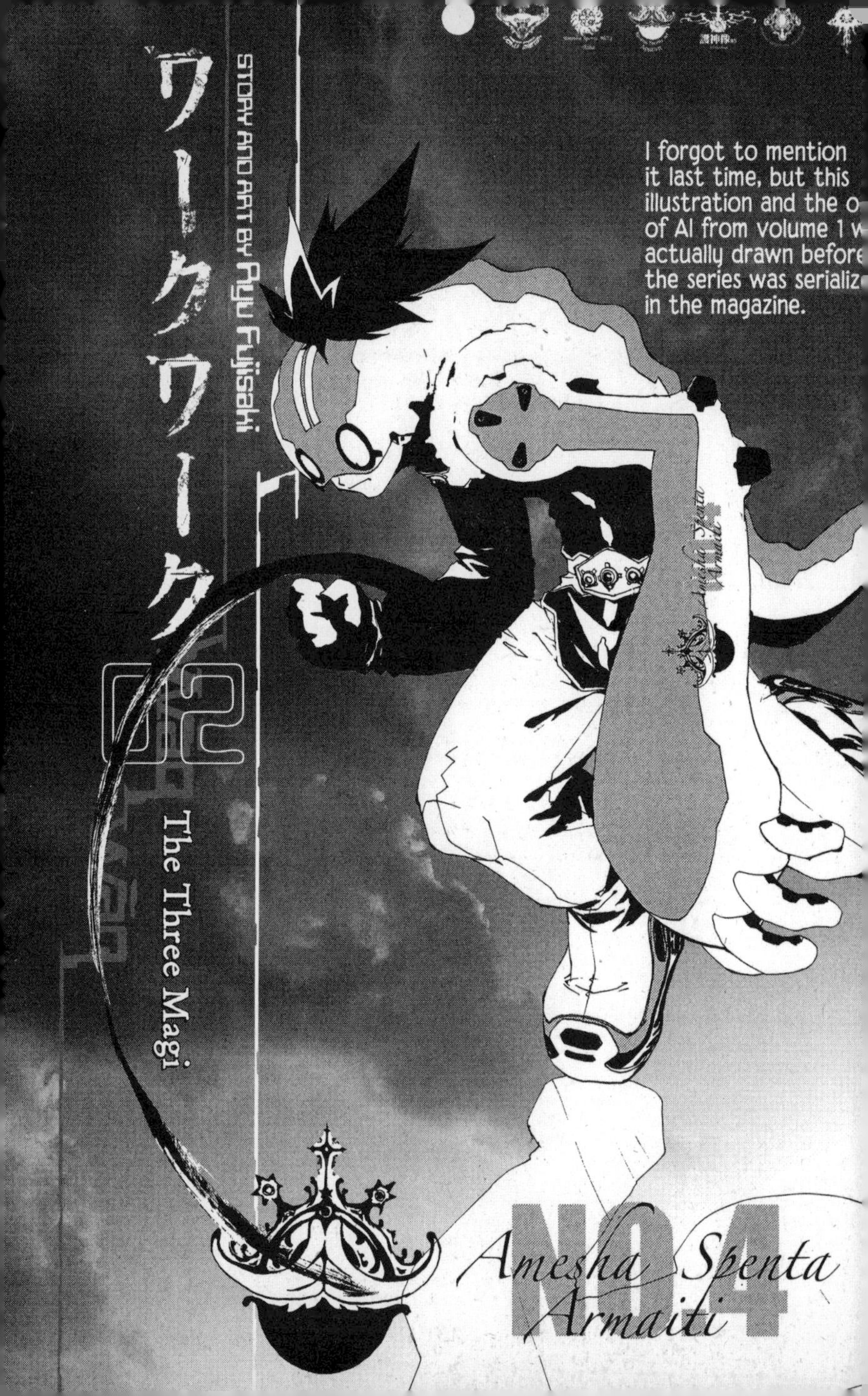

ワークワーク
STORY AND ART BY Ryu Fujisaki
02
The Three Magi
I forgot to mention
it last time, but this
illustration and the o
of AI from volume 1 w
actually drawn before
the series was serializ
in the magazine.
NO.4
Amesha Spenta
Armaiti

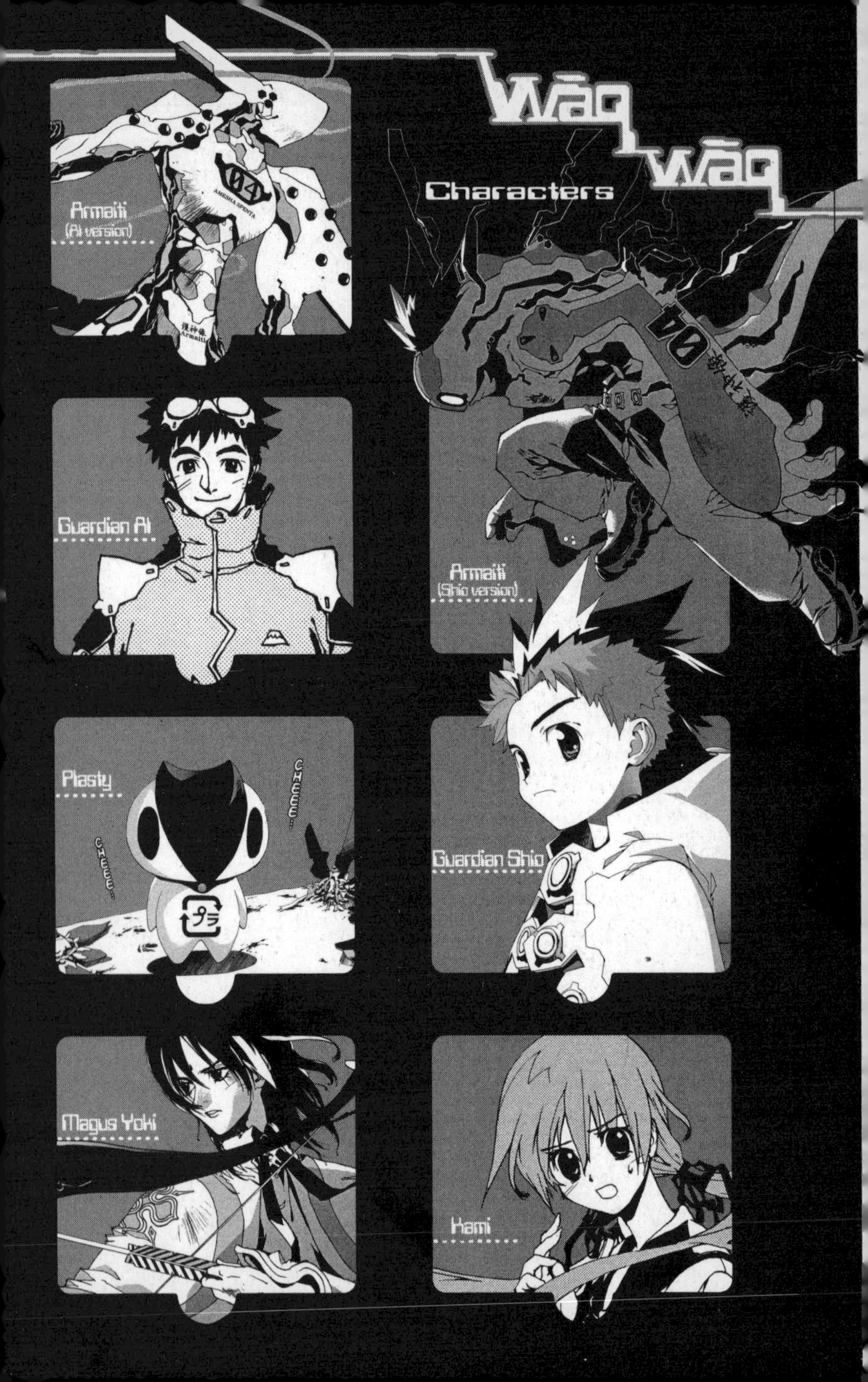
Wāq Wāq
Characters
Armaiti
(Ai version)
AMESHA SPENTA
04
Armaiti
(Shio version)
Guardian Ai
Guardian Shio
Plasty
CHEEE...
CHEEE...
Kami
Magus Yoki

Khshathra

Wāqwāq So Far

WELCOME TO A WORLD IN CHAOS! IN THE ULTIMATE BATTLE OF MAN VS. MACHINE, ALL HOPE LIES WITH A TEENAGE GIRL!

IN A WORLD IN CHAOS, WHERE THE LAST SURVIVING HUMANS OF THE BLACK-BLOOD RACE BAND TOGETHER IN SMALL MAKESHIFT TOWNS AND RELY ON THE GUARDIANS TO PROTECT THEM FROM THE MACHINES, YOUNG SHIO IS ATTACKED, AND HIS GUARDIAN FATHER, AL, IS KILLED. TO SAVE HIS OWN LIFE, SHIO BONDS HIMSELF TO HIS FATHER'S GOJIN-ZOU, THE MACHINE-WEAPON CALLED ARMAITI, TO BECOME A GUARDIAN HIMSELF.

IN THE AFTERMATH OF THE BATTLE, SHIO VOWS TO PROTECT A MYSTERIOUS RED-BLOOD GIRL HE BELIEVES IS THE KAMI, PROPHESIZED LONG AGO TO BE THE ONE TRUE SAVIOR OF THE PEOPLE OF WĀQWĀQ. SHIO AND KAMI JOURNEY TO SPIDER'S THREAD, LOCATED AT THE HEART OF THE WORLD OF WĀQWĀQ TO FIND OUT IF THE PROPHECY, WHICH SAYS THAT THE PROTECTOR OF THE KAMI WILL BE GRANTED ONE SINGLE WISH, IS TRUE. ALONG THE WAY, THEY ARE CONFRONTED BY THE GUARDIAN LEO, WHO WANTS HIS OWN WISH GRANTED...

Guardian Qaf

...THE KAMI!

Asha

Guardian Leo

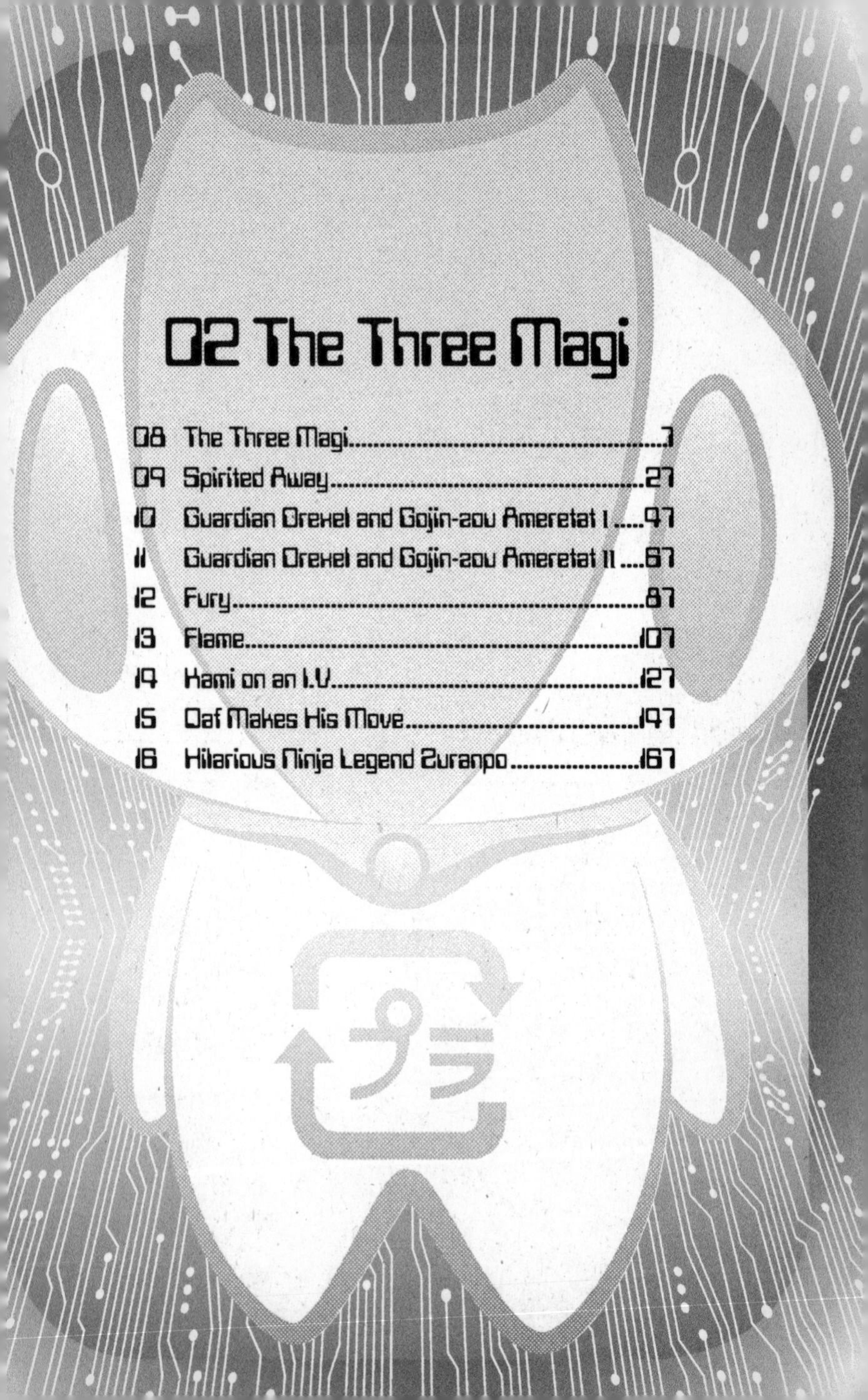

02 The Three Magi

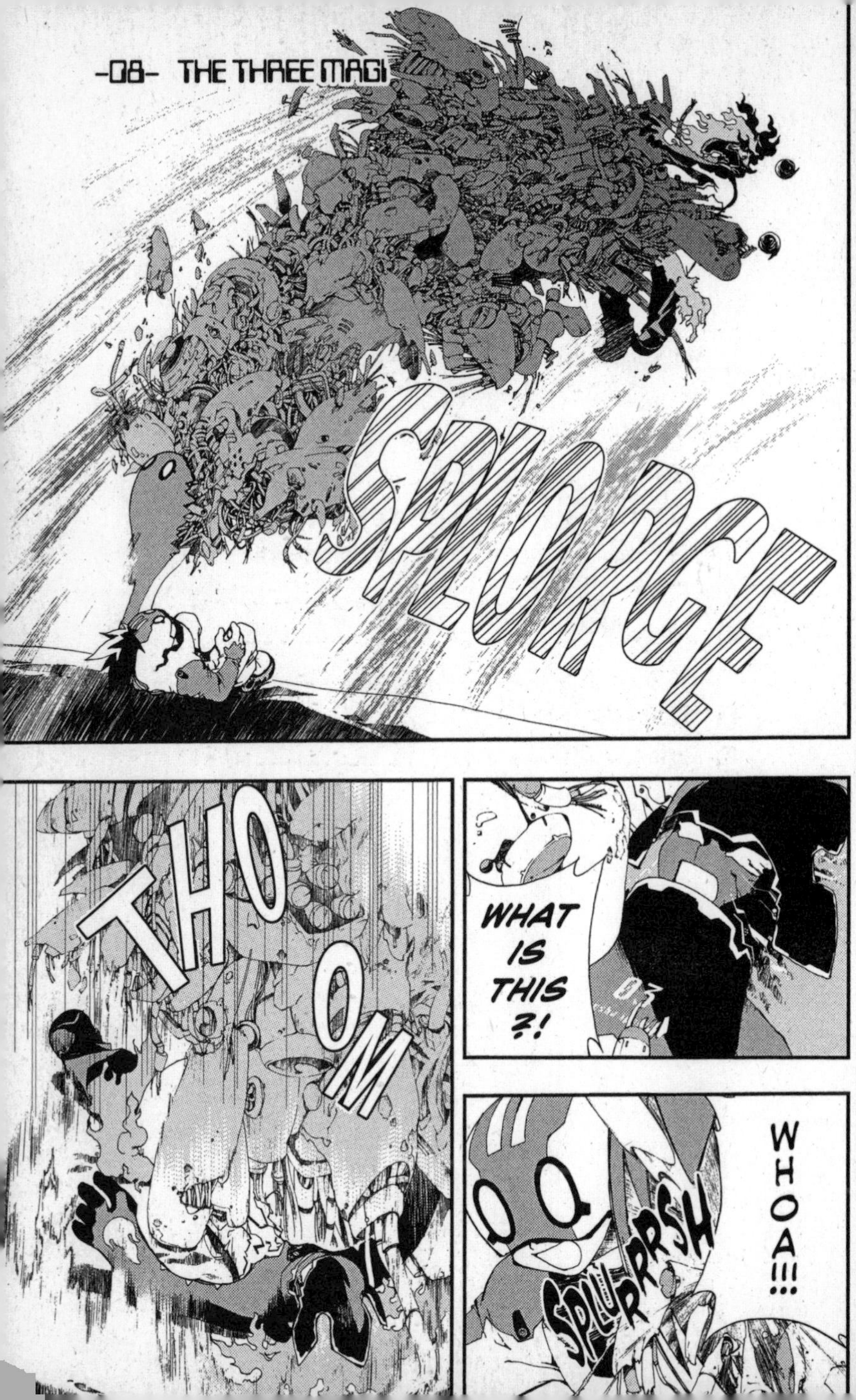
-08- THE THREE MAGI
WHAT IS THIS?!
WHOA!!!
SPLURRSH
THOOM

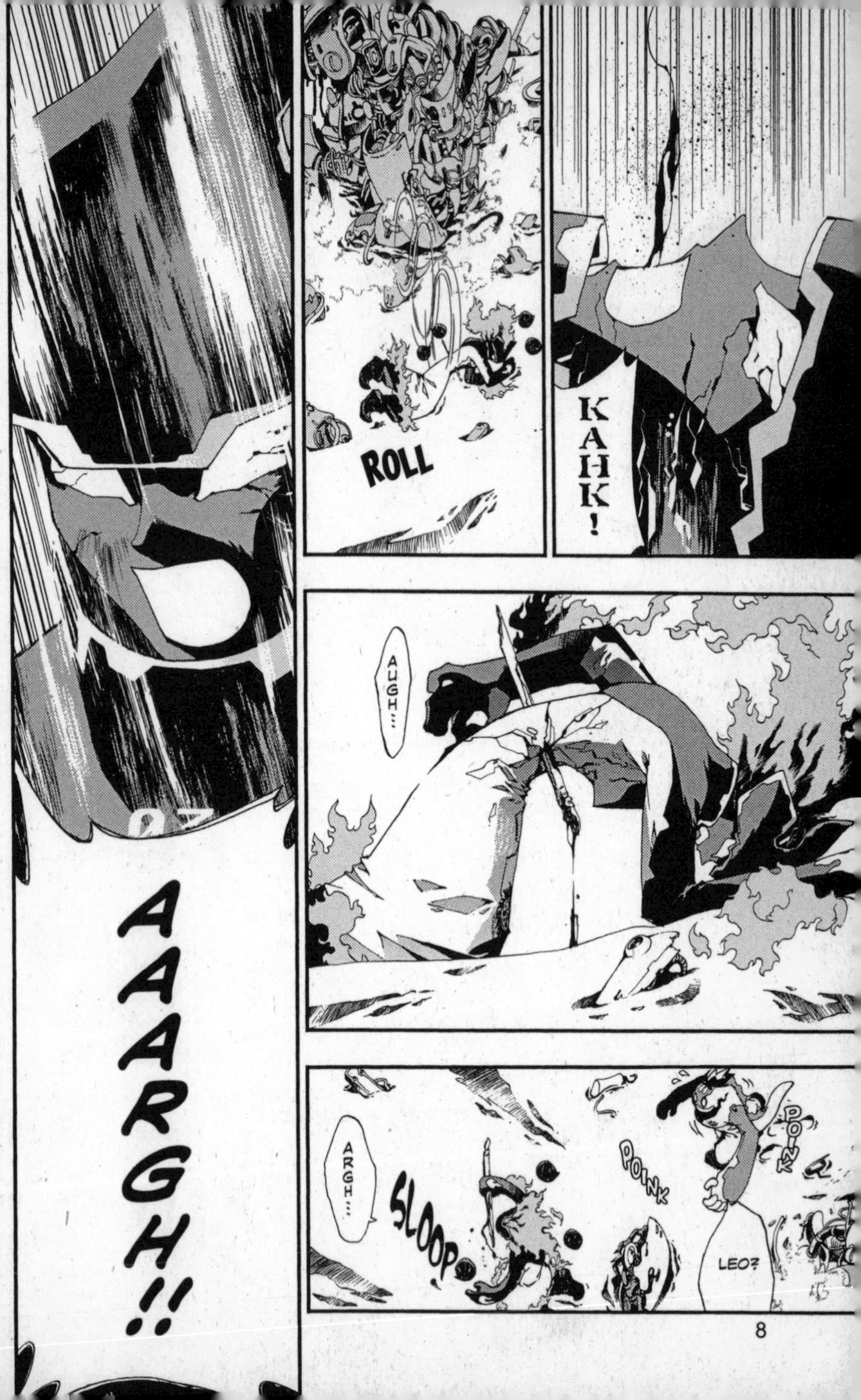
KAHHK!
ROLL
AUGH...
POINK
POINK
LEO?
SLOOP
ARGH...
AAAARGH!!

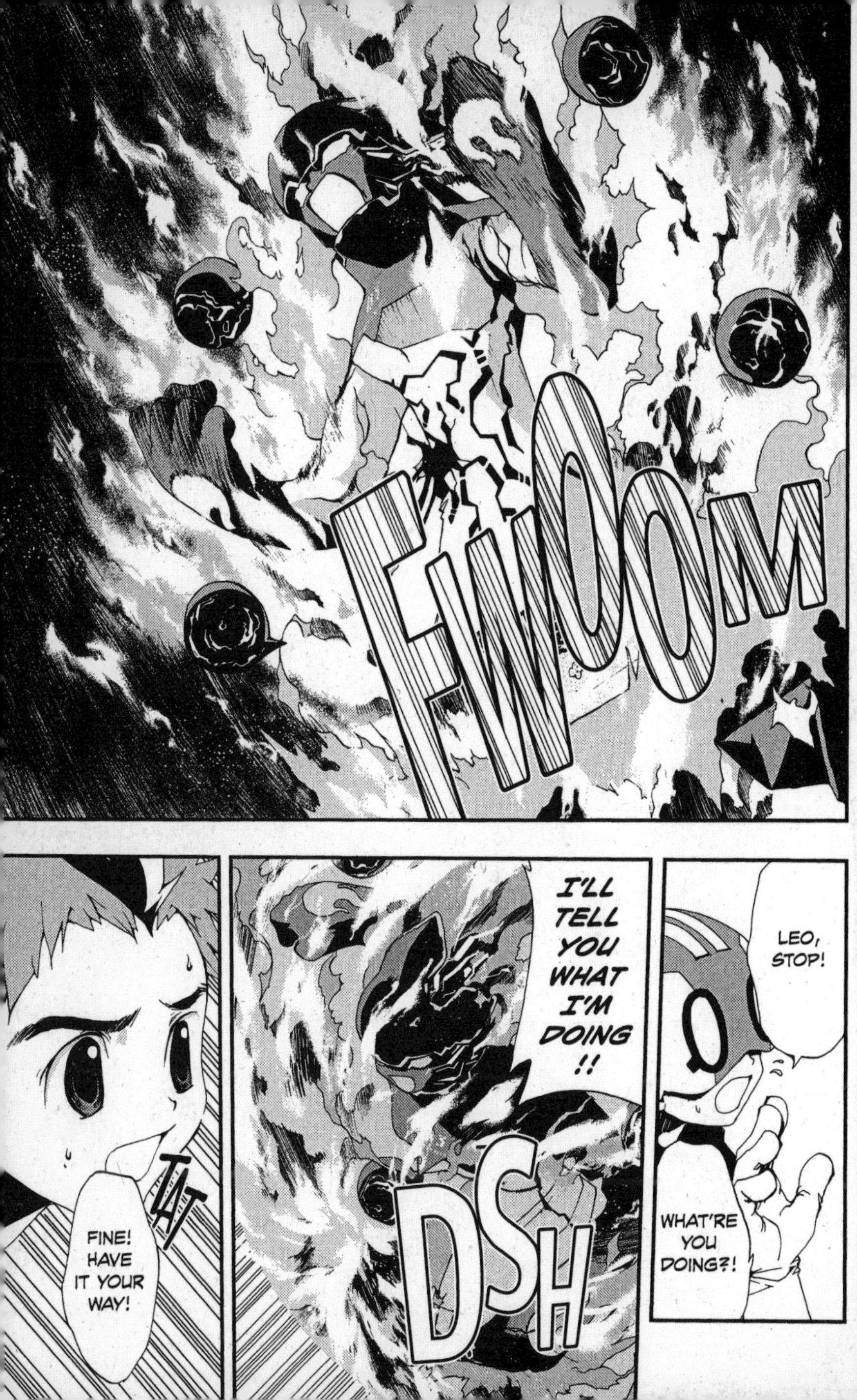
FWOOM
LEO, STOP!
WHAT'RE YOU DOING?!
I'LL TELL YOU WHAT I'M DOING!!
DSH
TAT
FINE! HAVE IT YOUR WAY!

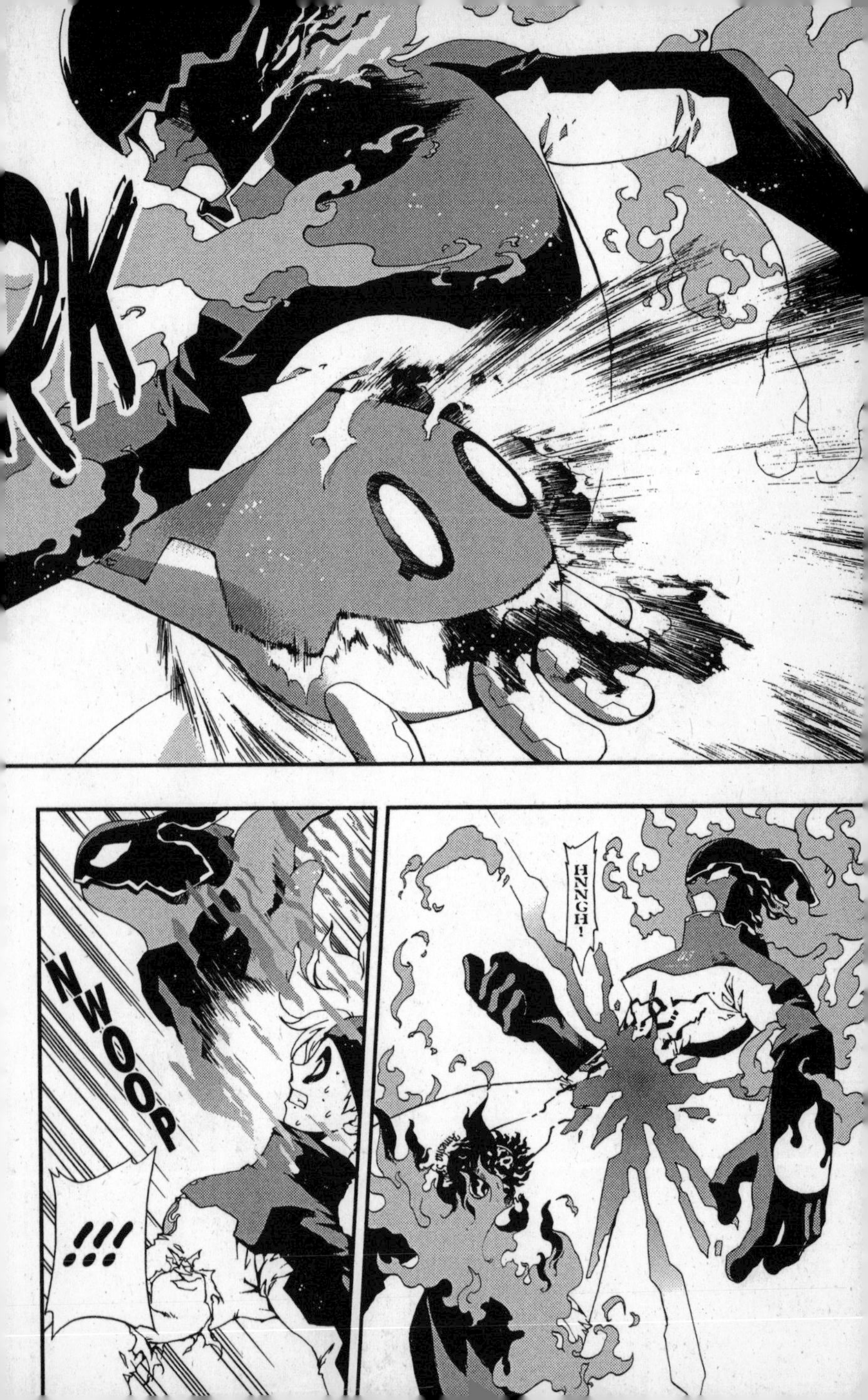
RK
HNNGH!
NWOOP
!!!

-08- THE THREE MAGI

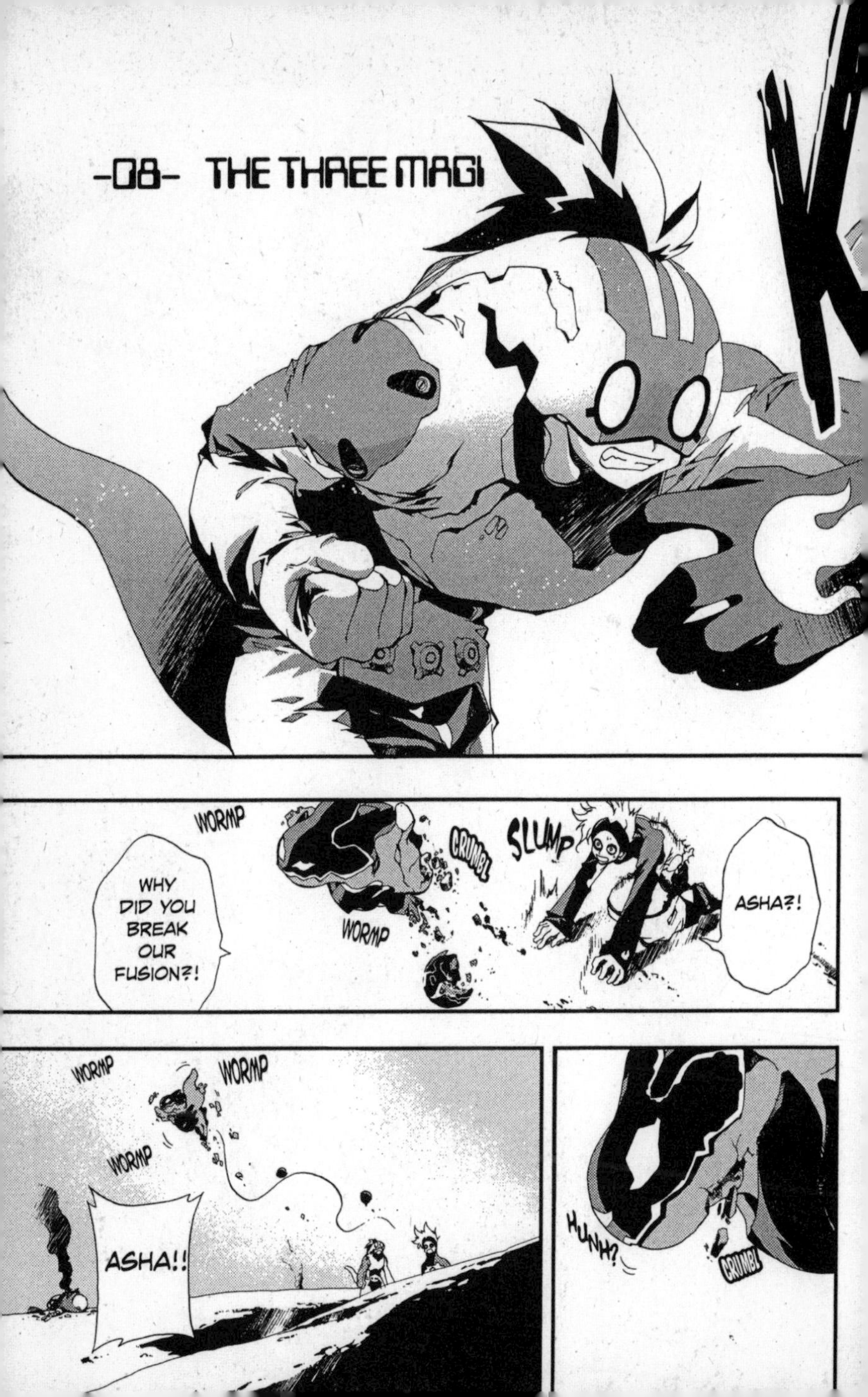
ASHA?!
SLUMP
CRUMBL
WORMP
WORMP
WHY DID YOU BREAK OUR FUSION?!
HUNH?
CRUMBL
WORMP
WORMP
WORMP
ASHA!!

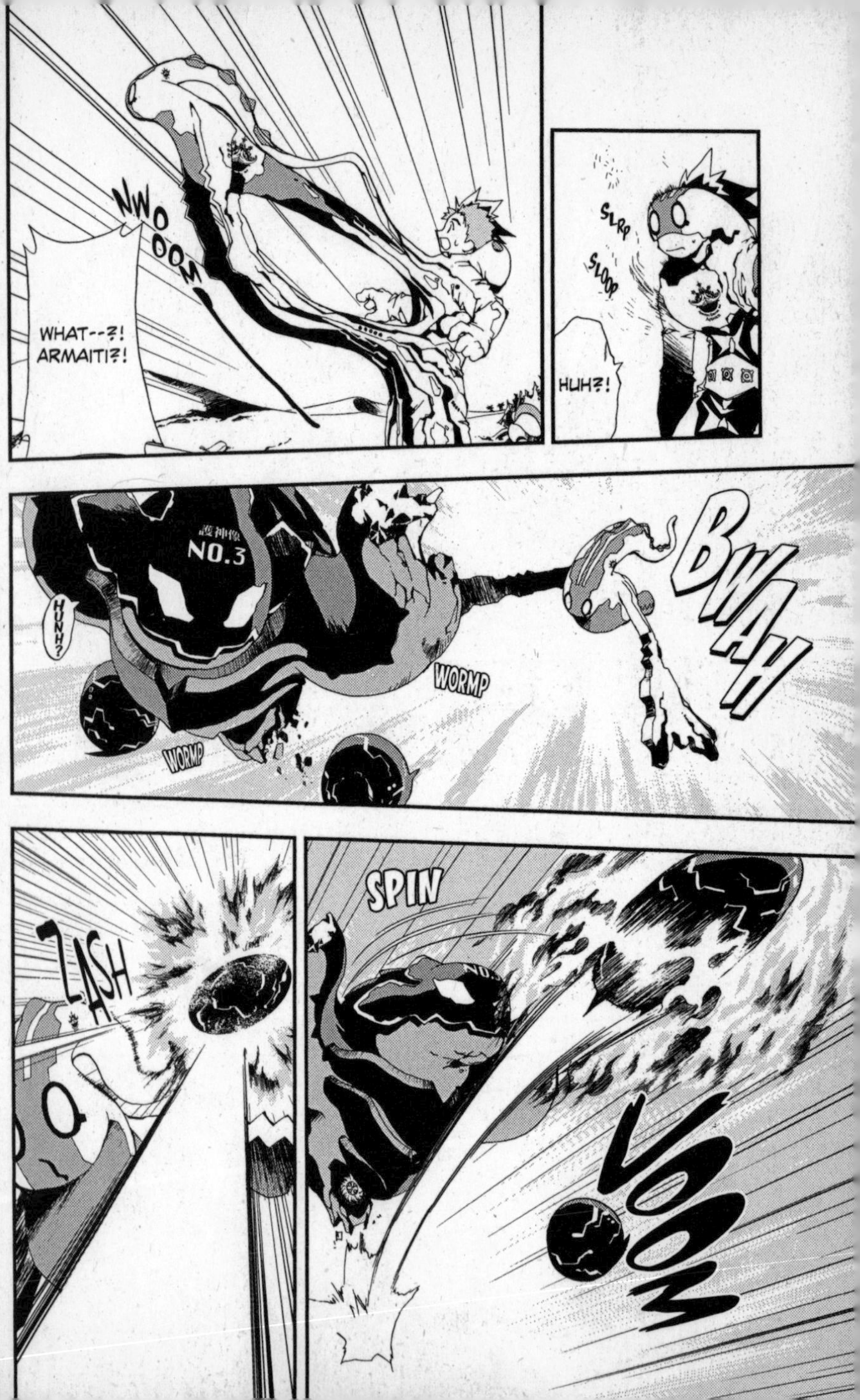
SLRP
SLOOP
HUH?!
NWOOOM
WHAT--?!
ARMAITI?!
BWAH
護神像
NO.3
HUNH?
WORMP
WORMP
SPIN
VOOM
ZASH

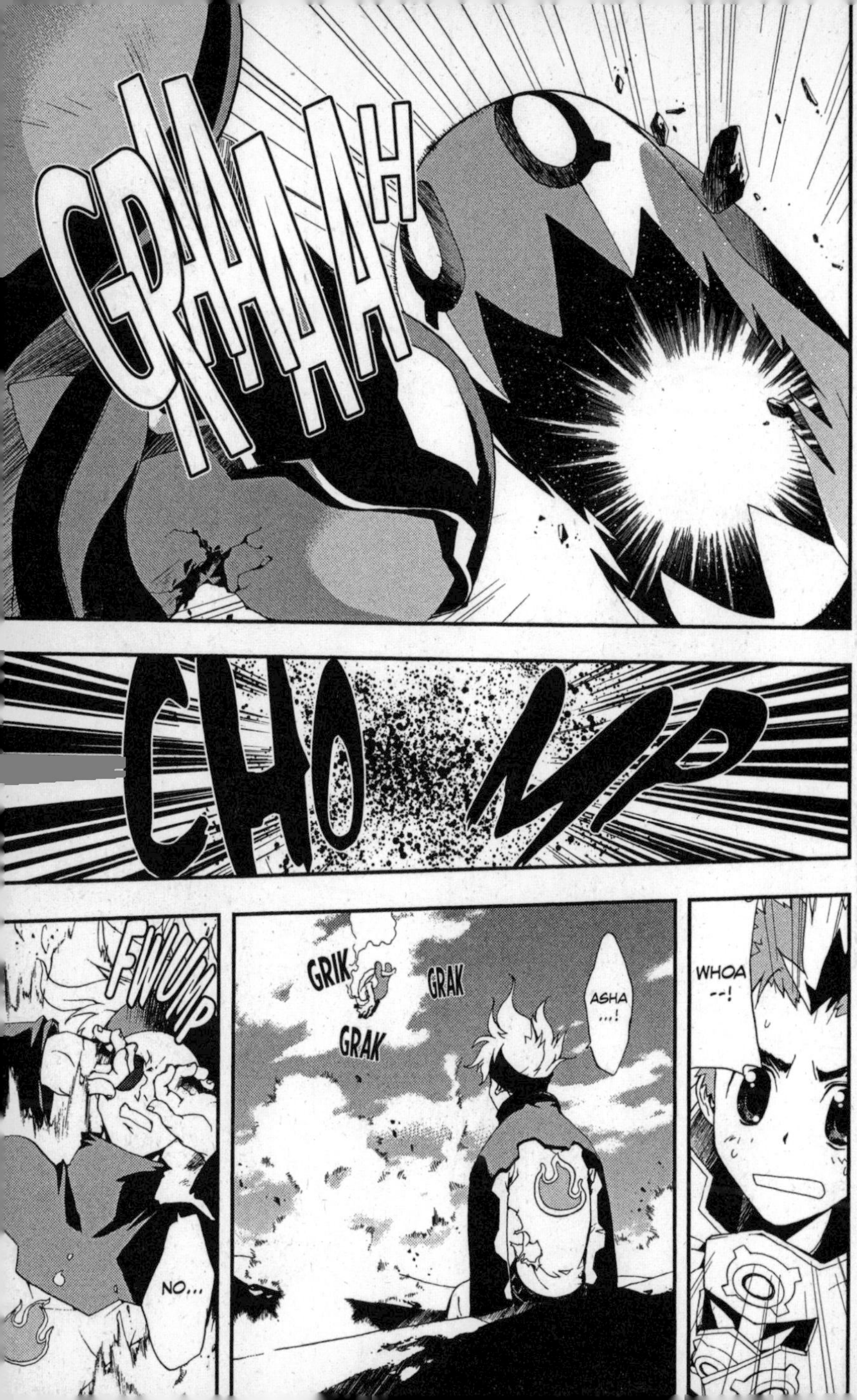
GRHAAAH
CHOMP
WHOA --!
ASHA ...!
GRIK
GRAK
GRAK
FWUMP
NO...

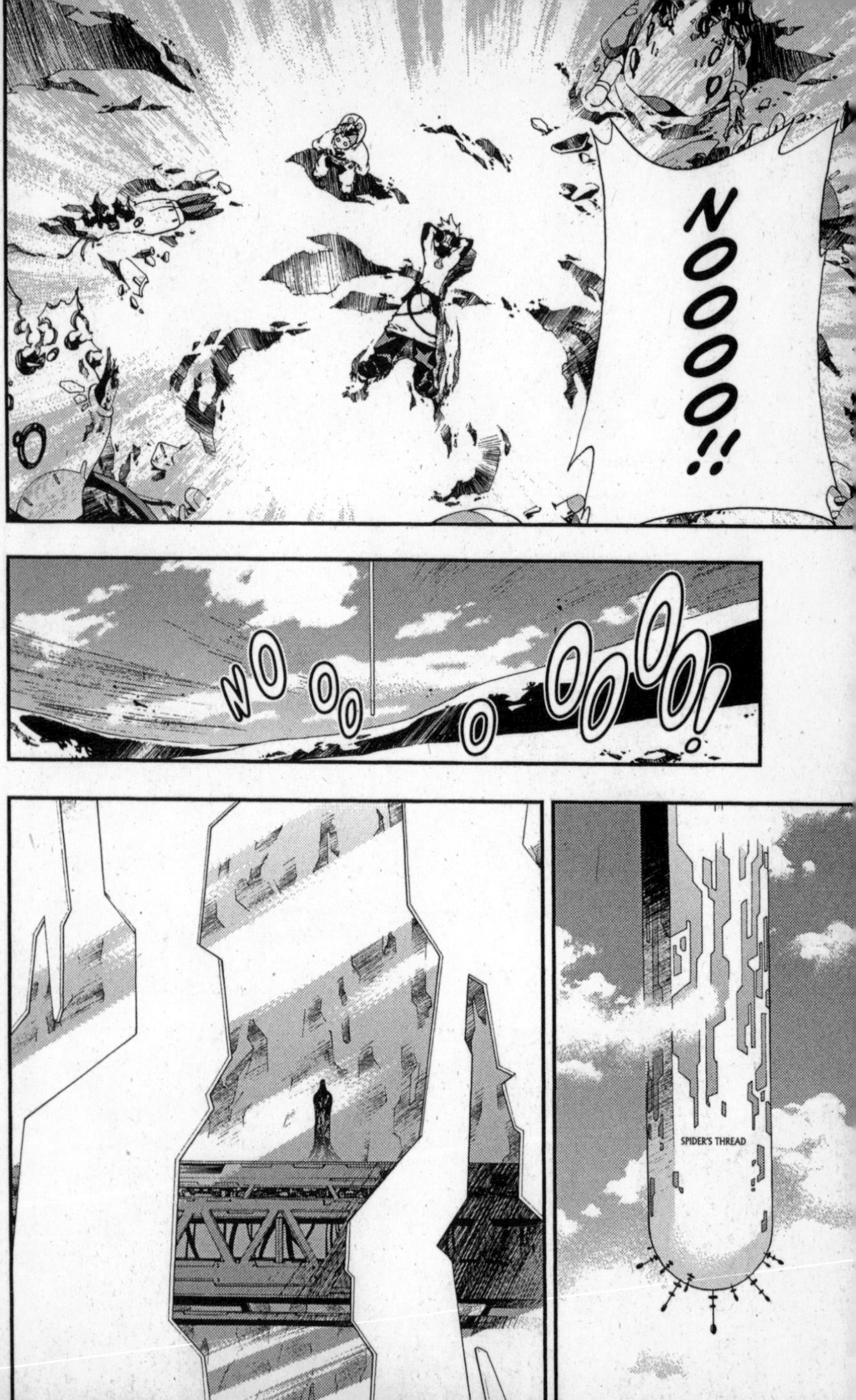
NOOOOO!!
NOOOOOOOOO!
SPIDER'S THREAD

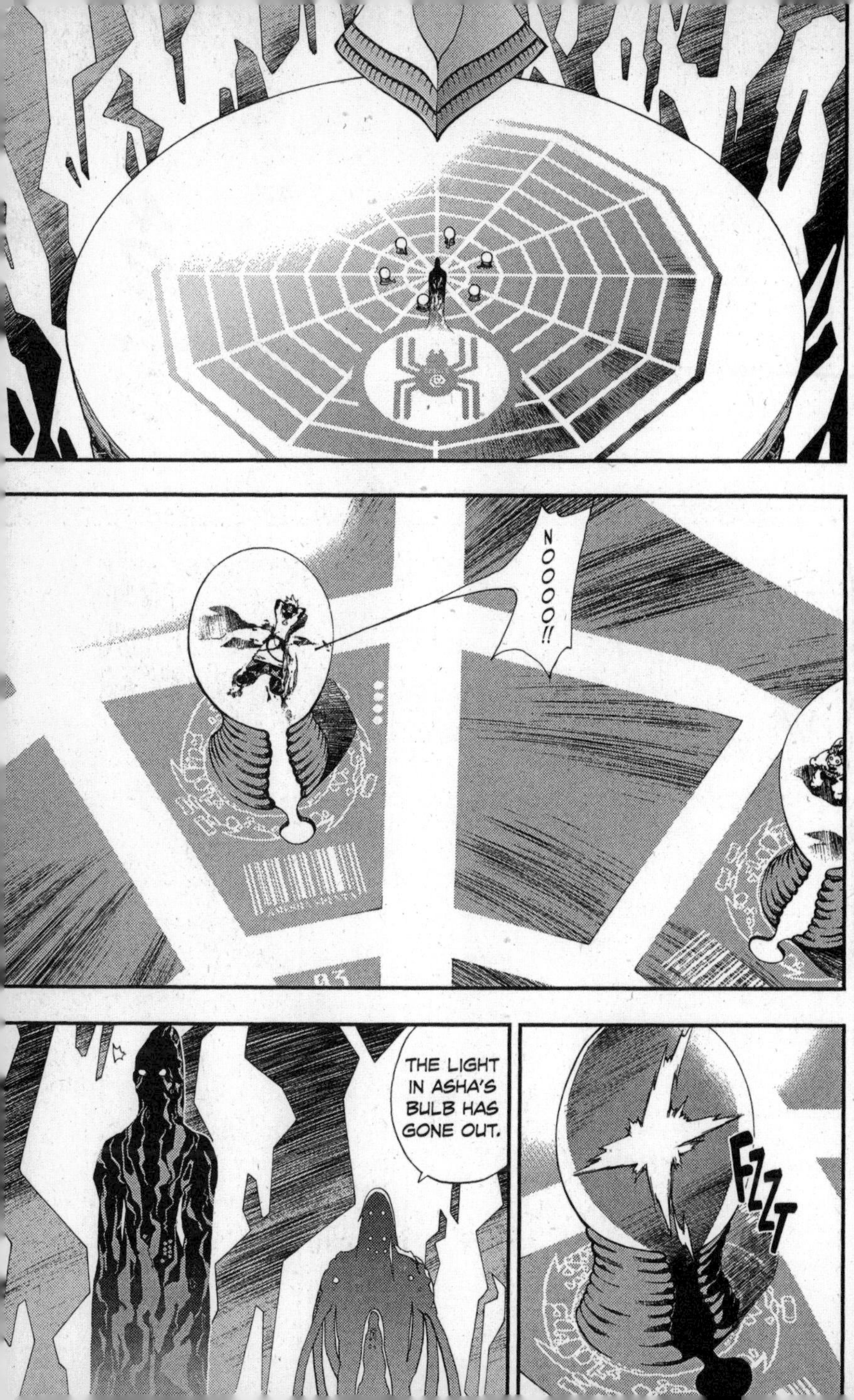
NOOOO!!
FZZT
THE LIGHT IN ASHA'S BULB HAS GONE OUT.

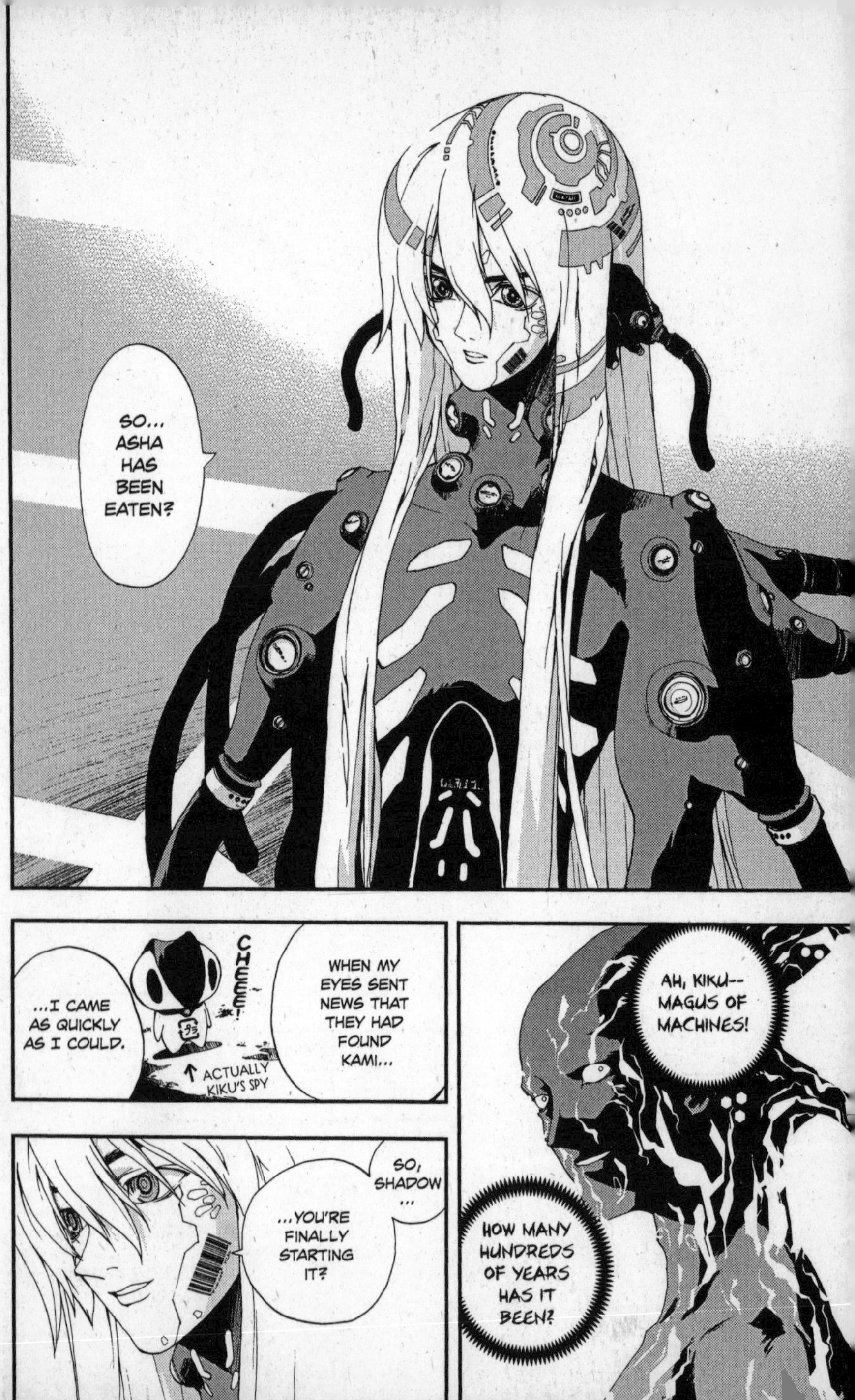
SO... ASHA HAS BEEN EATEN?
AH, KIKU-- MAGUS OF MACHINES!
HOW MANY HUNDREDS OF YEARS HAS IT BEEN?
WHEN MY EYES SENT NEWS THAT THEY HAD FOUND KAMI...
CHEEEE!
...I CAME AS QUICKLY AS I COULD.
↑ ACTUALLY KIKU'S SPY
SO, SHADOW...
...YOU'RE FINALLY STARTING IT?

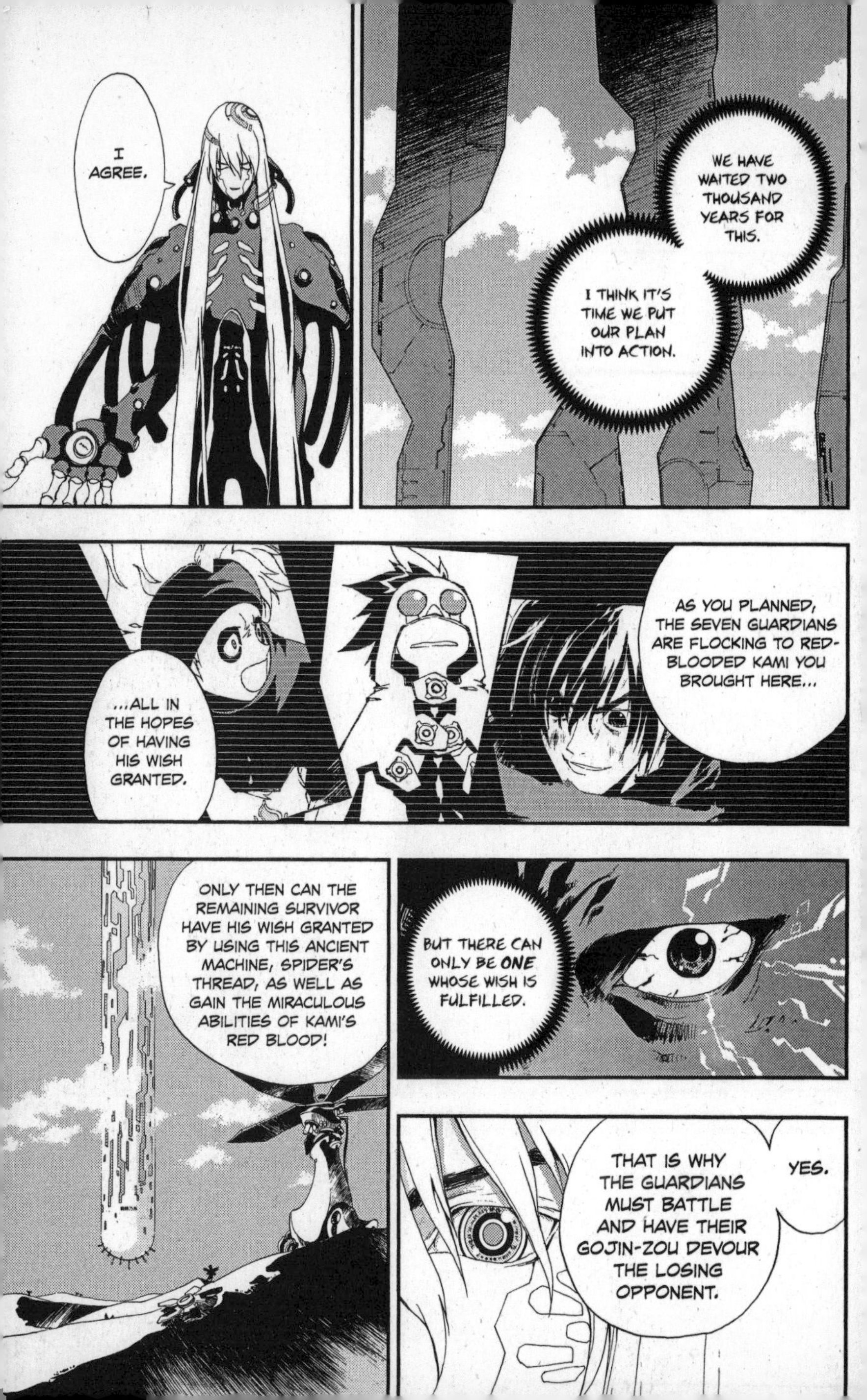
WE HAVE WAITED TWO THOUSAND YEARS FOR THIS.
I THINK IT'S TIME WE PUT OUR PLAN INTO ACTION.
I AGREE.
AS YOU PLANNED, THE SEVEN GUARDIANS ARE FLOCKING TO RED-BLOODED KAMI YOU BROUGHT HERE...
...ALL IN THE HOPES OF HAVING HIS WISH GRANTED.
BUT THERE CAN ONLY BE *ONE* WHOSE WISH IS FULFILLED.
YES.
THAT IS WHY THE GUARDIANS MUST BATTLE AND HAVE THEIR GOJIN-ZOU DEVOUR THE LOSING OPPONENT.
ONLY THEN CAN THE REMAINING SURVIVOR HAVE HIS WISH GRANTED BY USING THIS ANCIENT MACHINE, SPIDER'S THREAD, AS WELL AS GAIN THE MIRACULOUS ABILITIES OF KAMI'S RED BLOOD!

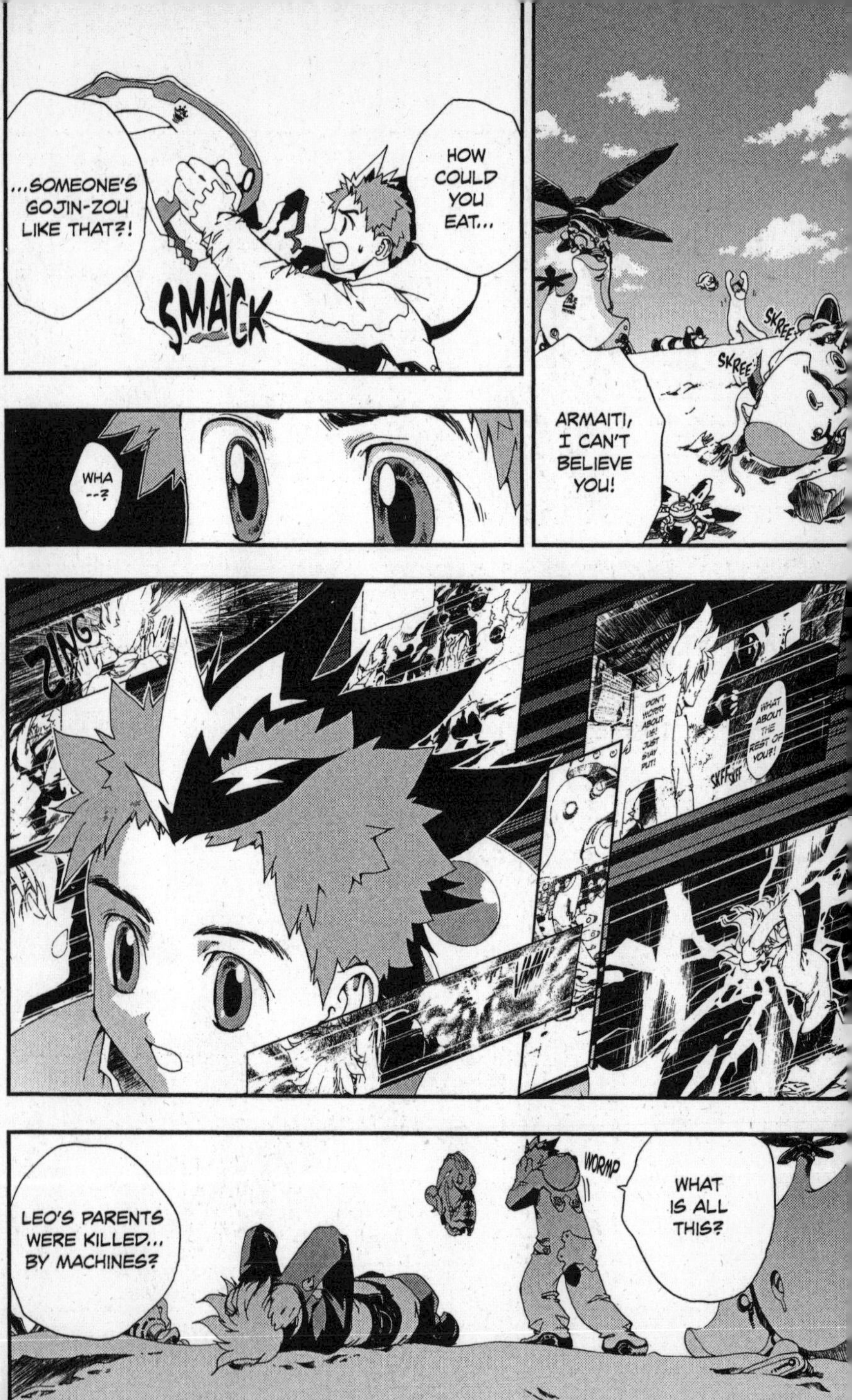
SKREE
SKREE
ARMAITI, I CAN'T BELIEVE YOU!
HOW COULD YOU EAT...
...SOMEONE'S GOJIN-ZOU LIKE THAT?!
SMACK
WHA--?
ZING
WHAT ABOUT THE REST OF YOU?!
SKFF SKFF
DON'T WORRY ABOUT US! JUST STAY PUT!
WHAT IS ALL THIS?
WORMP
LEO'S PARENTS WERE KILLED... BY MACHINES?

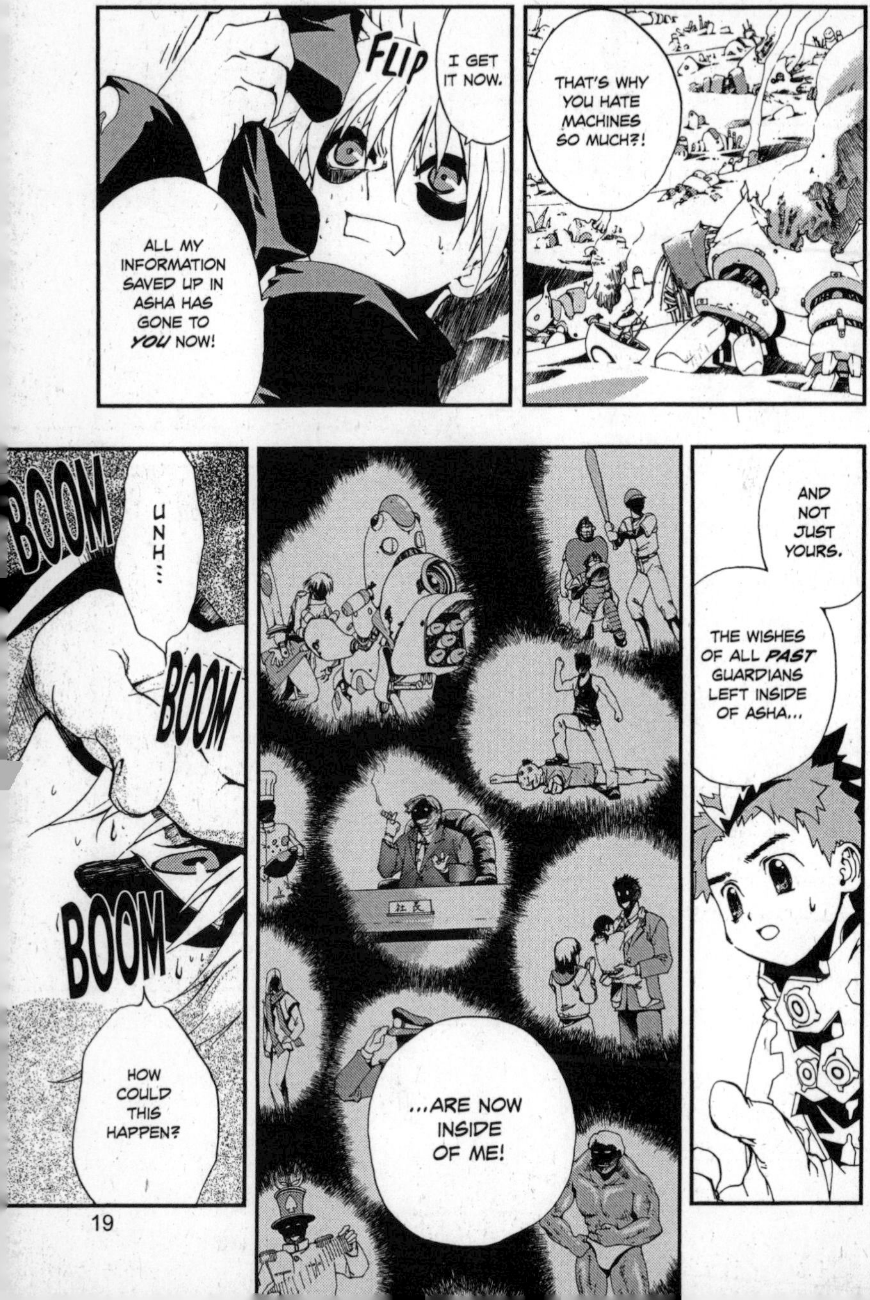
THAT'S WHY YOU HATE MACHINES SO MUCH?!
FLIP
I GET IT NOW.
ALL MY INFORMATION SAVED UP IN ASHA HAS GONE TO *YOU* NOW!
AND NOT JUST YOURS.
THE WISHES OF ALL *PAST* GUARDIANS LEFT INSIDE OF ASHA...
...ARE NOW INSIDE OF ME!
UNH...
BOOM
BOOM
BOOM
HOW COULD THIS HAPPEN?

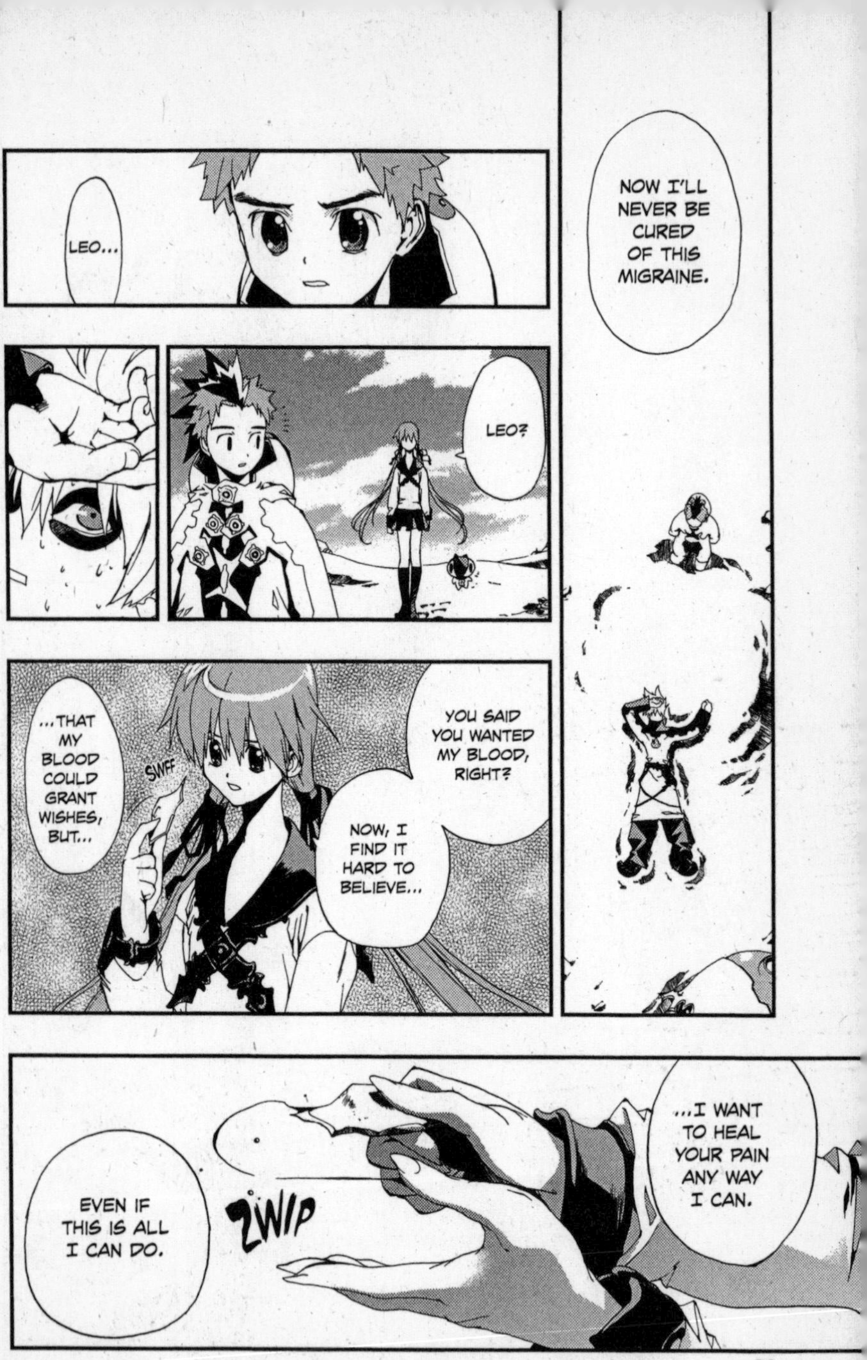
NOW I'LL NEVER BE CURED OF THIS MIGRAINE.
LEO...
LEO?
YOU SAID YOU WANTED MY BLOOD, RIGHT?
NOW, I FIND IT HARD TO BELIEVE...
...THAT MY BLOOD COULD GRANT WISHES, BUT...
SWFF
...I WANT TO HEAL YOUR PAIN ANY WAY I CAN.
ZWIP
EVEN IF THIS IS ALL I CAN DO.

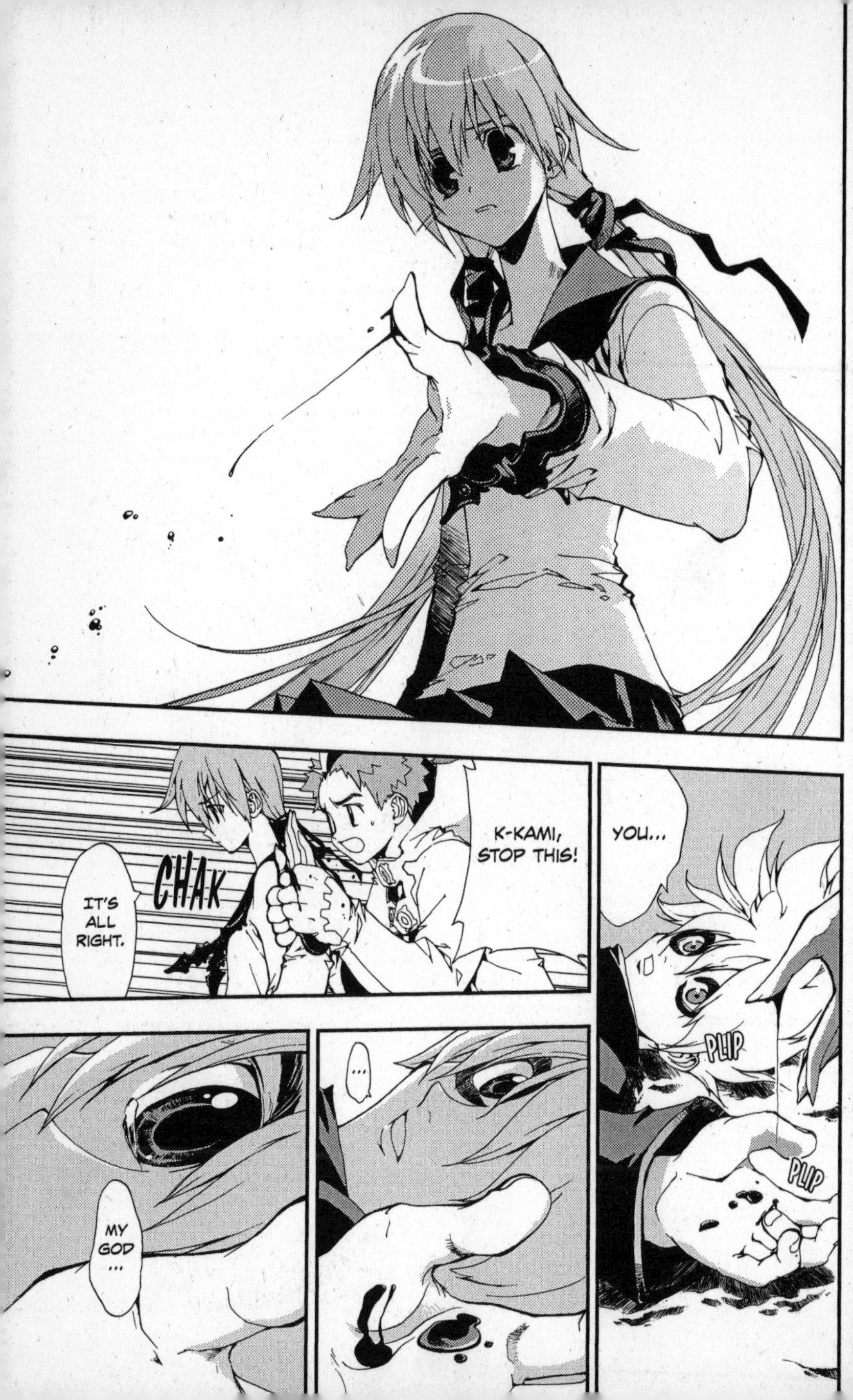
YOU...
PLIP
PLIP
K-KAMI, STOP THIS!
CHAK
IT'S ALL RIGHT.
...
MY GOD ...

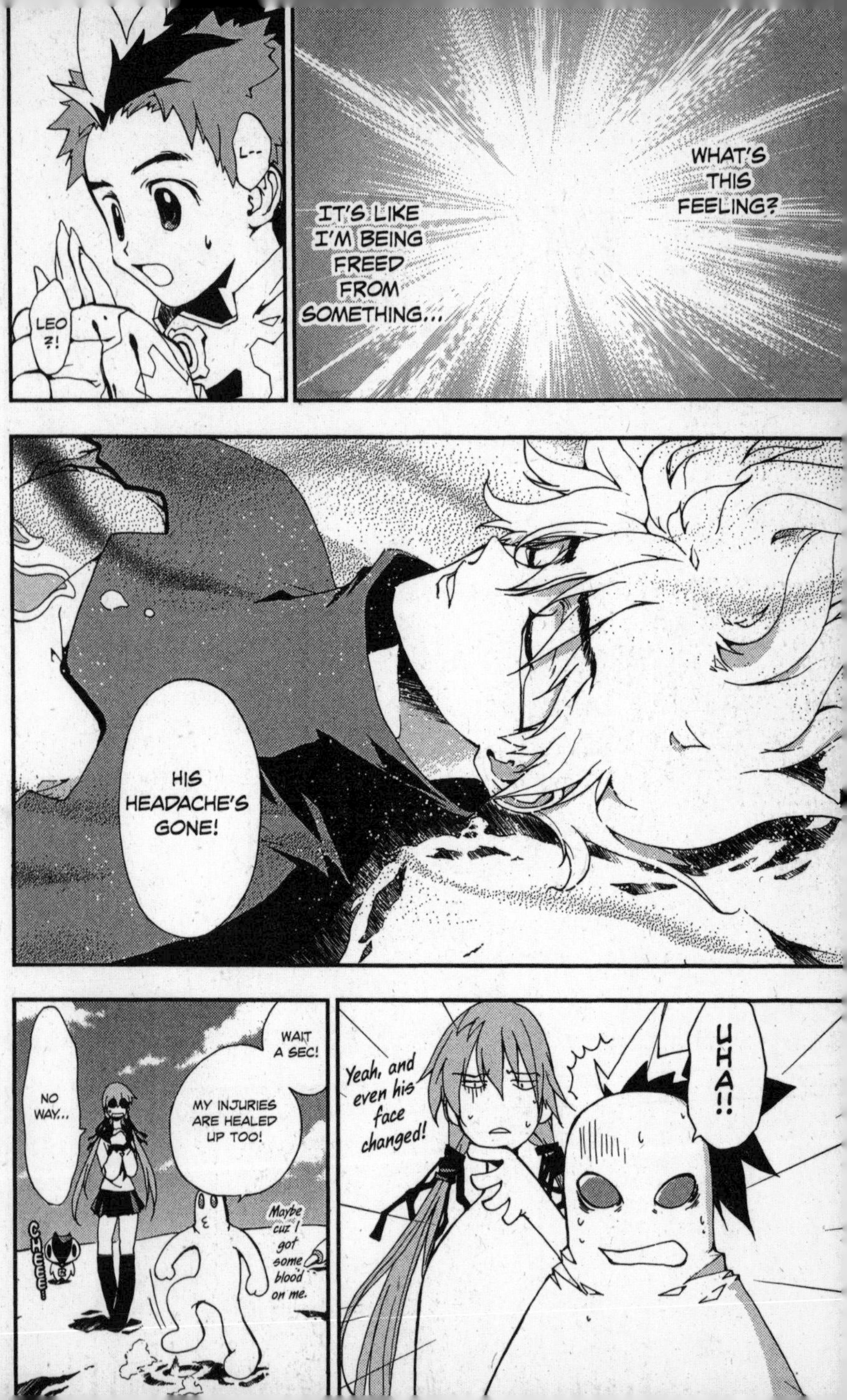
WHAT'S THIS FEELING?
IT'S LIKE I'M BEING FREED FROM SOMETHING...
L--
LEO ?!
HIS HEADACHE'S GONE!
UHA!!
Yeah, and even his face changed!
WAIT A SEC!
MY INJURIES ARE HEALED UP TOO!
NO WAY...
Maybe cuz I got some blood on me.
CHEEE!

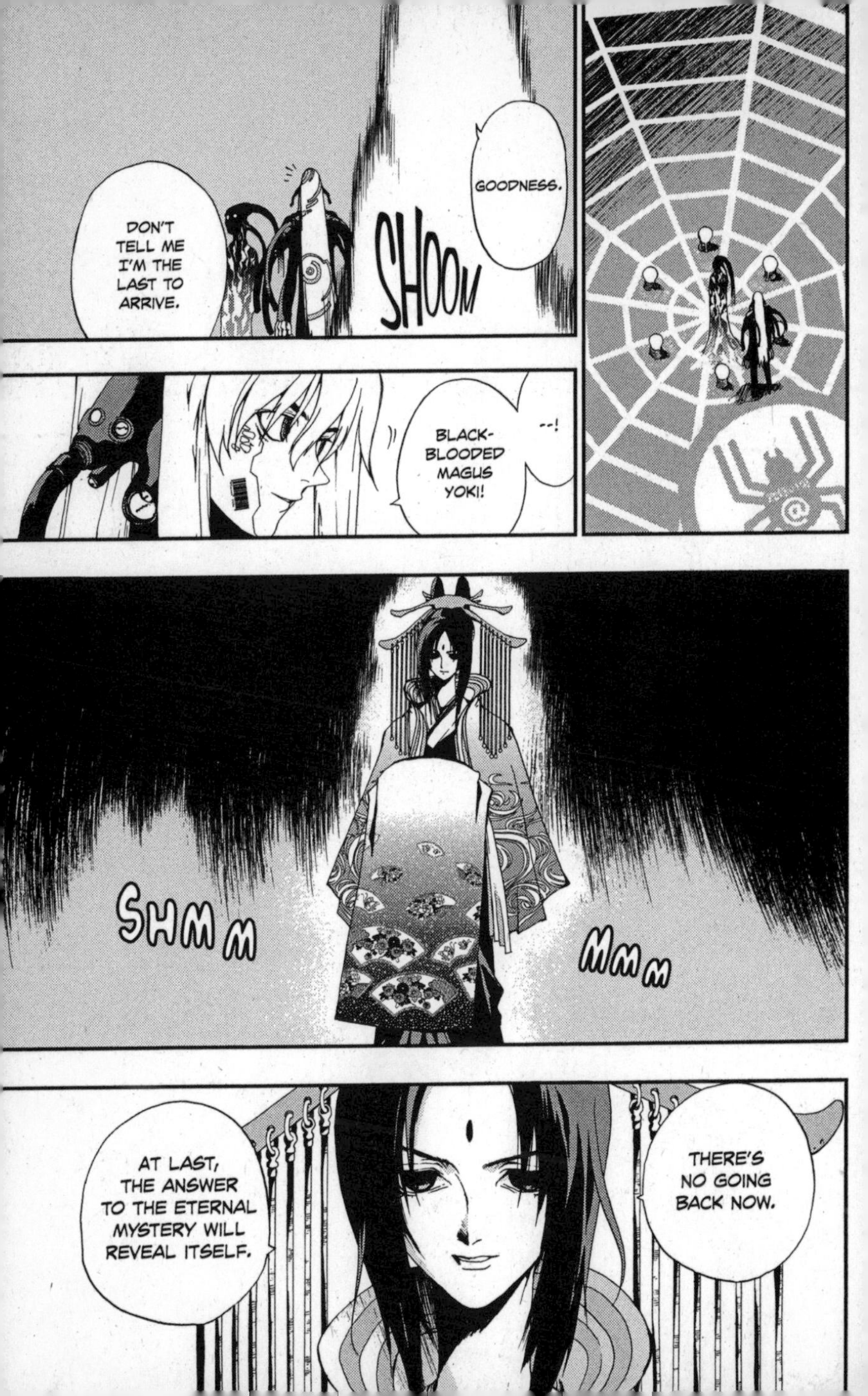
GOODNESS.
SHOOM
DON'T TELL ME I'M THE LAST TO ARRIVE.
--!
BLACK-BLOODED MAGUS YOKI!
SHMMM
MMMM
THERE'S NO GOING BACK NOW.
AT LAST, THE ANSWER TO THE ETERNAL MYSTERY WILL REVEAL ITSELF.

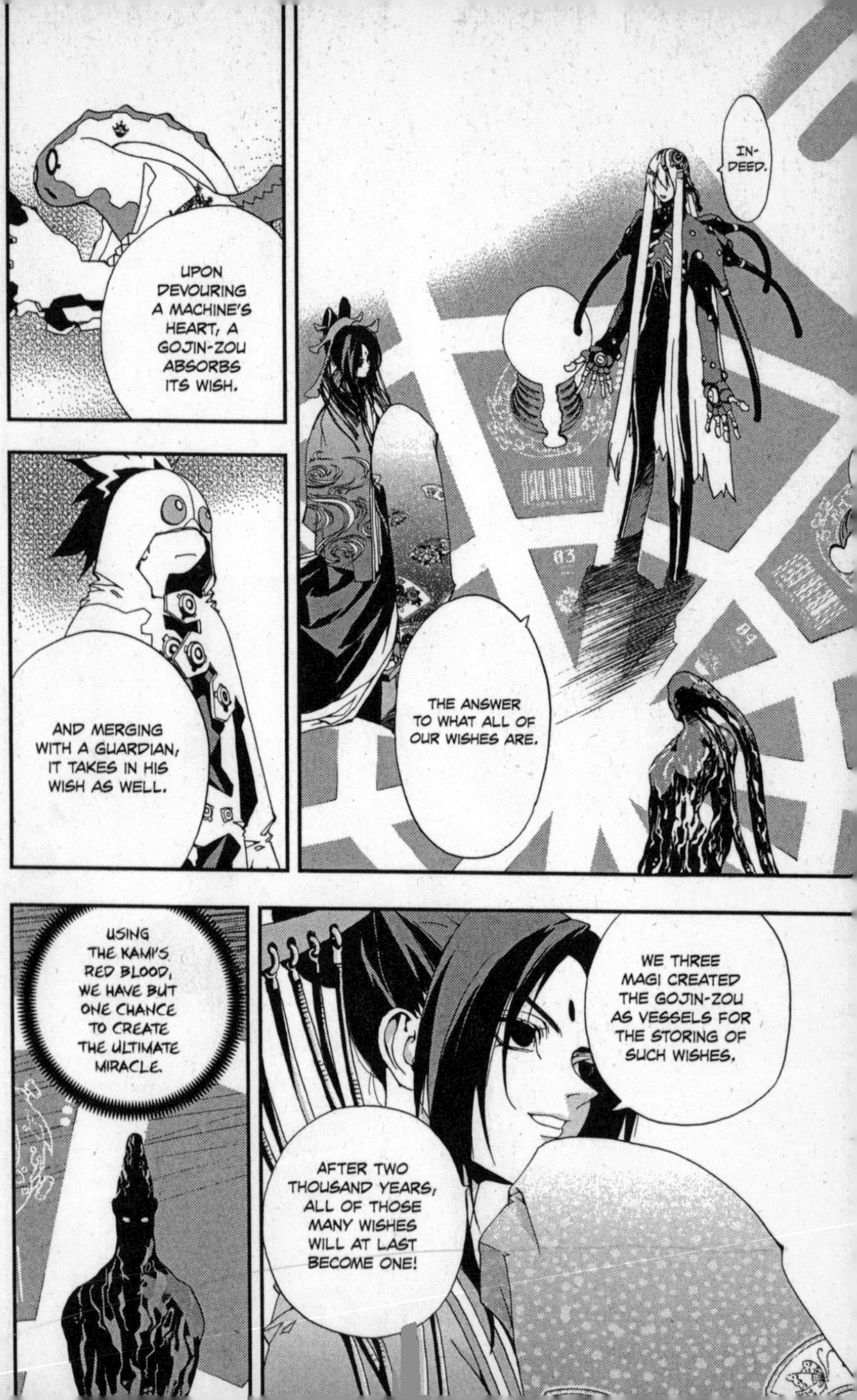
IN-DEED.
THE ANSWER TO WHAT ALL OF OUR WISHES ARE.
UPON DEVOURING A MACHINE'S HEART, A GOJIN-ZOU ABSORBS ITS WISH.
AND MERGING WITH A GUARDIAN, IT TAKES IN HIS WISH AS WELL.
WE THREE MAGI CREATED THE GOJIN-ZOU AS VESSELS FOR THE STORING OF SUCH WISHES.
AFTER TWO THOUSAND YEARS, ALL OF THOSE MANY WISHES WILL AT LAST BECOME ONE!
USING THE KAMI'S RED BLOOD, WE HAVE BUT ONE CHANCE TO CREATE THE ULTIMATE MIRACLE.

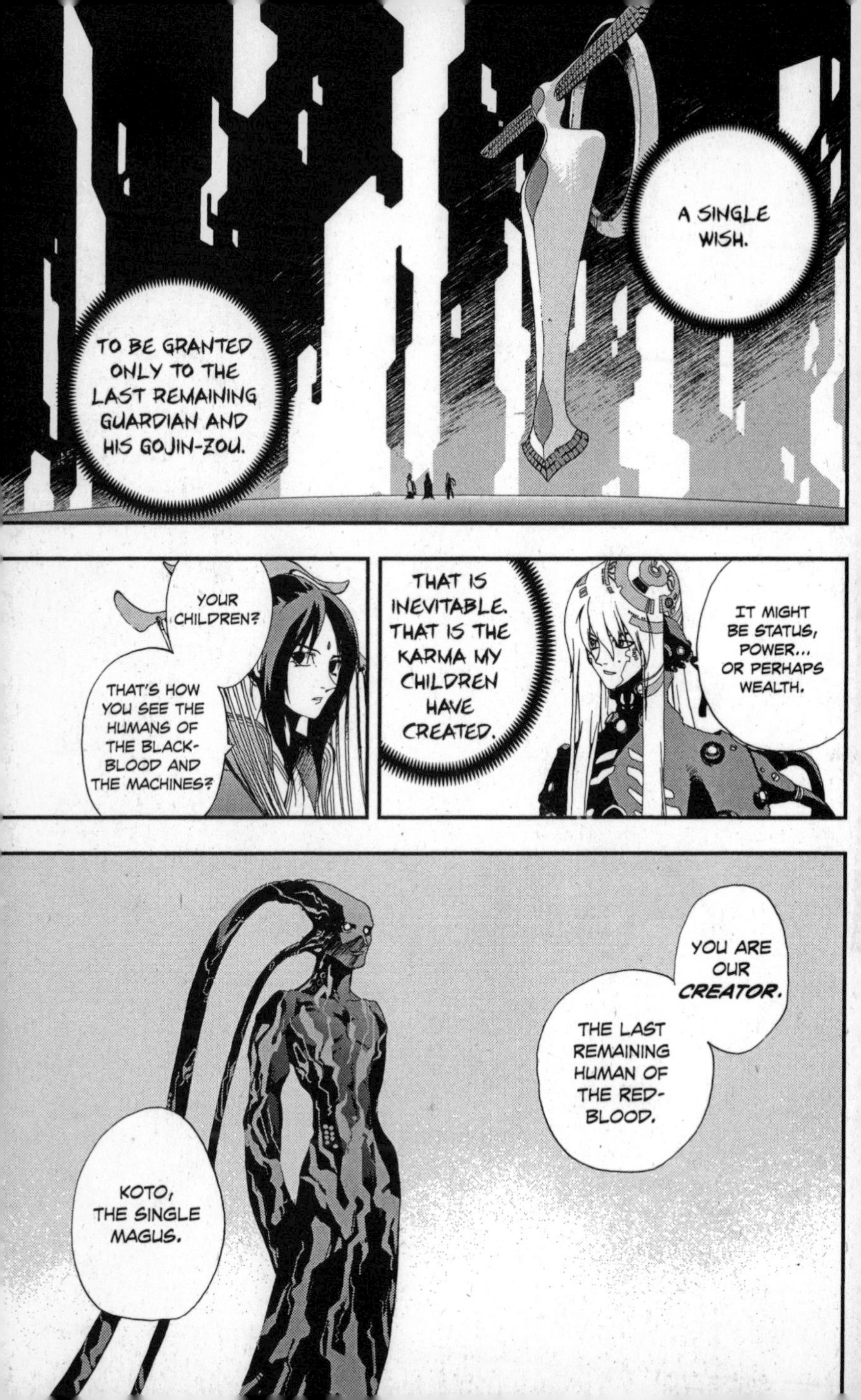
A SINGLE WISH.
TO BE GRANTED ONLY TO THE LAST REMAINING GUARDIAN AND HIS GOJIN-ZOU.
IT MIGHT BE STATUS, POWER... OR PERHAPS WEALTH.
THAT IS INEVITABLE. THAT IS THE KARMA MY CHILDREN HAVE CREATED.
YOUR CHILDREN?
THAT'S HOW YOU SEE THE HUMANS OF THE BLACK-BLOOD AND THE MACHINES?
YOU ARE OUR **CREATOR**.
THE LAST REMAINING HUMAN OF THE RED-BLOOD.
KOTO, THE SINGLE MAGUS.

WaqWaq

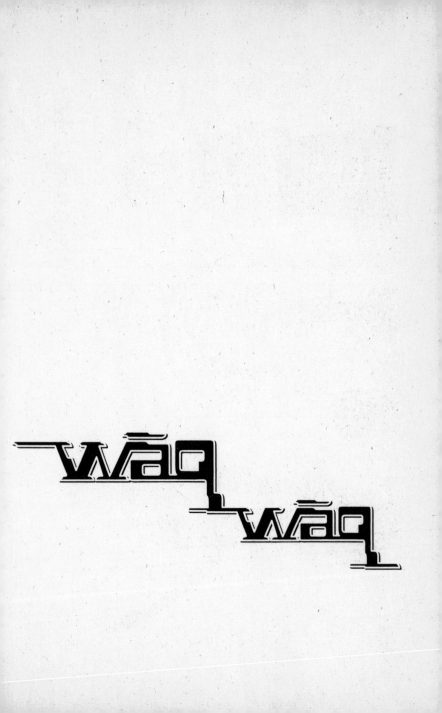

-09- SPIRITED AWAY

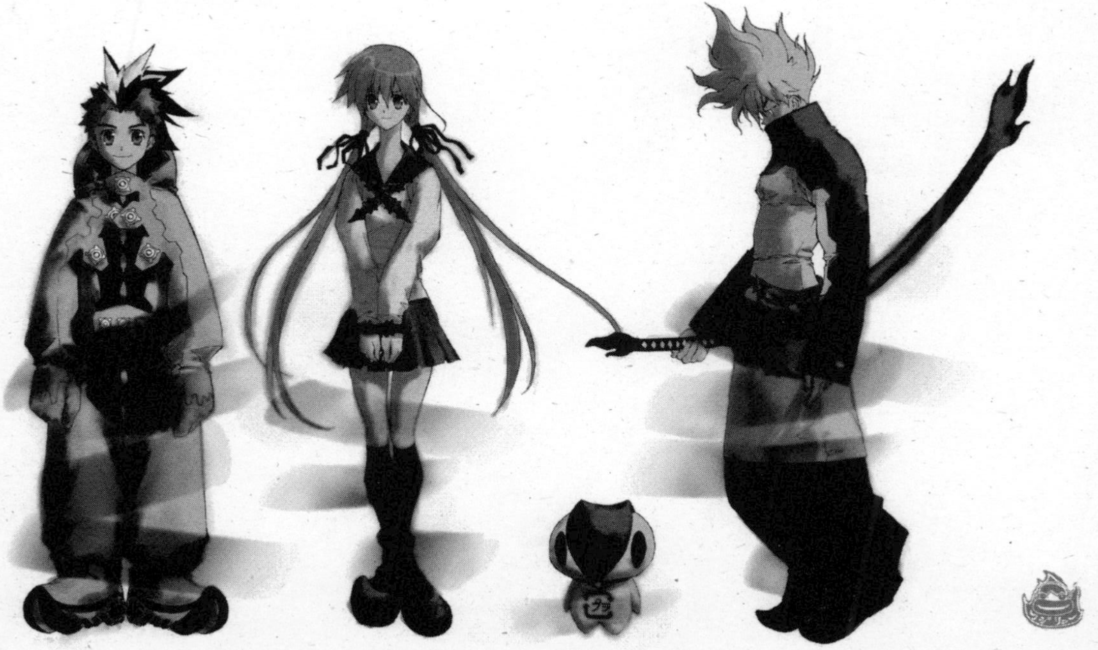

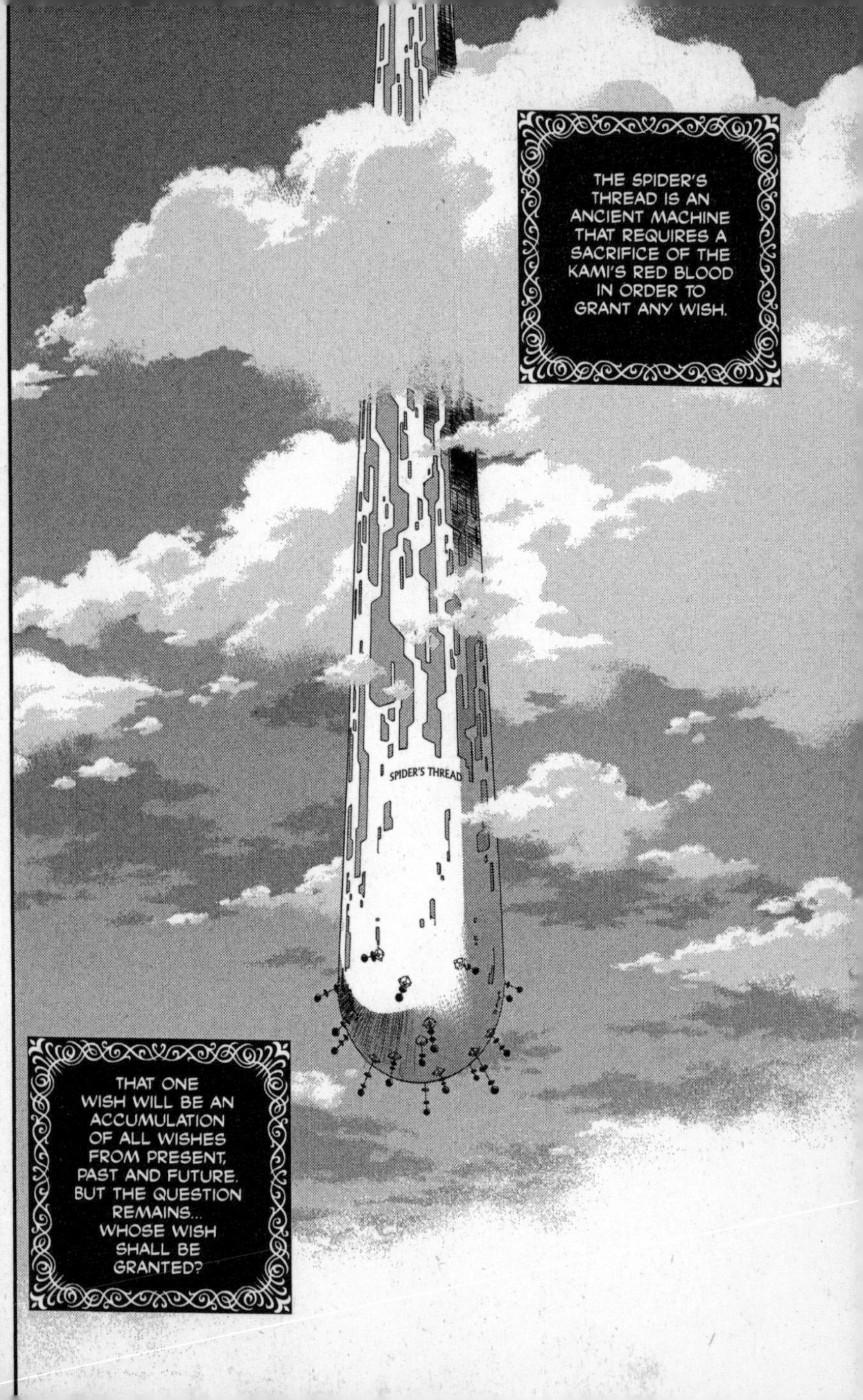
THE SPIDER'S THREAD IS AN ANCIENT MACHINE THAT REQUIRES A SACRIFICE OF THE KAMI'S RED BLOOD IN ORDER TO GRANT ANY WISH.
SPIDER'S THREAD
THAT ONE WISH WILL BE AN ACCUMULATION OF ALL WISHES FROM PRESENT, PAST AND FUTURE. BUT THE QUESTION REMAINS... WHOSE WISH SHALL BE GRANTED?

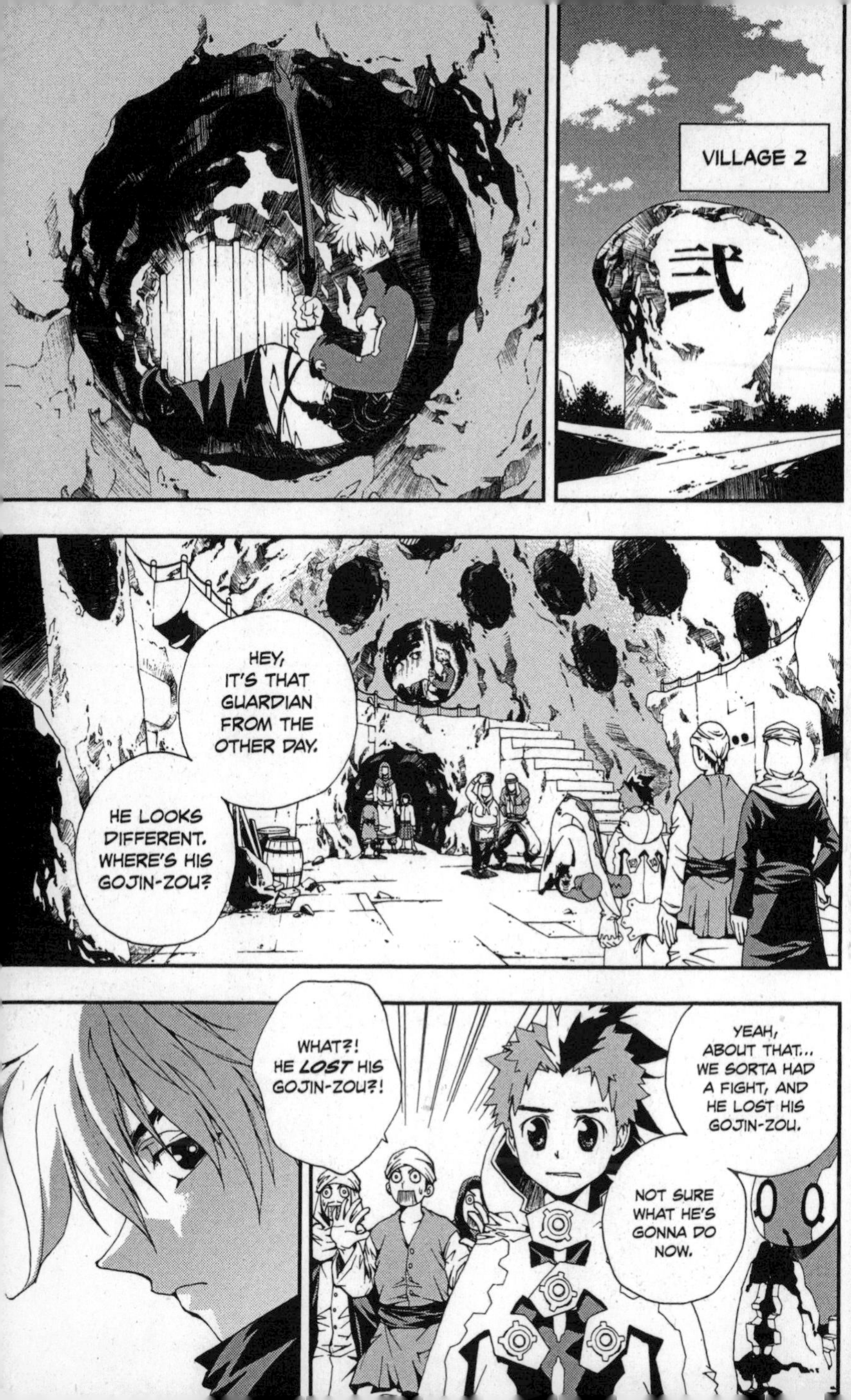
VILLAGE 2
弐
HEY, IT'S THAT GUARDIAN FROM THE OTHER DAY.
HE LOOKS DIFFERENT. WHERE'S HIS GOJIN-ZOU?
..
YEAH, ABOUT THAT... WE SORTA HAD A FIGHT, AND HE LOST HIS GOJIN-ZOU.
WHAT?! HE *LOST* HIS GOJIN-ZOU?!
NOT SURE WHAT HE'S GONNA DO NOW.

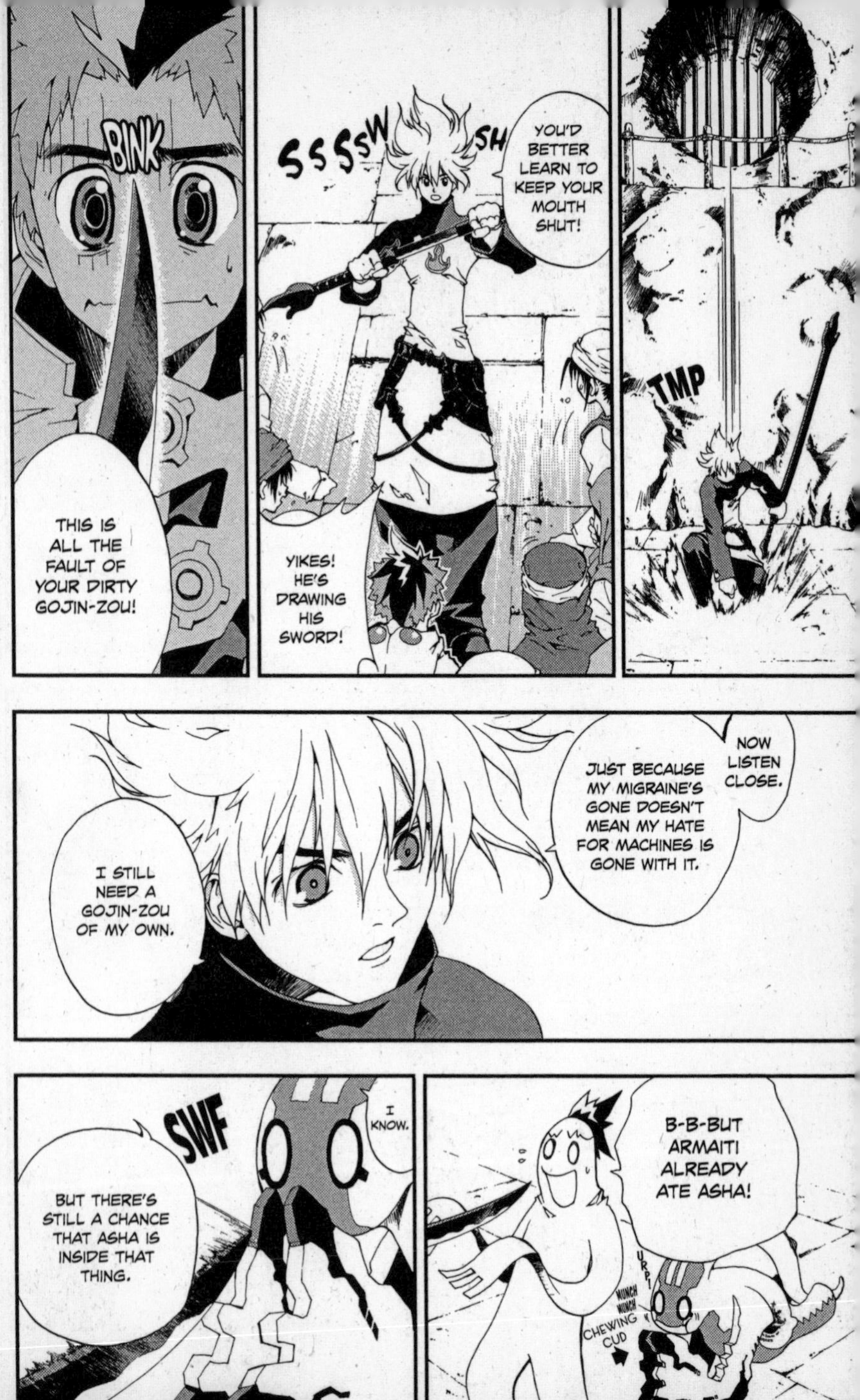

TMP
SSSSWSH
YOU'D BETTER LEARN TO KEEP YOUR MOUTH SHUT!
YIKES! HE'S DRAWING HIS SWORD!
BINK
THIS IS ALL THE FAULT OF YOUR DIRTY GOJIN-ZOU!
NOW LISTEN CLOSE.
JUST BECAUSE MY MIGRAINE'S GONE DOESN'T MEAN MY HATE FOR MACHINES IS GONE WITH IT.
I STILL NEED A GOJIN-ZOU OF MY OWN.
B-B-BUT ARMAITI ALREADY ATE ASHA!
URP!
MUNCH MUNCH
CHEWING CUD
I KNOW.
SWF
BUT THERE'S STILL A CHANCE THAT ASHA IS INSIDE THAT THING.

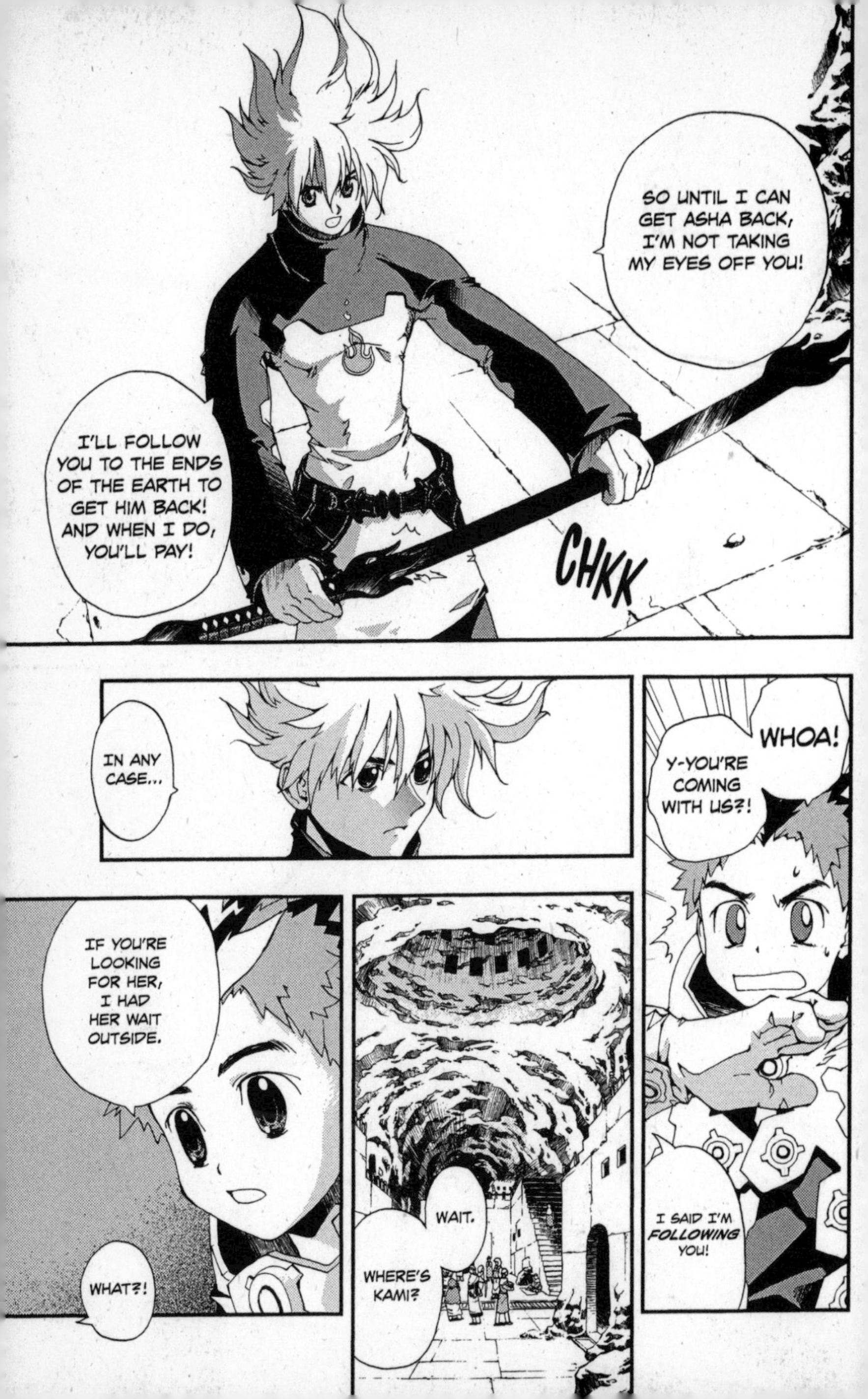
SO UNTIL I CAN GET ASHA BACK, I'M NOT TAKING MY EYES OFF YOU!
I'LL FOLLOW YOU TO THE ENDS OF THE EARTH TO GET HIM BACK! AND WHEN I DO, YOU'LL PAY!
CHKK
WHOA!
Y-YOU'RE COMING WITH US?!
I SAID I'M *FOLLOWING* YOU!
IN ANY CASE...
WAIT.
WHERE'S KAMI?
IF YOU'RE LOOKING FOR HER, I HAD HER WAIT OUTSIDE.
WHAT?!

IMBECILE!
HUH?
WHAT'S THE BIG DEAL?
TMP TMP
DON'T FORGET, EVERY GUARDIAN OUT THERE IS AFTER HER.
AND I CAN'T HAVE HER KIDNAPPED BEFORE MY WISH IS FULFILLED.
UHA! WAIT A SECOND! I'M COMING TOO!
BOW
EXIT
WELL, FOLKS. THIS IS WHERE WE SAY GOODBYE!

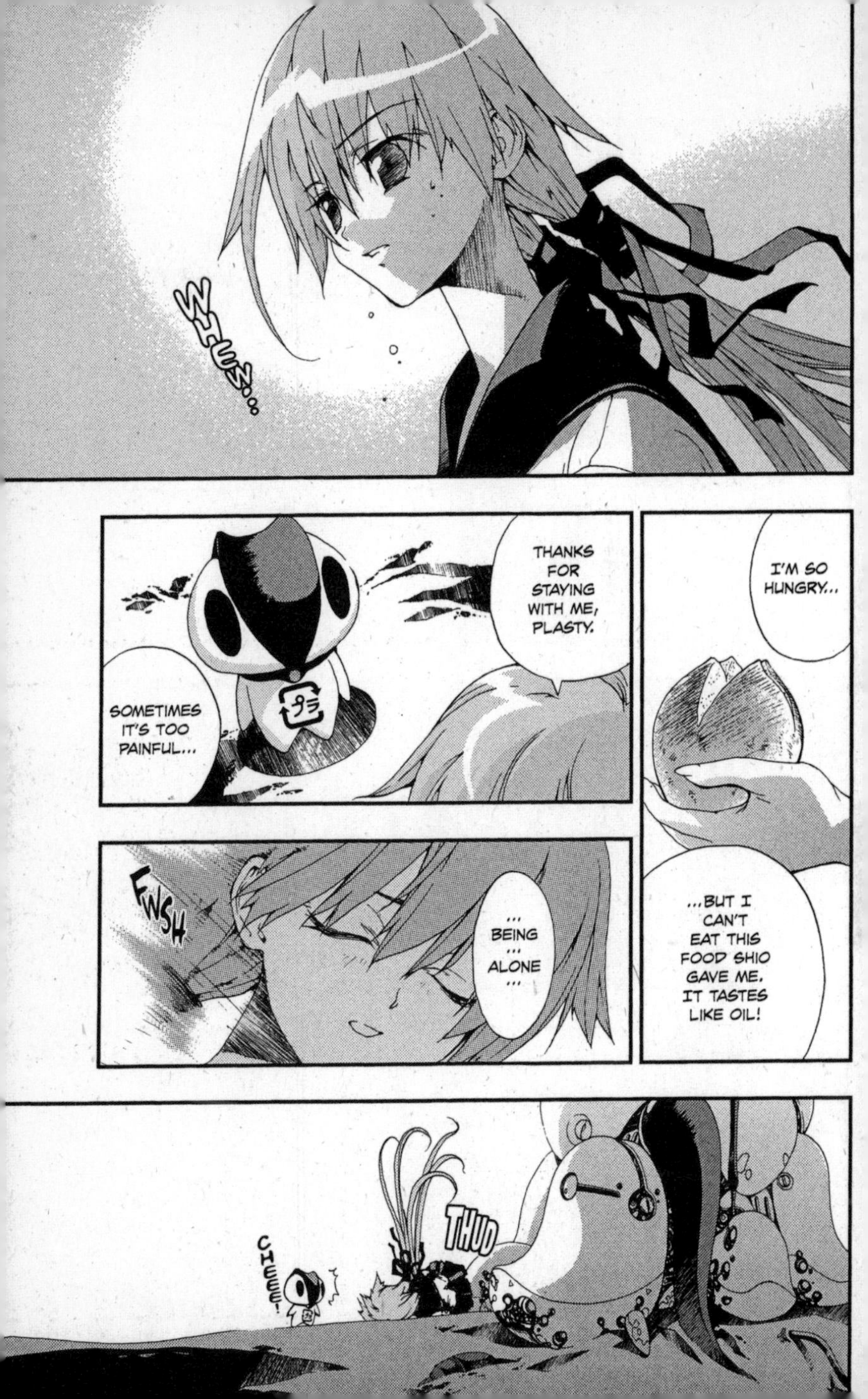
WHEW...
I'M SO HUNGRY...
...BUT I CAN'T EAT THIS FOOD SHIO GAVE ME. IT TASTES LIKE OIL!
THANKS FOR STAYING WITH ME, PLASTY.
SOMETIMES IT'S TOO PAINFUL...
...BEING...ALONE...
FWSH
THUD
CHEEE!

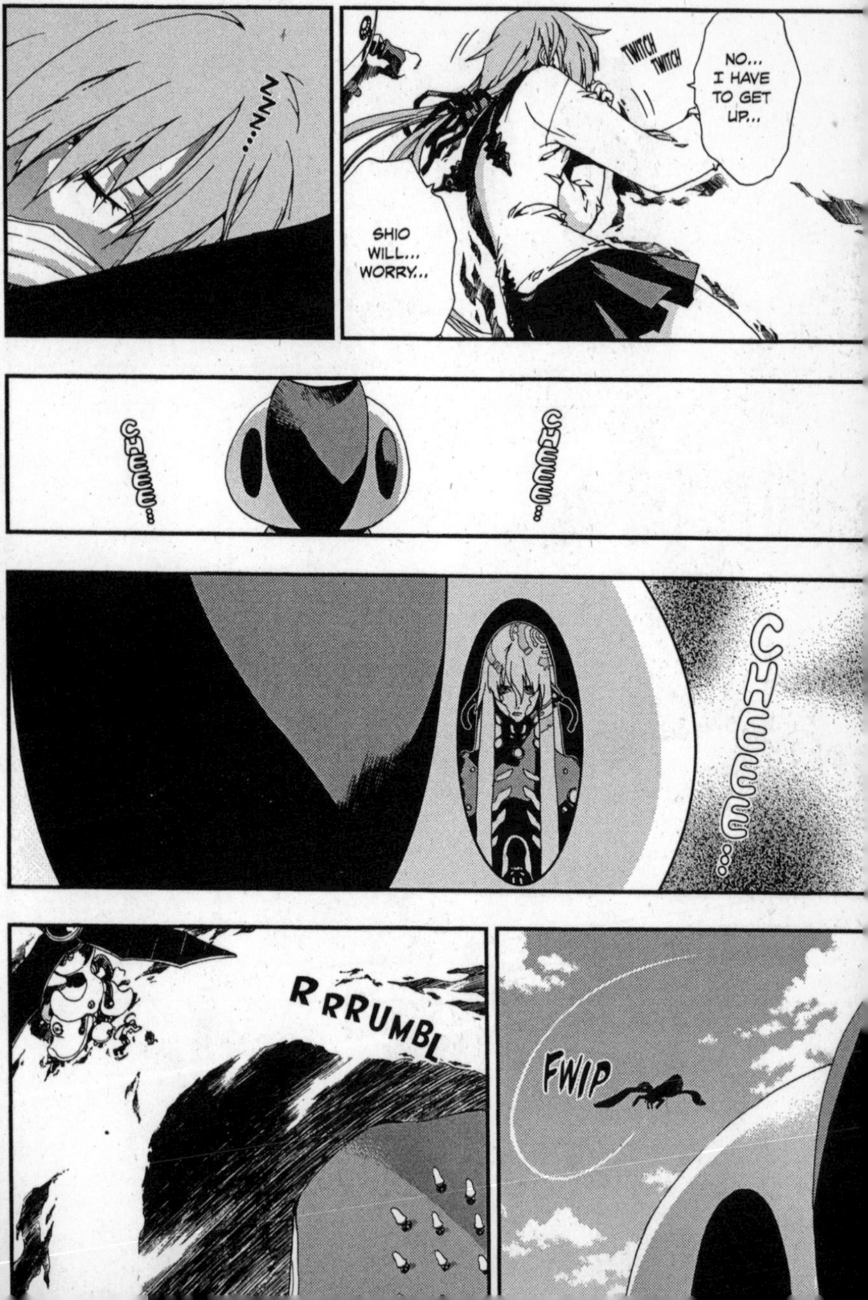
TWITCH TWITCH
NO... I HAVE TO GET UP...
SHIO WILL... WORRY...
NNN...
CHEEEE...
CHEEEE...
CHEEEE...
FWIP
R RRUMBL

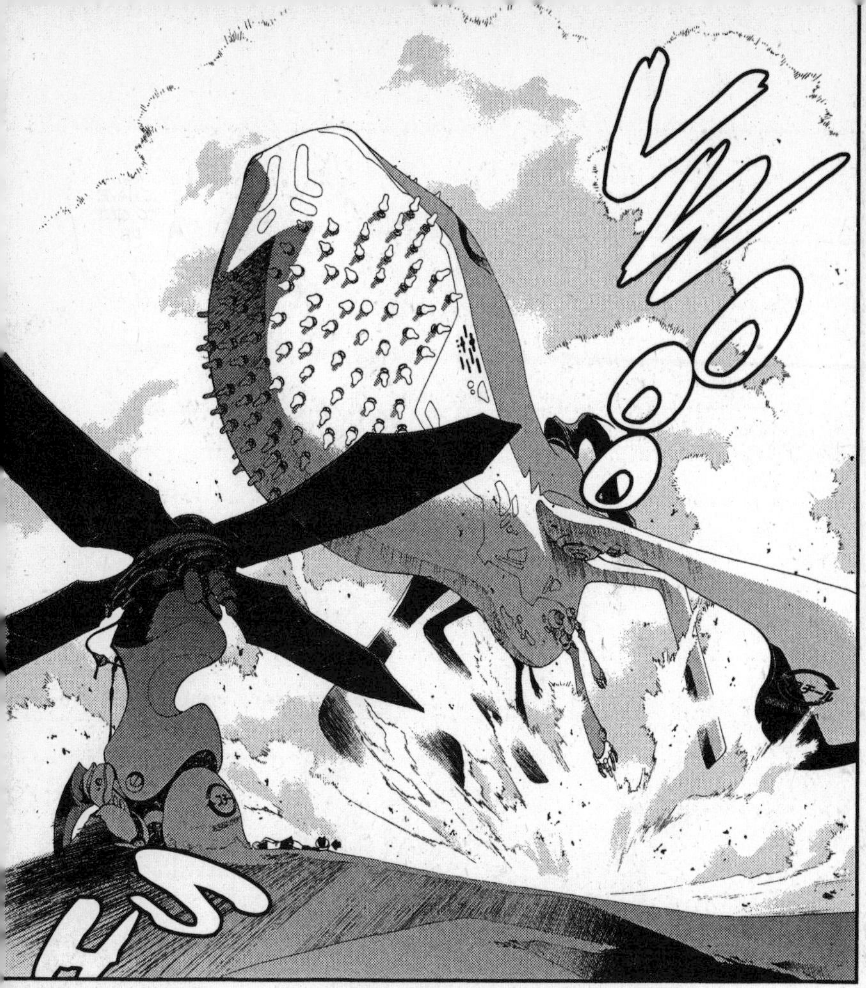
VWOOOO
SH
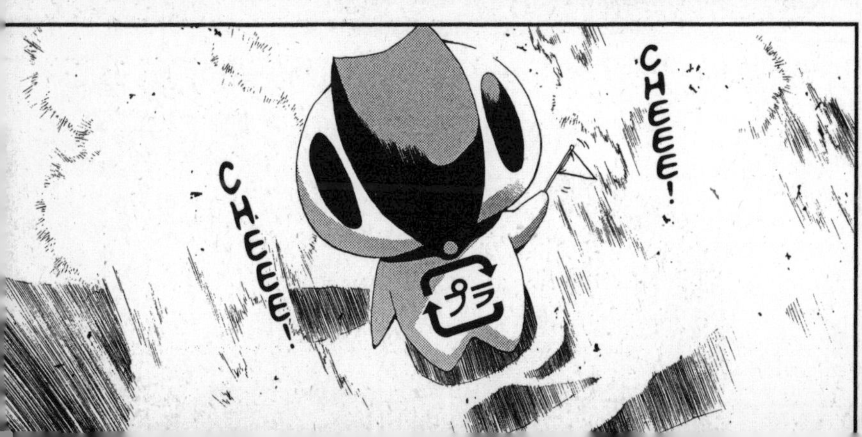
CHEEE!
CHEEEE!

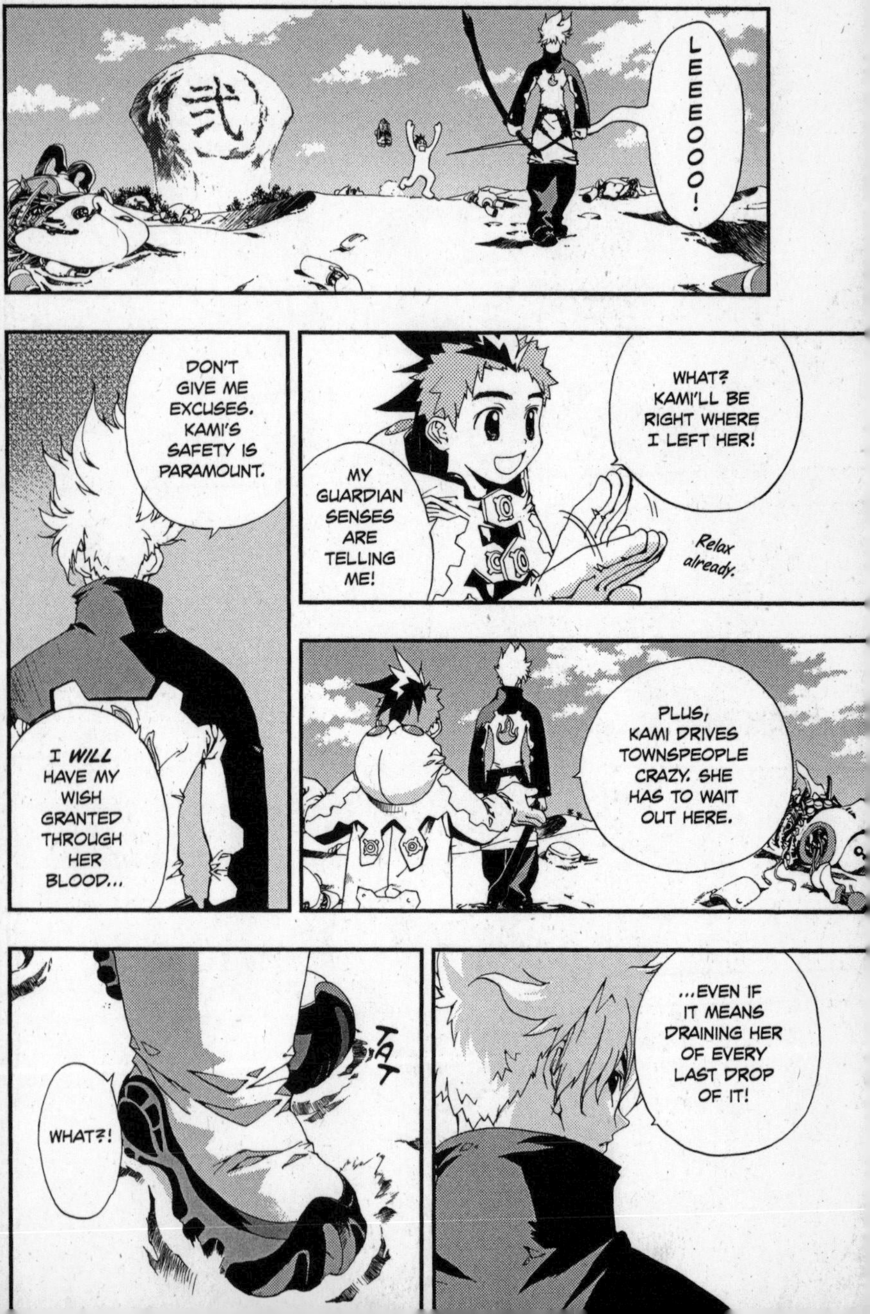
LEEEOOOO!
WHAT? KAMI'LL BE RIGHT WHERE I LEFT HER!
Relax already.
MY GUARDIAN SENSES ARE TELLING ME!
PLUS, KAMI DRIVES TOWNSPEOPLE CRAZY. SHE HAS TO WAIT OUT HERE.
DON'T GIVE ME EXCUSES. KAMI'S SAFETY IS PARAMOUNT.
I WILL HAVE MY WISH GRANTED THROUGH HER BLOOD...
...EVEN IF IT MEANS DRAINING HER OF EVERY LAST DROP OF IT!
TAT
WHAT?!

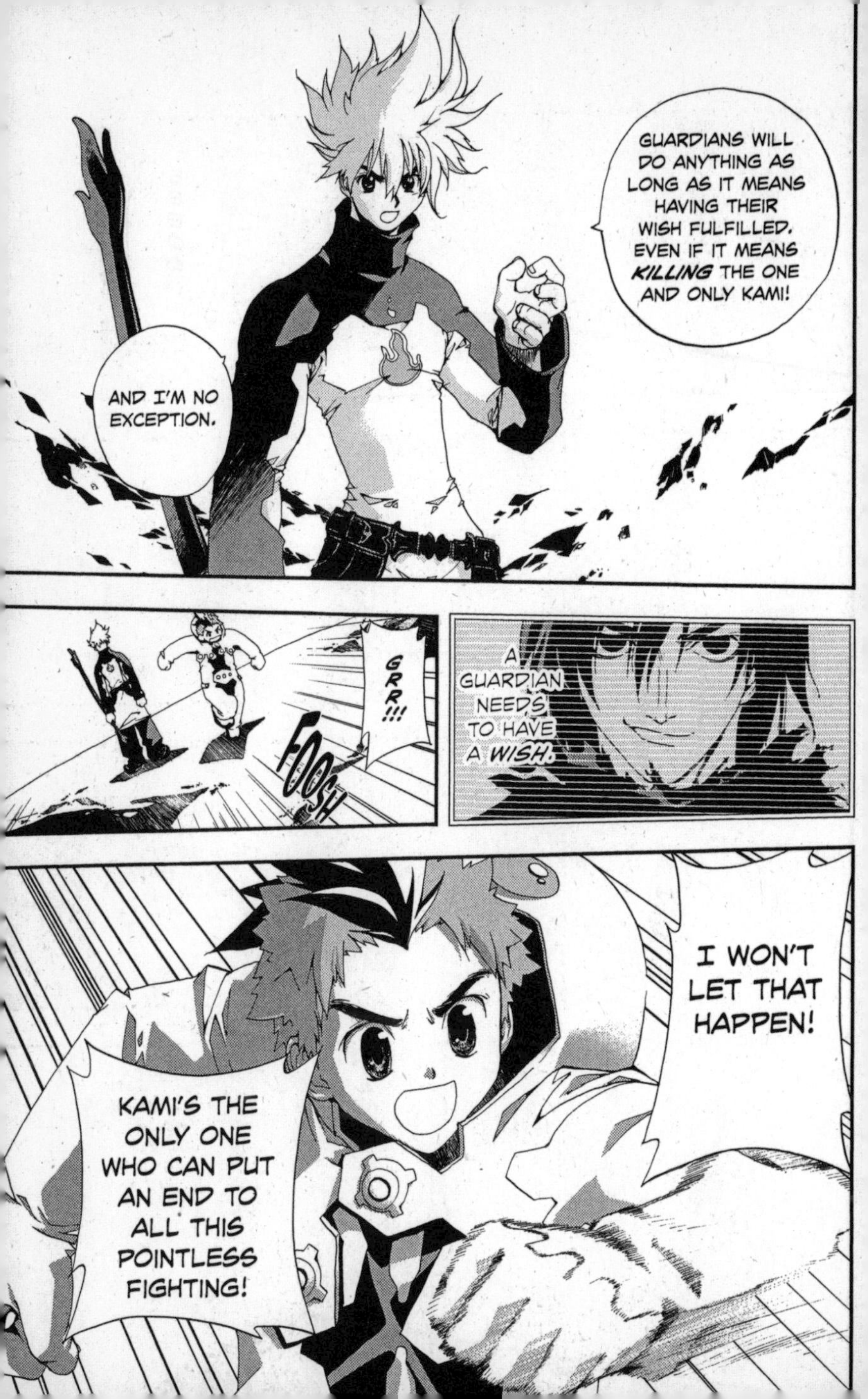
GUARDIANS WILL DO ANYTHING AS LONG AS IT MEANS HAVING THEIR WISH FULFILLED. EVEN IF IT MEANS KILLING THE ONE AND ONLY KAMI!
AND I'M NO EXCEPTION.
A GUARDIAN NEEDS TO HAVE A WISH.
GRR!!!
FOOSH
I WON'T LET THAT HAPPEN!
KAMI'S THE ONLY ONE WHO CAN PUT AN END TO ALL THIS POINTLESS FIGHTING!

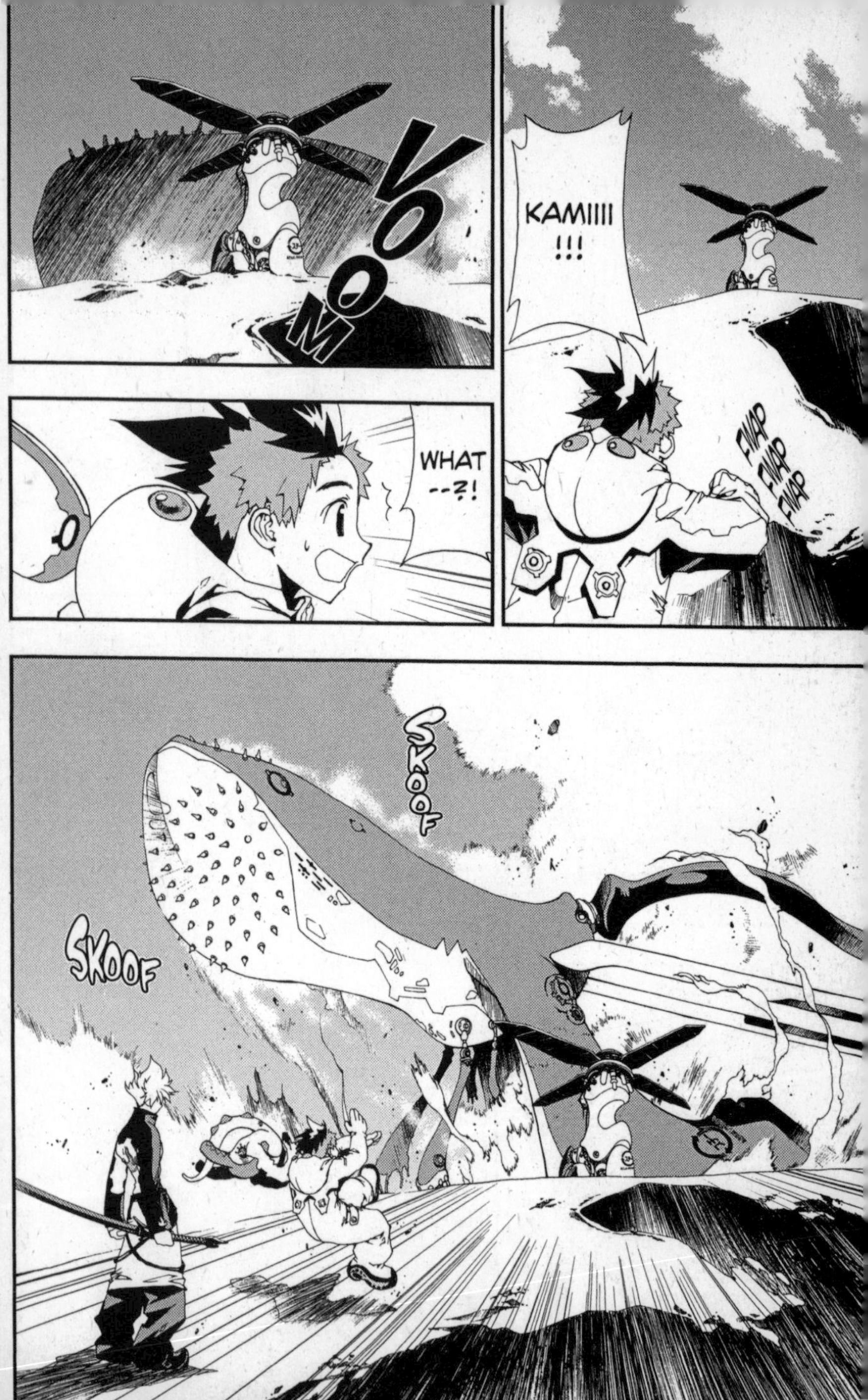
KAMIIIII !!!
FWAP FWAP FWAP
VOOM
WHAT --?!
SKOOF
SKOOF

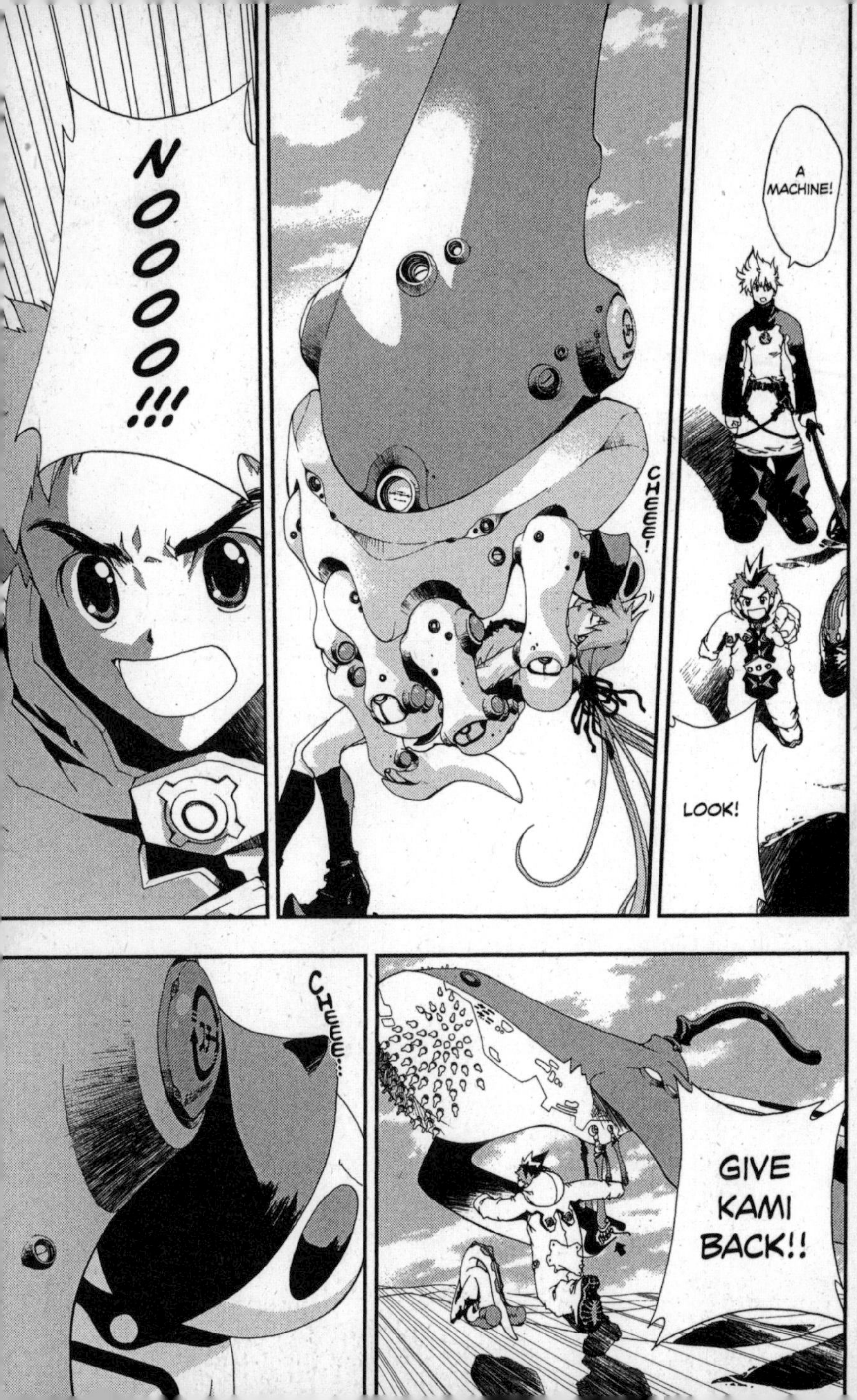
A MACHINE!
LOOK!
CHEEE!
NOOOOO!!!
GIVE KAMI BACK!!
CHEEE...

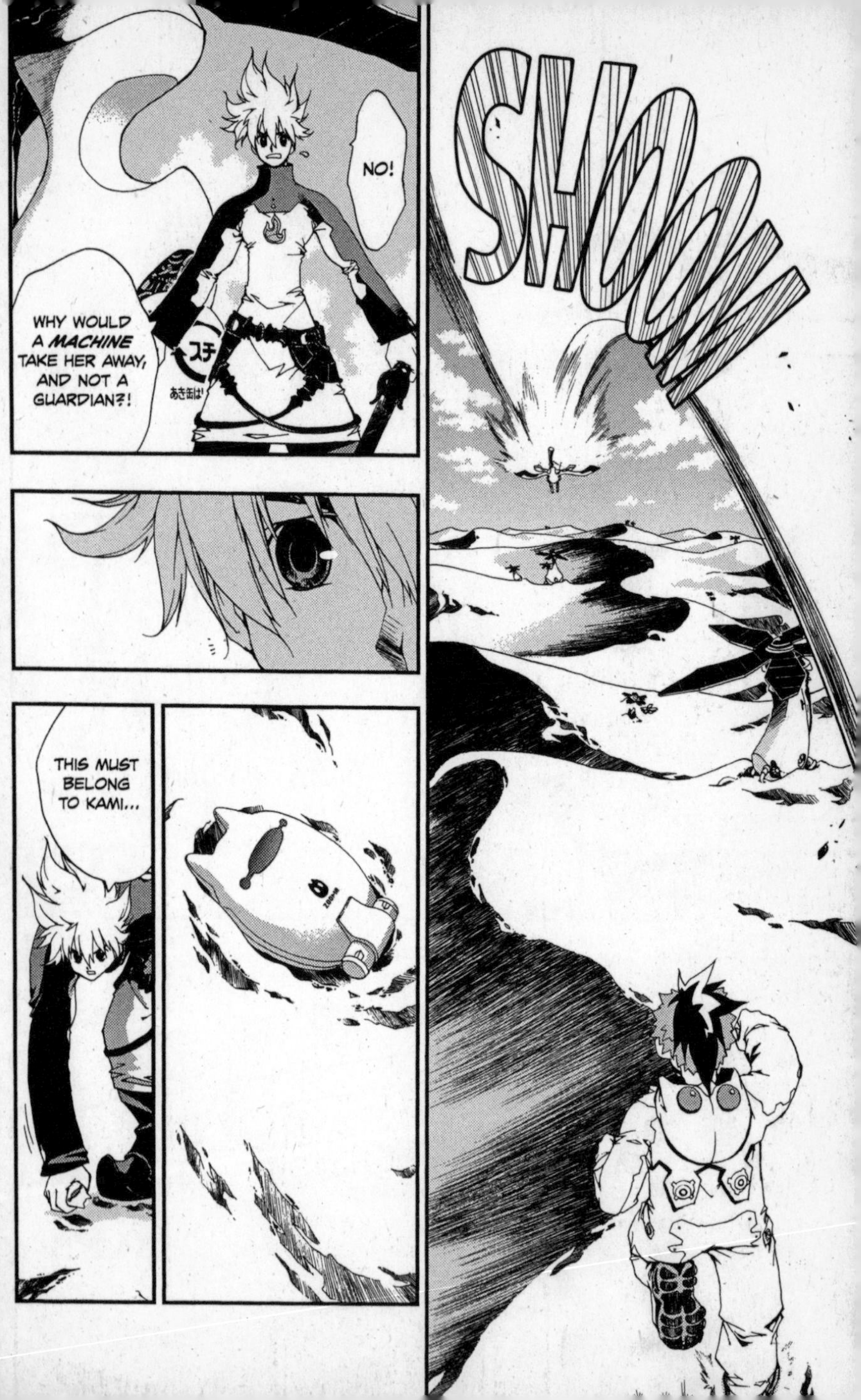
SHOOM
NO!
WHY WOULD A *MACHINE* TAKE HER AWAY, AND NOT A GUARDIAN?!
スチ
THIS MUST BELONG TO KAMI...

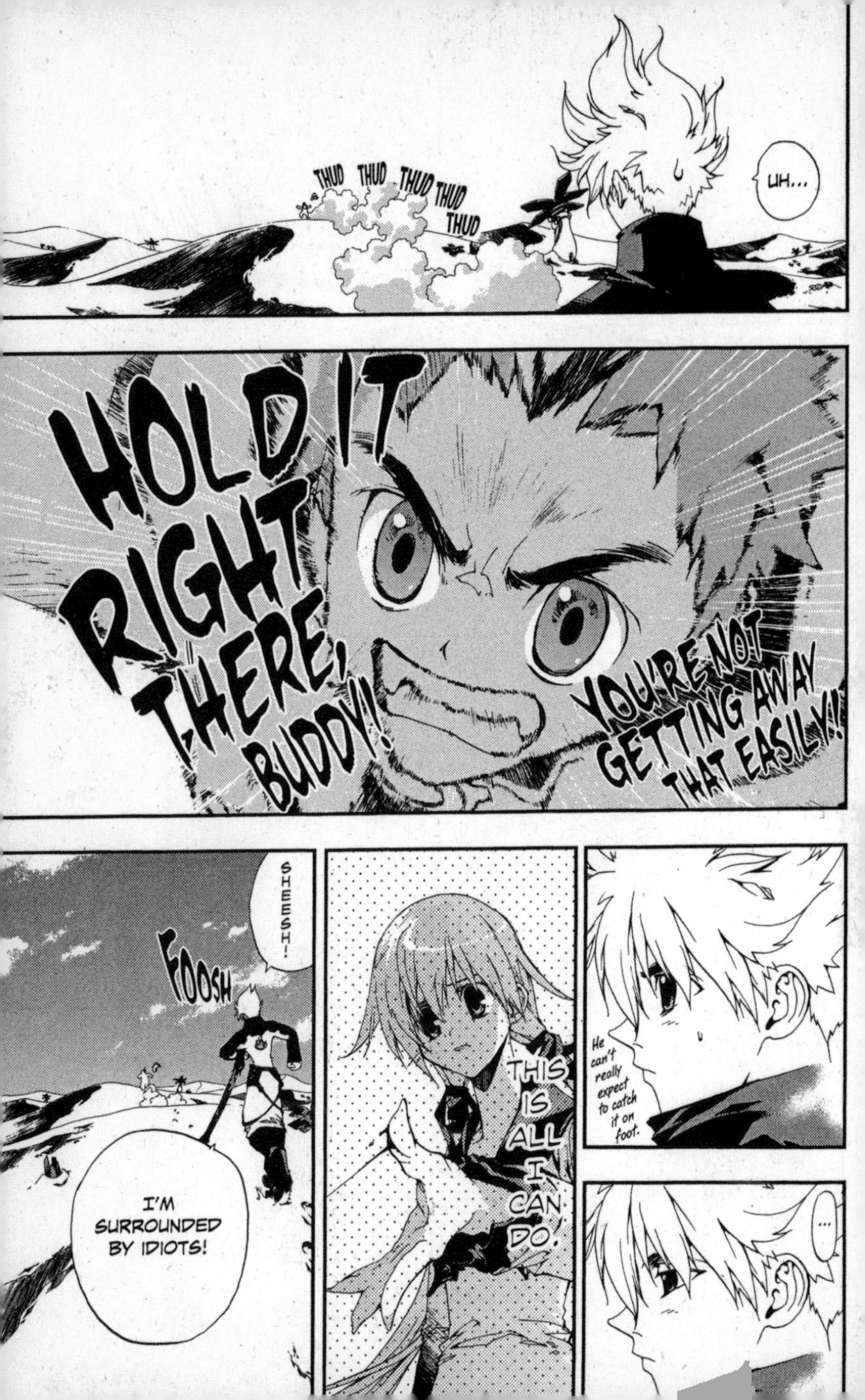
UH...
THUD THUD THUD THUD THUD
HOLD IT RIGHT THERE, BUDDY!
YOU'RE NOT GETTING AWAY THAT EASILY!!
He can't really expect to catch it on foot.
...
THIS IS ALL I CAN DO.
SHEESH!
FOOSH
I'M SURROUNDED BY IDIOTS!

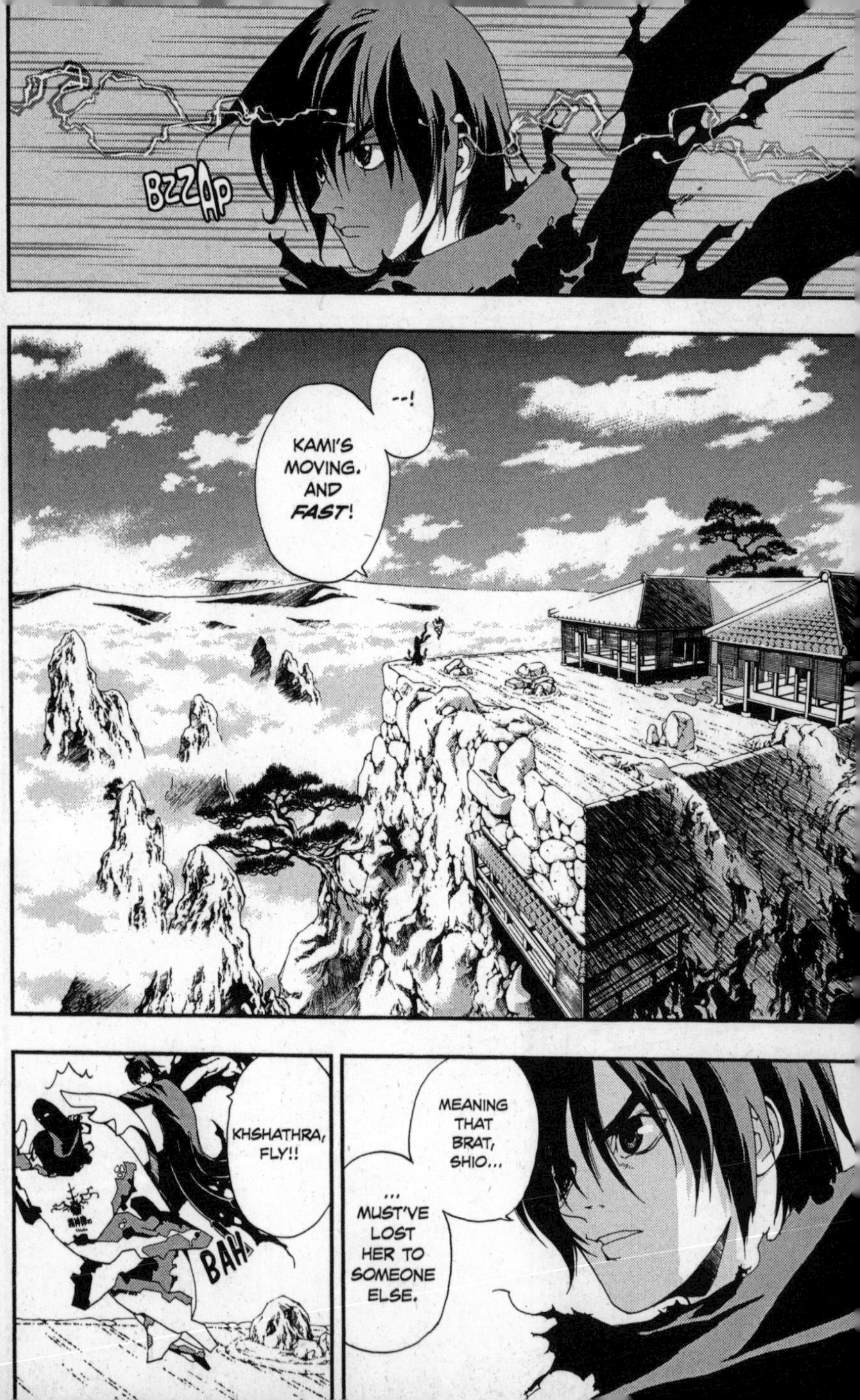
BZZAP
--!
KAMI'S MOVING. AND *FAST*!
MEANING THAT BRAT, SHIO...
... MUST'VE LOST HER TO SOMEONE ELSE.
KHSHATHRA, FLY!!
BAH

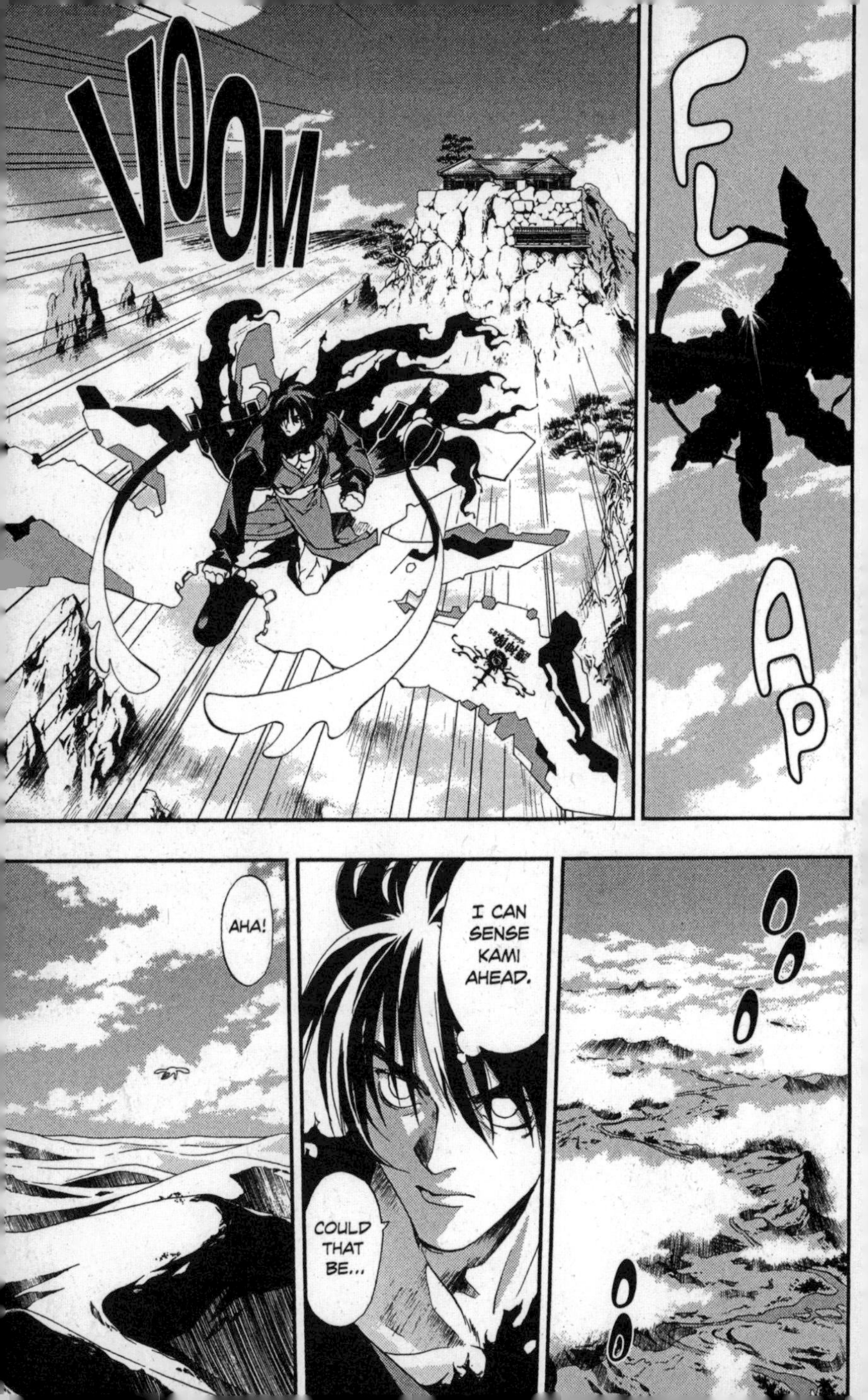
FLAP
VOOM
OOOO
OO
I CAN SENSE KAMI AHEAD.
COULD THAT BE...
AHA!

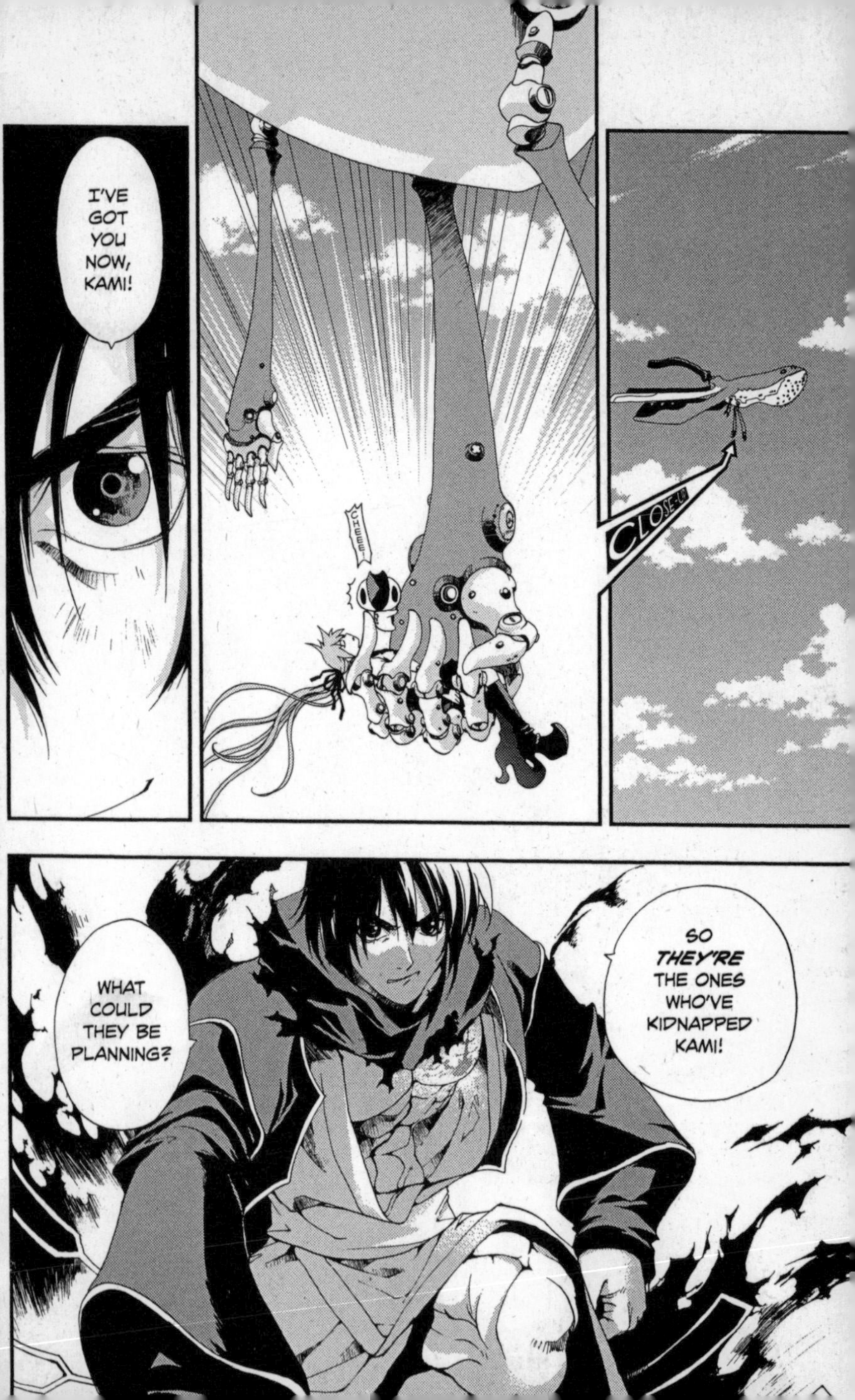
CLOSE-UP
CHEEE!
I'VE GOT YOU NOW, KAMI!
SO *THEY'RE* THE ONES WHO'VE KIDNAPPED KAMI!
WHAT COULD THEY BE PLANNING?

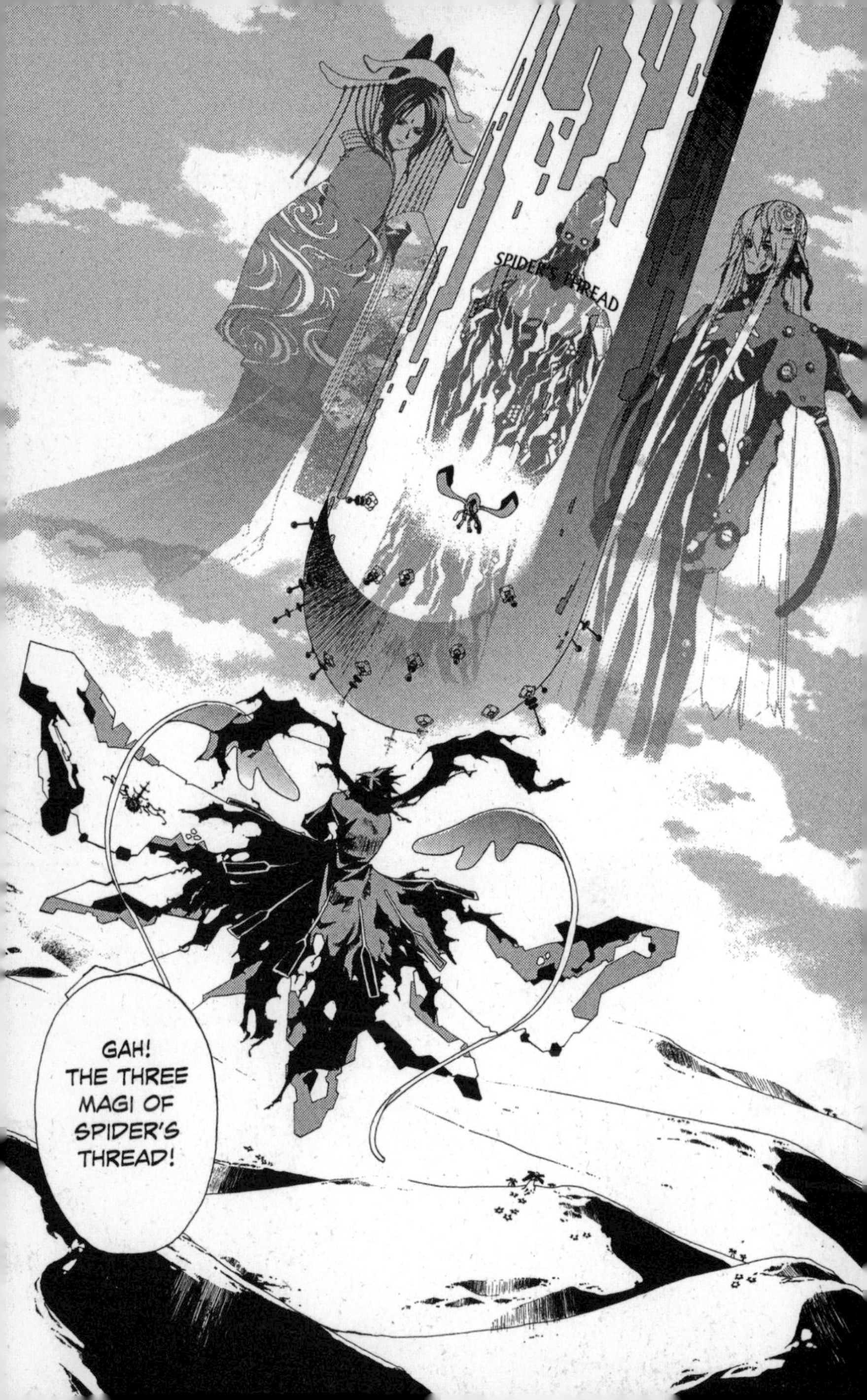
SPIDER'S THREAD
GAH! THE THREE MAGI OF SPIDER'S THREAD!

Wāq
Wāq

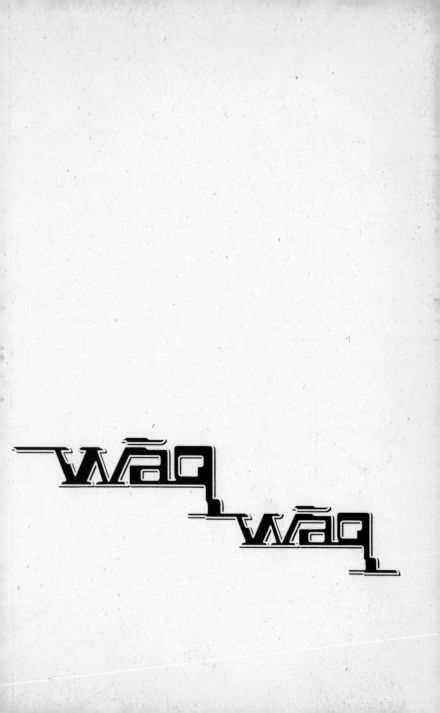

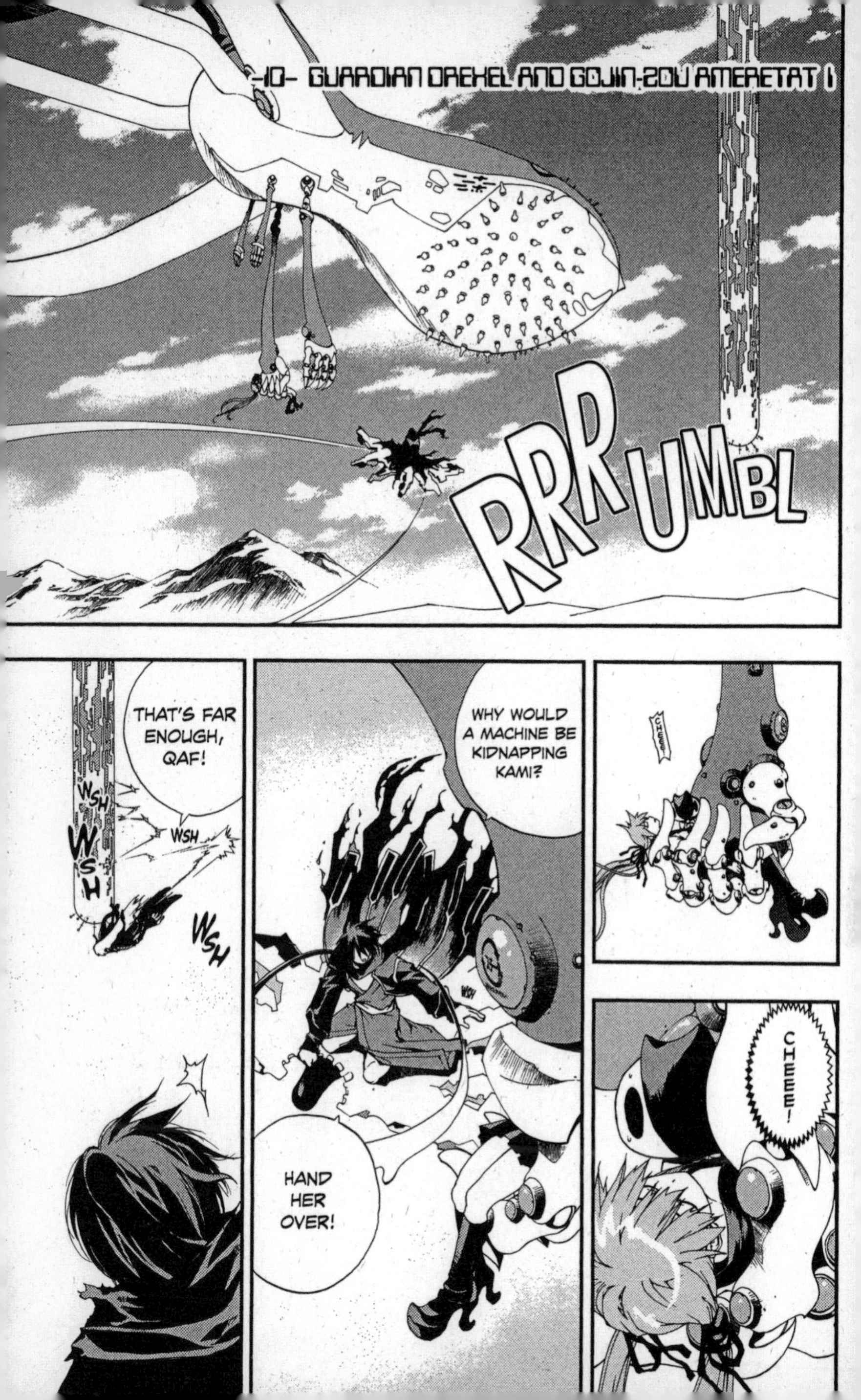
-10- GUARDIAN DREXEL AND GOJIN-ZOU AMERETAT I
RRRUMBL
CHEEE!
CHEEE!
WHY WOULD A MACHINE BE KIDNAPPING KAMI?
WSH
HAND HER OVER!
THAT'S FAR ENOUGH, QAF!
WSH
WSH
WSH
WSH
WSH

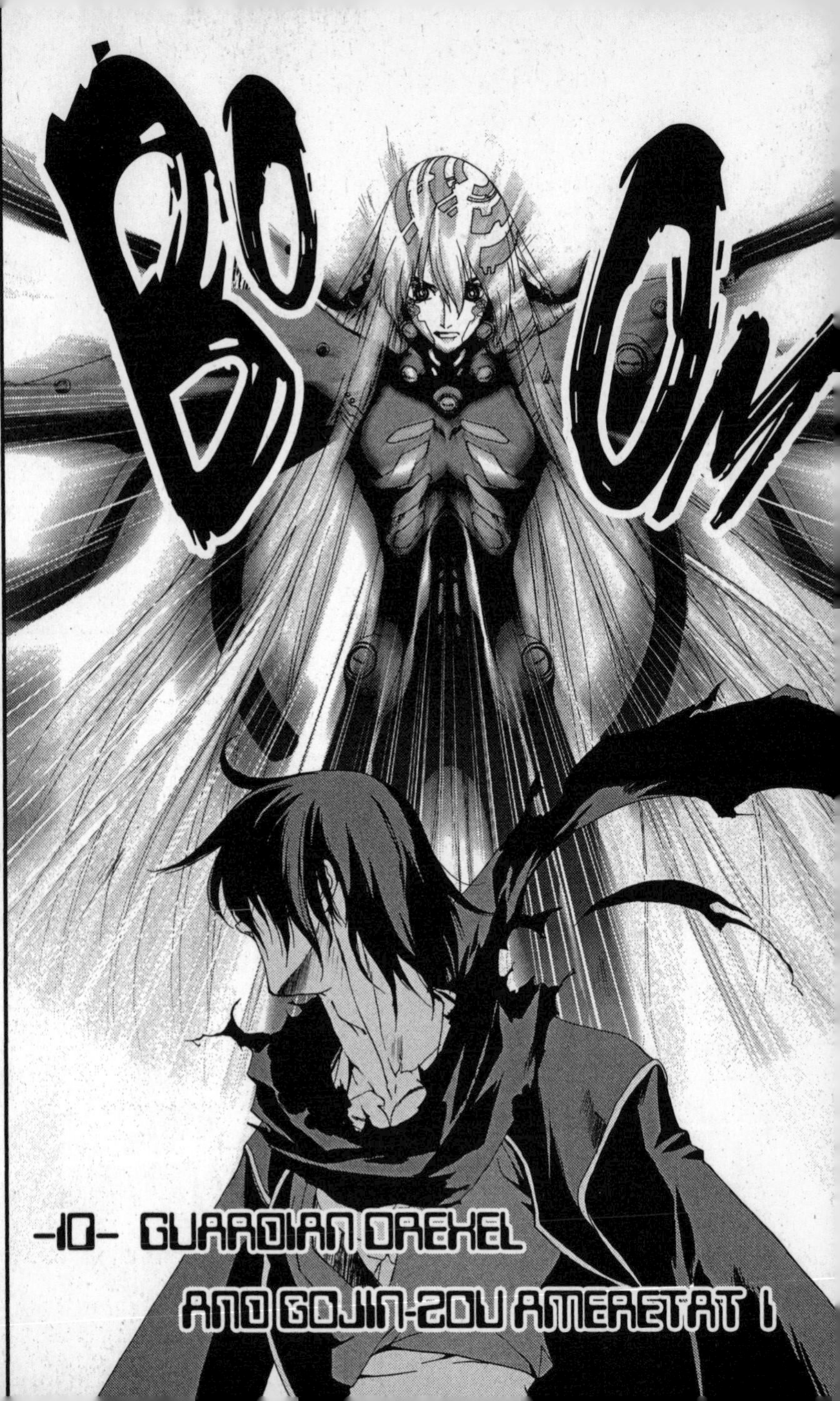
BOOM
-10- GUARDIAN DREXEL
AND GOJIN-ZOU AMERETAT I

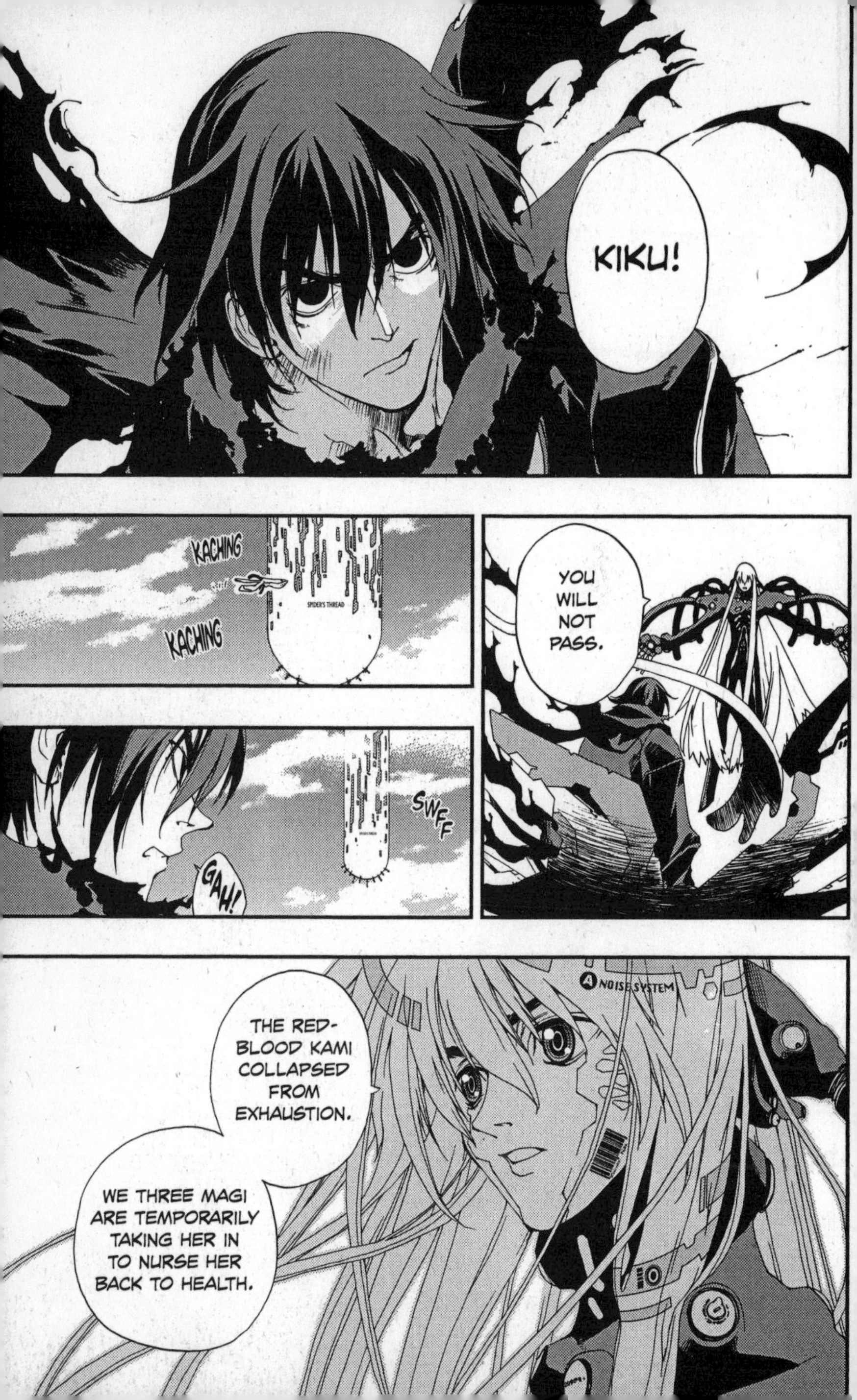
KIKU!
YOU WILL NOT PASS.
SPIDER'S THREAD
KACHING
KACHING
SWFF
GAH!
NOISE SYSTEM
THE RED-BLOOD KAMI COLLAPSED FROM EXHAUSTION.
WE THREE MAGI ARE TEMPORARILY TAKING HER IN TO NURSE HER BACK TO HEALTH.

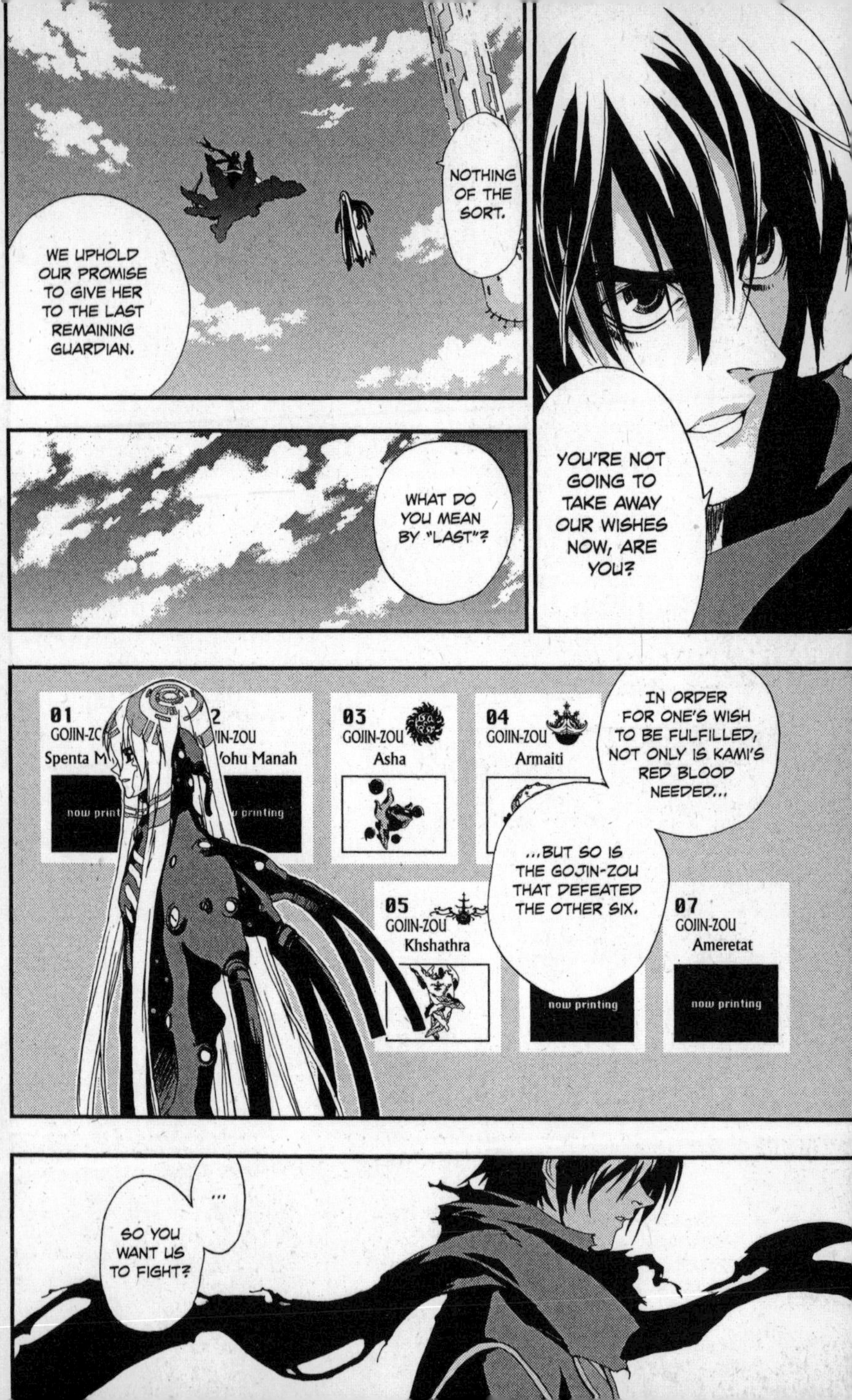
YOU'RE NOT GOING TO TAKE AWAY OUR WISHES NOW, ARE YOU?
NOTHING OF THE SORT.
WE UPHOLD OUR PROMISE TO GIVE HER TO THE LAST REMAINING GUARDIAN.
WHAT DO YOU MEAN BY "LAST"?
IN ORDER FOR ONE'S WISH TO BE FULFILLED, NOT ONLY IS KAMI'S RED BLOOD NEEDED...
...BUT SO IS THE GOJIN-ZOU THAT DEFEATED THE OTHER SIX.
01 GOJIN-ZO Spenta M
now print
2 IN-ZOU Vohu Manah
printing
03 GOJIN-ZOU Asha
04 GOJIN-ZOU Armaiti
05 GOJIN-ZOU Khshathra
now printing
07 GOJIN-ZOU Ameretat
now printing
...
SO YOU WANT US TO FIGHT?

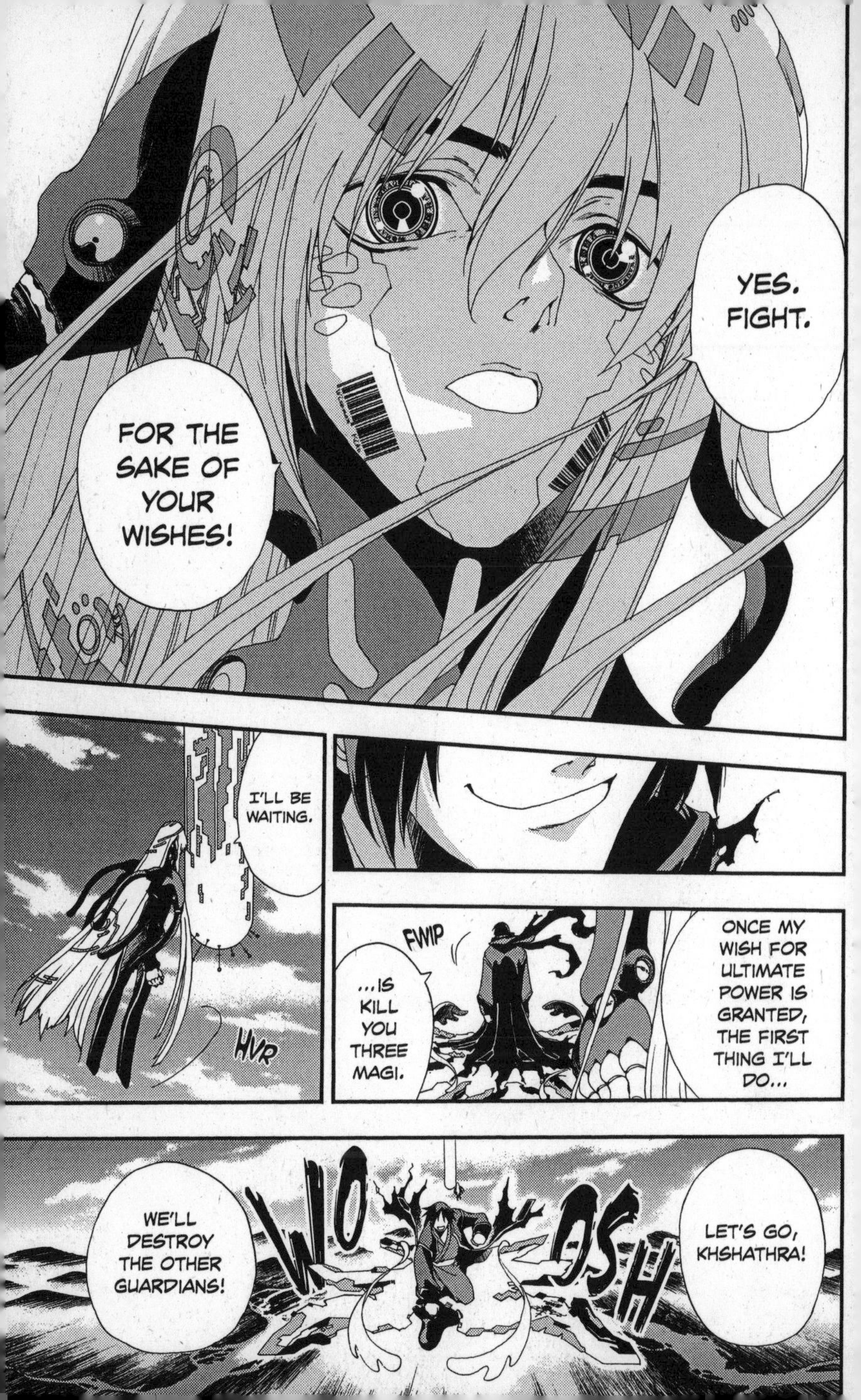
YES. FIGHT.
FOR THE SAKE OF YOUR WISHES!
ONCE MY WISH FOR ULTIMATE POWER IS GRANTED, THE FIRST THING I'LL DO...
FWIP
...IS KILL YOU THREE MAGI.
I'LL BE WAITING.
HVR
LET'S GO, KHSHATHRA!
WOOSH
WE'LL DESTROY THE OTHER GUARDIANS!

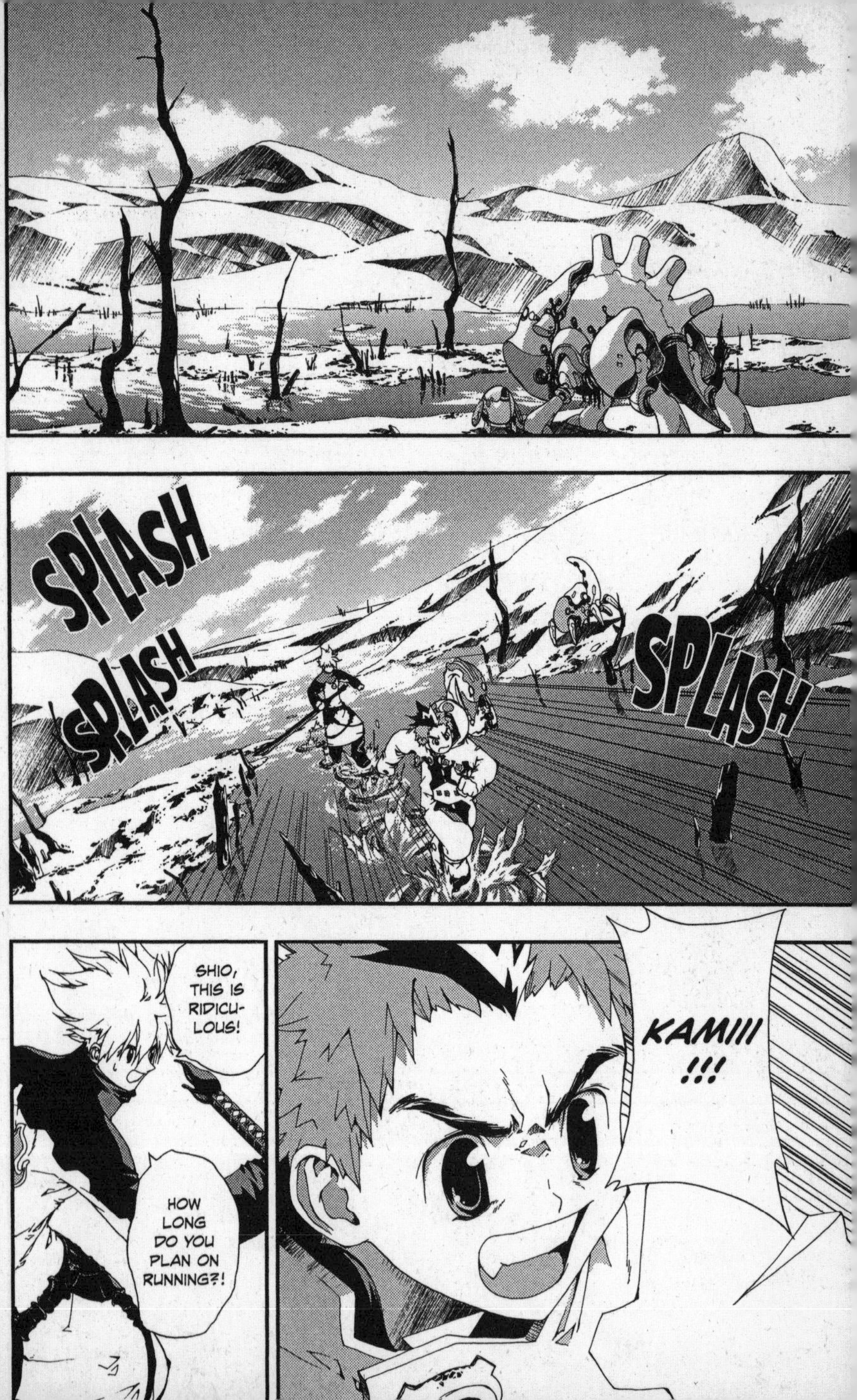
SPLASH
SPLASH
SPLASH
KAMIII !!!
SHIO, THIS IS RIDICU-LOUS!
HOW LONG DO YOU PLAN ON RUNNING?!

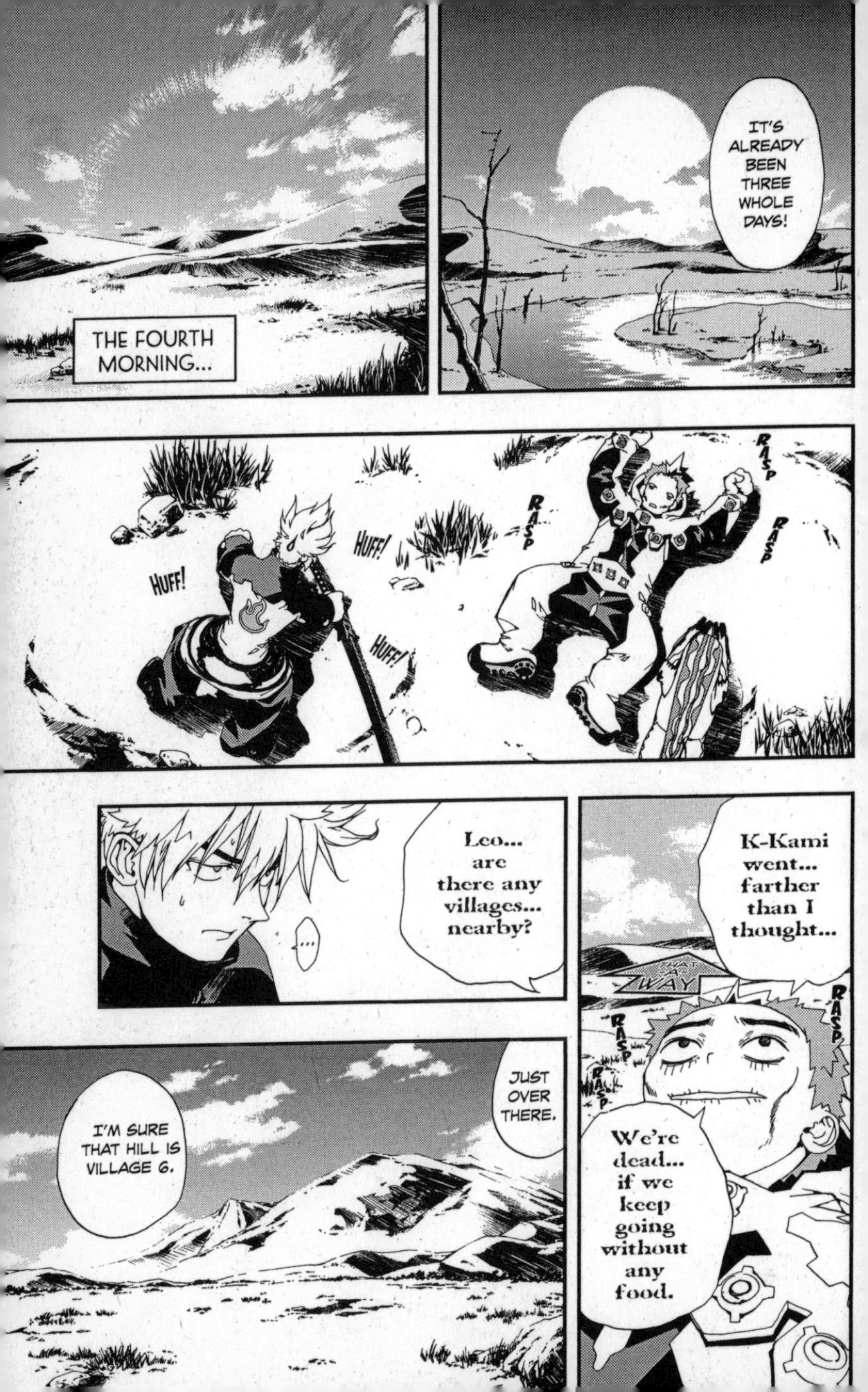
IT'S ALREADY BEEN THREE WHOLE DAYS!
THE FOURTH MORNING...
RASP
RASP
RASP
HUFF!
HUFF!
HUFF!
K-Kami went... farther than I thought...
THAT A WAY
RASP
RASP
RASP
We're dead... if we keep going without any food.
Leo... are there any villages... nearby?
...
JUST OVER THERE.
I'M SURE THAT HILL IS VILLAGE 6.

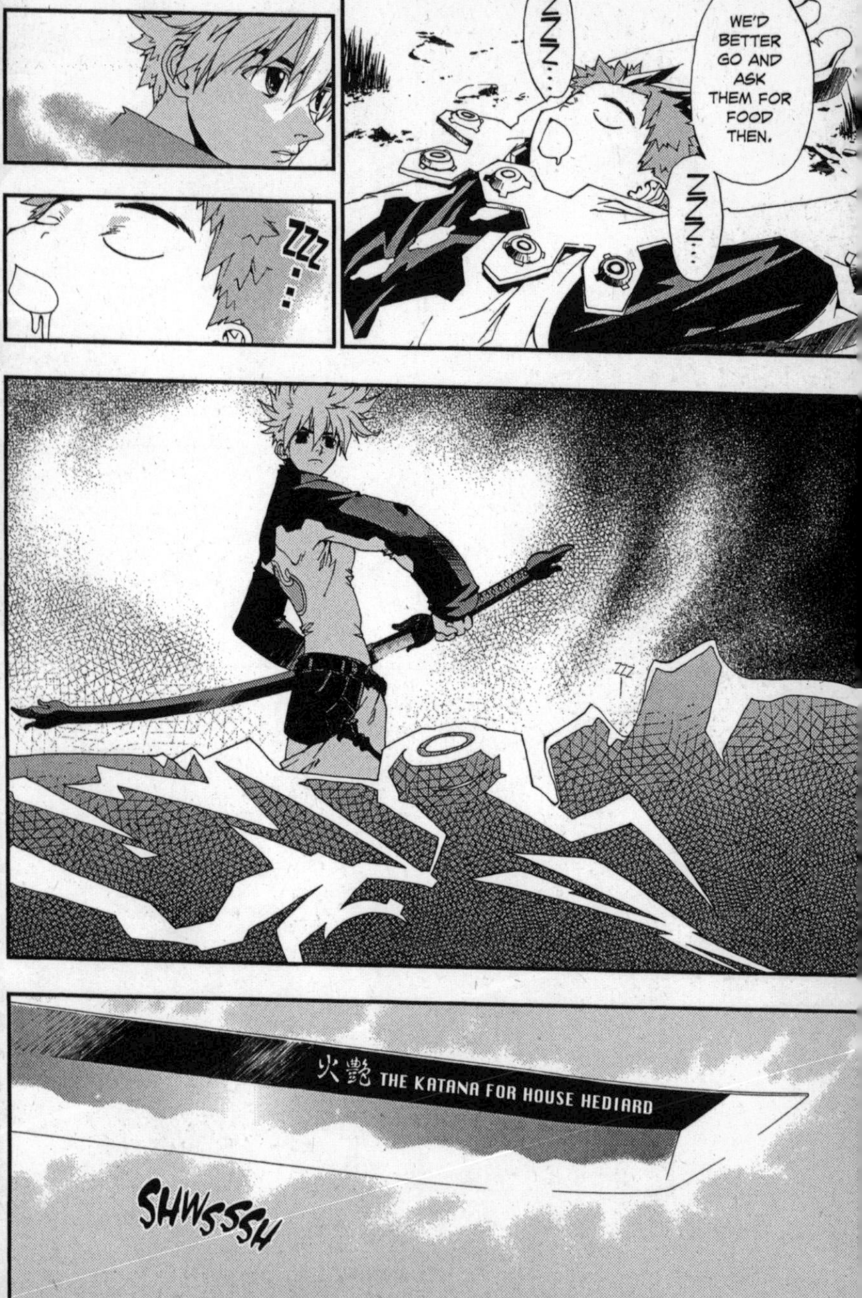
WE'D BETTER GO AND ASK THEM FOR FOOD THEN.
ZZZ...
ZZZ...
ZZZ...
ZZZ
火艶 THE KATANA FOR HOUSE HEDIARD
SHWSSSH

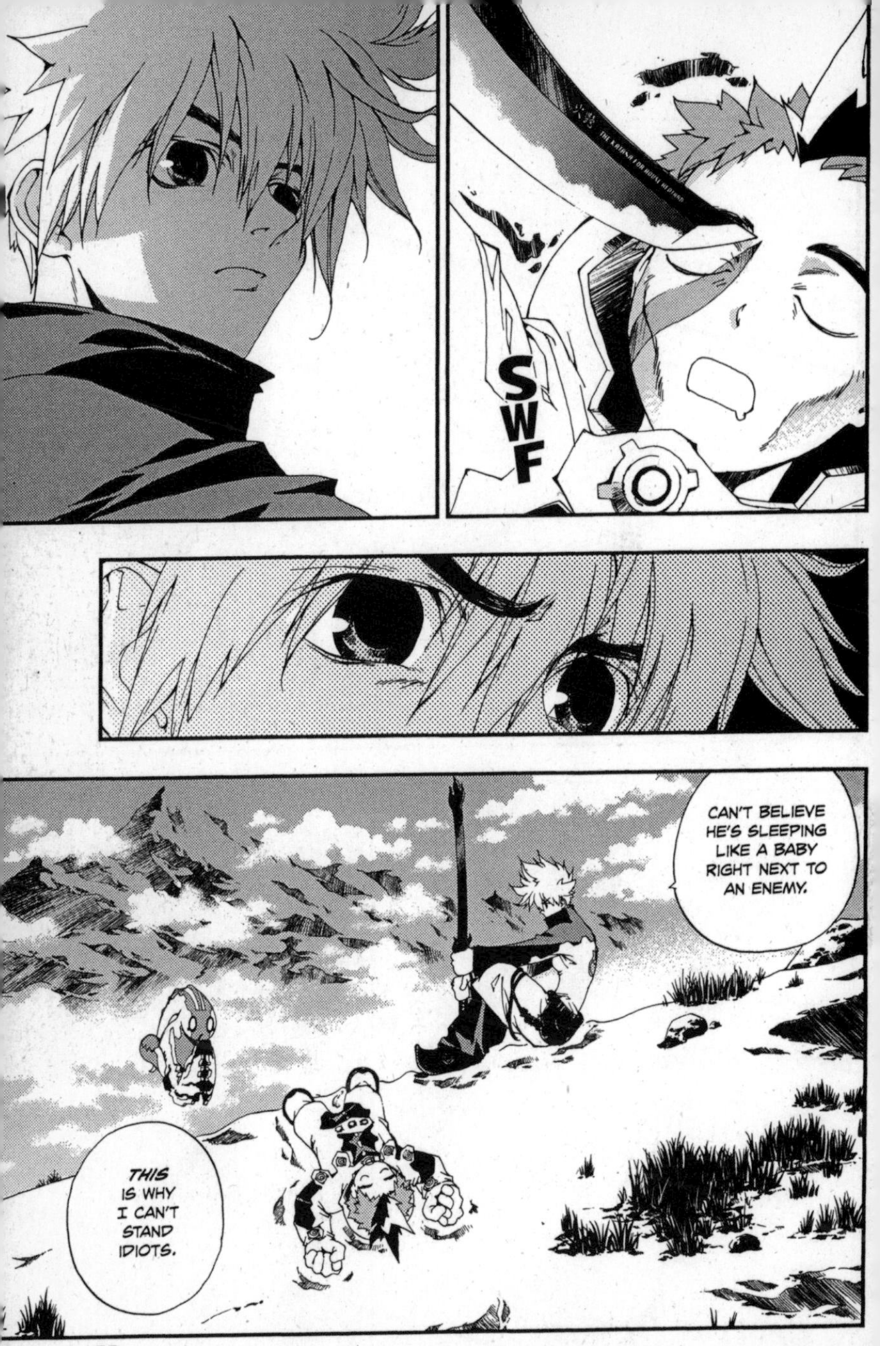
SWF
CAN'T BELIEVE HE'S SLEEPING LIKE A BABY RIGHT NEXT TO AN ENEMY.
THIS IS WHY I CAN'T STAND IDIOTS.

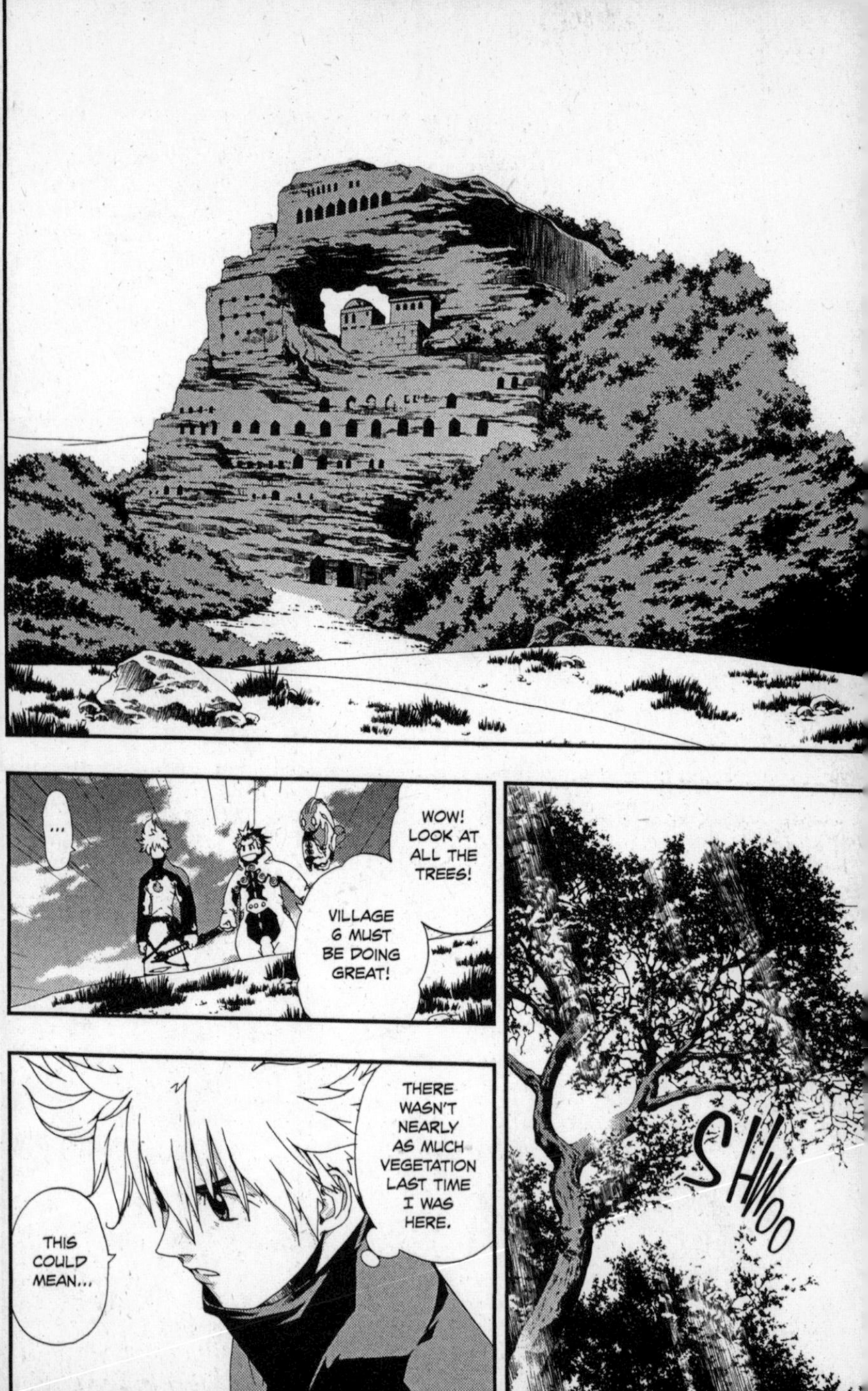
SHWOO
WOW! LOOK AT ALL THE TREES!
VILLAGE 6 MUST BE DOING GREAT!
...
THERE WASN'T NEARLY AS MUCH VEGETATION LAST TIME I WAS HERE.
THIS COULD MEAN...

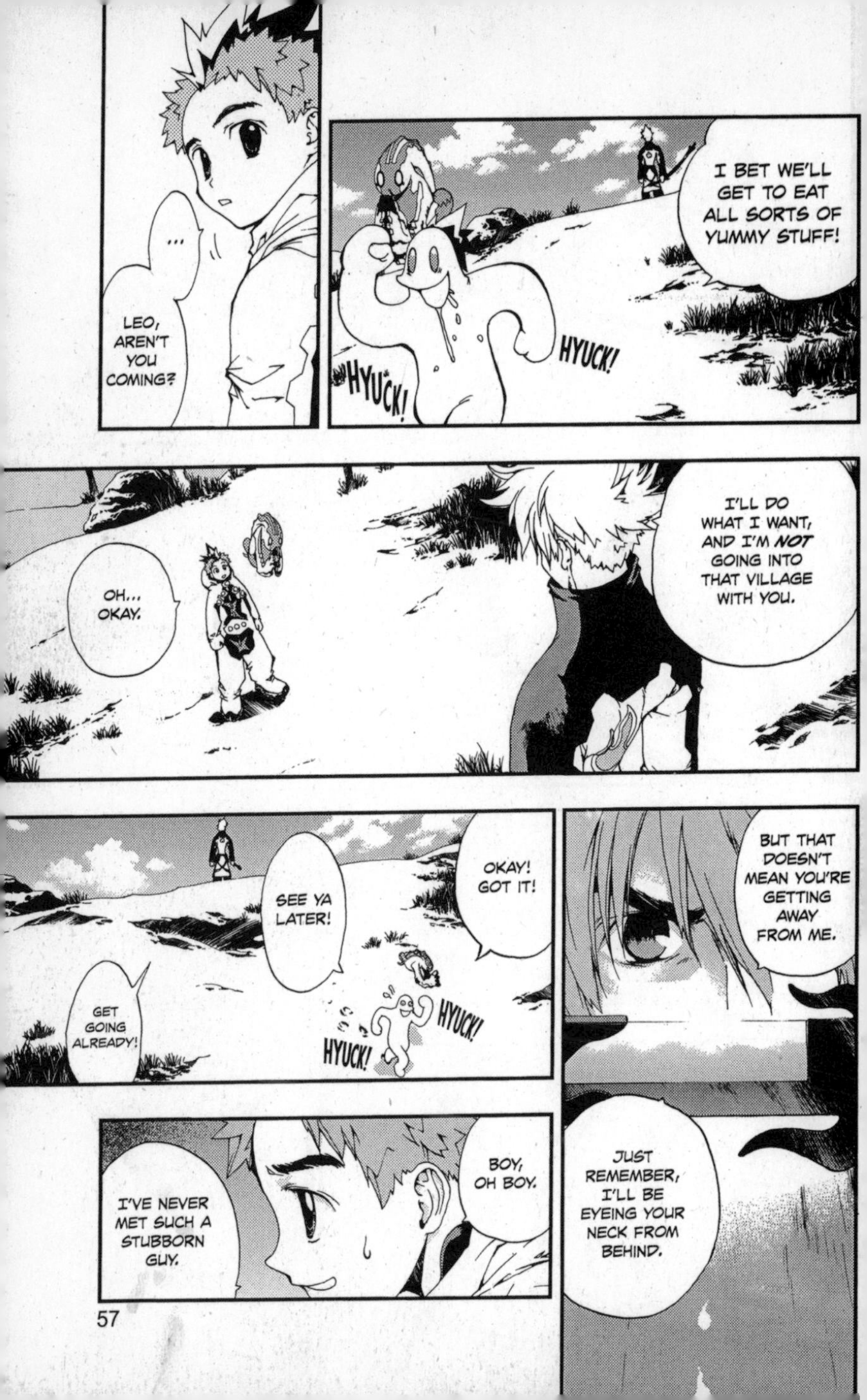
I BET WE'LL GET TO EAT ALL SORTS OF YUMMY STUFF!
HYUCK!
HYUCK!
...
LEO, AREN'T YOU COMING?
I'LL DO WHAT I WANT, AND I'M *NOT* GOING INTO THAT VILLAGE WITH YOU.
OH... OKAY.
BUT THAT DOESN'T MEAN YOU'RE GETTING AWAY FROM ME.
JUST REMEMBER, I'LL BE EYEING YOUR NECK FROM BEHIND.
OKAY! GOT IT!
SEE YA LATER!
HYUCK!
HYUCK!
GET GOING ALREADY!
BOY, OH BOY.
I'VE NEVER MET SUCH A STUBBORN GUY.

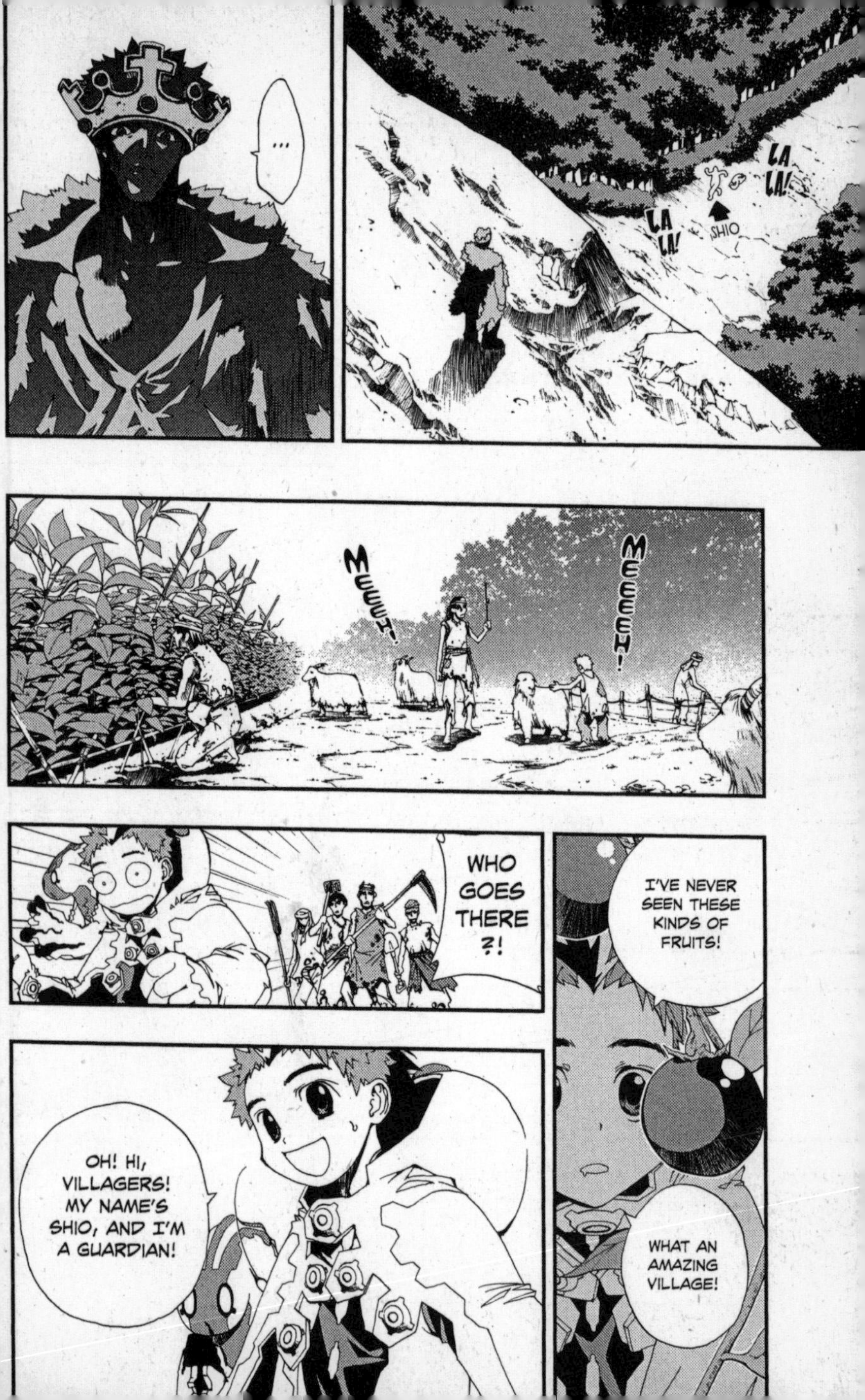
LA LA!
LA LA!
SHIO
...
MEEEEEH!
MEEEH!
I'VE NEVER SEEN THESE KINDS OF FRUITS!
WHAT AN AMAZING VILLAGE!
WHO GOES THERE ?!
OH! HI, VILLAGERS! MY NAME'S SHIO, AND I'M A GUARDIAN!

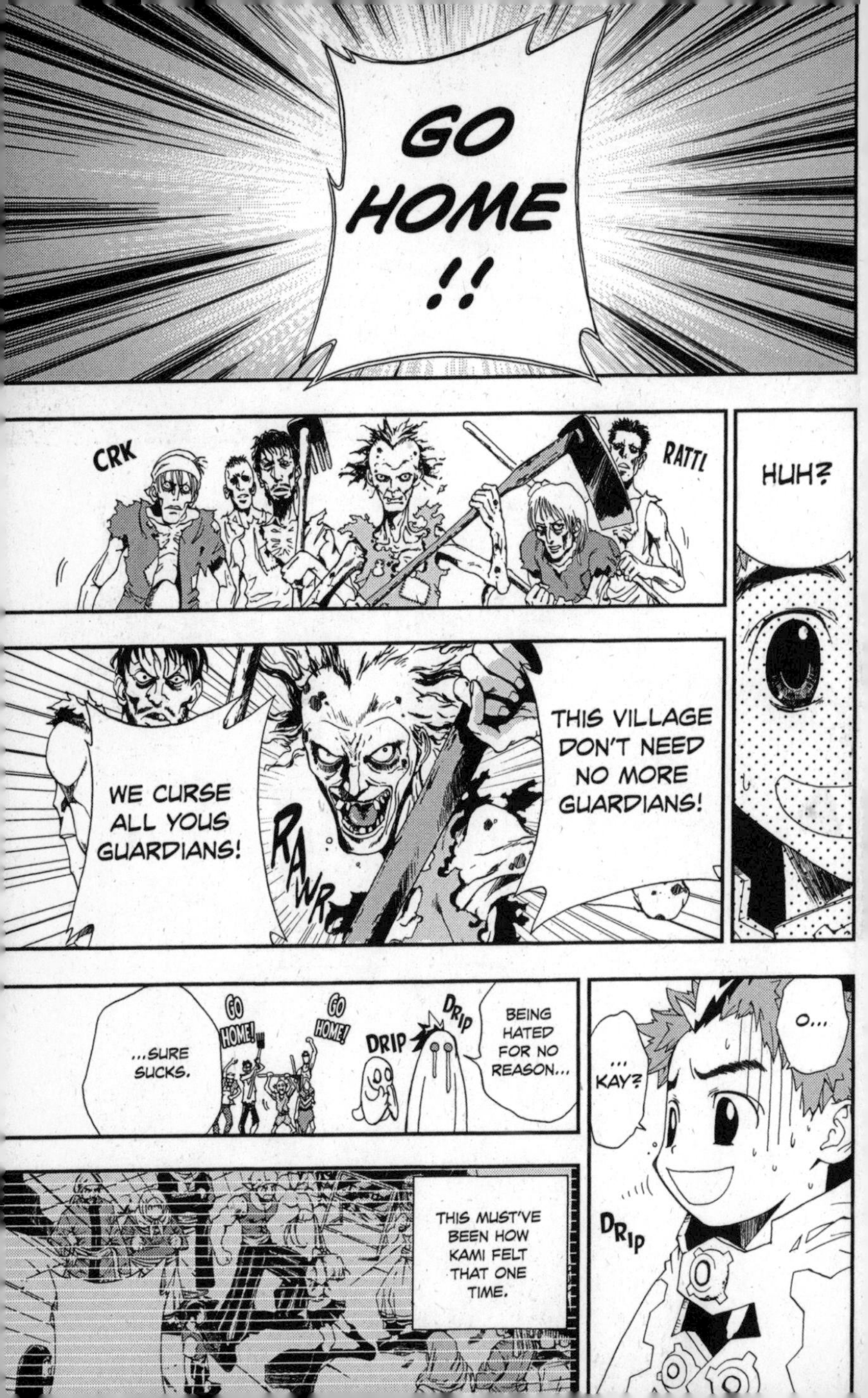
GO HOME !!
HUH?
RATTL
CRK
THIS VILLAGE DON'T NEED NO MORE GUARDIANS!
RAWR
WE CURSE ALL YOUS GUARDIANS!
O...
... KAY?
DRIP
BEING HATED FOR NO REASON...
DRIP
DRIP
GO HOME!
GO HOME!
...SURE SUCKS.
THIS MUST'VE BEEN HOW KAMI FELT THAT ONE TIME.

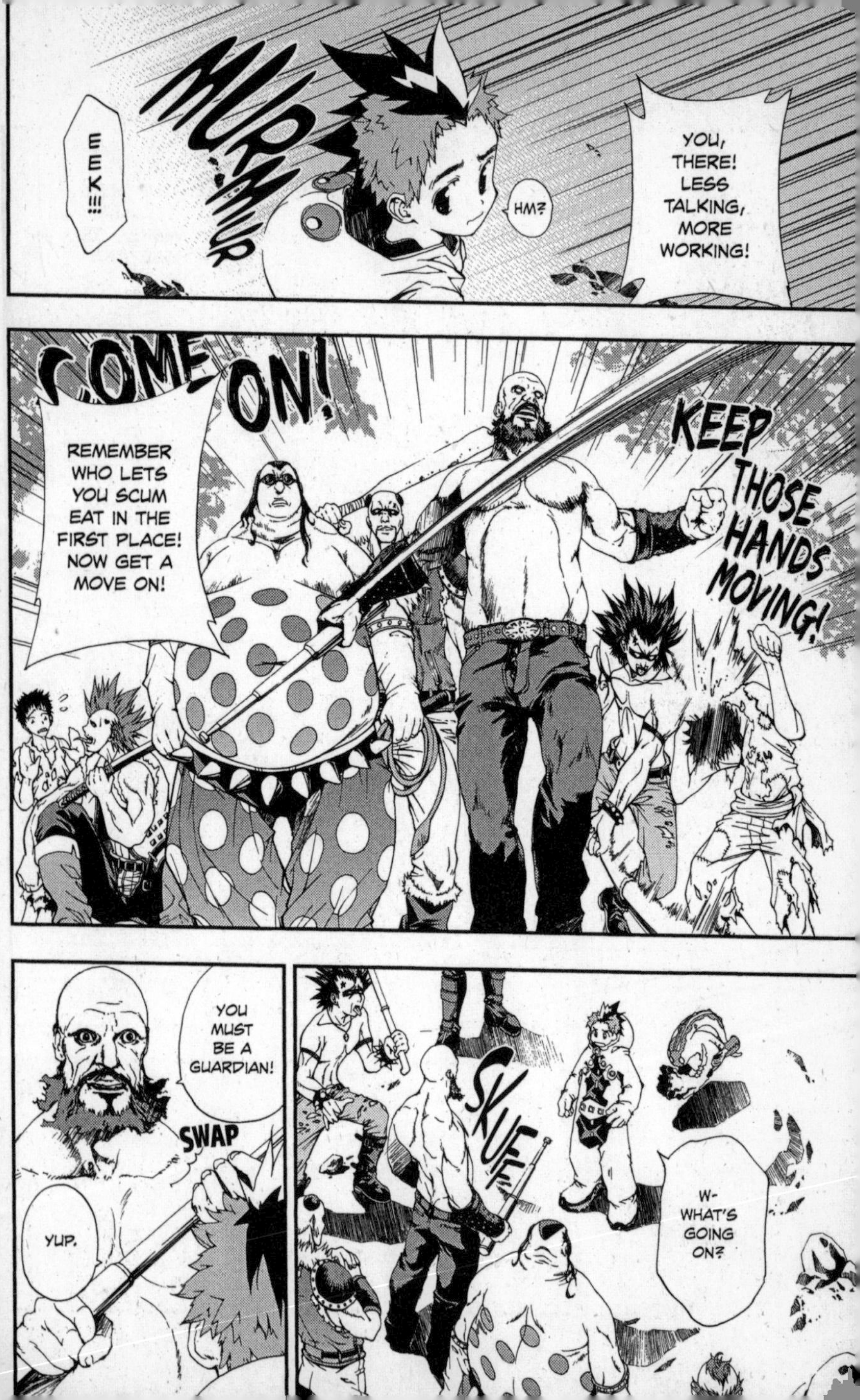
YOU, THERE! LESS TALKING, MORE WORKING!
HM?
MURMUR
EEK!!!
KEEP THOSE HANDS MOVING!
COME ON!
REMEMBER WHO LETS YOU SCUM EAT IN THE FIRST PLACE! NOW GET A MOVE ON!
W-WHAT'S GOING ON?
SKUFF
YOU MUST BE A GUARDIAN!
SWAP
YUP.

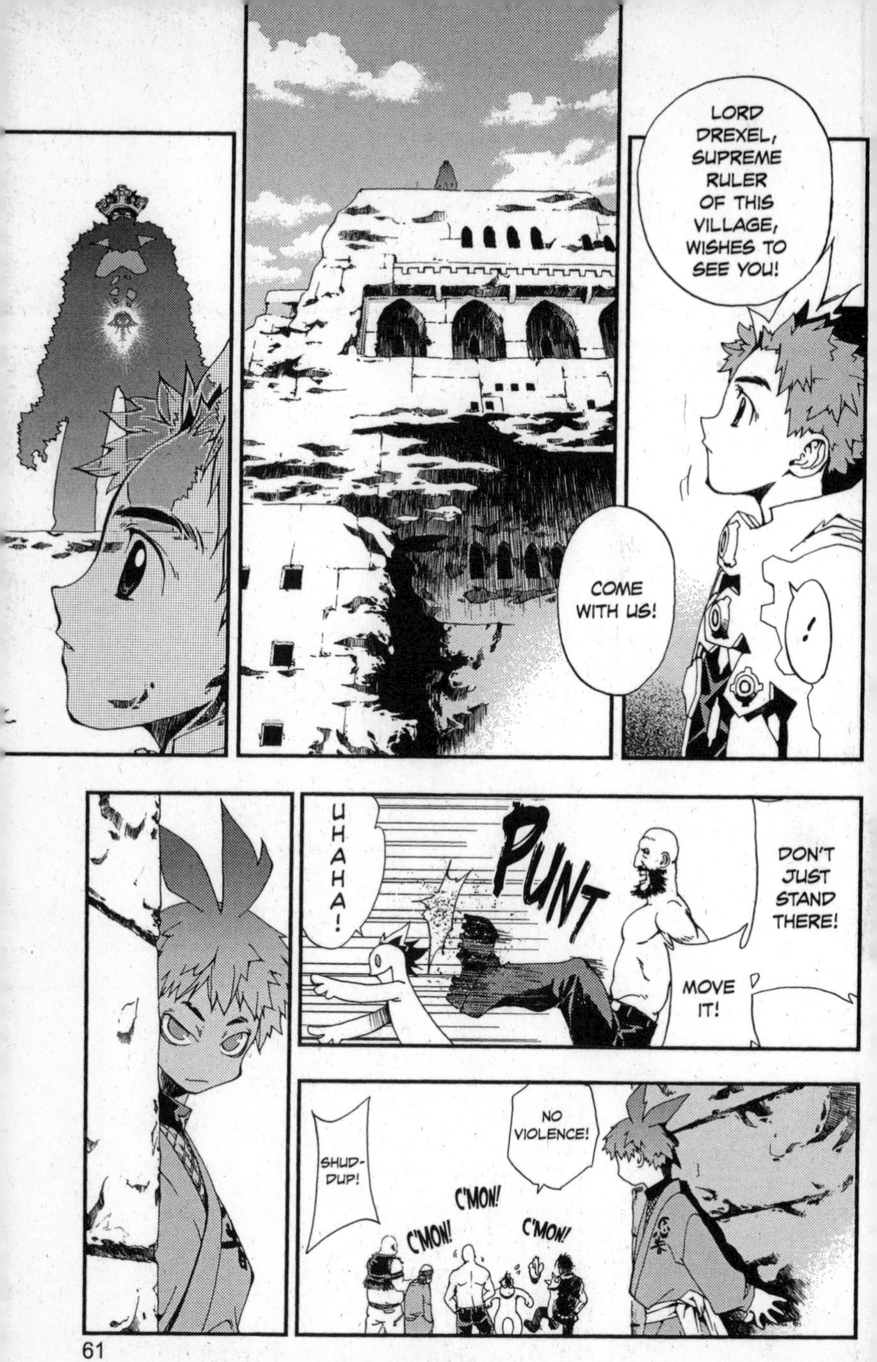

LORD DREXEL, SUPREME RULER OF THIS VILLAGE, WISHES TO SEE YOU!
COME WITH US!
!
DON'T JUST STAND THERE!
MOVE IT!
PUNT
UHAHA!
NO VIOLENCE!
C'MON!
SHUD-DUP!
C'MON!
C'MON!

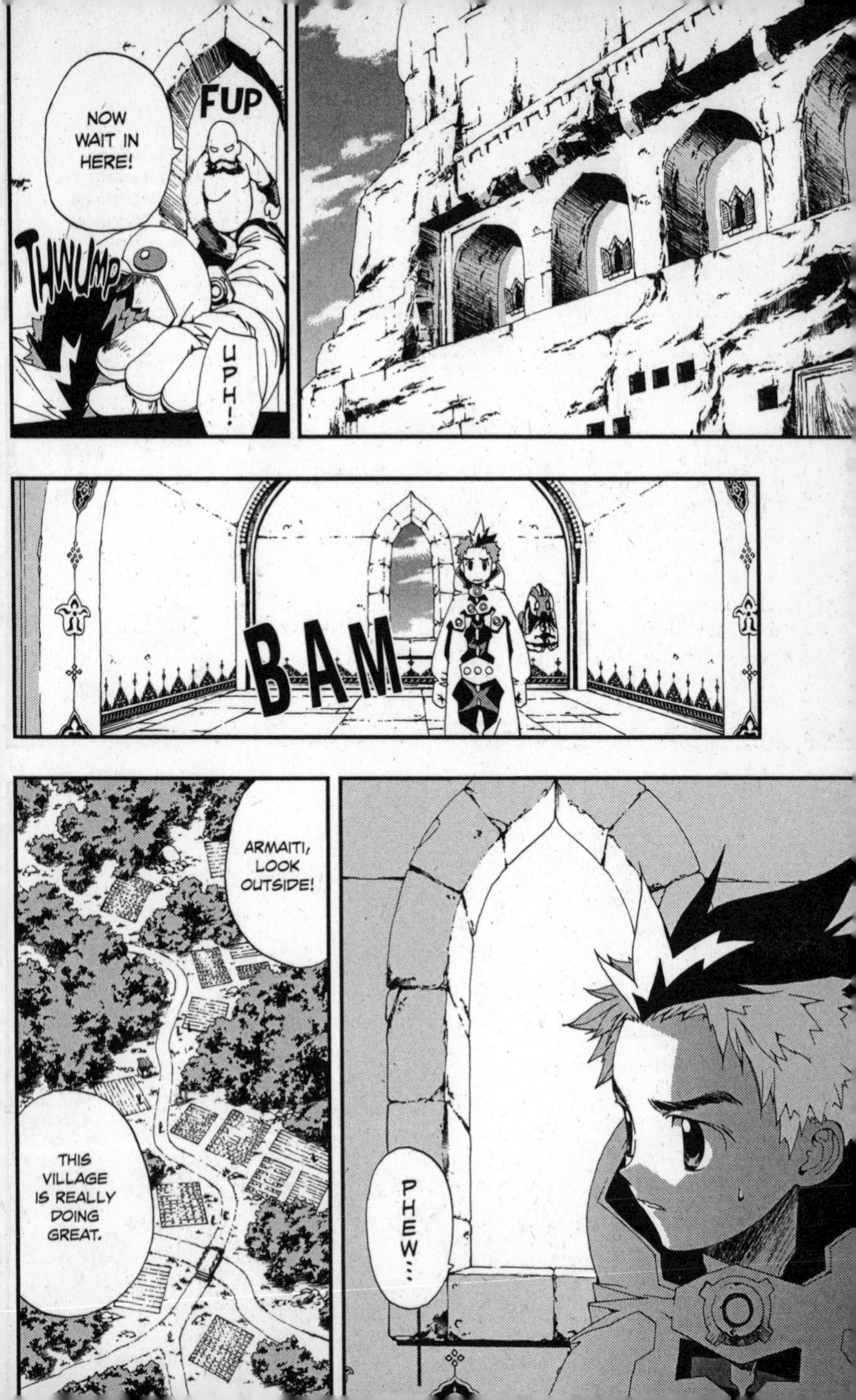
FUP
NOW WAIT IN HERE!
THWUMP
UPH!
BAM
PHEW...
ARMAITI, LOOK OUTSIDE!
THIS VILLAGE IS REALLY DOING GREAT.

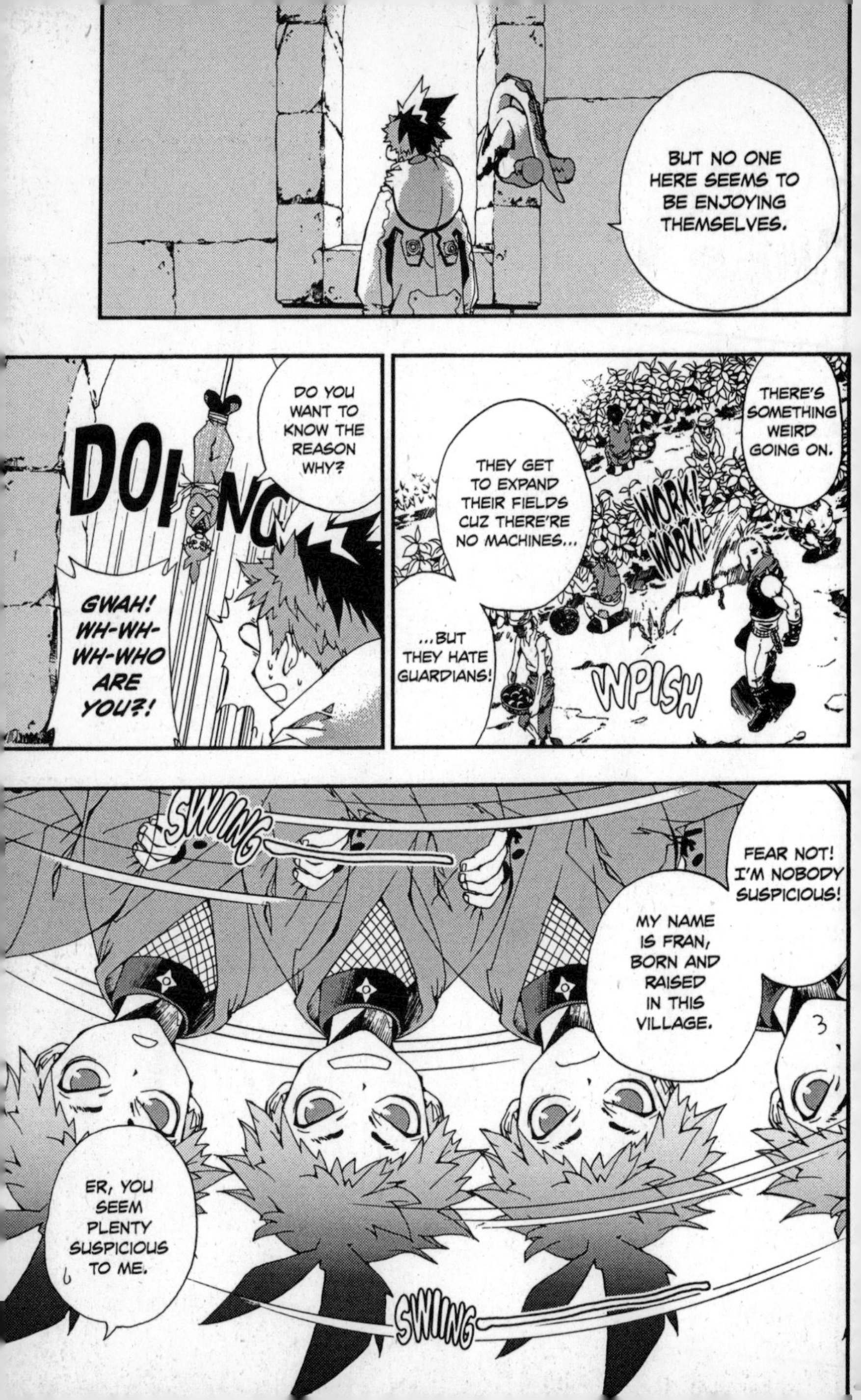
BUT NO ONE HERE SEEMS TO BE ENJOYING THEMSELVES.
THERE'S SOMETHING WEIRD GOING ON.
THEY GET TO EXPAND THEIR FIELDS CUZ THERE'RE NO MACHINES...
WORK! WORK!
...BUT THEY HATE GUARDIANS!
WPISH
DO YOU WANT TO KNOW THE REASON WHY?
DOING
GWAH! WH-WH-WH-WHO ARE YOU?!
FEAR NOT! I'M NOBODY SUSPICIOUS!
SWING
MY NAME IS FRAN, BORN AND RAISED IN THIS VILLAGE.
ER, YOU SEEM PLENTY SUSPICIOUS TO ME.
SWING

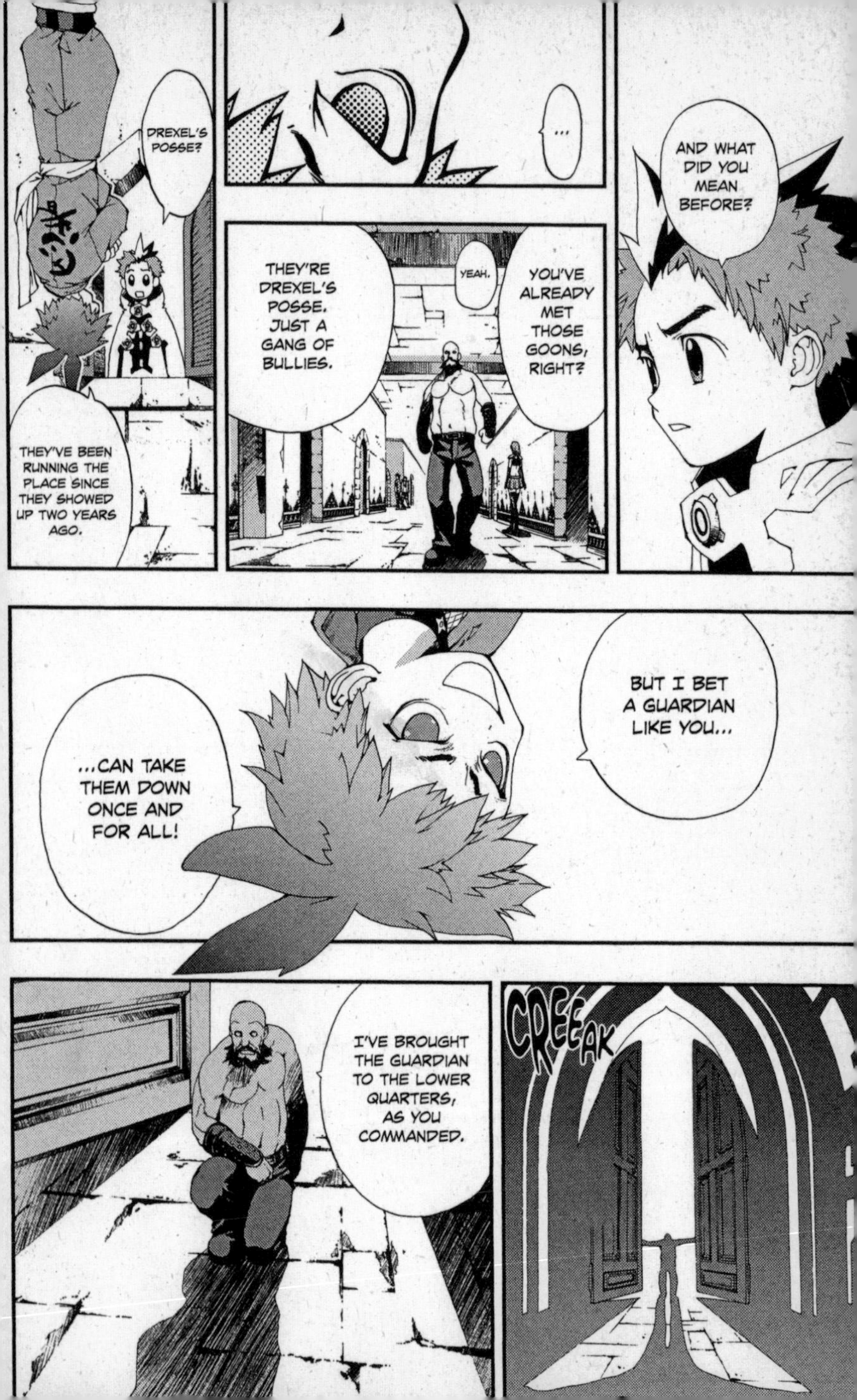
AND WHAT DID YOU MEAN BEFORE?
...
YOU'VE ALREADY MET THOSE GOONS, RIGHT?
YEAH.
THEY'RE DREXEL'S POSSE. JUST A GANG OF BULLIES.
DREXEL'S POSSE?
THEY'VE BEEN RUNNING THE PLACE SINCE THEY SHOWED UP TWO YEARS AGO.
BUT I BET A GUARDIAN LIKE YOU...
...CAN TAKE THEM DOWN ONCE AND FOR ALL!
CREEEAK
I'VE BROUGHT THE GUARDIAN TO THE LOWER QUARTERS, AS YOU COMMANDED.

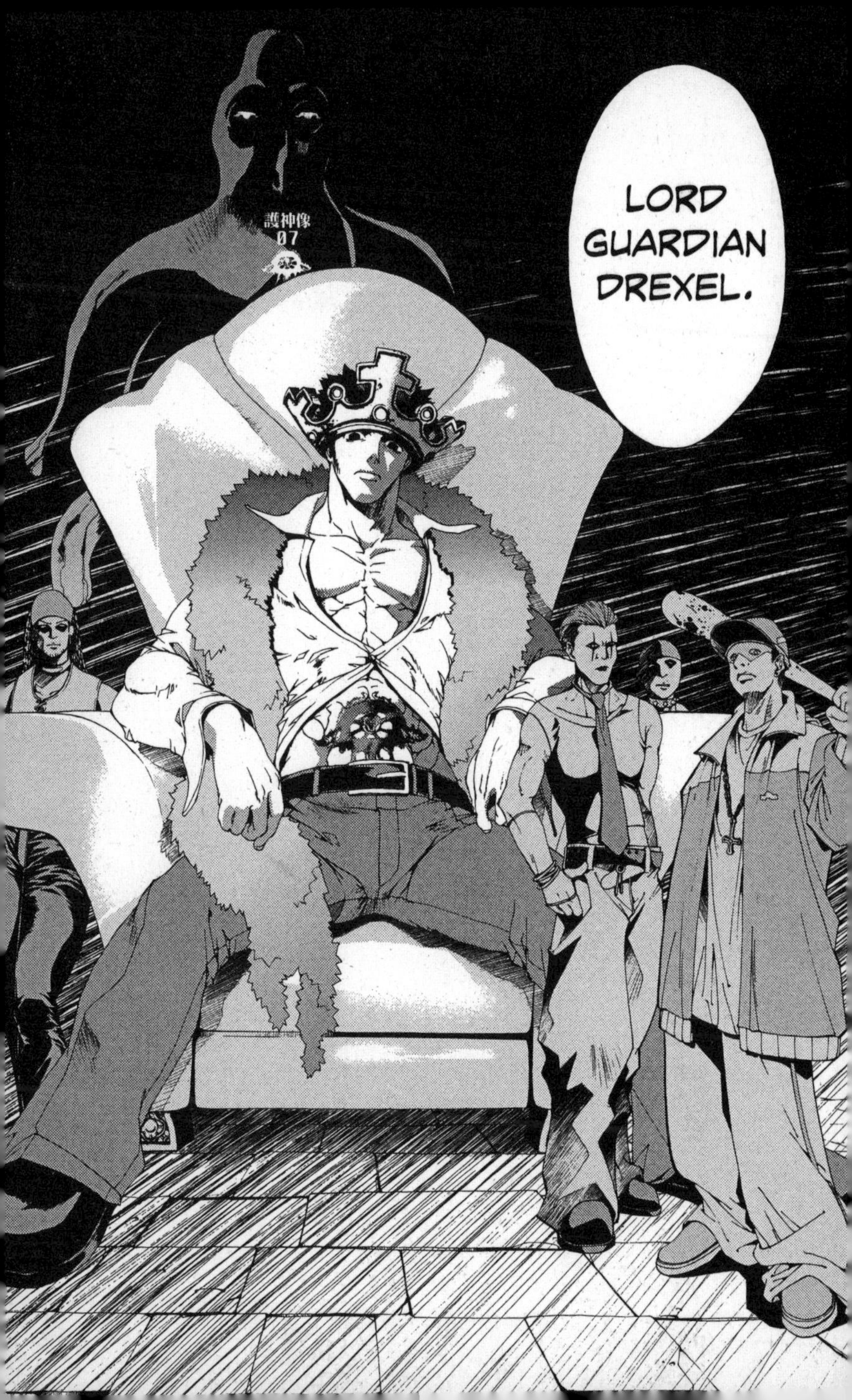
LORD GUARDIAN DREXEL.
護神像
07

WaqWaq

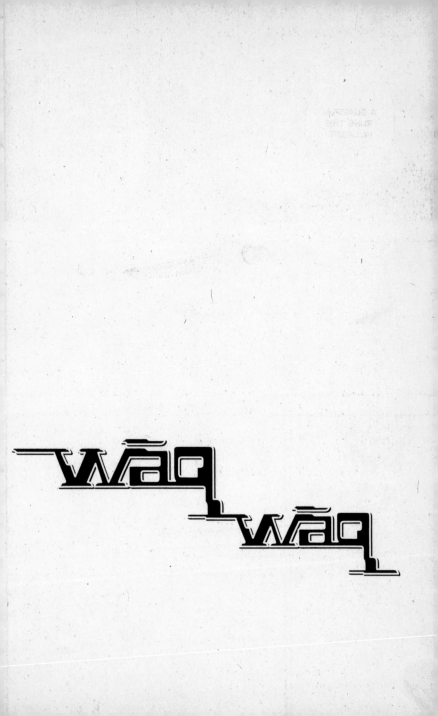

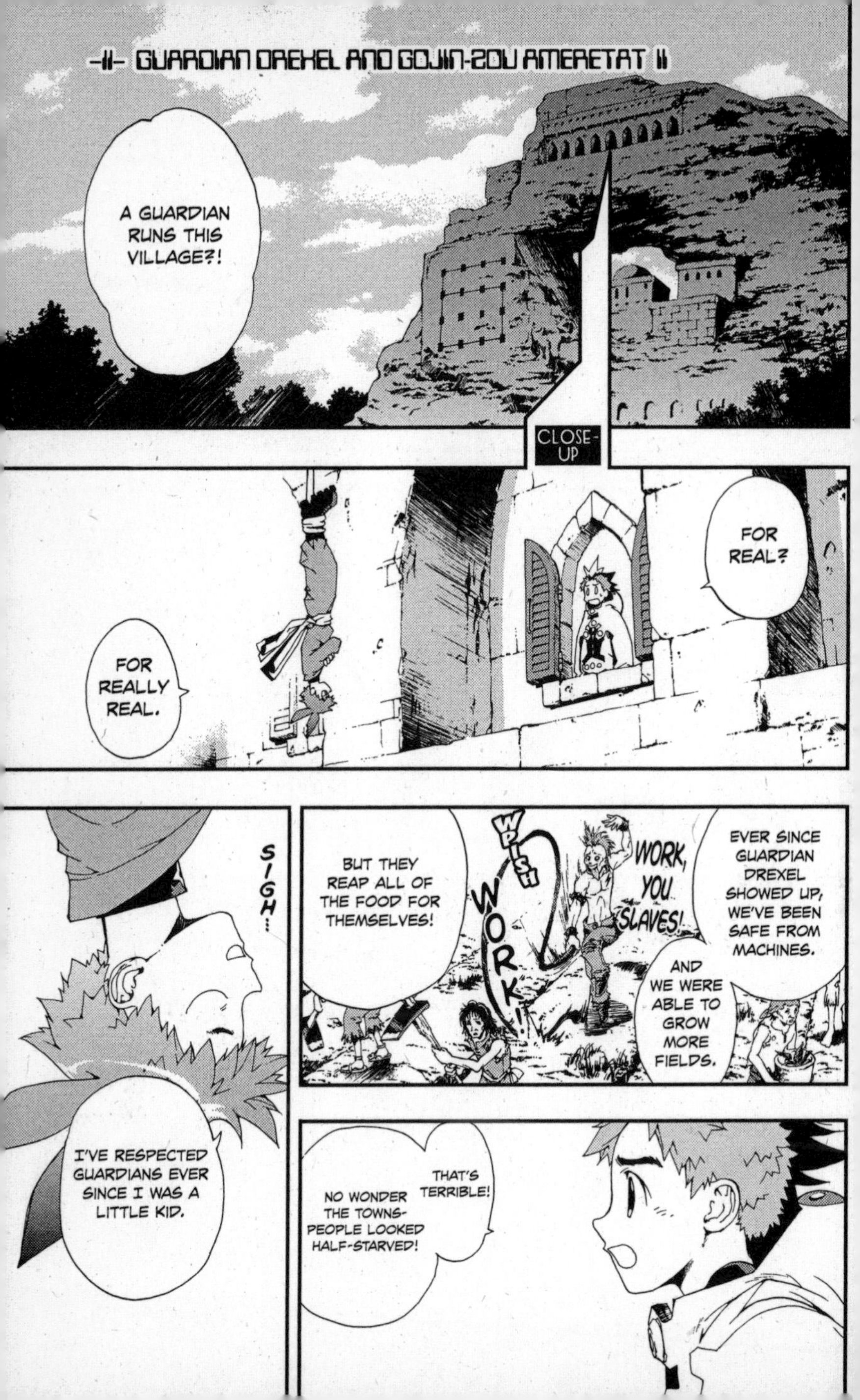
-11- GUARDIAN DREXEL AND GOJIN-ZOU AMERETAT 11
A GUARDIAN RUNS THIS VILLAGE?!
CLOSE-UP
FOR REAL?
FOR REALLY REAL.
EVER SINCE GUARDIAN DREXEL SHOWED UP, WE'VE BEEN SAFE FROM MACHINES.
AND WE WERE ABLE TO GROW MORE FIELDS.
WORK, YOU SLAVES!
WPISH
WORK WORK!
BUT THEY REAP ALL OF THE FOOD FOR THEMSELVES!
THAT'S TERRIBLE!
NO WONDER THE TOWNS-PEOPLE LOOKED HALF-STARVED!
SIGH...
I'VE RESPECTED GUARDIANS EVER SINCE I WAS A LITTLE KID.

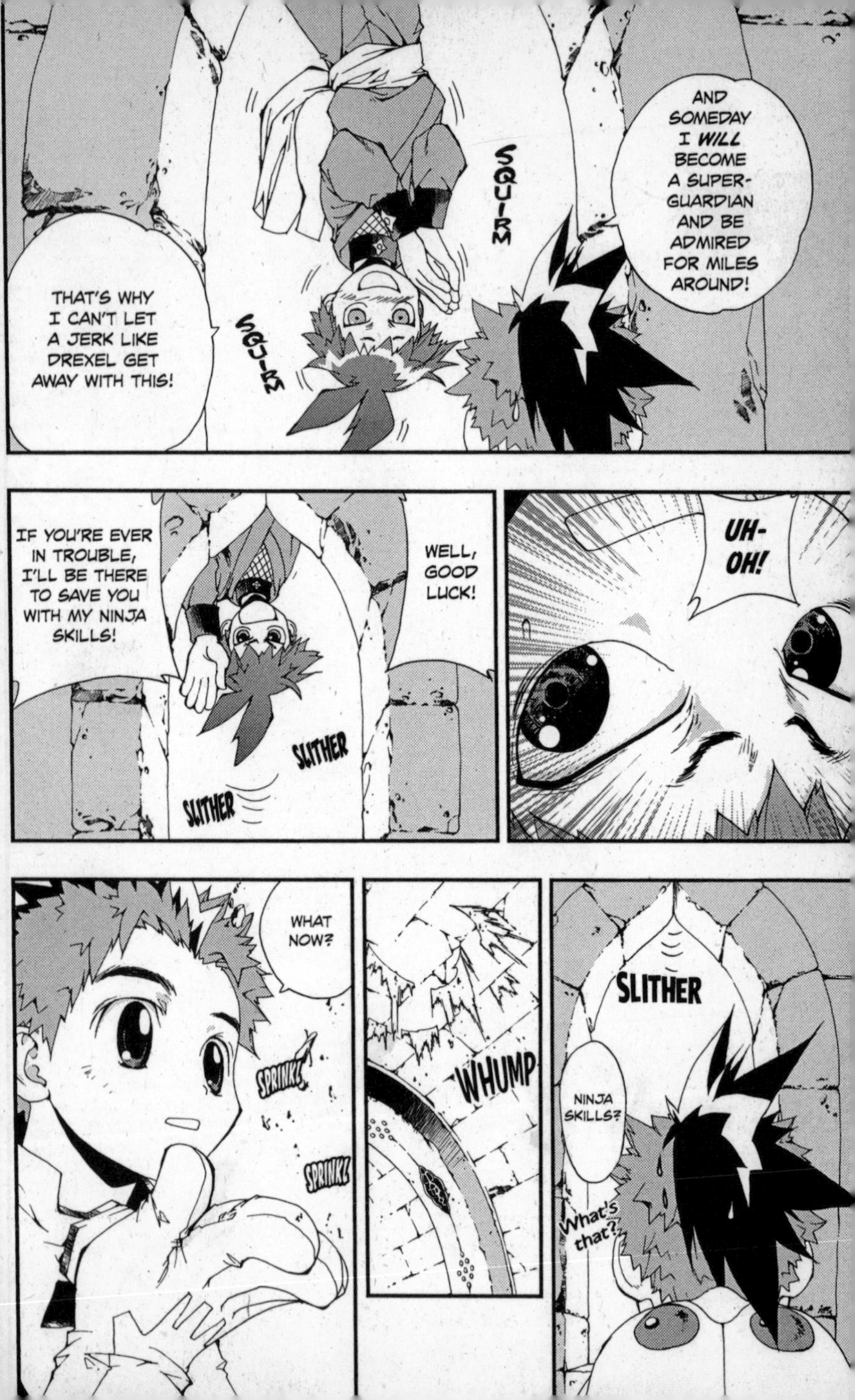
AND SOMEDAY I *WILL* BECOME A SUPER-GUARDIAN AND BE ADMIRED FOR MILES AROUND!
SQUIRM
SQUIRM
THAT'S WHY I CAN'T LET A JERK LIKE DREXEL GET AWAY WITH THIS!
UH-OH!
WELL, GOOD LUCK!
IF YOU'RE EVER IN TROUBLE, I'LL BE THERE TO SAVE YOU WITH MY NINJA SKILLS!
SLITHER
SLITHER
SLITHER
NINJA SKILLS?
What's that?
WHUMP
WHAT NOW?
SPRINK!
SPRINK!

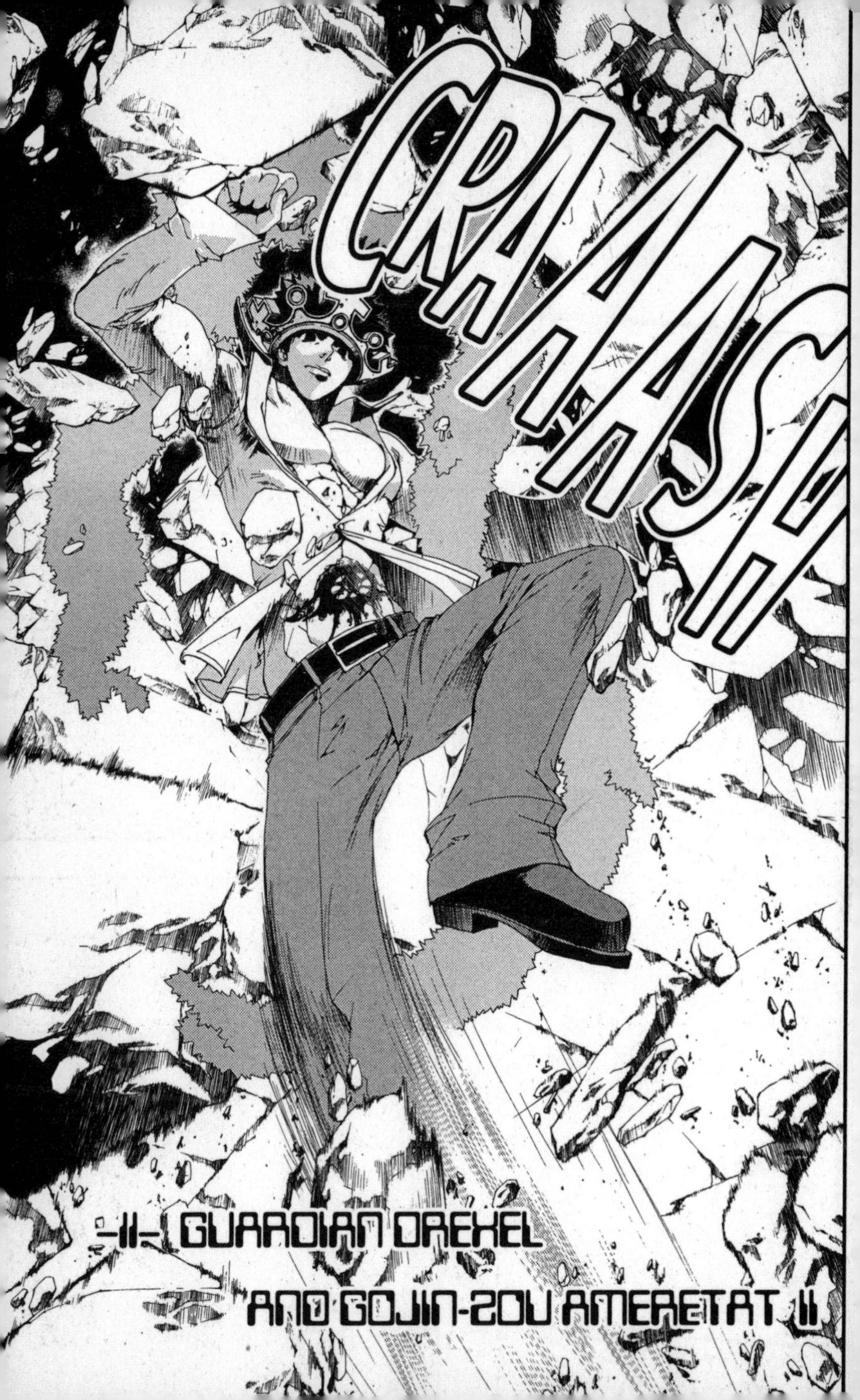
CRAAASH
-11- GUARDIAN DREXEL
AND GOJIN-ZOU AMERETAT II

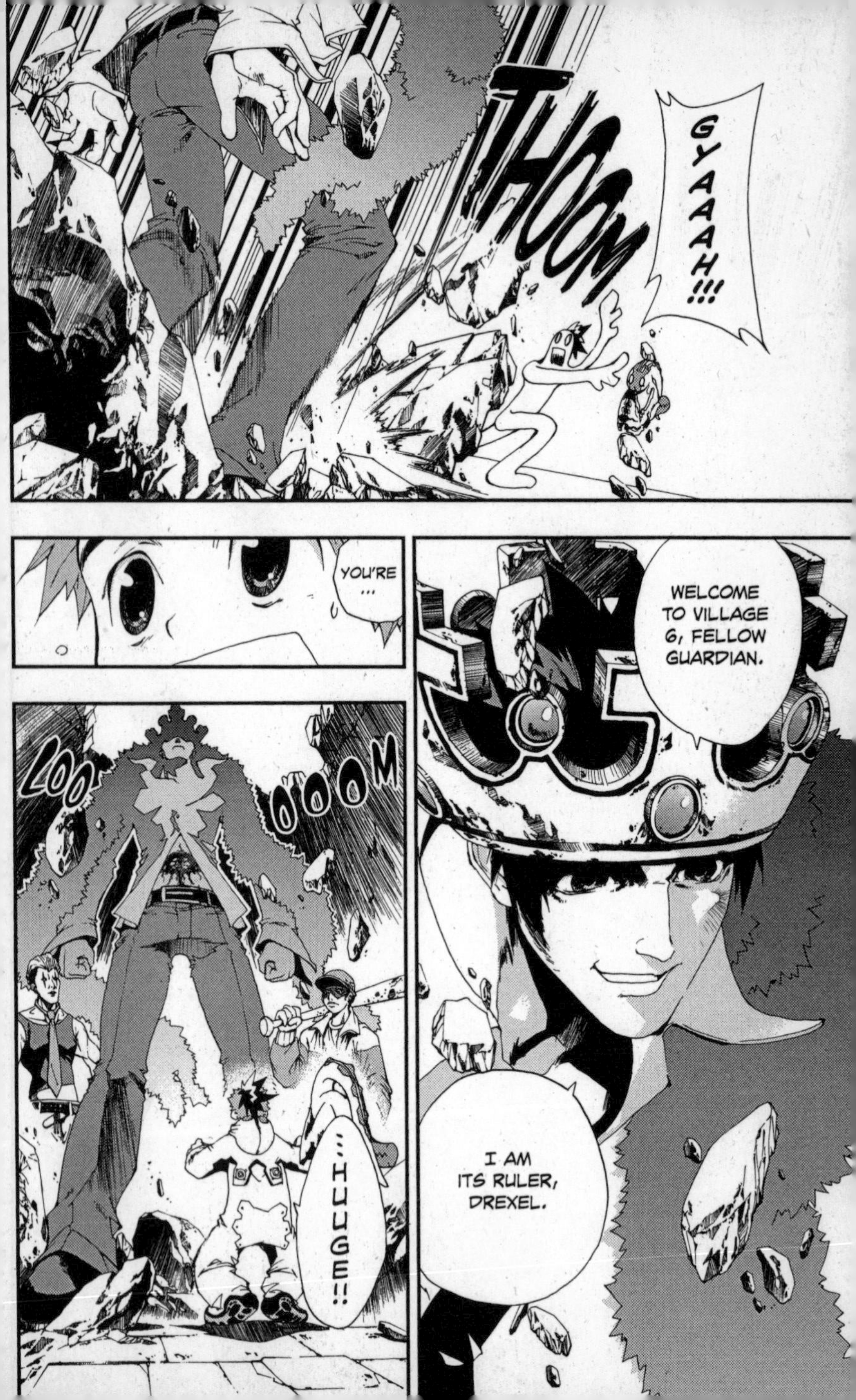
THOOM
GYAAAH!!!
WELCOME TO VILLAGE 6, FELLOW GUARDIAN.
I AM ITS RULER, DREXEL.
YOU'RE ...
LOOOOOM
...HUUGE!!

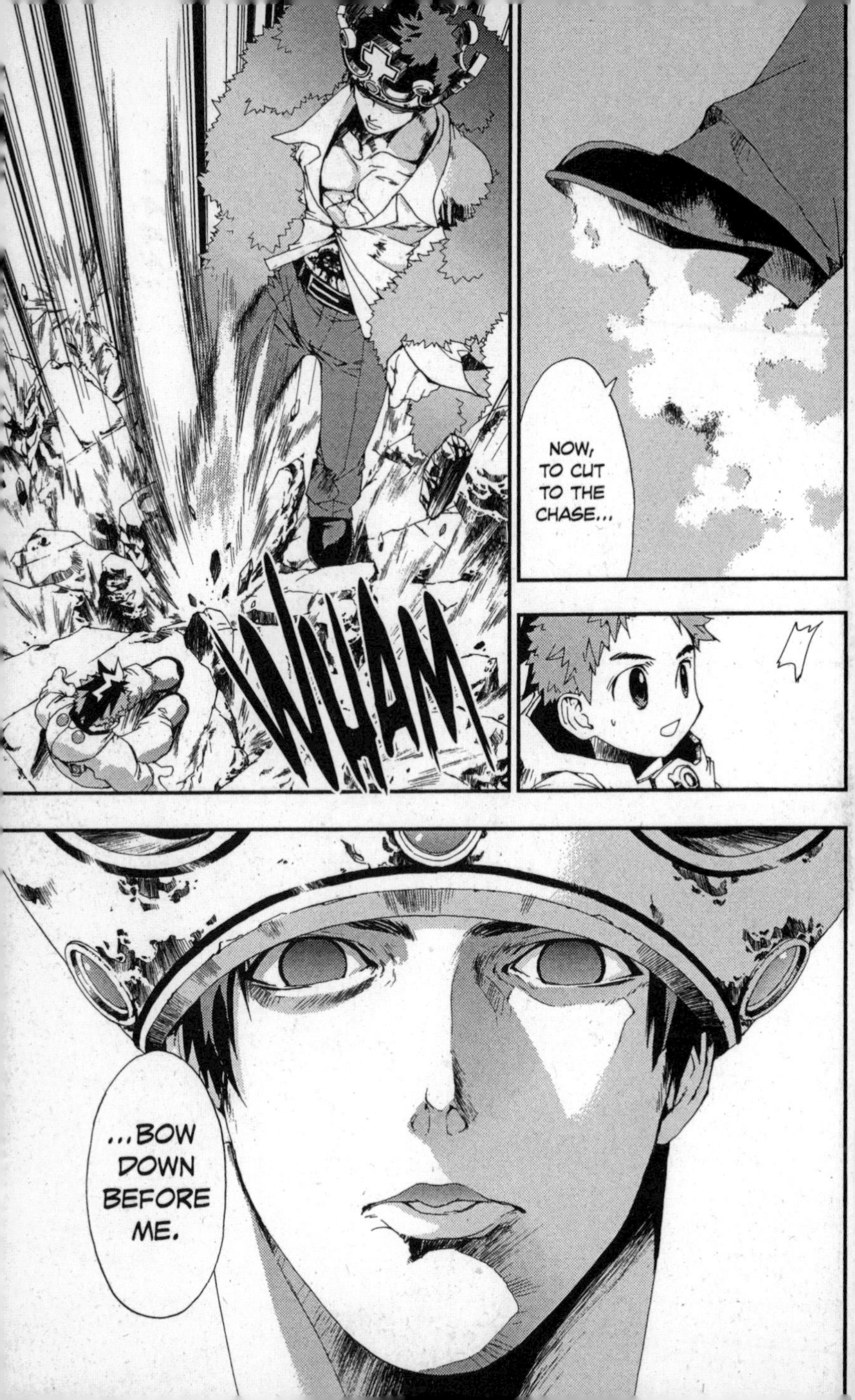
NOW, TO CUT TO THE CHASE...
WHAM
...BOW DOWN BEFORE ME.

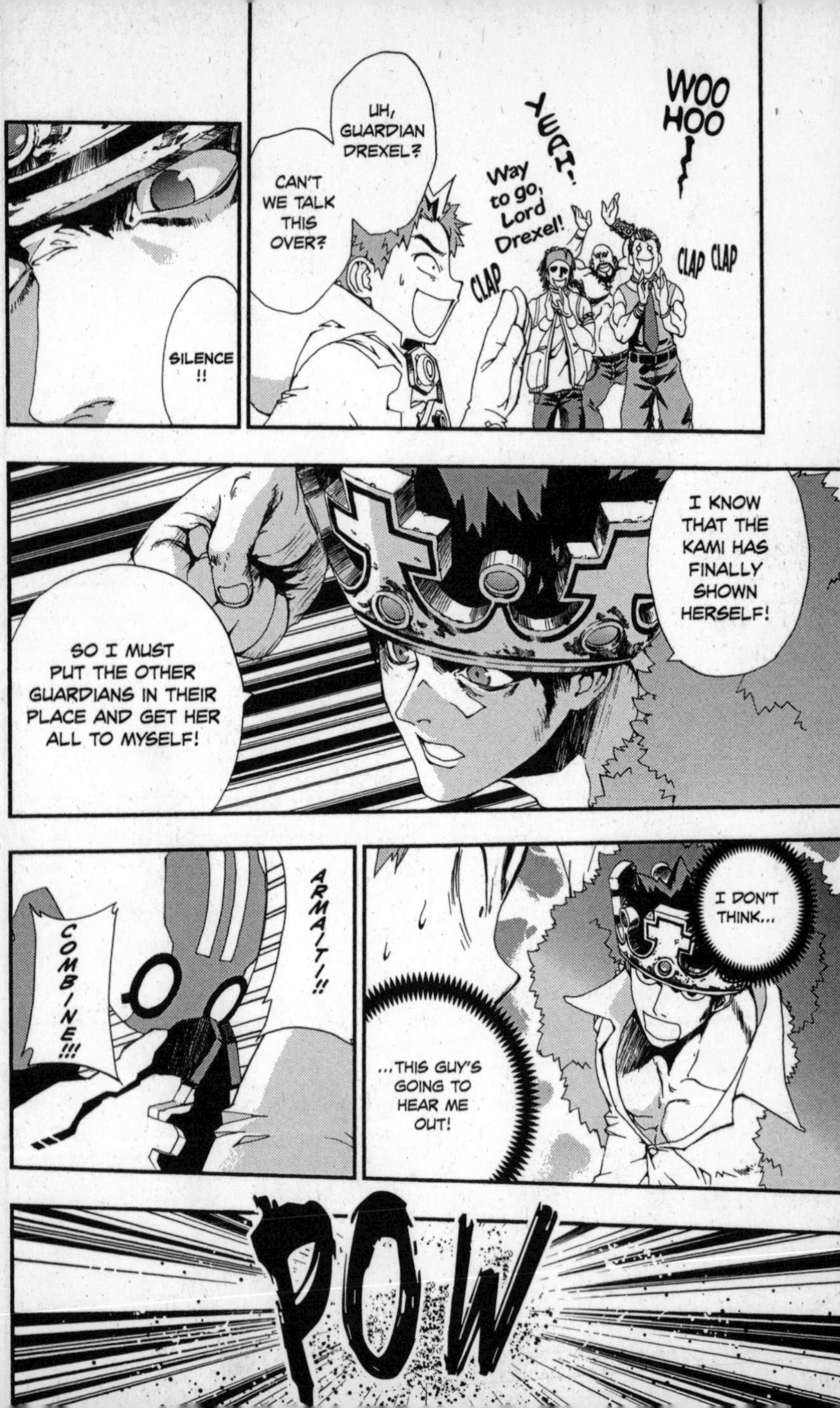
WOO HOO!
YEAH!
Way to go, Lord Drexel!
CLAP CLAP
CLAP
UH, GUARDIAN DREXEL?
CAN'T WE TALK THIS OVER?
SILENCE!!
I KNOW THAT THE KAMI HAS FINALLY SHOWN HERSELF!
SO I MUST PUT THE OTHER GUARDIANS IN THEIR PLACE AND GET HER ALL TO MYSELF!
I DON'T THINK...
...THIS GUY'S GOING TO HEAR ME OUT!
ARMAITI!!
COMBINE!!!
POW

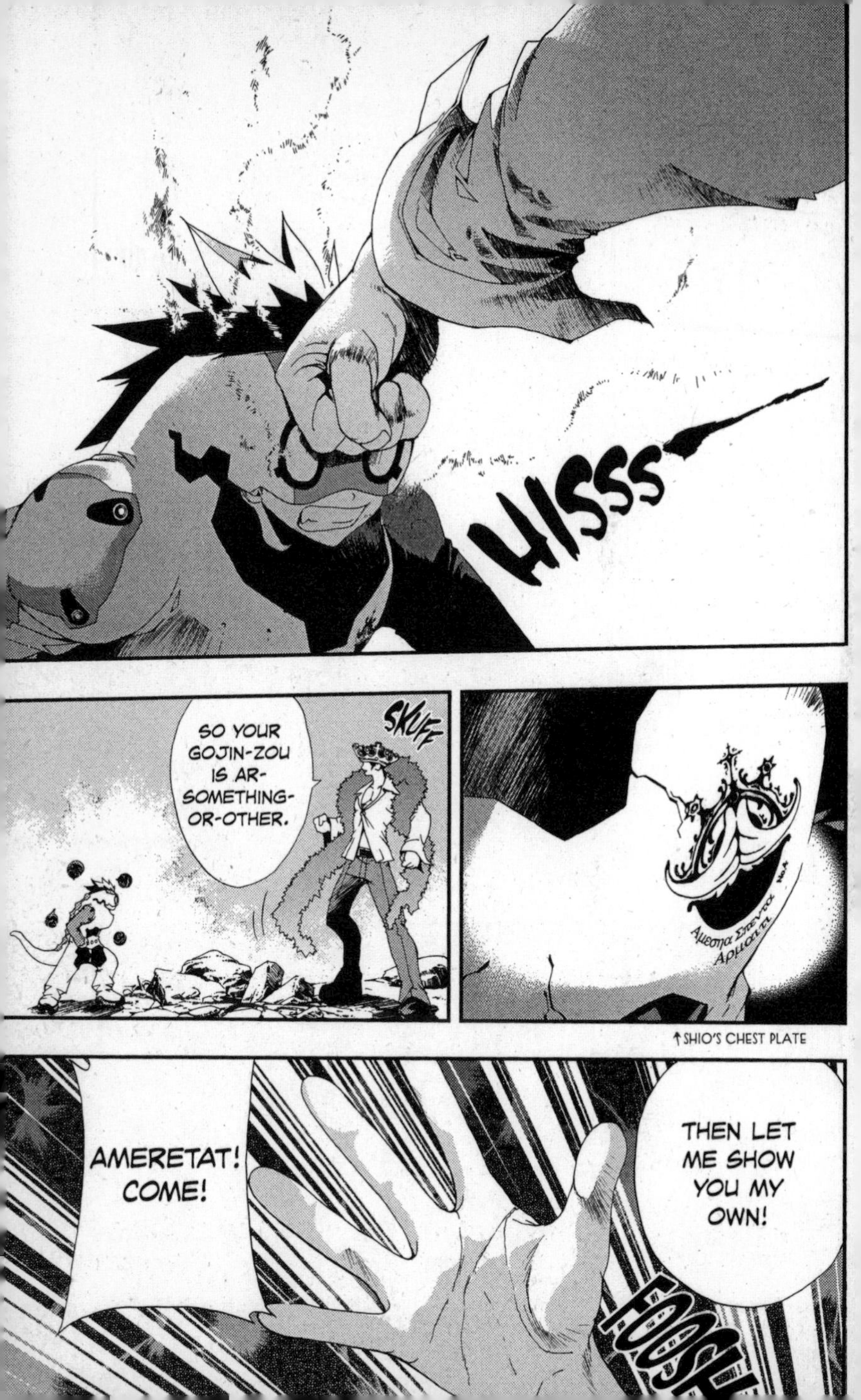
HISSS
SKUFF
SO YOUR GOJIN-ZOU IS AR-SOMETHING-OR-OTHER.
↑SHIO'S CHEST PLATE
THEN LET ME SHOW YOU MY OWN!
FOOSH
AMERETAT! COME!

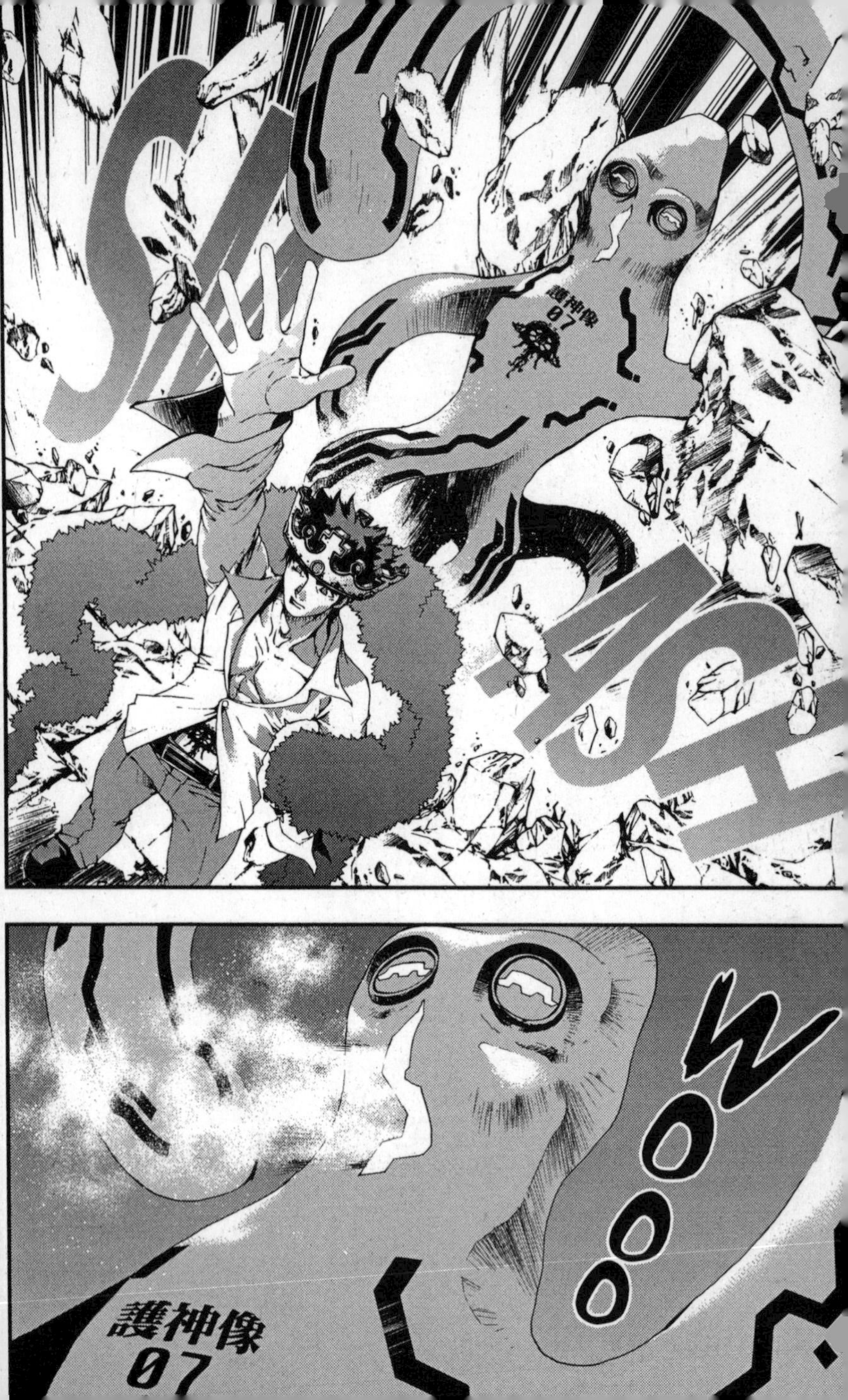
護神像
07
WOOO
護神像
07

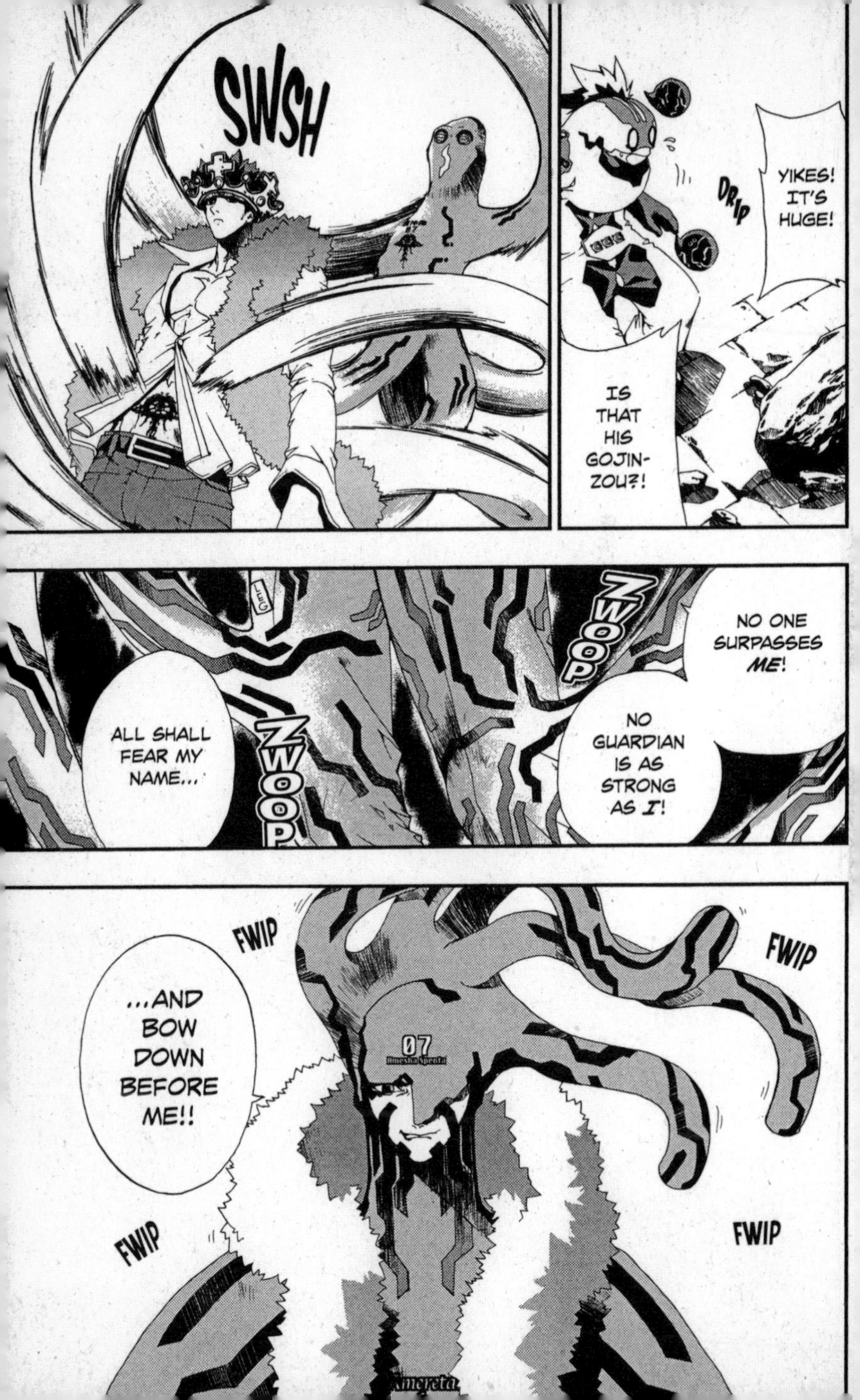
YIKES! IT'S HUGE!
DRIP
IS THAT HIS GOJIN-ZOU?!
SWSH
NO ONE SURPASSES ME!
ZWOOP
NO GUARDIAN IS AS STRONG AS I!
ZWOOP
ALL SHALL FEAR MY NAME...
FWIP
FWIP
...AND BOW DOWN BEFORE ME!!
07
Amesha Spenta
FWIP
FWIP

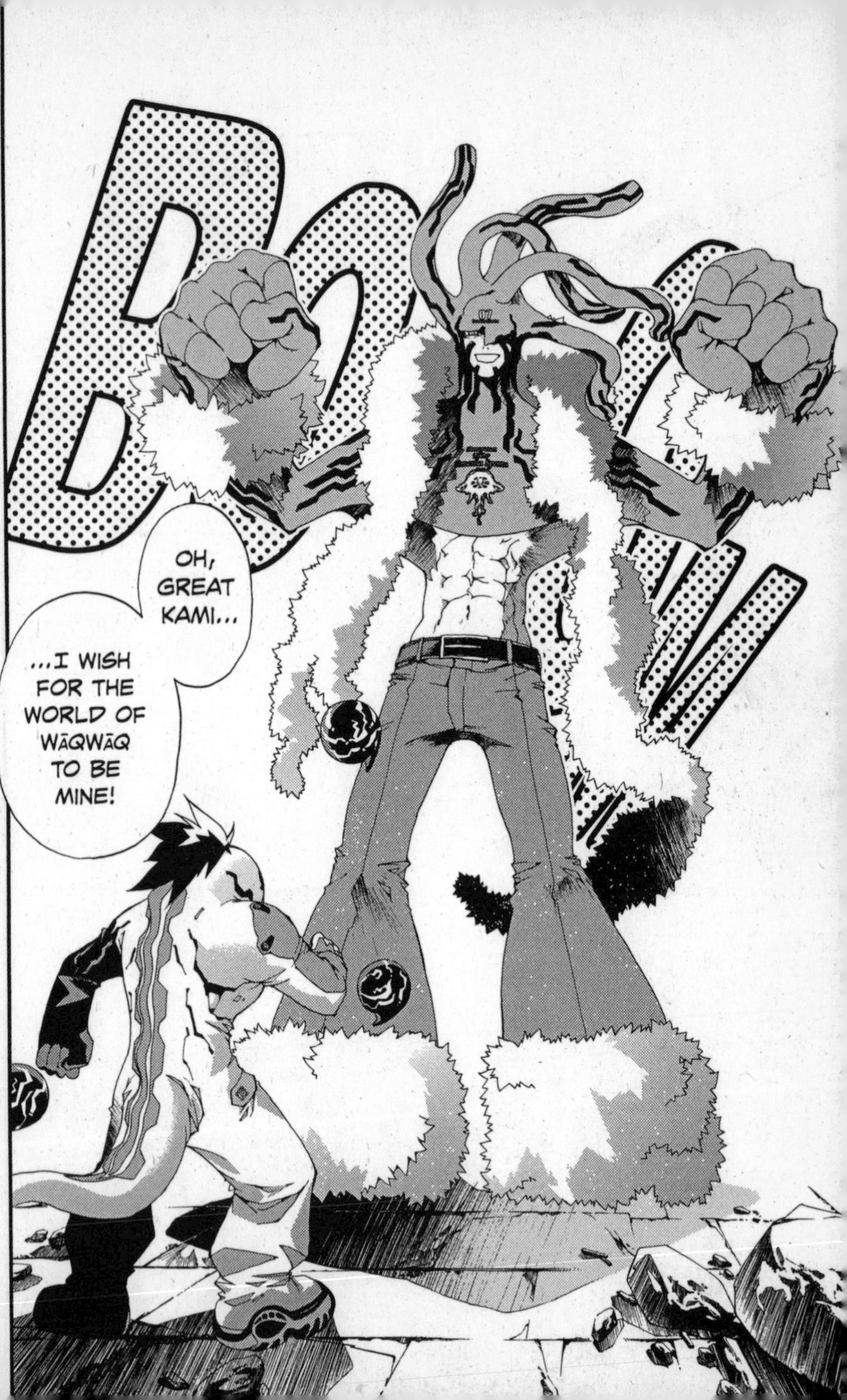
OH, GREAT KAMI...
...I WISH FOR THE WORLD OF WĀQWĀQ TO BE MINE!

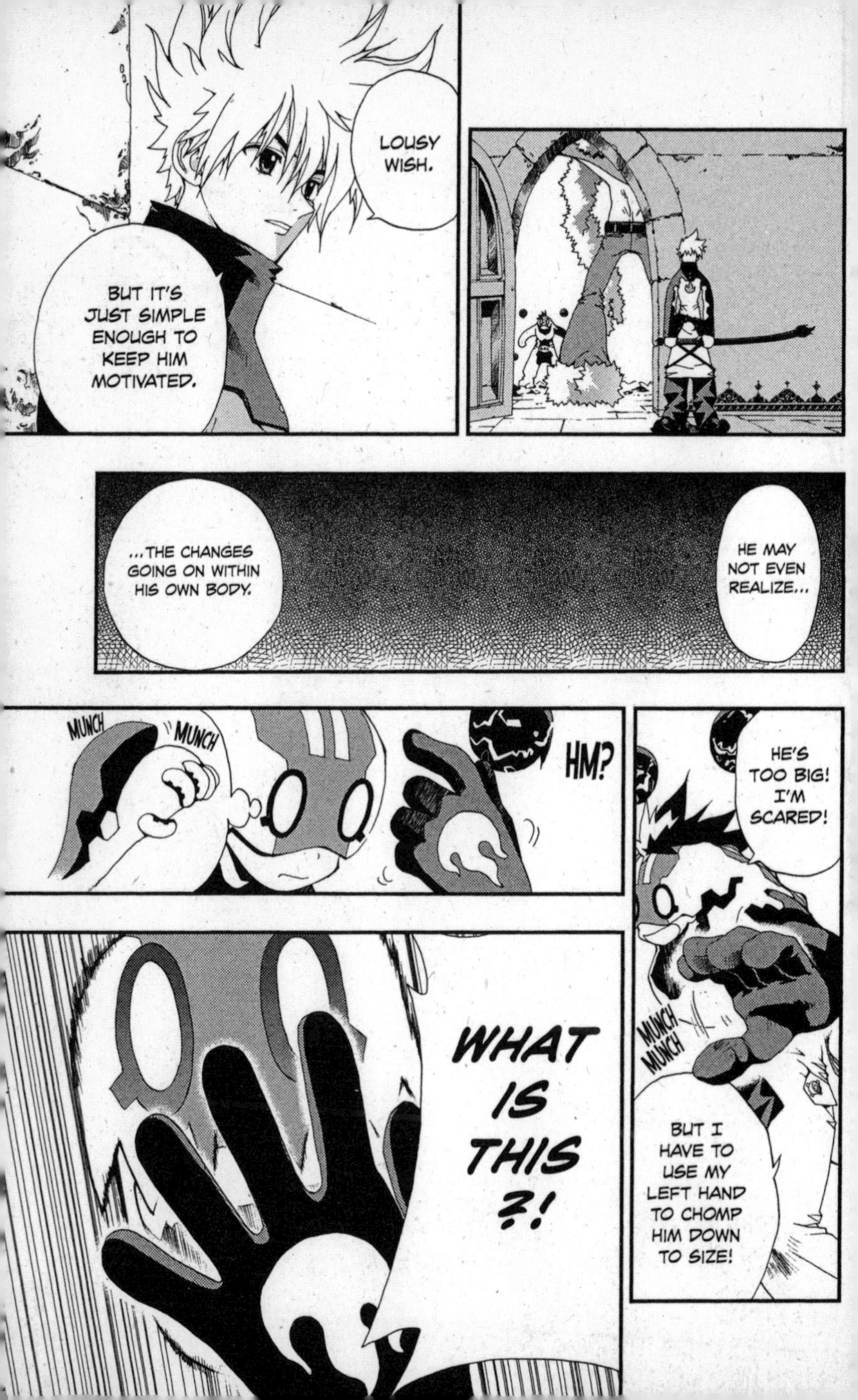
LOUSY WISH.
BUT IT'S JUST SIMPLE ENOUGH TO KEEP HIM MOTIVATED.
HE MAY NOT EVEN REALIZE...
...THE CHANGES GOING ON WITHIN HIS OWN BODY.
HE'S TOO BIG! I'M SCARED!
MUNCH MUNCH
BUT I HAVE TO USE MY LEFT HAND TO CHOMP HIM DOWN TO SIZE!
HM?
MUNCH
MUNCH
WHAT IS THIS ?!

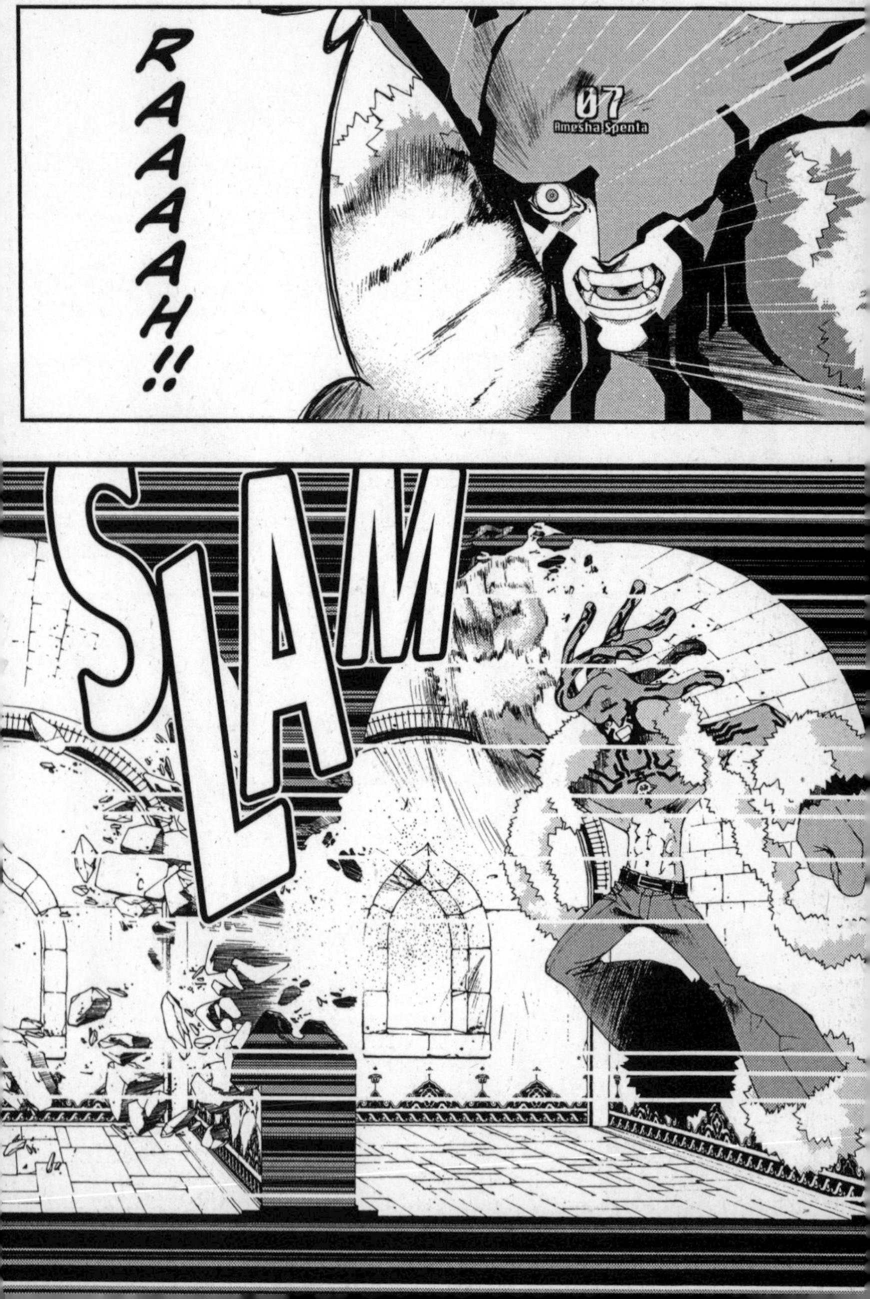
07
Amesha Spenta
RAAAAAH!!
SLAM

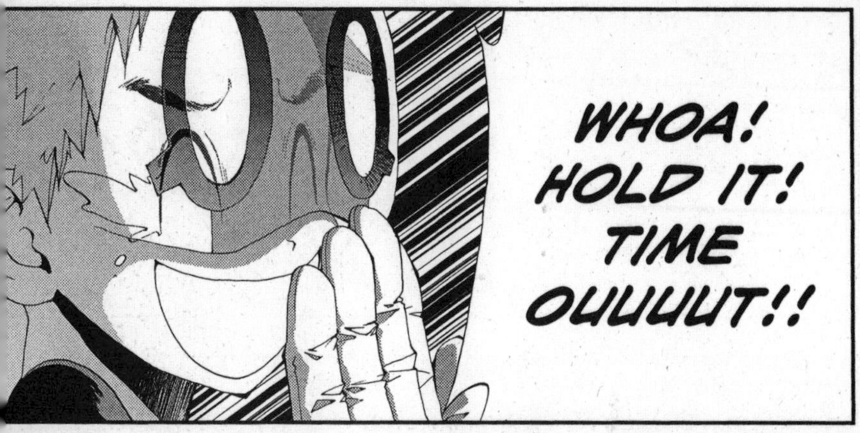
WHOA! HOLD IT! TIME OUUUUT!!
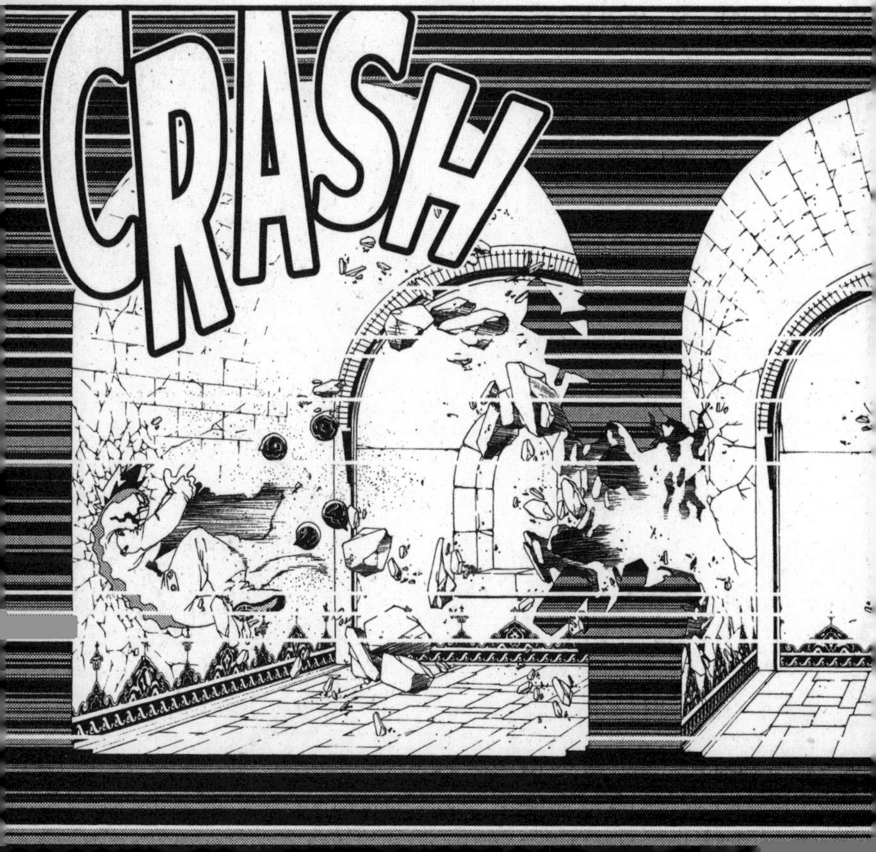
CRASH

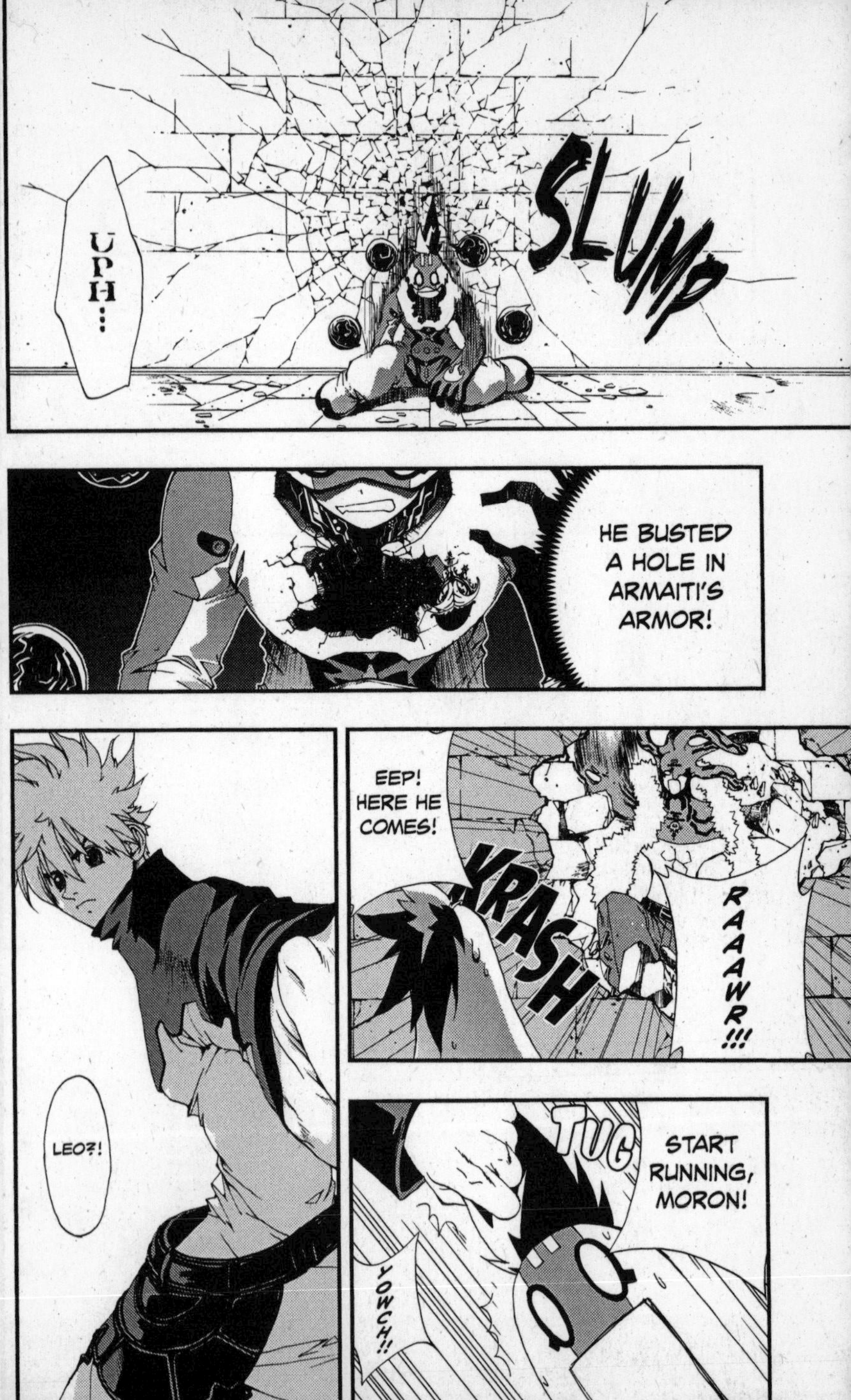
SLUMP
UPH...
HE BUSTED A HOLE IN ARMAITI'S ARMOR!
RAAAAWR!!!
EEP! HERE HE COMES!
KRASH
START RUNNING, MORON!
TUG
YOWCH!!
LEO?!

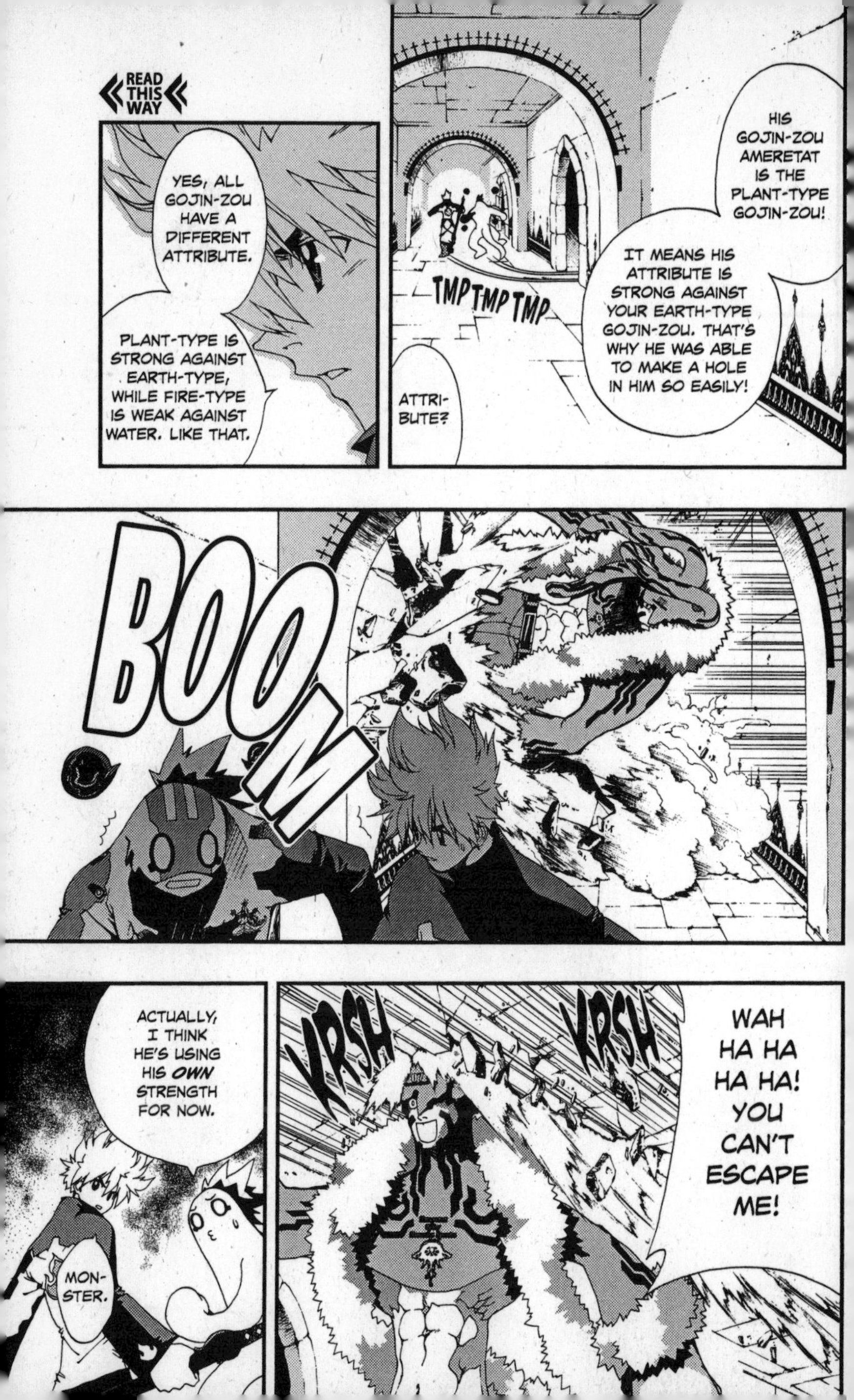
READ THIS WAY
HIS GOJIN-ZOU AMERETAT IS THE PLANT-TYPE GOJIN-ZOU!
IT MEANS HIS ATTRIBUTE IS STRONG AGAINST YOUR EARTH-TYPE GOJIN-ZOU. THAT'S WHY HE WAS ABLE TO MAKE A HOLE IN HIM SO EASILY!
TMP TMP TMP
ATTRI-BUTE?
YES, ALL GOJIN-ZOU HAVE A DIFFERENT ATTRIBUTE.
PLANT-TYPE IS STRONG AGAINST EARTH-TYPE, WHILE FIRE-TYPE IS WEAK AGAINST WATER. LIKE THAT.
BOOM
KRSH
KRSH
WAH HA HA HA HA! YOU CAN'T ESCAPE ME!
ACTUALLY, I THINK HE'S USING HIS *OWN* STRENGTH FOR NOW.
MON-STER.

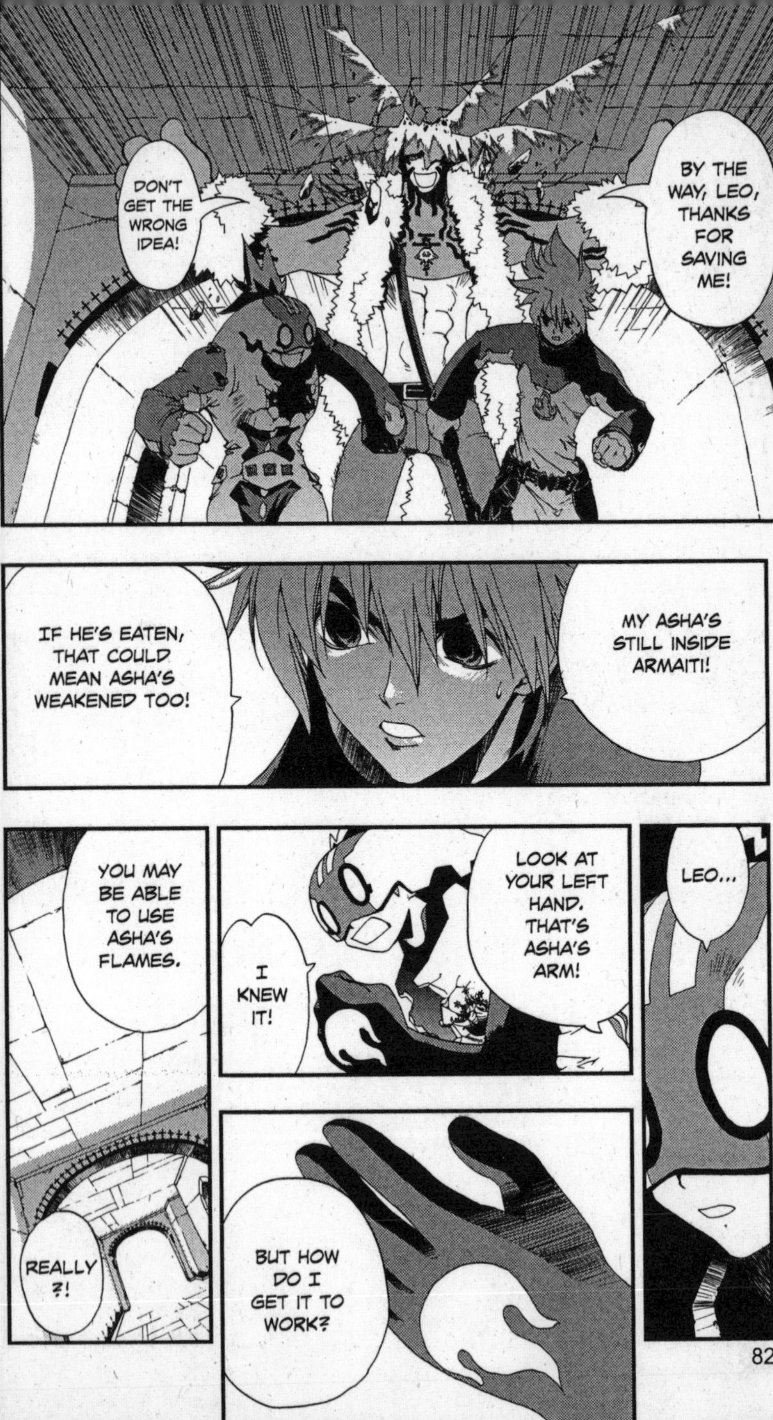
BY THE WAY, LEO, THANKS FOR SAVING ME!
DON'T GET THE WRONG IDEA!
MY ASHA'S STILL INSIDE ARMAITI!
IF HE'S EATEN, THAT COULD MEAN ASHA'S WEAKENED TOO!
LEO...
LOOK AT YOUR LEFT HAND. THAT'S ASHA'S ARM!
I KNEW IT!
BUT HOW DO I GET IT TO WORK?
YOU MAY BE ABLE TO USE ASHA'S FLAMES.
REALLY?!

READ THIS WAY

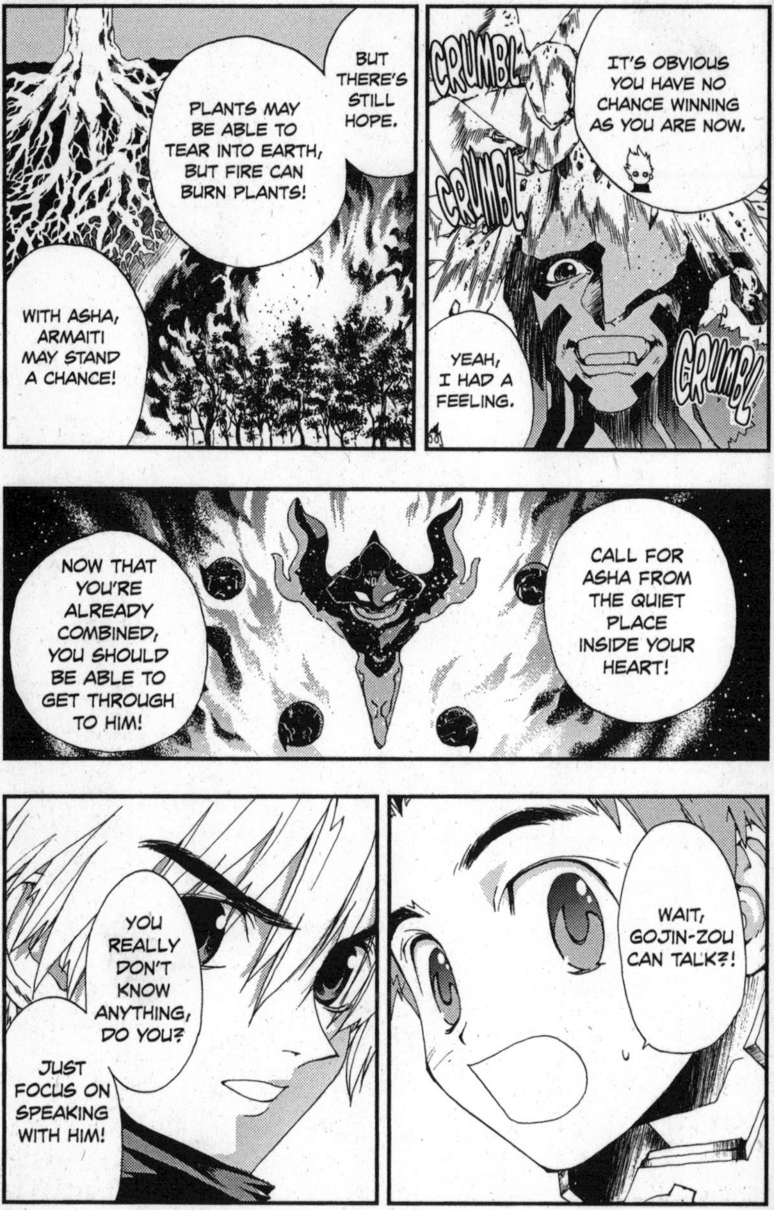

CRUMBL
CRUMBL
IT'S OBVIOUS YOU HAVE NO CHANCE WINNING AS YOU ARE NOW.
YEAH, I HAD A FEELING.
CRUMBL
BUT THERE'S STILL HOPE.
PLANTS MAY BE ABLE TO TEAR INTO EARTH, BUT FIRE CAN BURN PLANTS!
WITH ASHA, ARMAITI MAY STAND A CHANCE!
CALL FOR ASHA FROM THE QUIET PLACE INSIDE YOUR HEART!
NOW THAT YOU'RE ALREADY COMBINED, YOU SHOULD BE ABLE TO GET THROUGH TO HIM!
WAIT, GOJIN-ZOU CAN TALK?!
YOU REALLY DON'T KNOW ANYTHING, DO YOU?
JUST FOCUS ON SPEAKING WITH HIM!

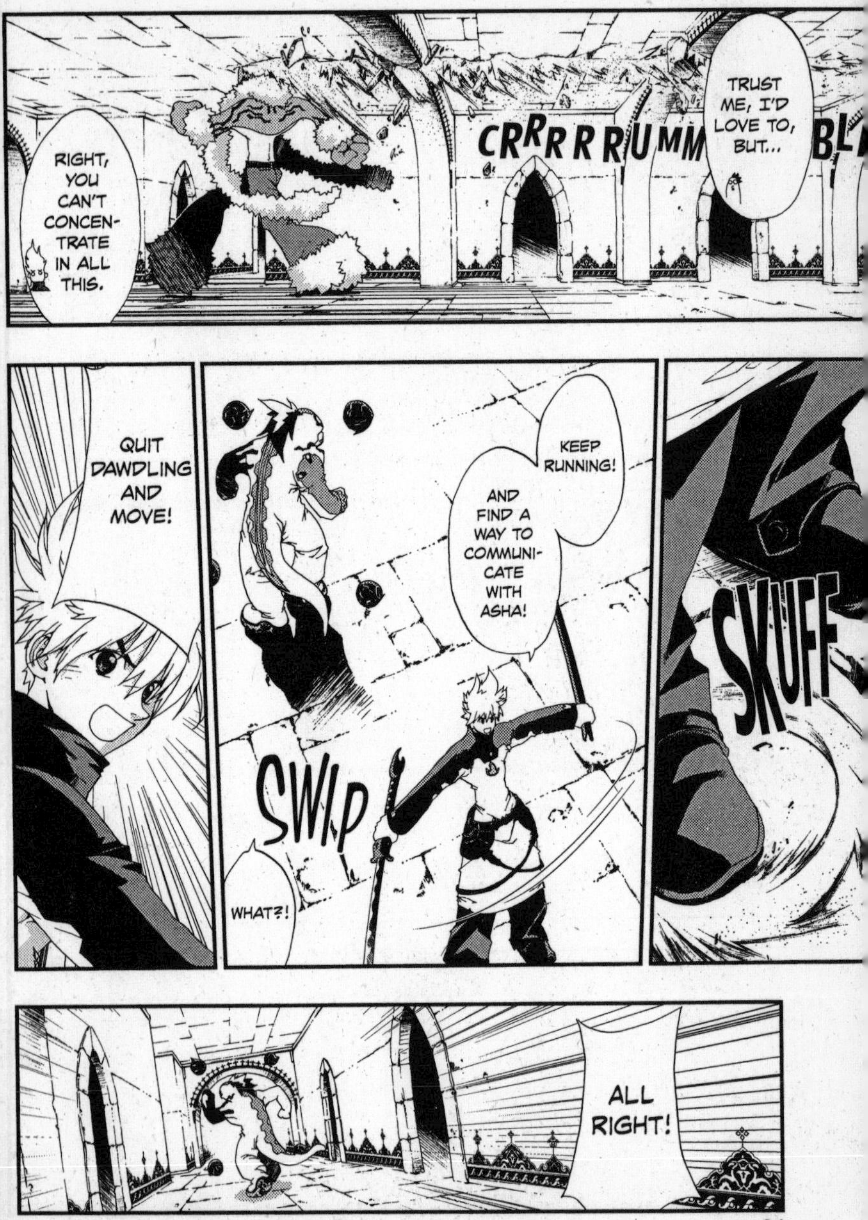
TRUST ME, I'D LOVE TO, BUT...
CRRRRRUMMBL
RIGHT, YOU CAN'T CONCEN-TRATE IN ALL THIS.
SKUFF
KEEP RUNNING!
AND FIND A WAY TO COMMUNI-CATE WITH ASHA!
SWIP
WHAT?!
QUIT DAWDLING AND MOVE!
ALL RIGHT!

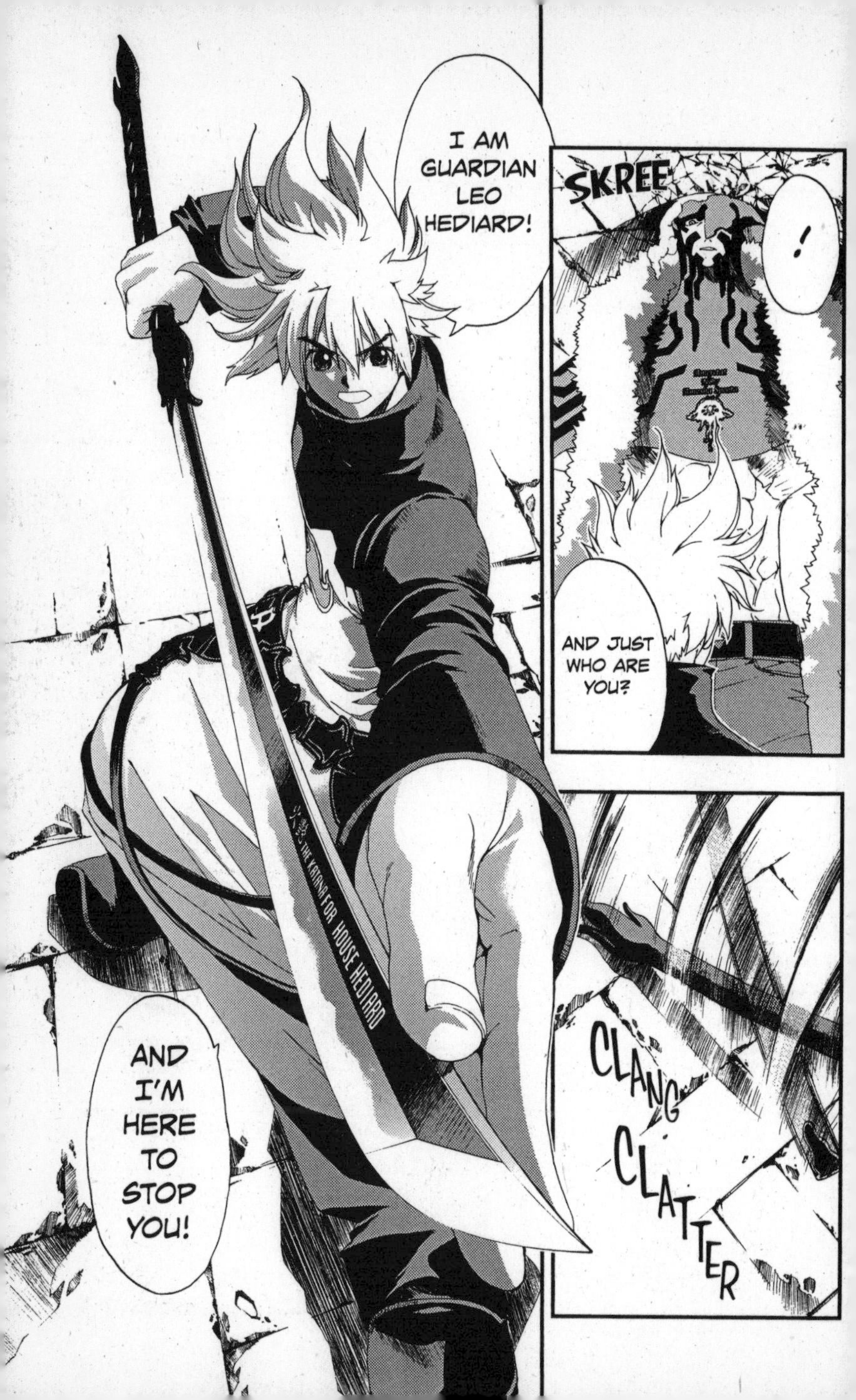
SKREE
!
AND JUST WHO ARE YOU?
CLANG
CLATTER
I AM GUARDIAN LEO HEDIARD!
THE KATANA FOR HOUSE HEDIARD
AND I'M HERE TO STOP YOU!

Wāq Wāq

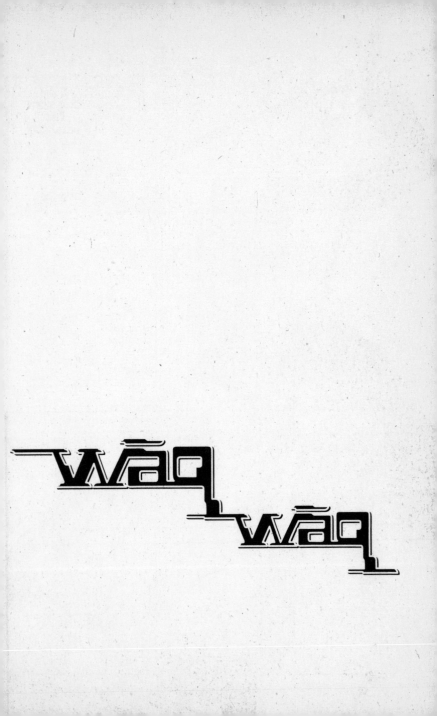

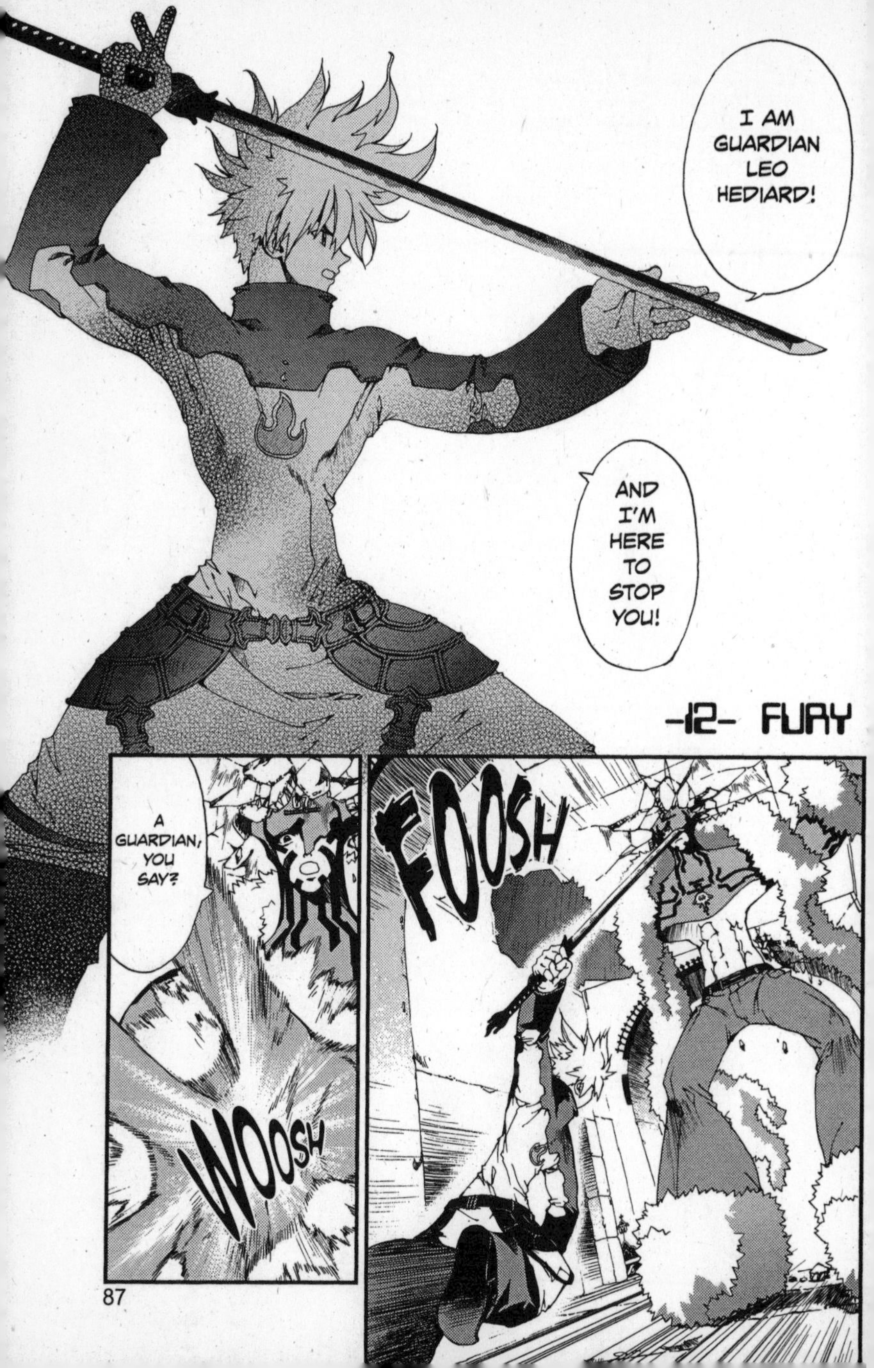
I AM GUARDIAN LEO HEDIARD!
AND I'M HERE TO STOP YOU!
-12- FURY
FOOSH
A GUARDIAN, YOU SAY?
WOOSH

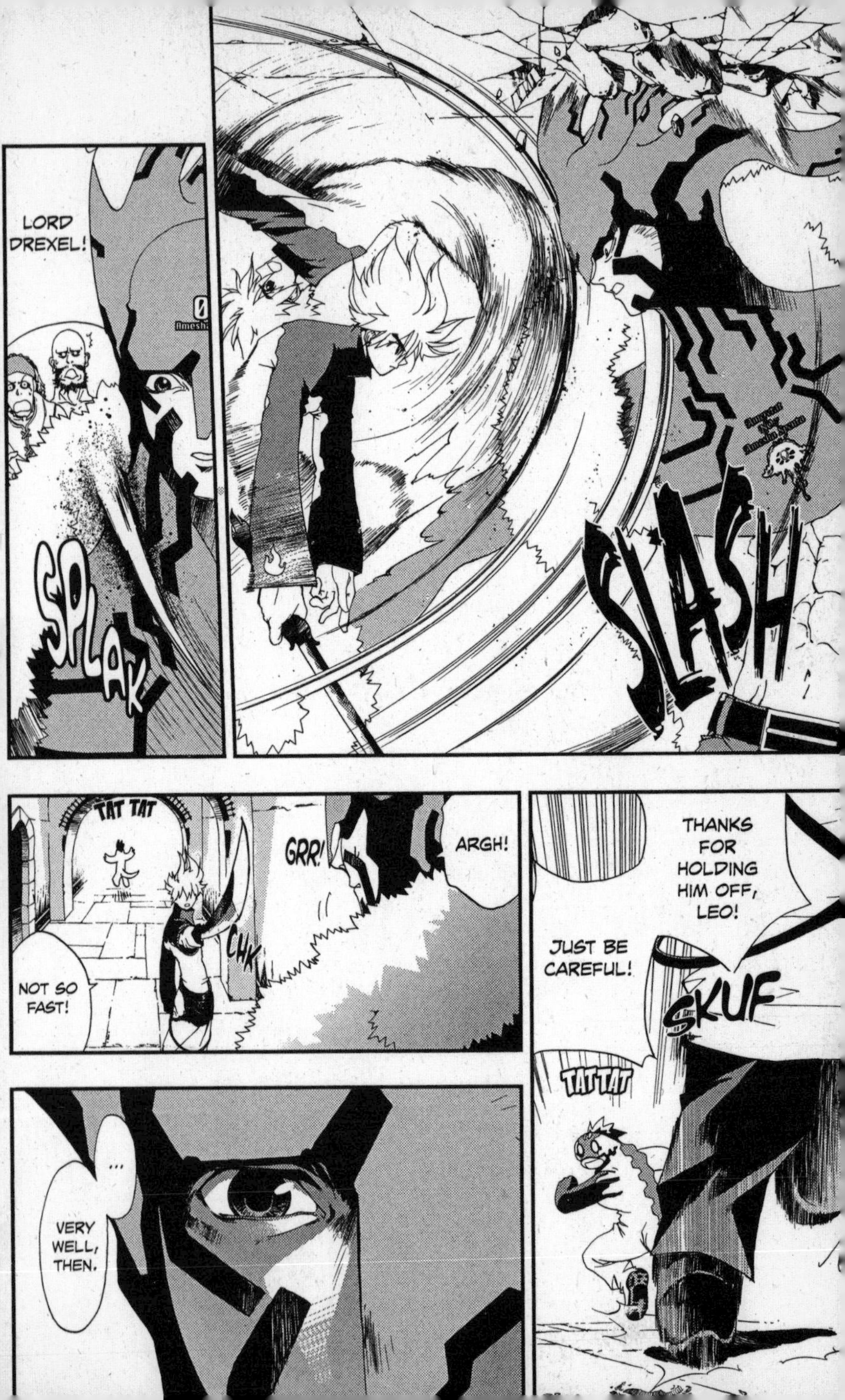
SLASH
LORD DREXEL!
SPLAK
THANKS FOR HOLDING HIM OFF, LEO!
JUST BE CAREFUL!
SKUF
TAT TAT
ARGH!
GRR!
TAT TAT
CHK
NOT SO FAST!
...
VERY WELL, THEN.

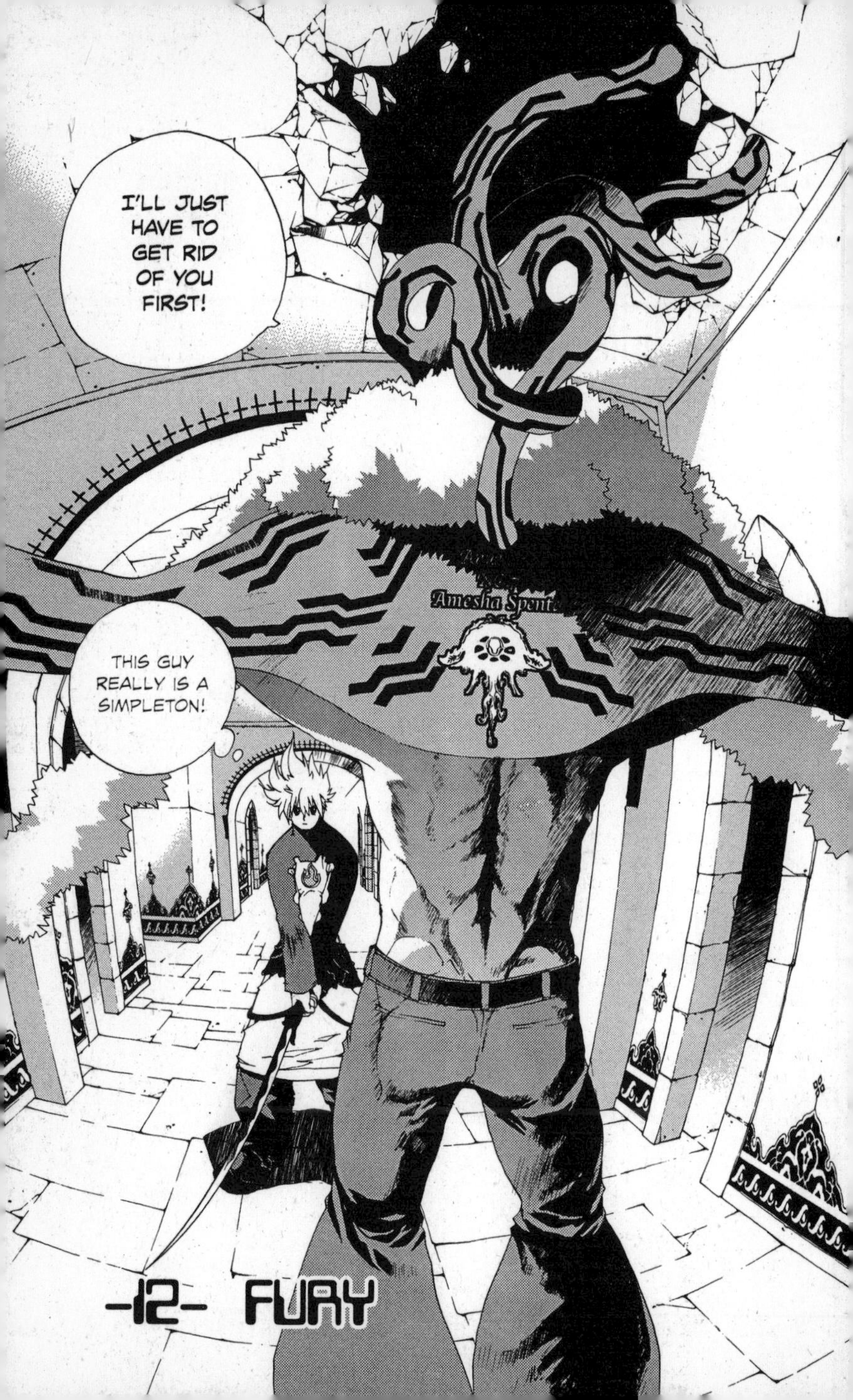
I'LL JUST HAVE TO GET RID OF YOU FIRST!
Ameshia Spenta
THIS GUY REALLY IS A SIMPLETON!
-12- FURY

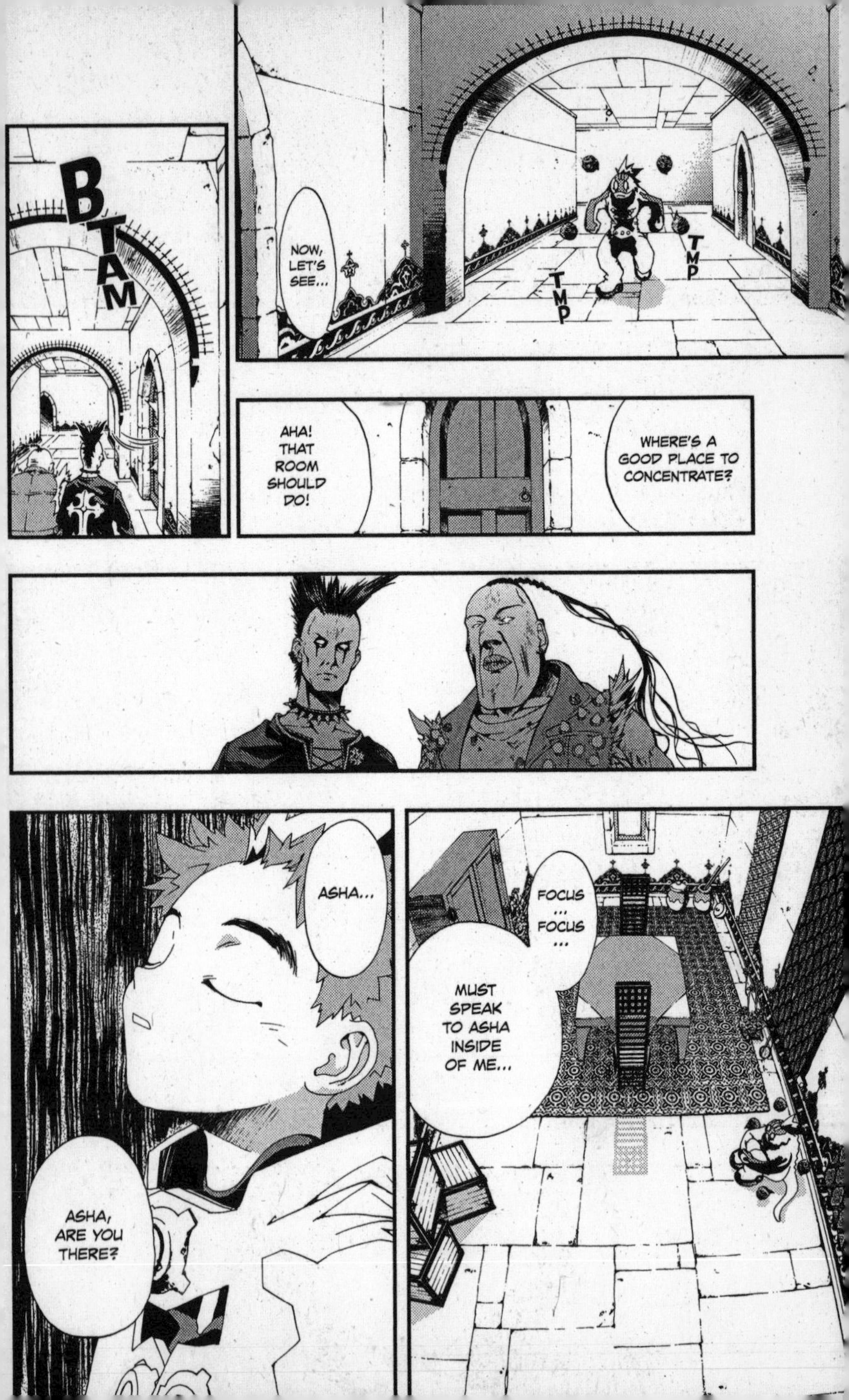
TMP
TMP
NOW, LET'S SEE...
WHERE'S A GOOD PLACE TO CONCENTRATE?
AHA! THAT ROOM SHOULD DO!
BTAM
FOCUS ... FOCUS ...
MUST SPEAK TO ASHA INSIDE OF ME...
ASHA...
ASHA, ARE YOU THERE?

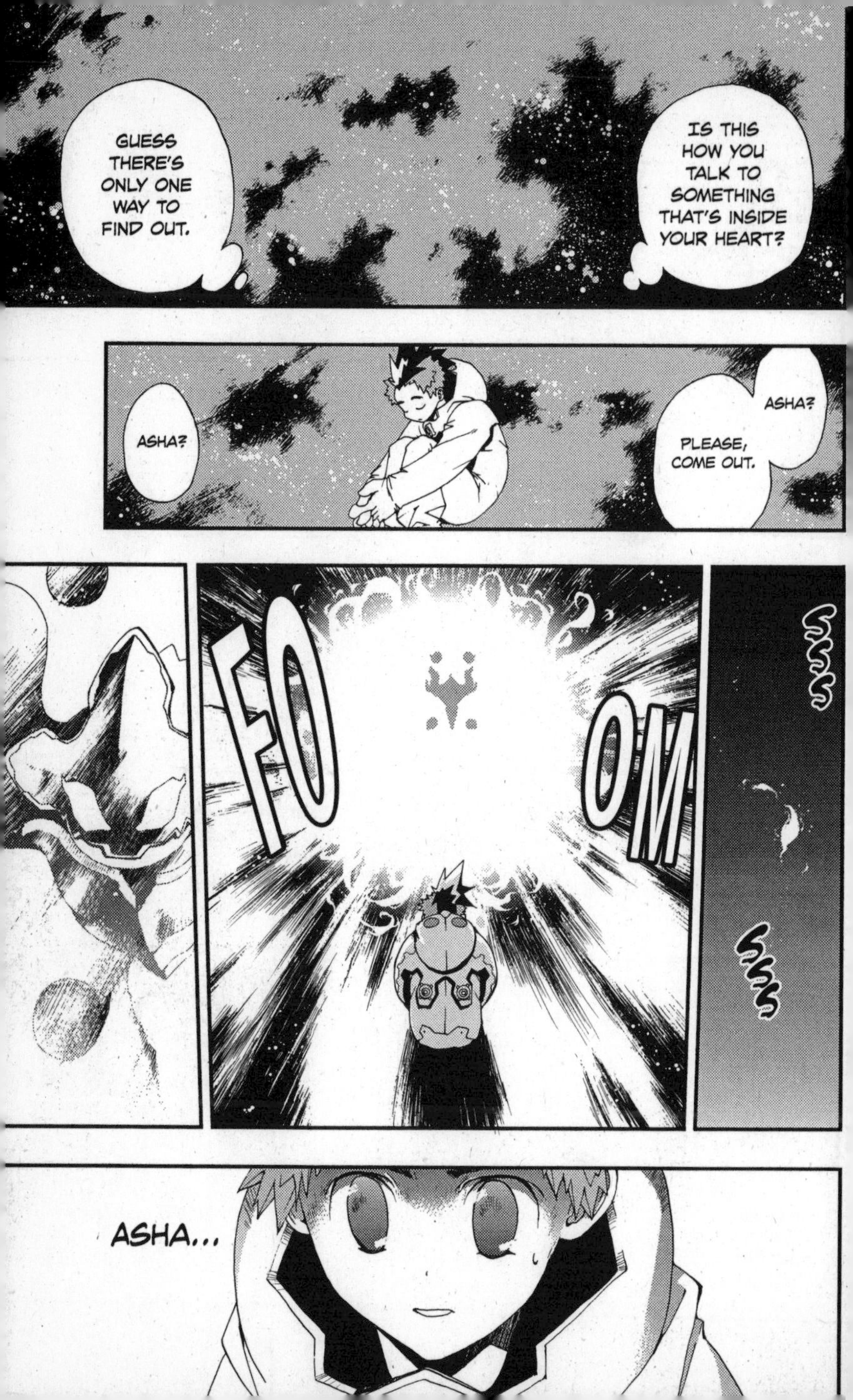
IS THIS HOW YOU TALK TO SOMETHING THAT'S INSIDE YOUR HEART?
GUESS THERE'S ONLY ONE WAY TO FIND OUT.
ASHA? PLEASE, COME OUT.
ASHA?
FOOM
ASHA...

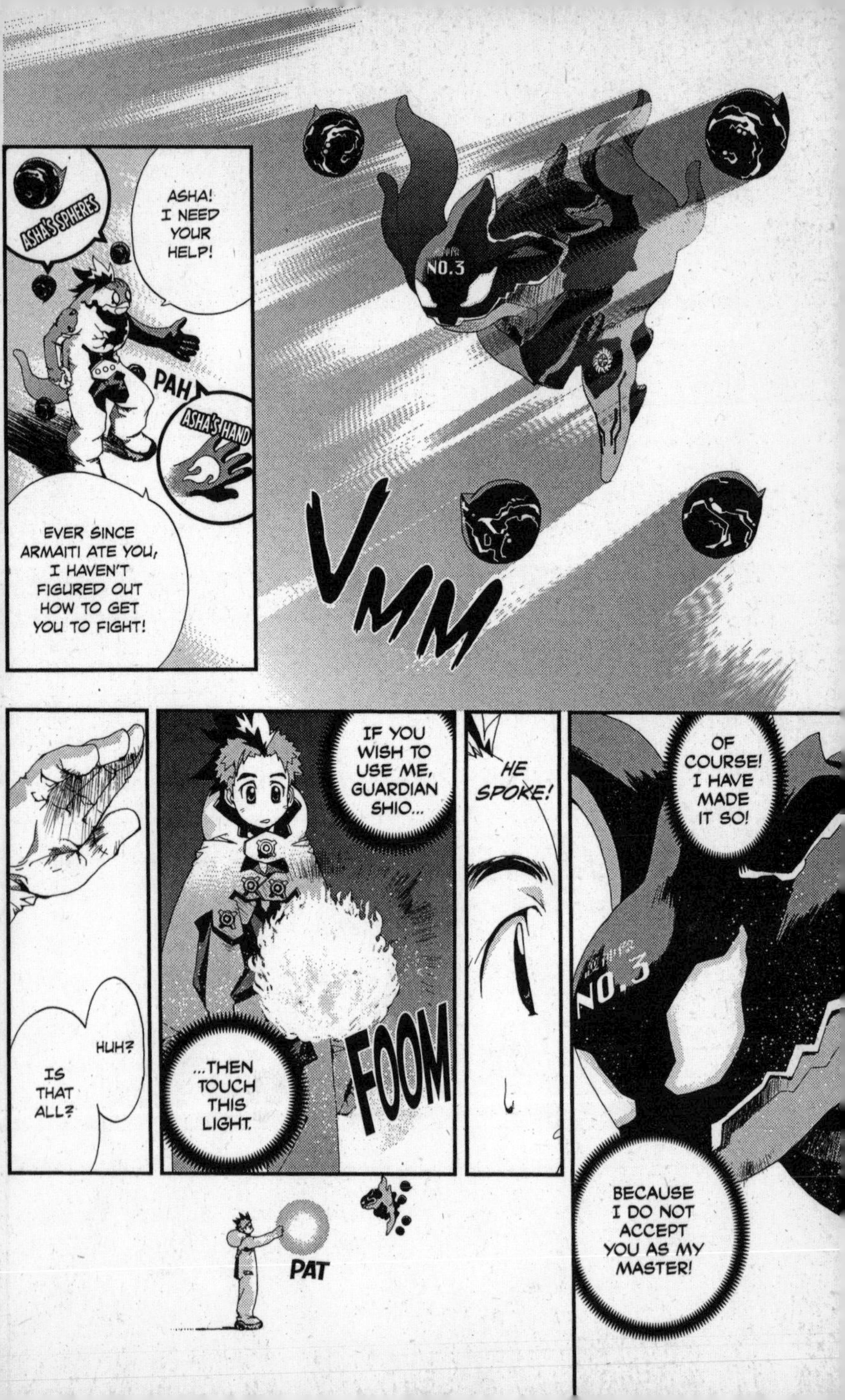
VMM
NO.3
ASHA! I NEED YOUR HELP!
ASHA'S SPHERES
PAH
ASHA'S HAND
EVER SINCE ARMAITI ATE YOU, I HAVEN'T FIGURED OUT HOW TO GET YOU TO FIGHT!
OF COURSE! I HAVE MADE IT SO!
NO.3
BECAUSE I DO NOT ACCEPT YOU AS MY MASTER!
HE SPOKE!
IF YOU WISH TO USE ME, GUARDIAN SHIO...
...THEN TOUCH THIS LIGHT.
FOOM
HUH?
IS THAT ALL?
PAT

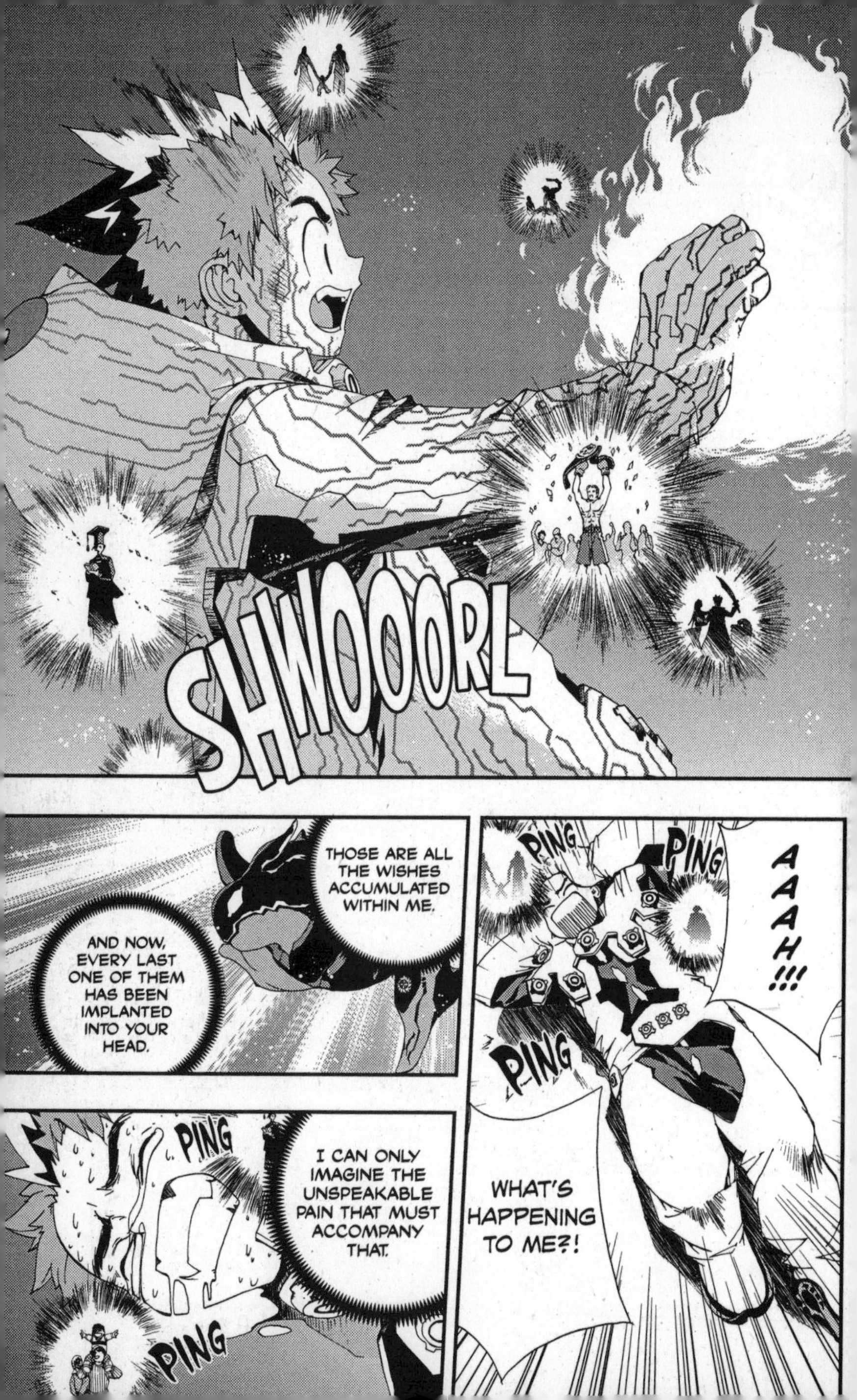
SHWOOORL
PING
PING
AAAH!!!
PING
WHAT'S HAPPENING TO ME?!
THOSE ARE ALL THE WISHES ACCUMULATED WITHIN ME.
AND NOW, EVERY LAST ONE OF THEM HAS BEEN IMPLANTED INTO YOUR HEAD.
PING
I CAN ONLY IMAGINE THE UNSPEAKABLE PAIN THAT MUST ACCOMPANY THAT.
PING

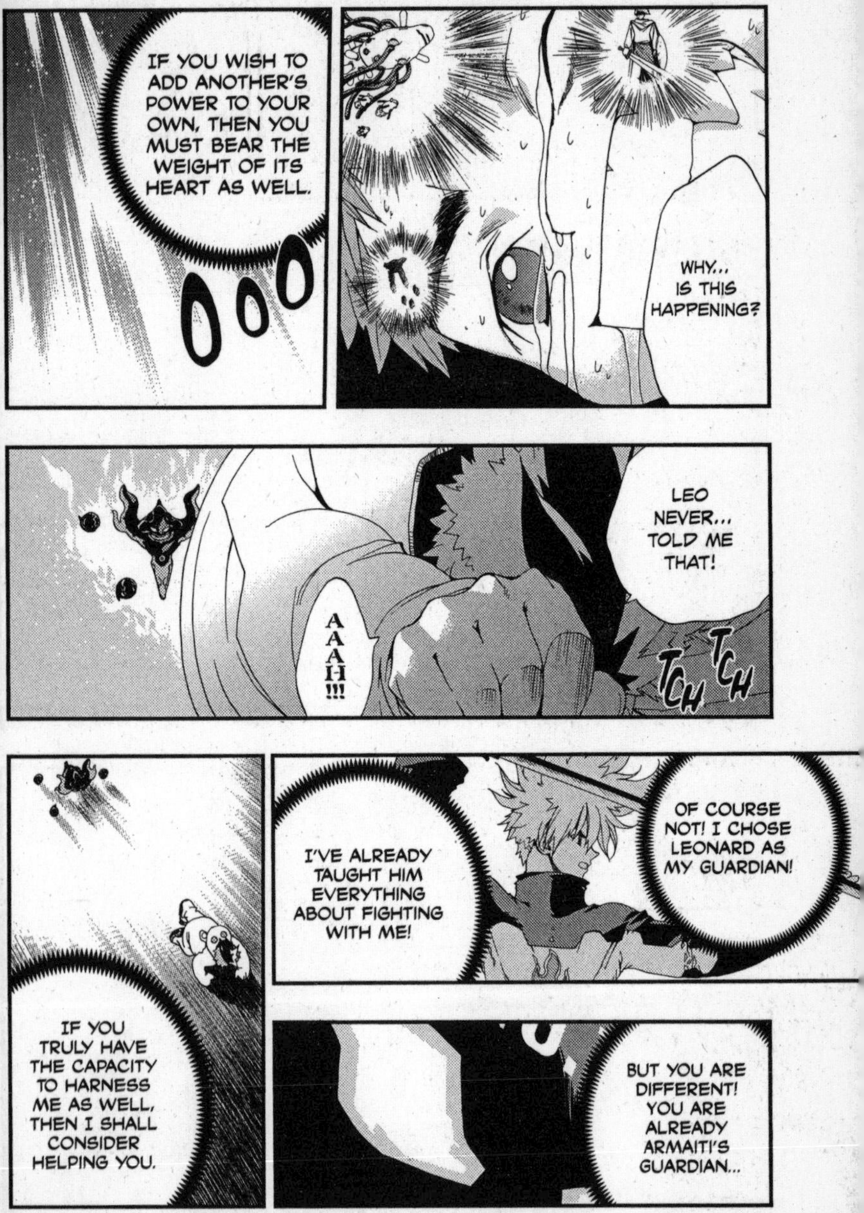
WHY... IS THIS HAPPENING?
IF YOU WISH TO ADD ANOTHER'S POWER TO YOUR OWN, THEN YOU MUST BEAR THE WEIGHT OF ITS HEART AS WELL.
LEO NEVER... TOLD ME THAT!
AAAH!!!
TCH TCH
OF COURSE NOT! I CHOSE LEONARD AS MY GUARDIAN!
I'VE ALREADY TAUGHT HIM EVERYTHING ABOUT FIGHTING WITH ME!
BUT YOU ARE DIFFERENT! YOU ARE ALREADY ARMAITI'S GUARDIAN...
IF YOU TRULY HAVE THE CAPACITY TO HARNESS ME AS WELL, THEN I SHALL CONSIDER HELPING YOU.

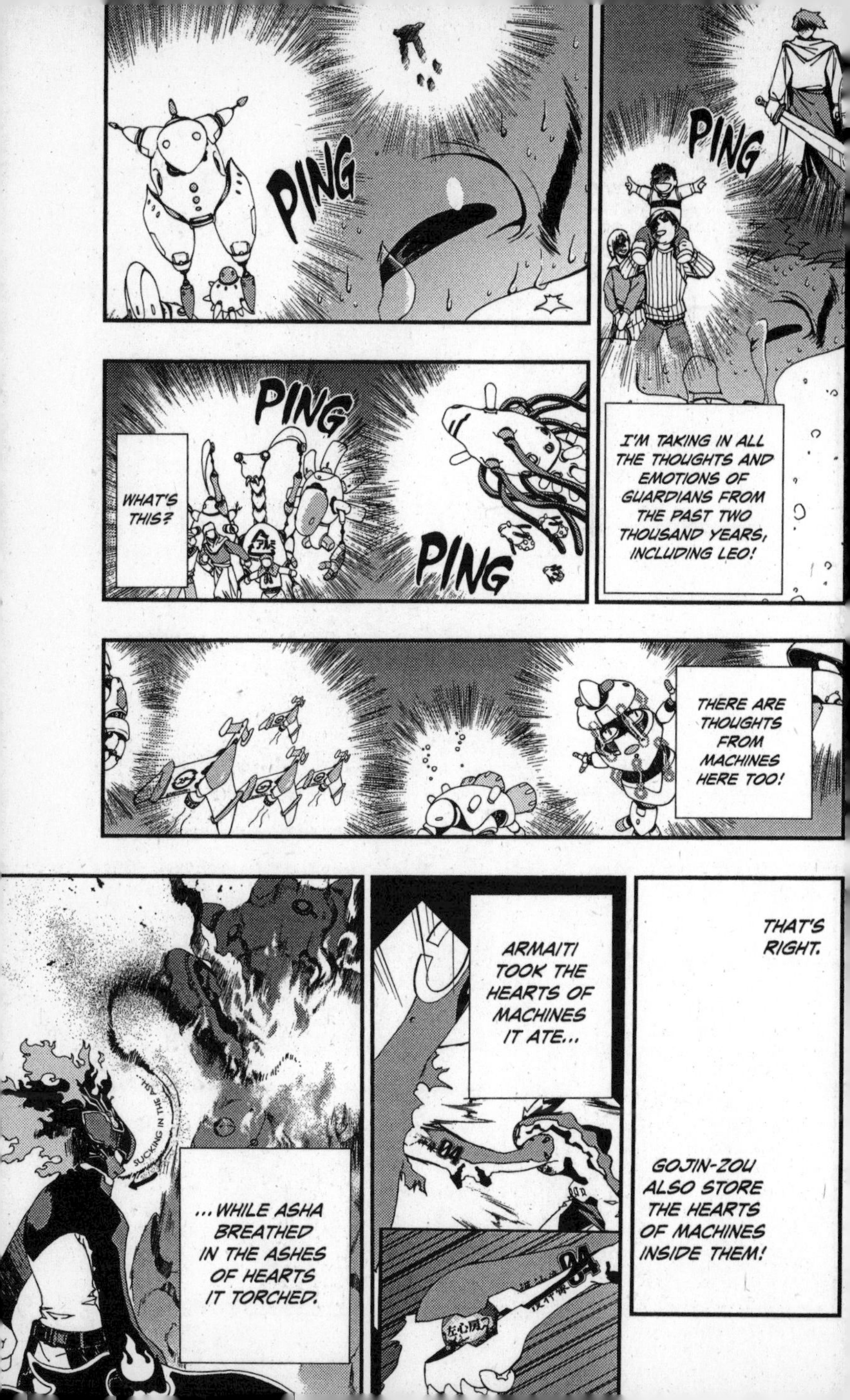
PING
I'M TAKING IN ALL THE THOUGHTS AND EMOTIONS OF GUARDIANS FROM THE PAST TWO THOUSAND YEARS, INCLUDING LEO!
PING
PING
PING
WHAT'S THIS?
THERE ARE THOUGHTS FROM MACHINES HERE TOO!
THAT'S RIGHT.
GOJIN-ZOU ALSO STORE THE HEARTS OF MACHINES INSIDE THEM!
ARMAITI TOOK THE HEARTS OF MACHINES IT ATE...
SUCKING IN THE ASH
...WHILE ASHA BREATHED IN THE ASHES OF HEARTS IT TORCHED.

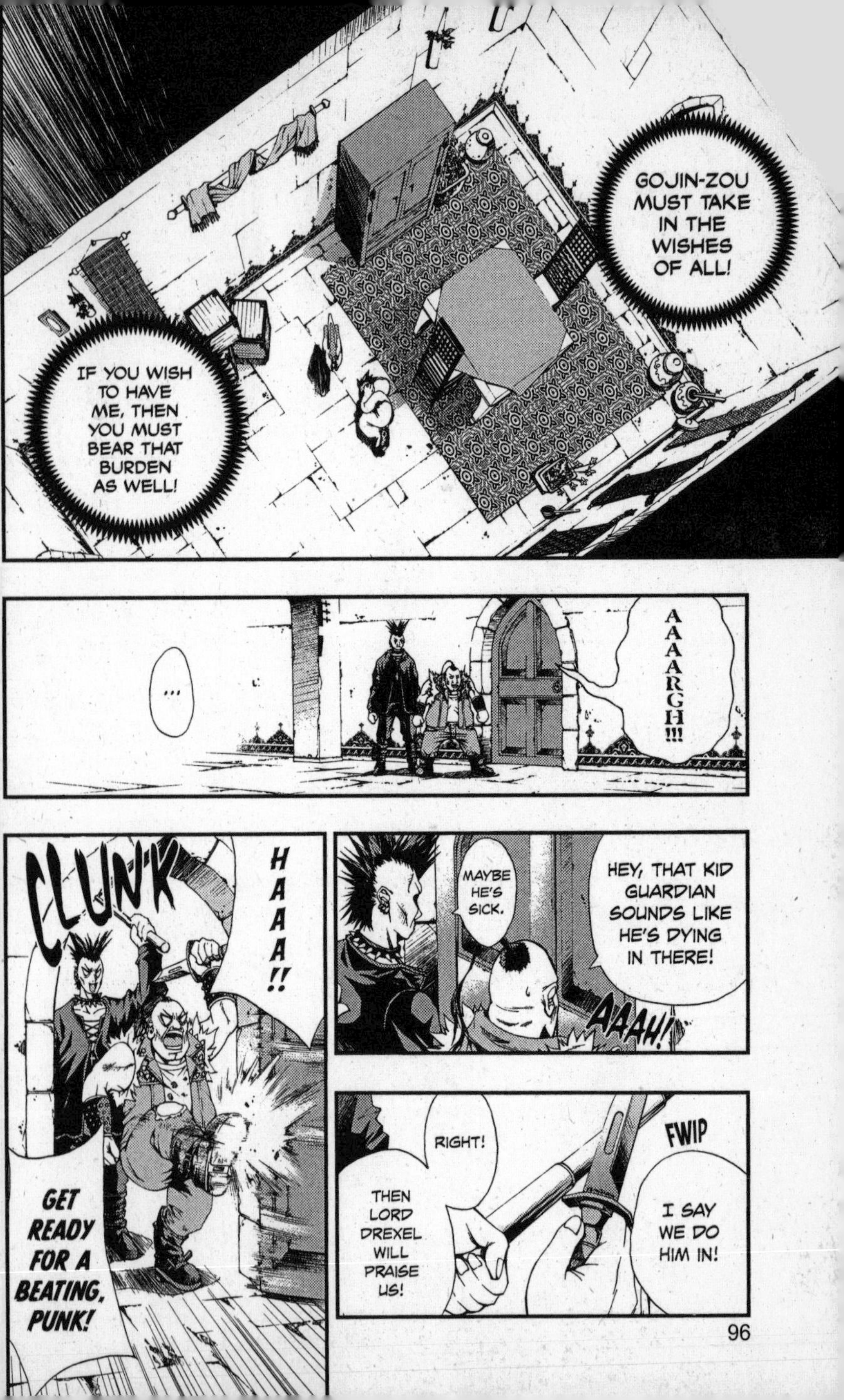
GOJIN-ZOU MUST TAKE IN THE WISHES OF ALL!
IF YOU WISH TO HAVE ME, THEN YOU MUST BEAR THAT BURDEN AS WELL!
AAAARGH!!!
...
HEY, THAT KID GUARDIAN SOUNDS LIKE HE'S DYING IN THERE!
MAYBE HE'S SICK.
AAAH!
I SAY WE DO HIM IN!
FWIP
RIGHT!
THEN LORD DREXEL WILL PRAISE US!
HAAAA!!
CLUNK
GET READY FOR A BEATING, PUNK!

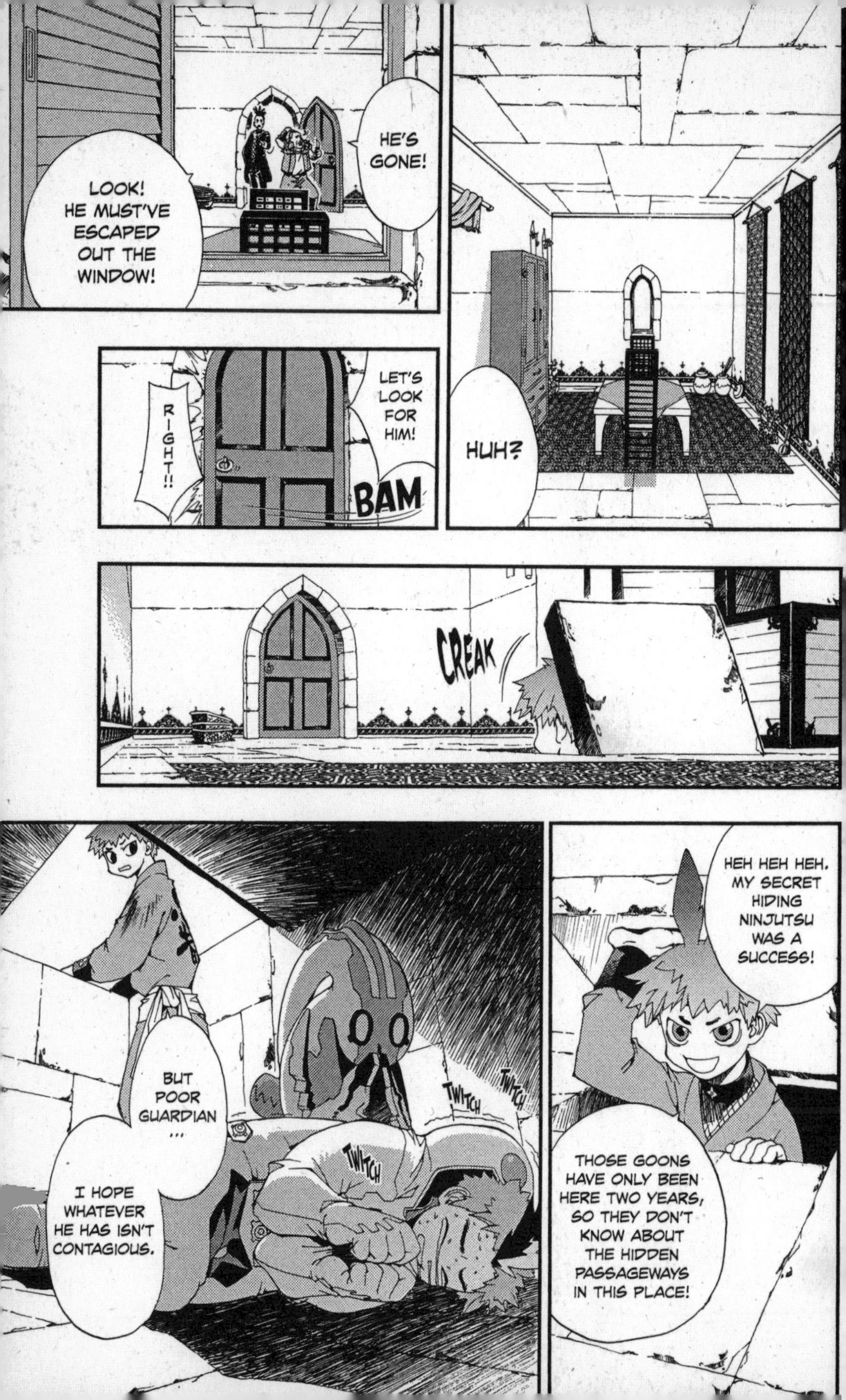
HUH?
HE'S GONE!
LOOK! HE MUST'VE ESCAPED OUT THE WINDOW!
LET'S LOOK FOR HIM!
BAM
RIGHT!!
CREAK
HEH HEH HEH. MY SECRET HIDING NINJUTSU WAS A SUCCESS!
THOSE GOONS HAVE ONLY BEEN HERE TWO YEARS, SO THEY DON'T KNOW ABOUT THE HIDDEN PASSAGEWAYS IN THIS PLACE!
TWITCH
TWITCH
TWITCH
BUT POOR GUARDIAN...
I HOPE WHATEVER HE HAS ISN'T CONTAGIOUS.

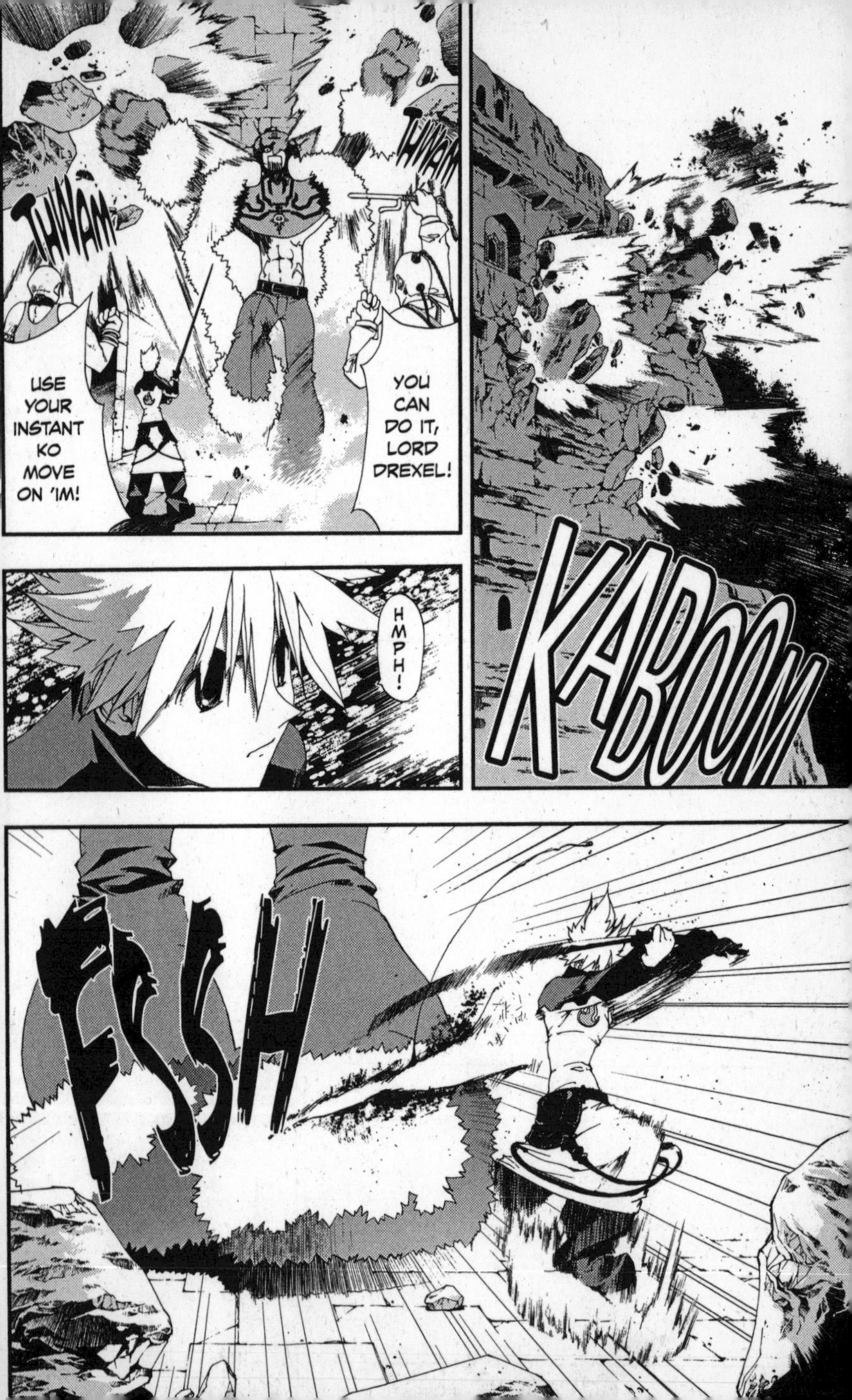
KABOOM
THWAM
THWAM
YOU CAN DO IT, LORD DREXEL!
USE YOUR INSTANT KO MOVE ON 'IM!
HMPH!
FSSH

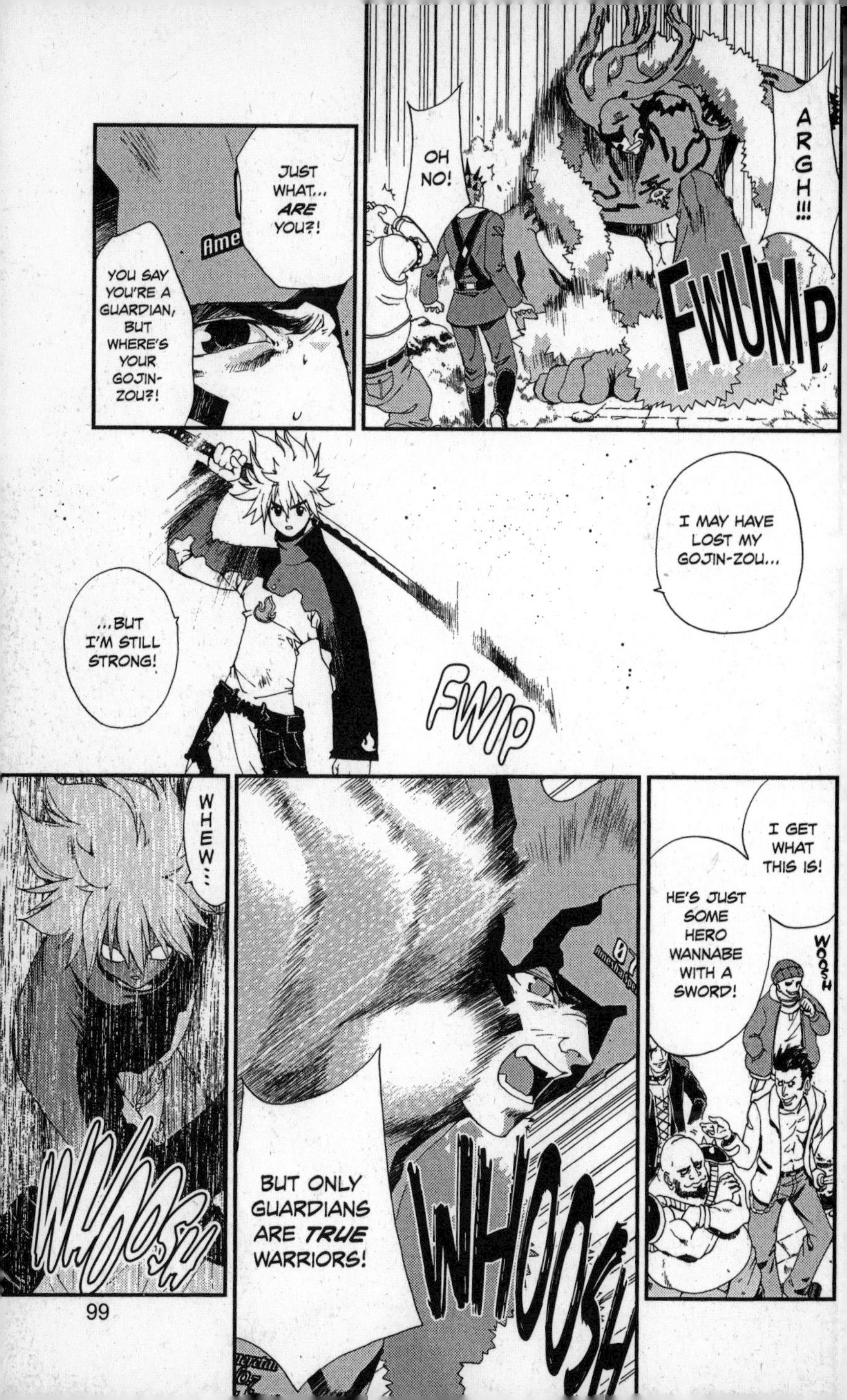
ARGH!!!
OH NO!
FWUMP
JUST WHAT... *ARE* YOU?!
YOU SAY YOU'RE A GUARDIAN, BUT WHERE'S YOUR GOJIN-ZOU?!
I MAY HAVE LOST MY GOJIN-ZOU...
FWIP
...BUT I'M STILL STRONG!
I GET WHAT THIS IS!
HE'S JUST SOME HERO WANNABE WITH A SWORD!
WOOSH
BUT ONLY GUARDIANS ARE *TRUE* WARRIORS!
WHOOSH
WHEW...
WHOOSH

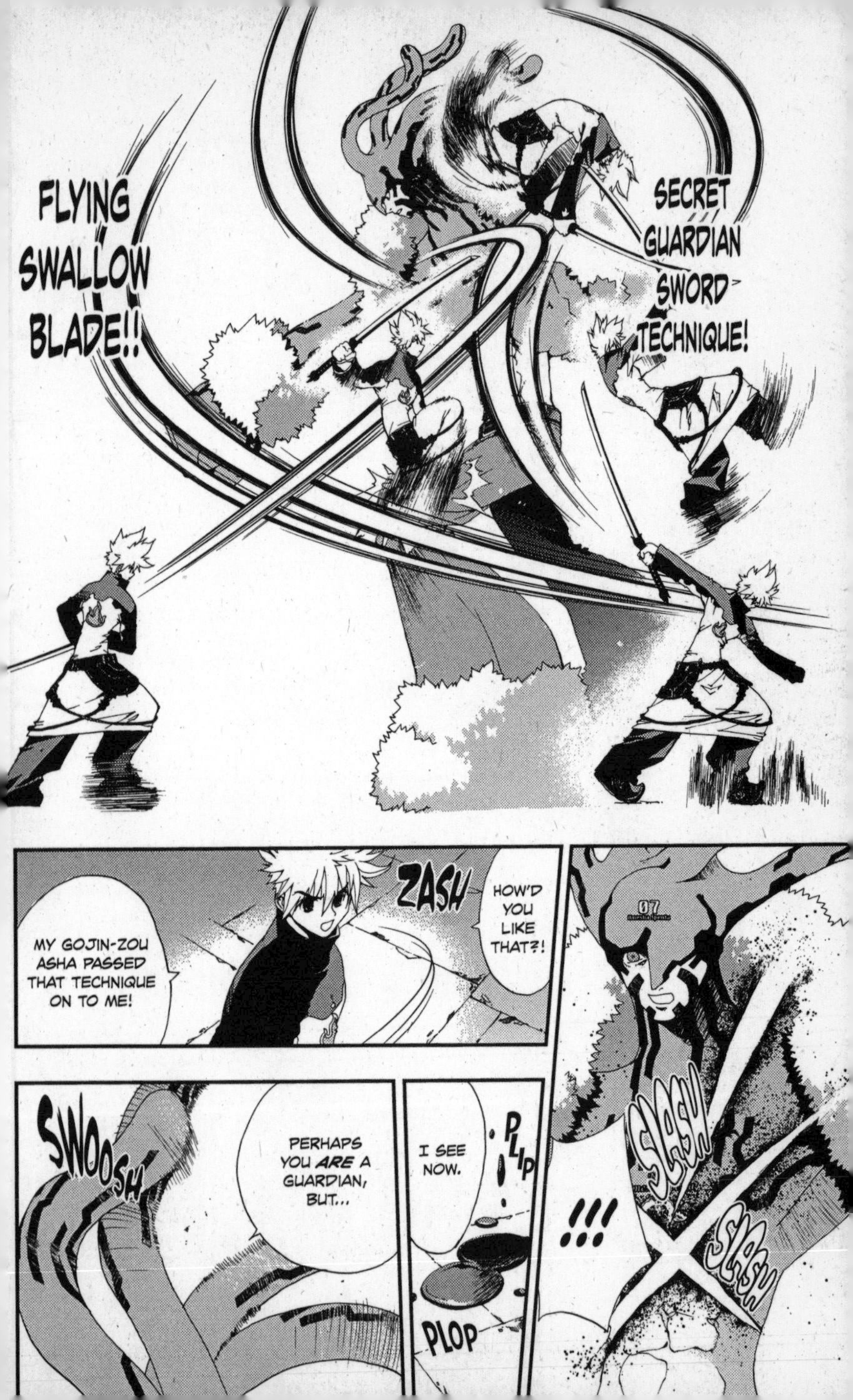
SECRET GUARDIAN SWORD TECHNIQUE!
FLYING SWALLOW BLADE!!
SLASH
SLASH
!!!
ZASH
HOW'D YOU LIKE THAT?!
MY GOJIN-ZOU ASHA PASSED THAT TECHNIQUE ON TO ME!
I SEE NOW.
PLIP
PLOP
PERHAPS YOU *ARE* A GUARDIAN, BUT...
SWOOSH

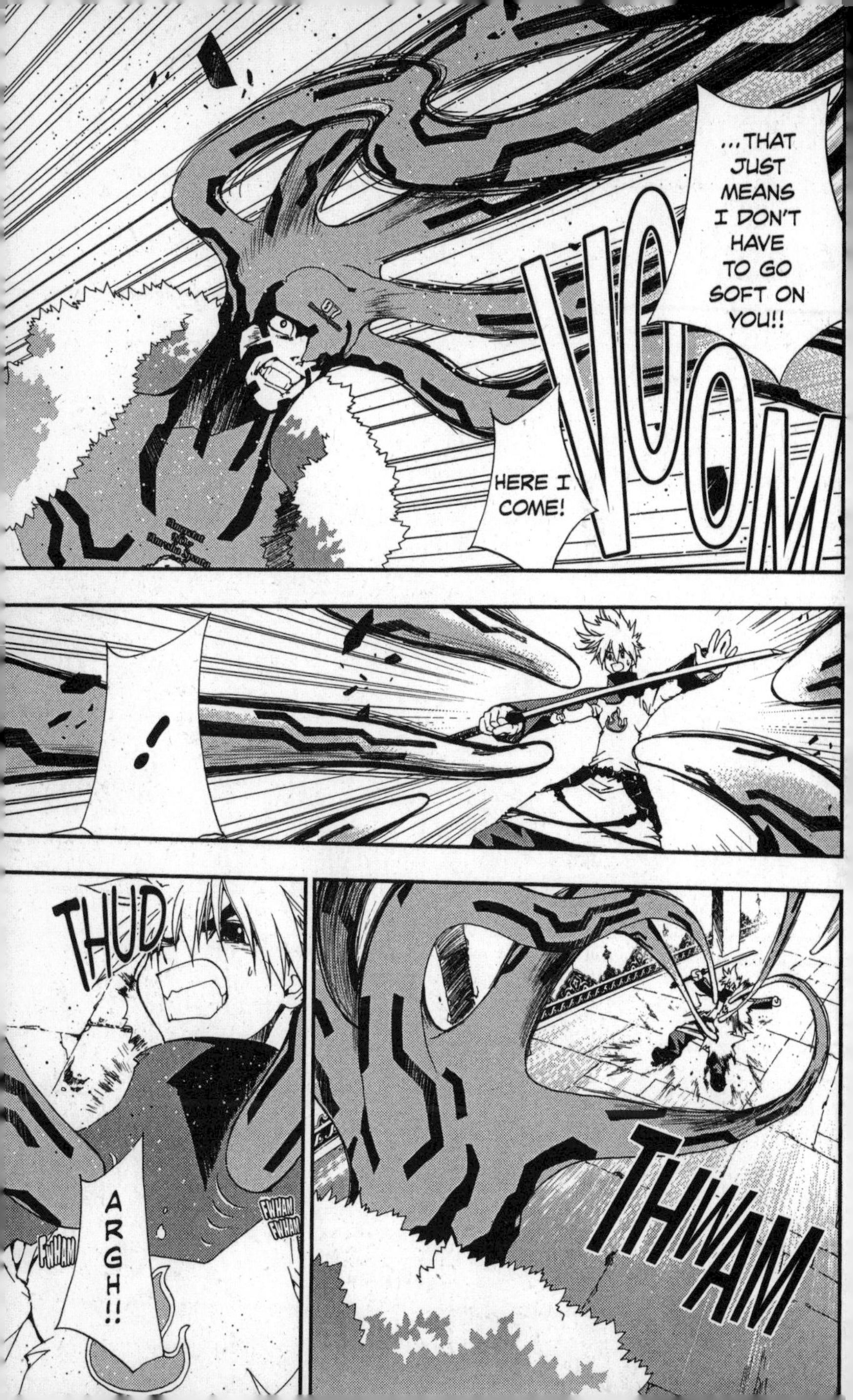
...THAT JUST MEANS I DON'T HAVE TO GO SOFT ON YOU!!
VOOM
HERE I COME!
!
THWAM
THUD
FWHAM FWHAM
ARGH!!
FWHAM

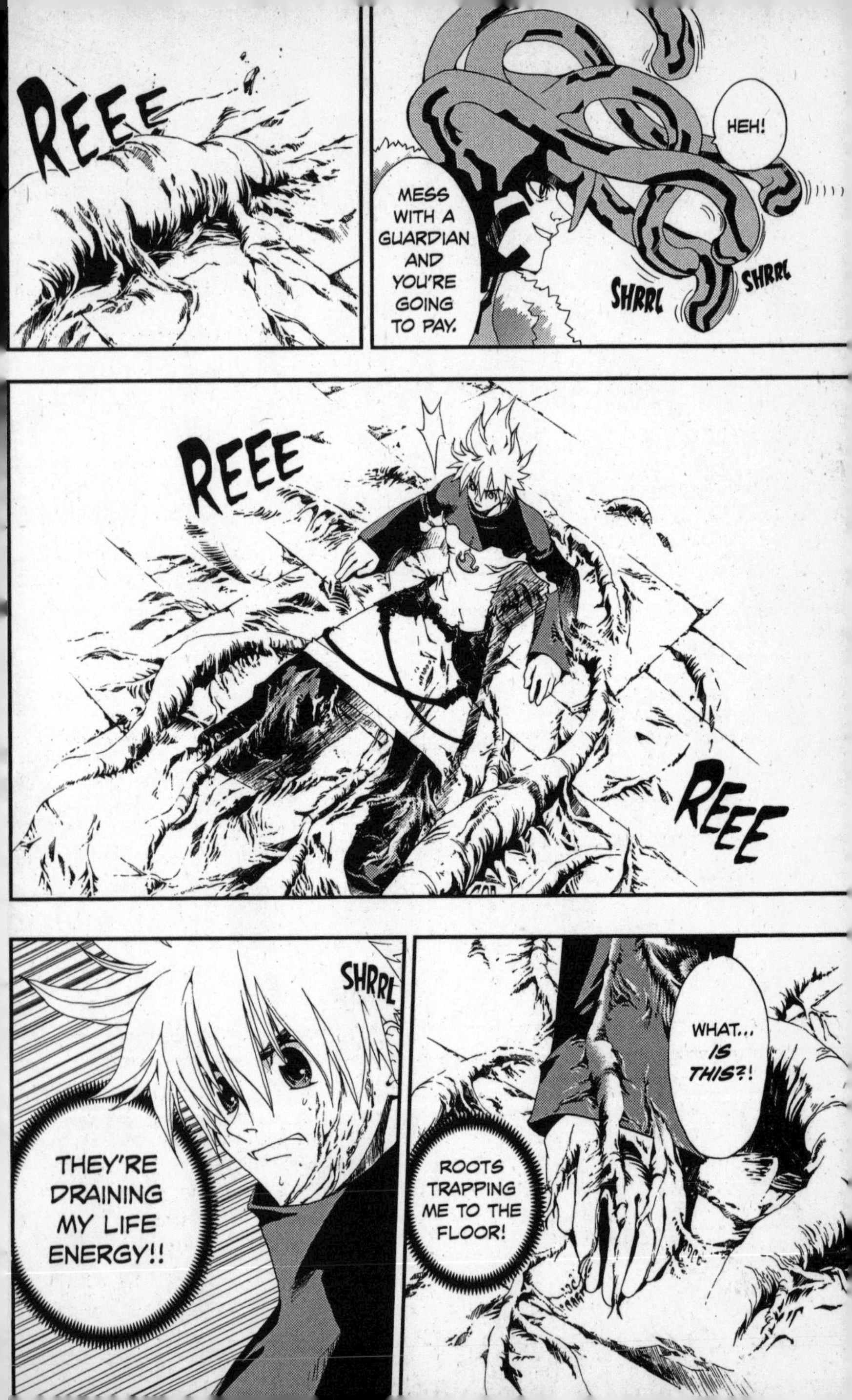
HEH!
MESS WITH A GUARDIAN AND YOU'RE GOING TO PAY.
SHRRL
SHRRL
REEE
REEE
REEE
WHAT... IS THIS?!
ROOTS TRAPPING ME TO THE FLOOR!
SHRRL
THEY'RE DRAINING MY LIFE ENERGY!!

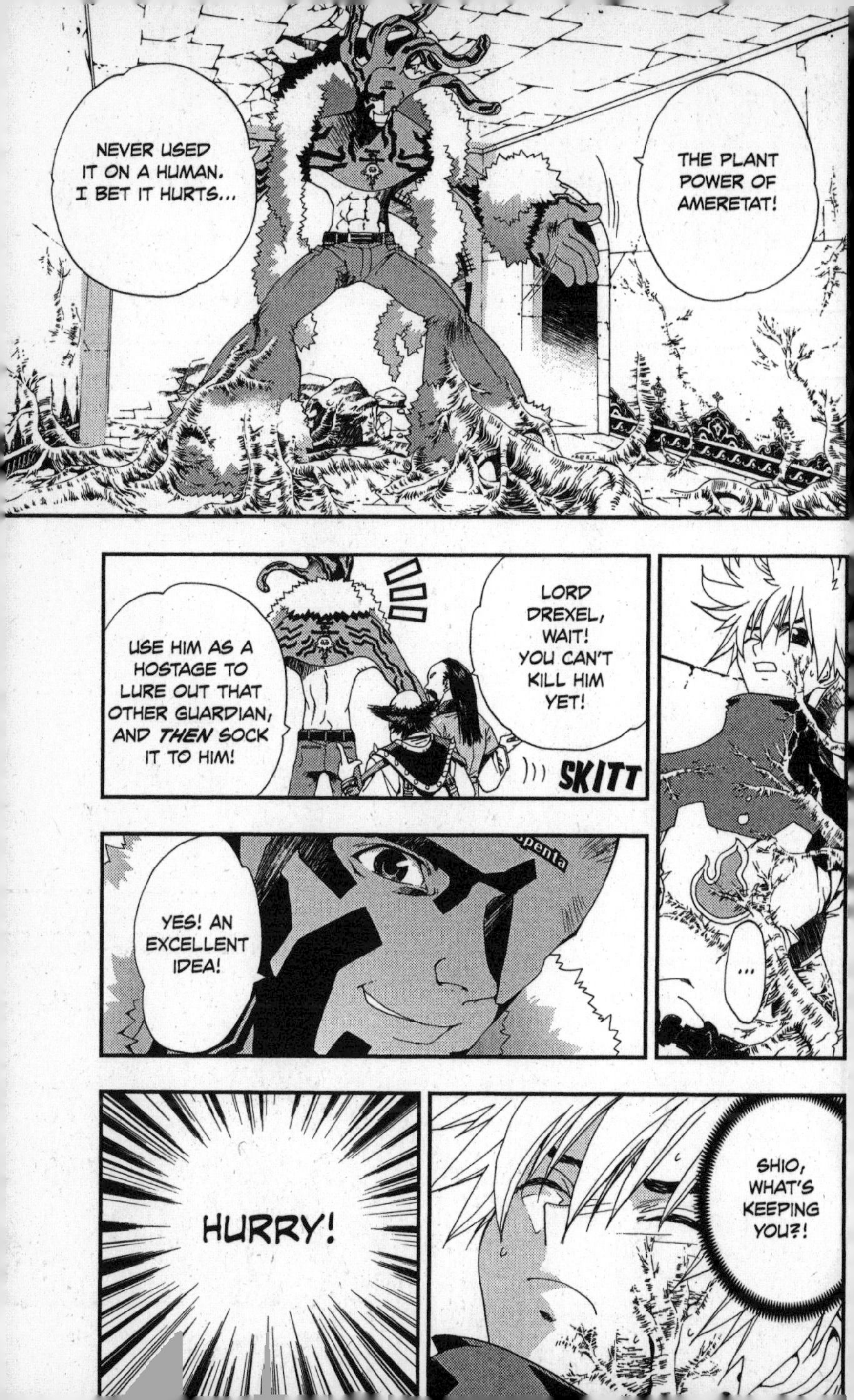
THE PLANT POWER OF AMERETAT!
NEVER USED IT ON A HUMAN. I BET IT HURTS...
...
LORD DREXEL, WAIT! YOU CAN'T KILL HIM YET!
SKITT
USE HIM AS A HOSTAGE TO LURE OUT THAT OTHER GUARDIAN, AND *THEN* SOCK IT TO HIM!
YES! AN EXCELLENT IDEA!
SHIO, WHAT'S KEEPING YOU?!
HURRY!

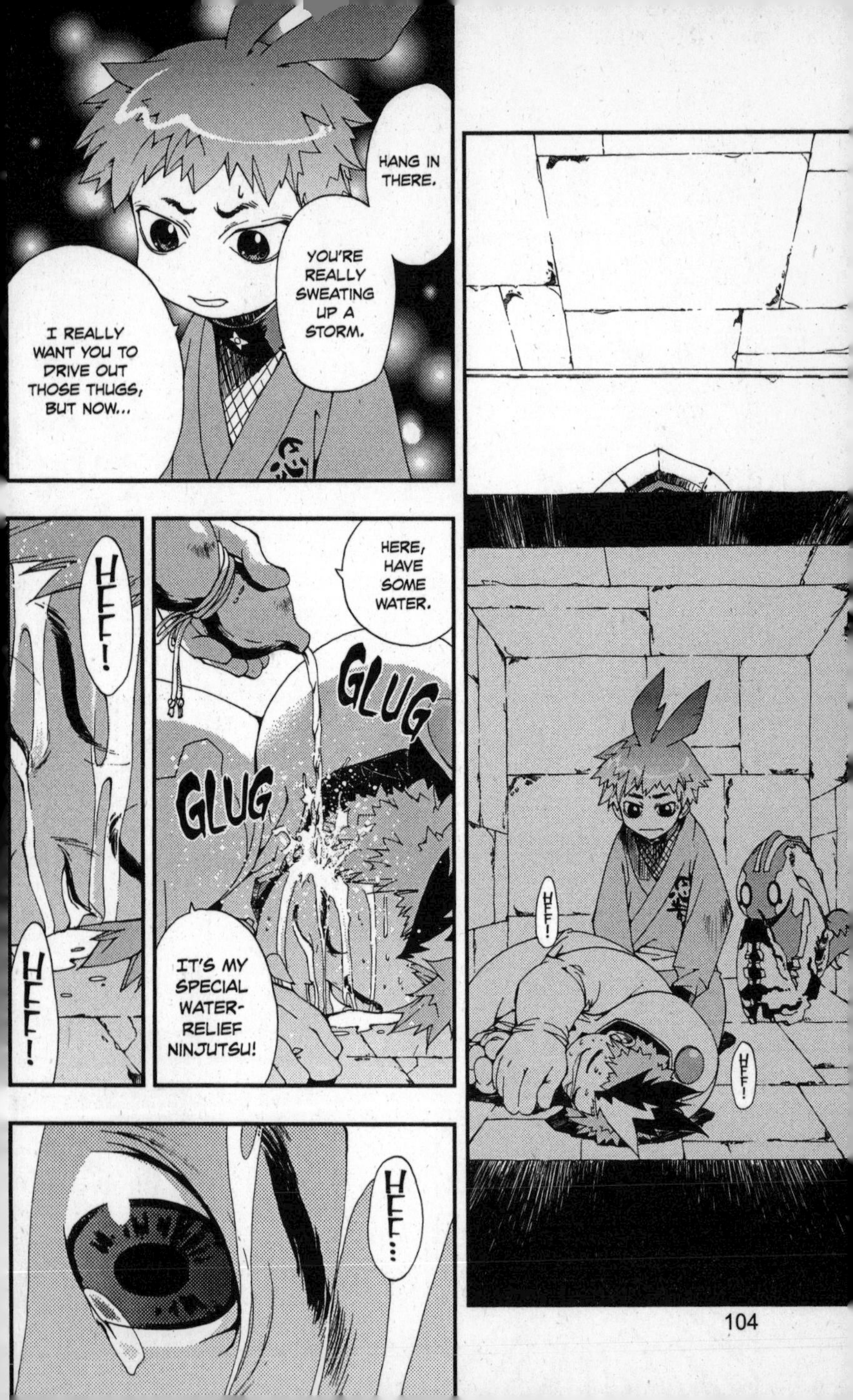
HFF!
HFF!
HANG IN THERE.
YOU'RE REALLY SWEATING UP A STORM.
I REALLY WANT YOU TO DRIVE OUT THOSE THUGS, BUT NOW...
HERE, HAVE SOME WATER.
GLUG
GLUG
IT'S MY SPECIAL WATER-RELIEF NINJUTSU!
HFF!
HFF!
HFF...

READ THIS WAY

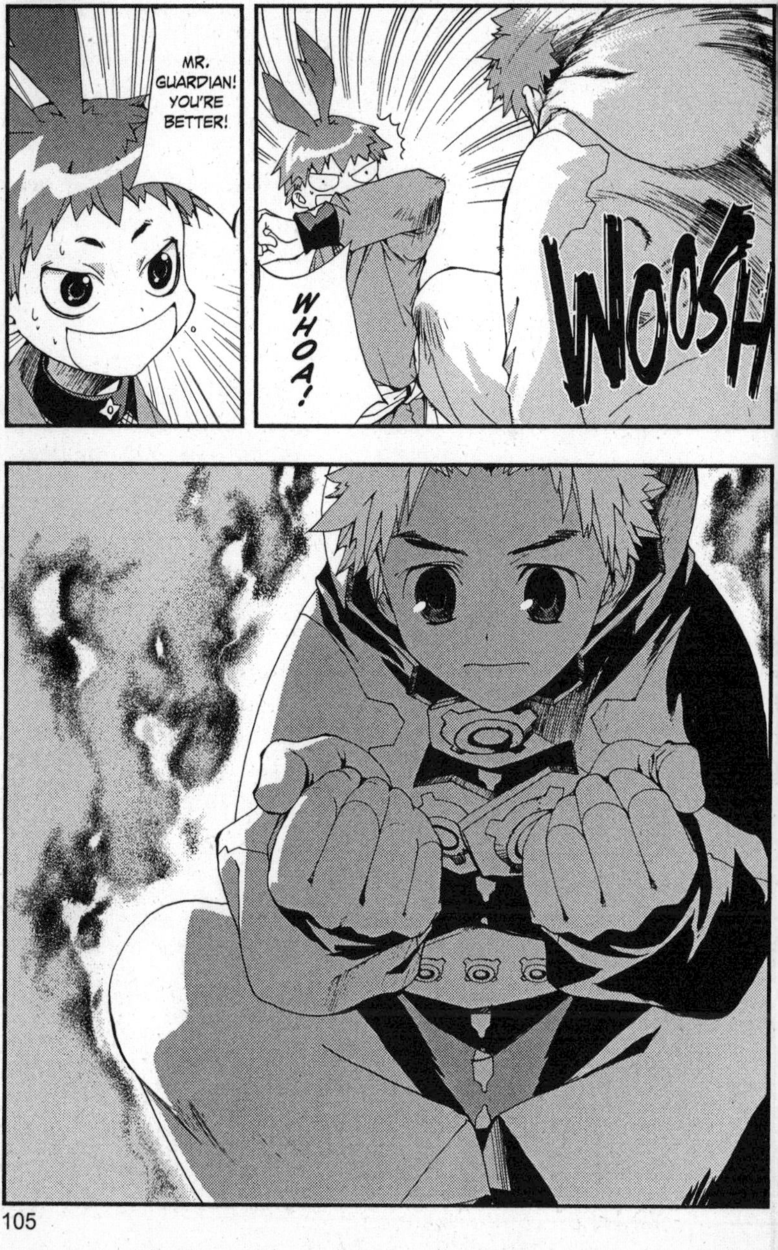
WOOSH
WHOA!
MR. GUARDIAN! YOU'RE BETTER!

wāq wāq

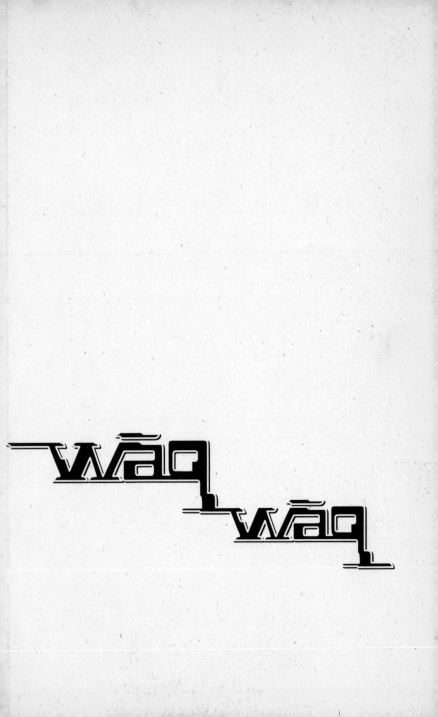

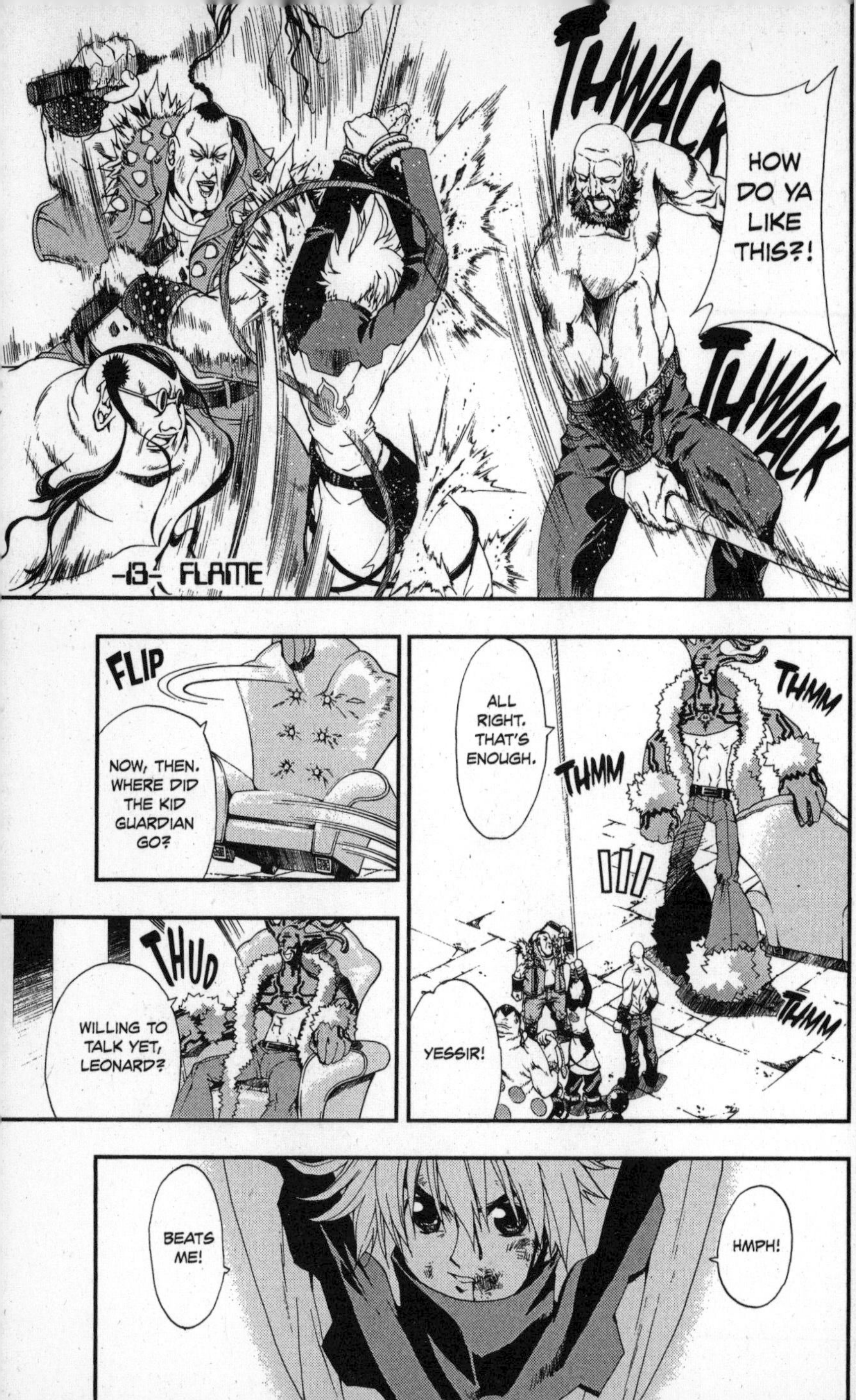
THWACK
HOW DO YA LIKE THIS?!
THWACK
-13- FLAME
ALL RIGHT. THAT'S ENOUGH.
THMM
THMM
YESSIR!
THMM
FLIP
NOW, THEN. WHERE DID THE KID GUARDIAN GO?
THUD
WILLING TO TALK YET, LEONARD?
HMPH!
BEATS ME!

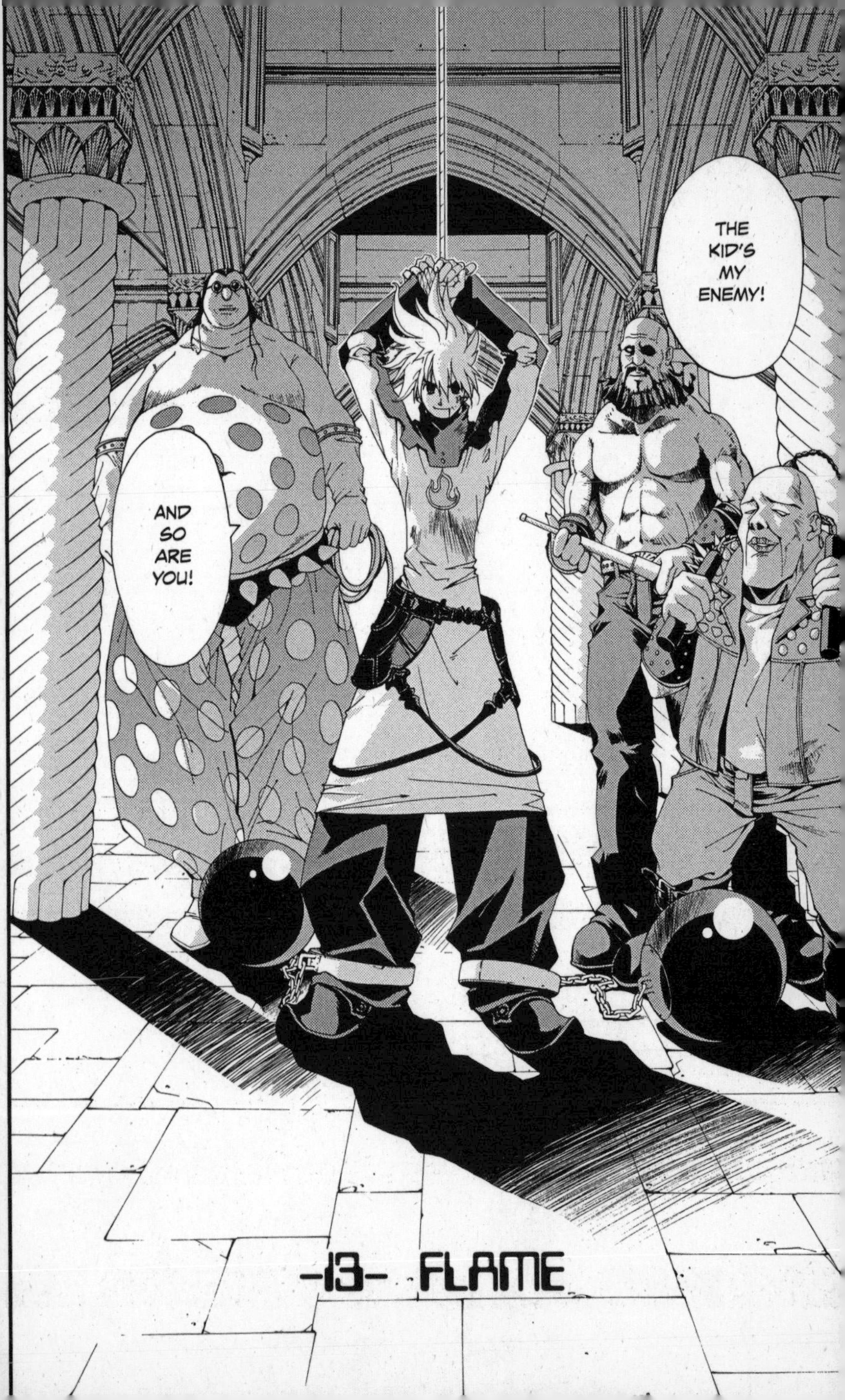
THE KID'S MY ENEMY!
AND SO ARE YOU!
-13- FLAME

READ THIS WAY

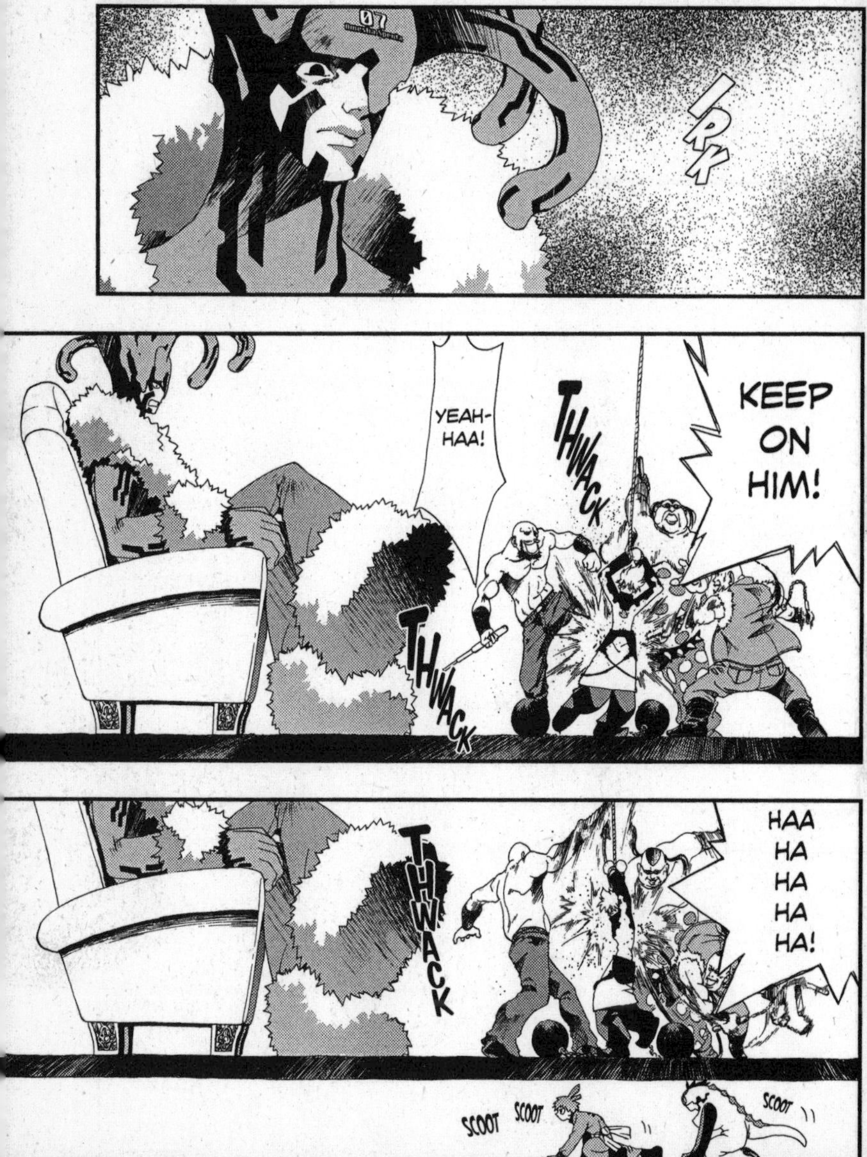

IRK
KEEP ON HIM!
THWACK
YEAH-HAA!
THWACK
HAA HA HA HA HA!
THWACK
SCOOT
SCOOT
SCOOT

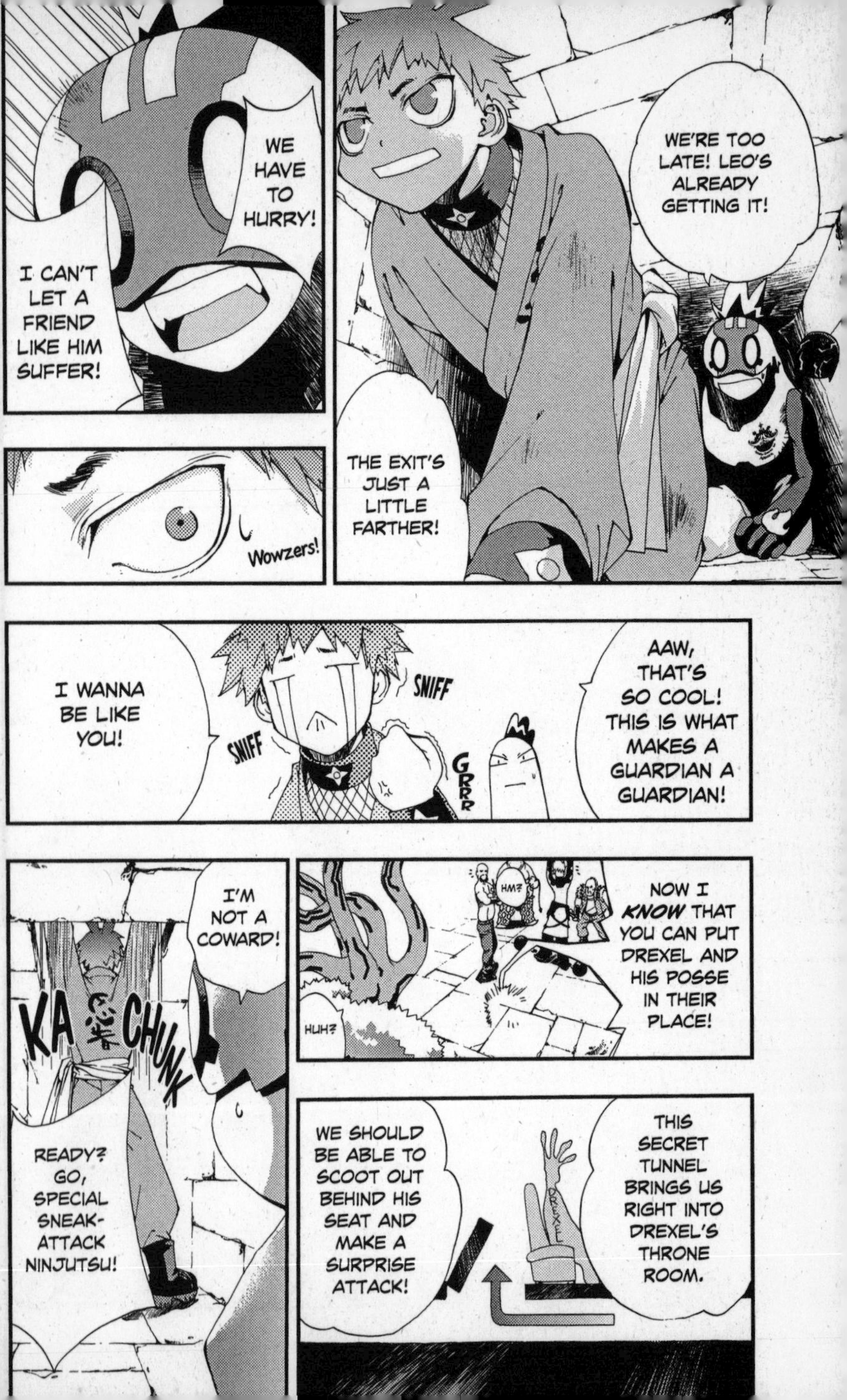
WE'RE TOO LATE! LEO'S ALREADY GETTING IT!
THE EXIT'S JUST A LITTLE FARTHER!
WE HAVE TO HURRY!
I CAN'T LET A FRIEND LIKE HIM SUFFER!
Wowzers!
AAW, THAT'S SO COOL! THIS IS WHAT MAKES A GUARDIAN A GUARDIAN!
GRRR
SNIFF
SNIFF
I WANNA BE LIKE YOU!
NOW I KNOW THAT YOU CAN PUT DREXEL AND HIS POSSE IN THEIR PLACE!
HM?
HUH?
THIS SECRET TUNNEL BRINGS US RIGHT INTO DREXEL'S THRONE ROOM.
DREXEL
WE SHOULD BE ABLE TO SCOOT OUT BEHIND HIS SEAT AND MAKE A SURPRISE ATTACK!
I'M NOT A COWARD!
KA CHUNK
READY? GO, SPECIAL SNEAK-ATTACK NINJUTSU!

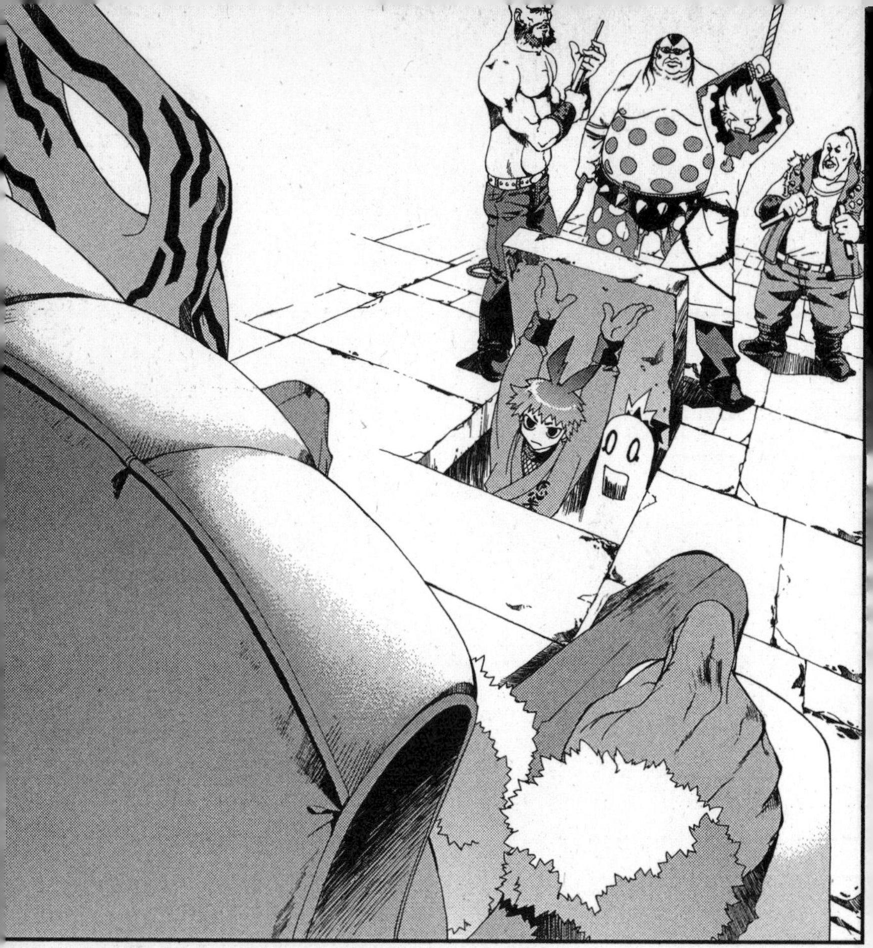

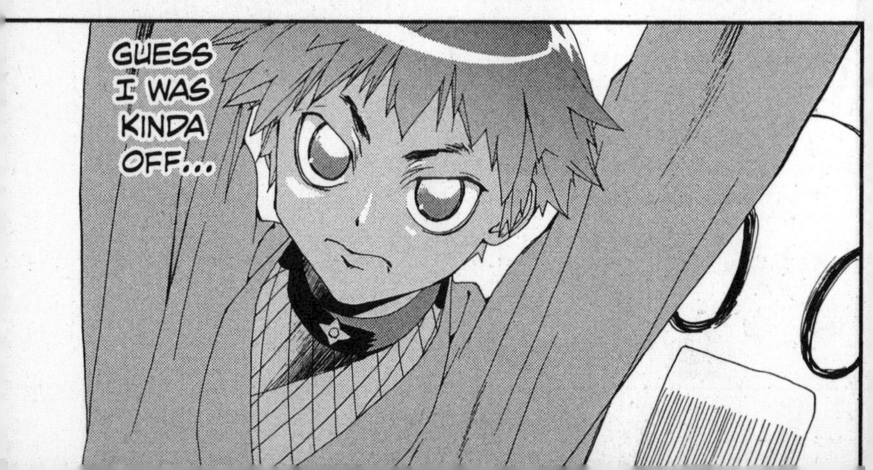
GUESS I WAS KINDA OFF...

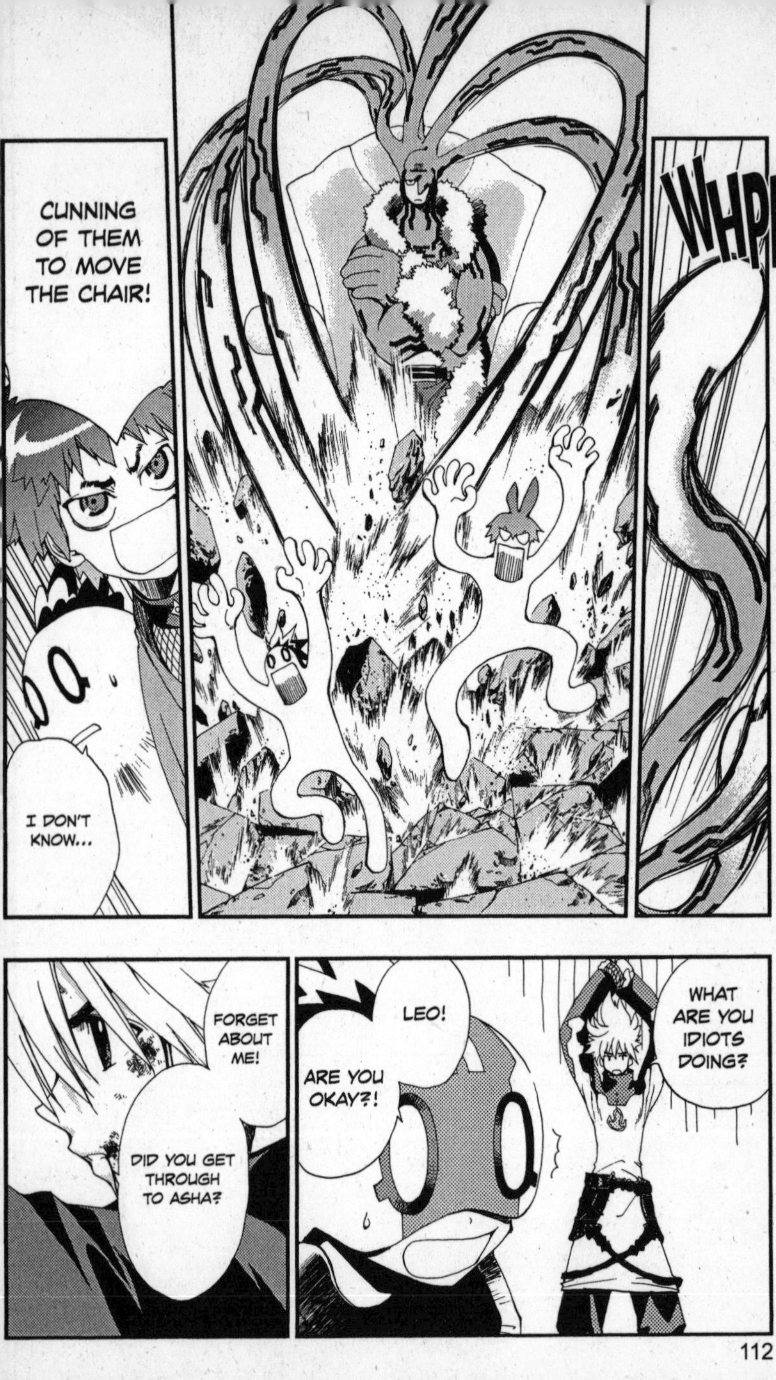
WHPP
CUNNING OF THEM TO MOVE THE CHAIR!
I DON'T KNOW...
WHAT ARE YOU IDIOTS DOING?
LEO!
ARE YOU OKAY?!
FORGET ABOUT ME!
DID YOU GET THROUGH TO ASHA?

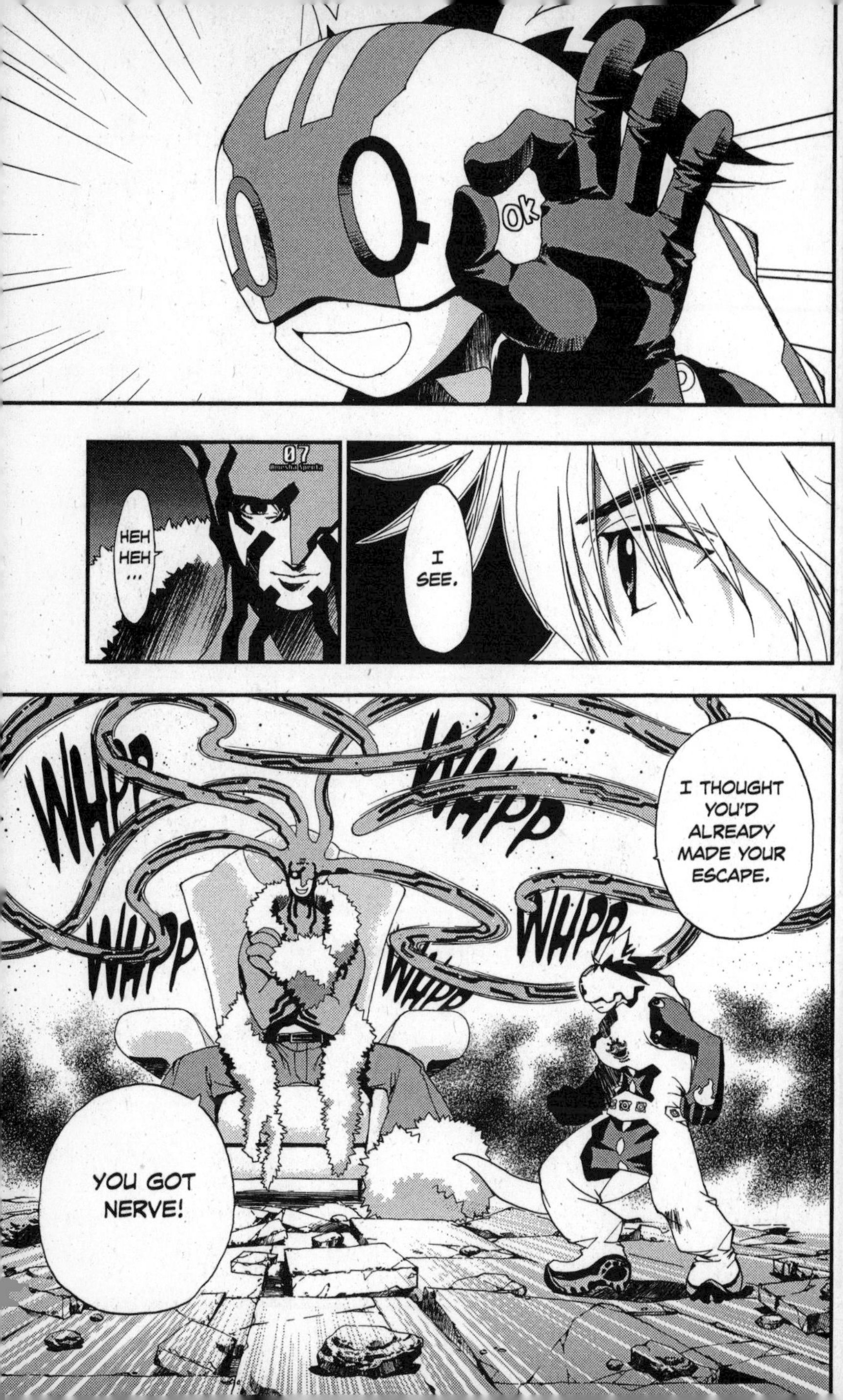
OK
I SEE.
07
Amesha Spenta
HEH HEH ...
I THOUGHT YOU'D ALREADY MADE YOUR ESCAPE.
WHPP
WHPP
WHPP
WHPP
WHPP
YOU GOT NERVE!

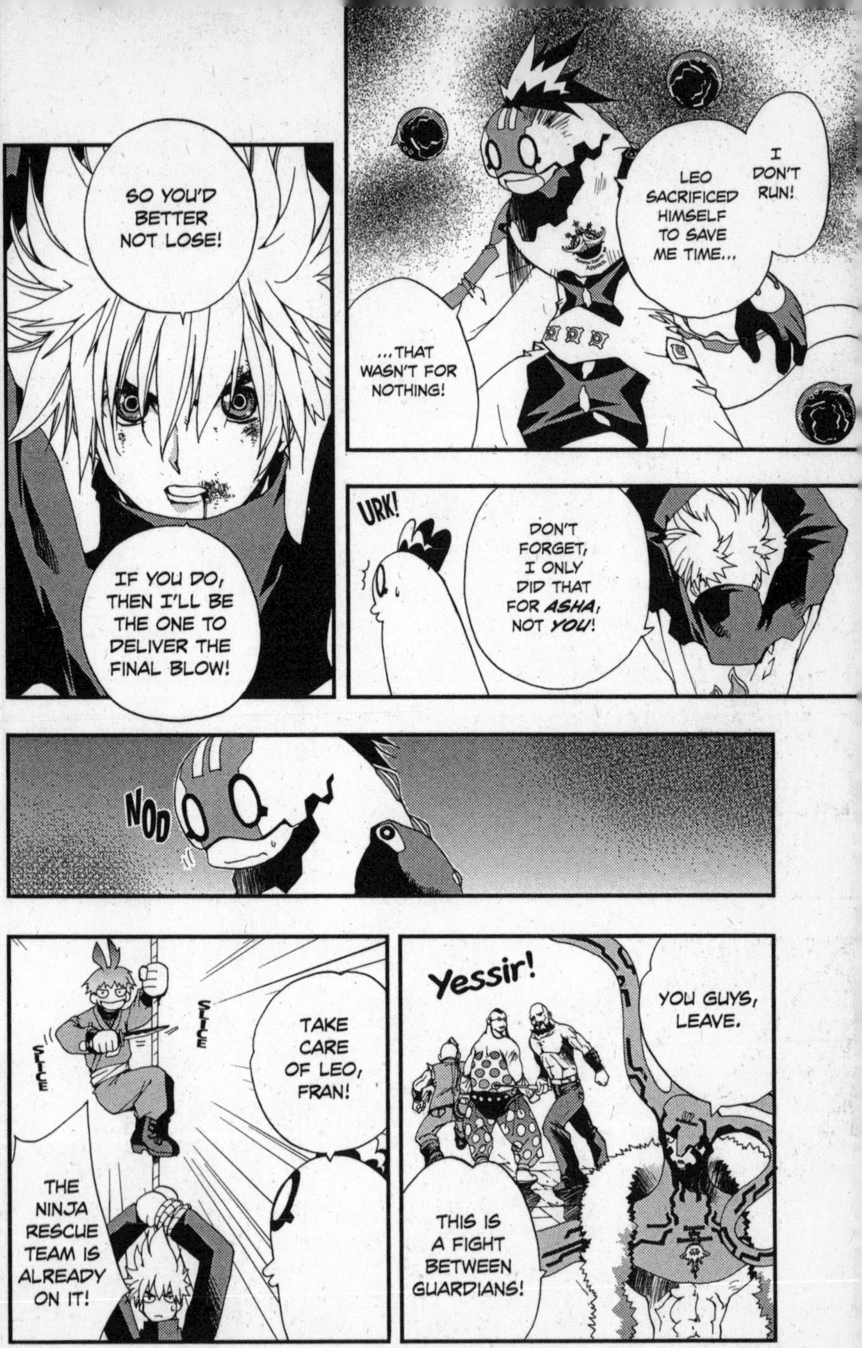
I DON'T RUN!
LEO SACRIFICED HIMSELF TO SAVE ME TIME...
...THAT WASN'T FOR NOTHING!
URK!
DON'T FORGET, I ONLY DID THAT FOR *ASHA*, NOT *YOU*!
SO YOU'D BETTER NOT LOSE!
IF YOU DO, THEN I'LL BE THE ONE TO DELIVER THE FINAL BLOW!
NOD
YOU GUYS, LEAVE.
Yessir!
THIS IS A FIGHT BETWEEN GUARDIANS!
TAKE CARE OF LEO, FRAN!
SLICE
SLICE
THE NINJA RESCUE TEAM IS ALREADY ON IT!

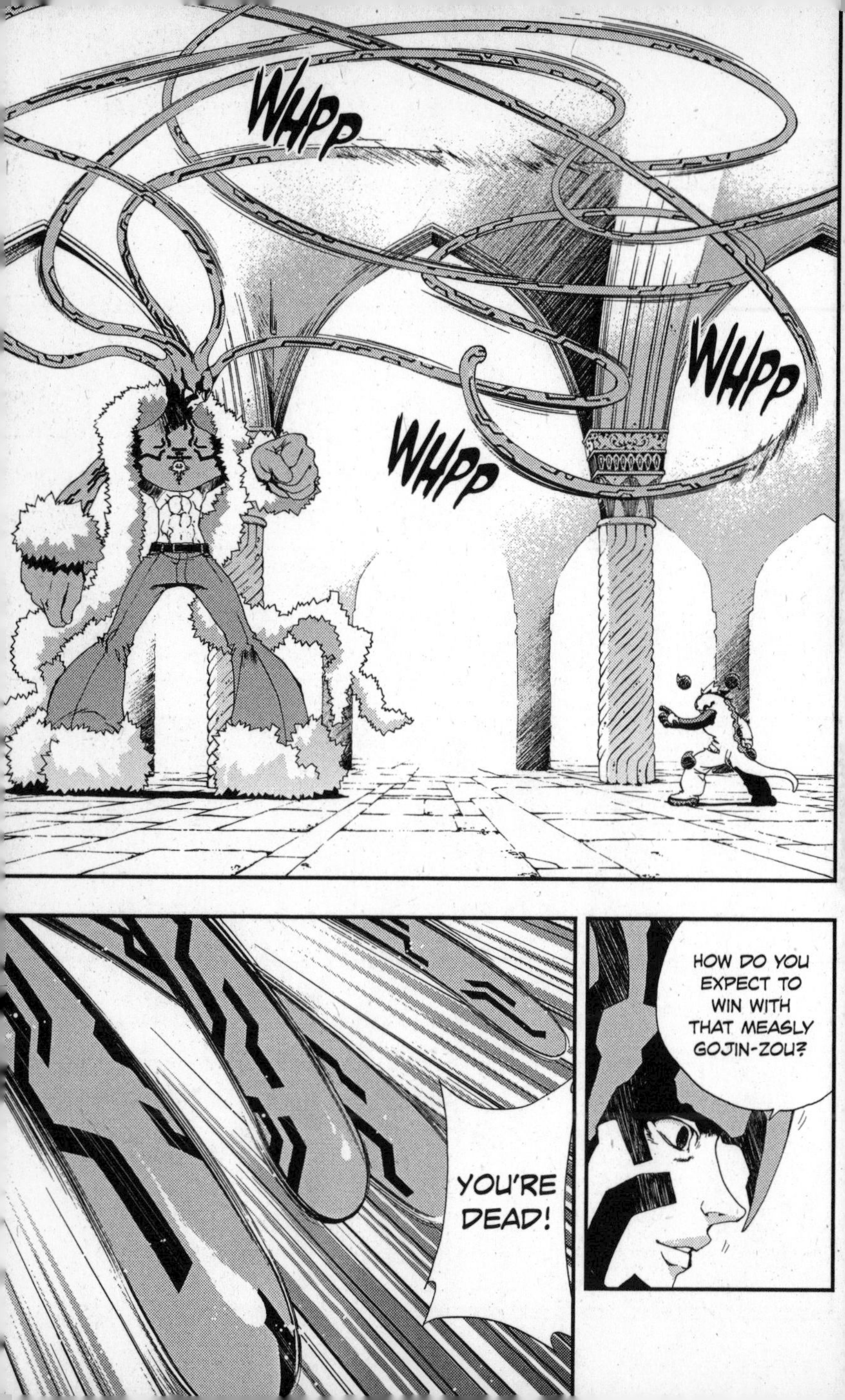
WHPP
WHPP
WHPP
HOW DO YOU EXPECT TO WIN WITH THAT MEASLY GOJIN-ZOU?
YOU'RE DEAD!

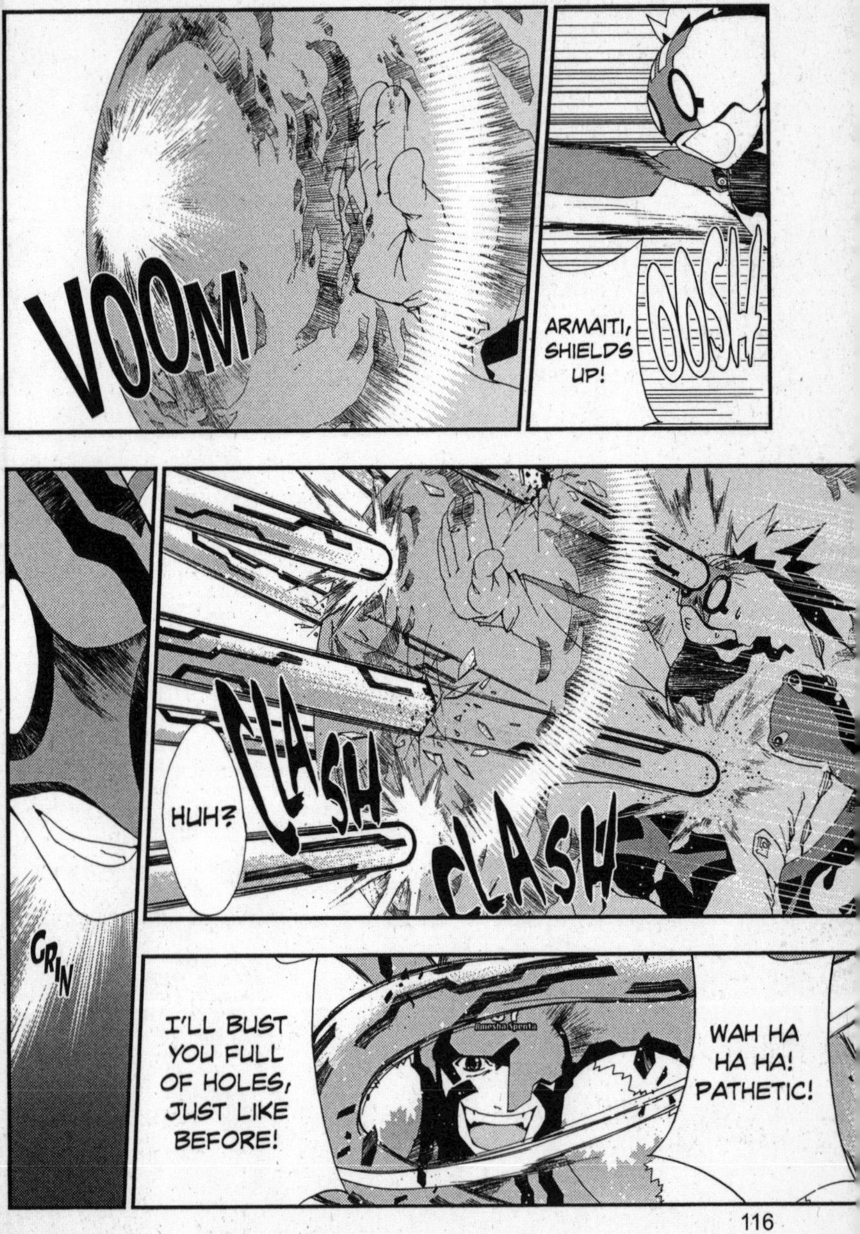
OOSH
ARMAITI, SHIELDS UP!
VOOM
CLASH
CLASH
HUH?
WAH HA HA HA! PATHETIC!
Amesha Spenta
I'LL BUST YOU FULL OF HOLES, JUST LIKE BEFORE!
GRIN

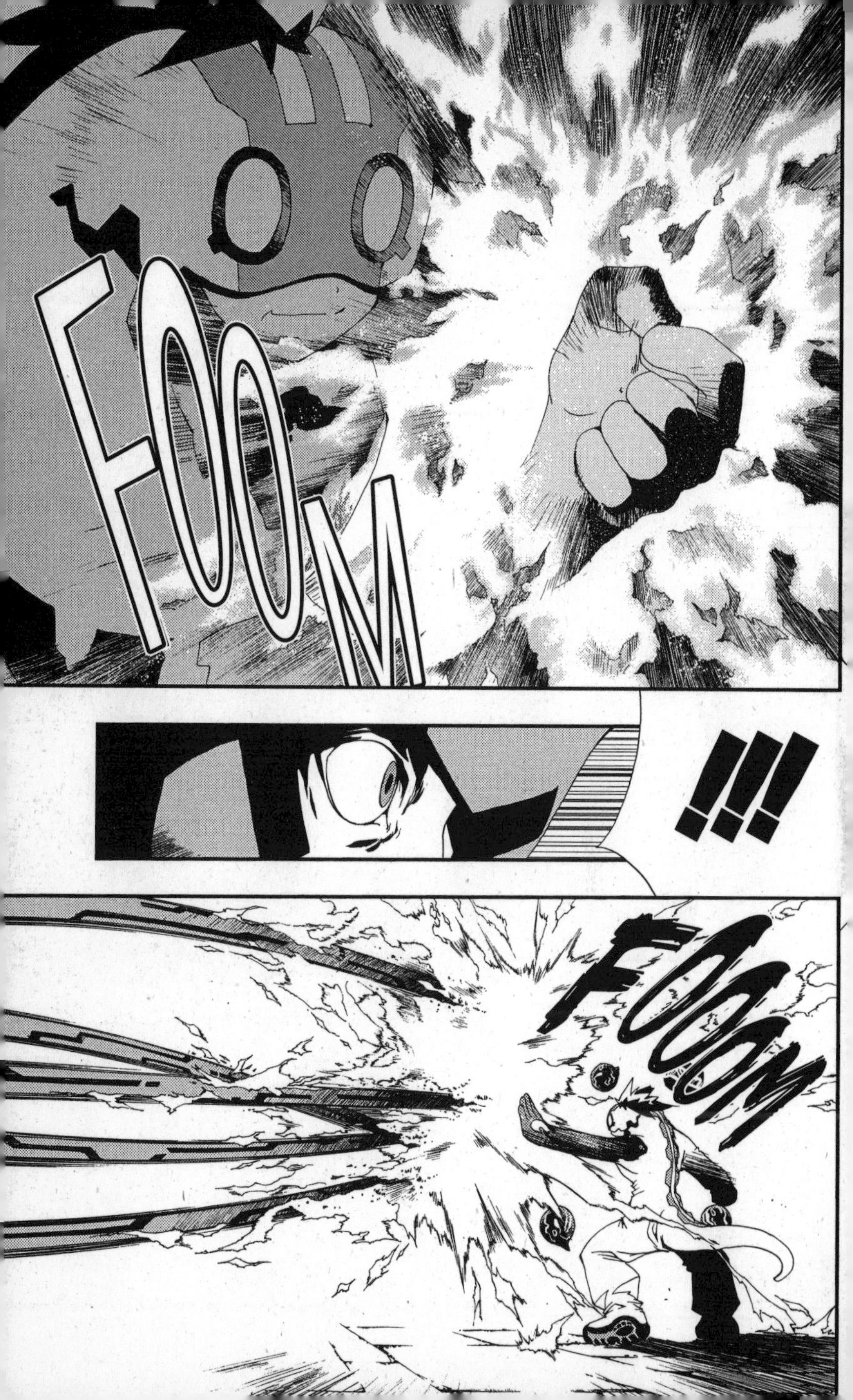
FOOM
!!!
FOOM

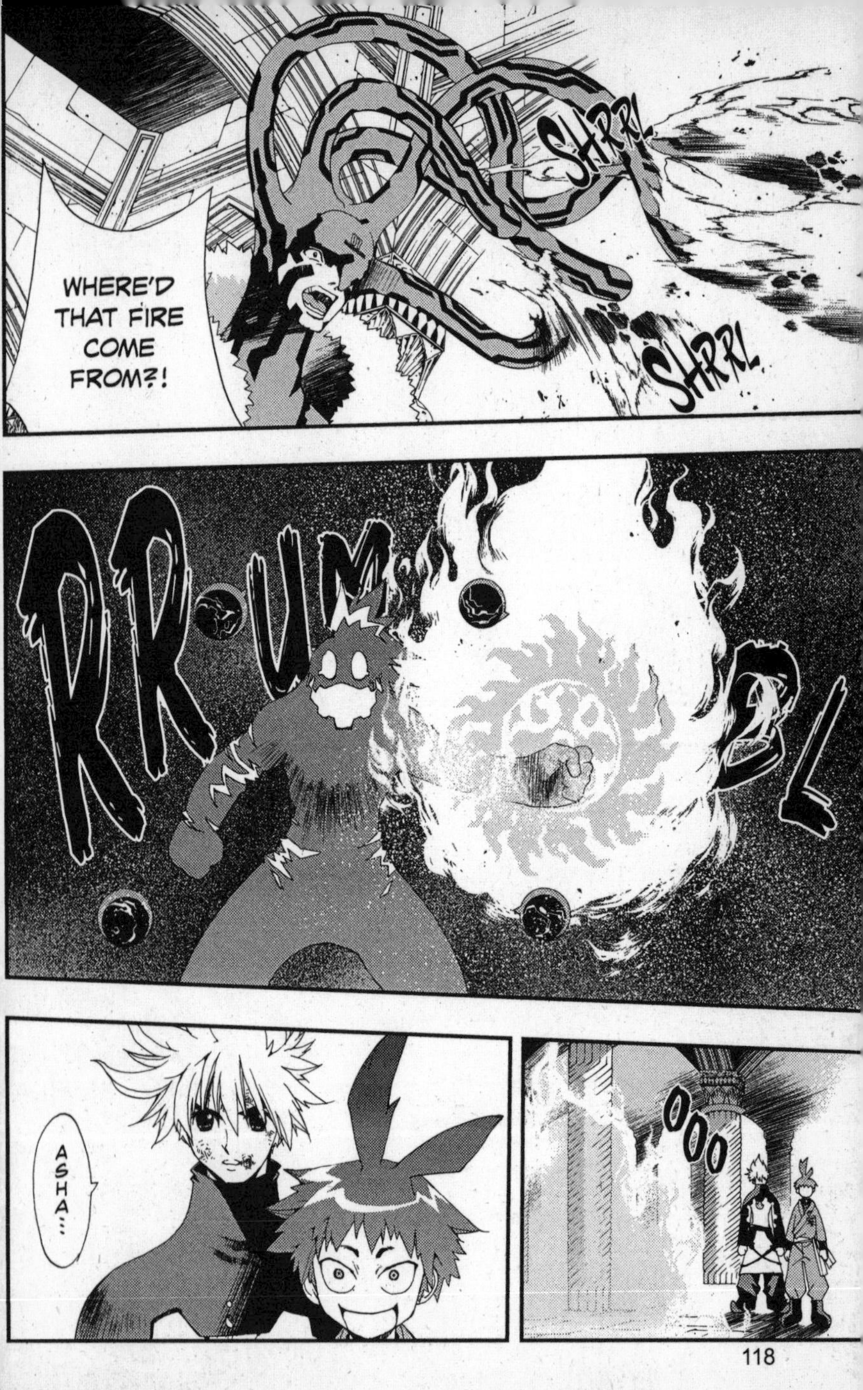
WHERE'D THAT FIRE COME FROM?!
SHRRL
SHRRL
RR-UMBL
OOO
ASHA...

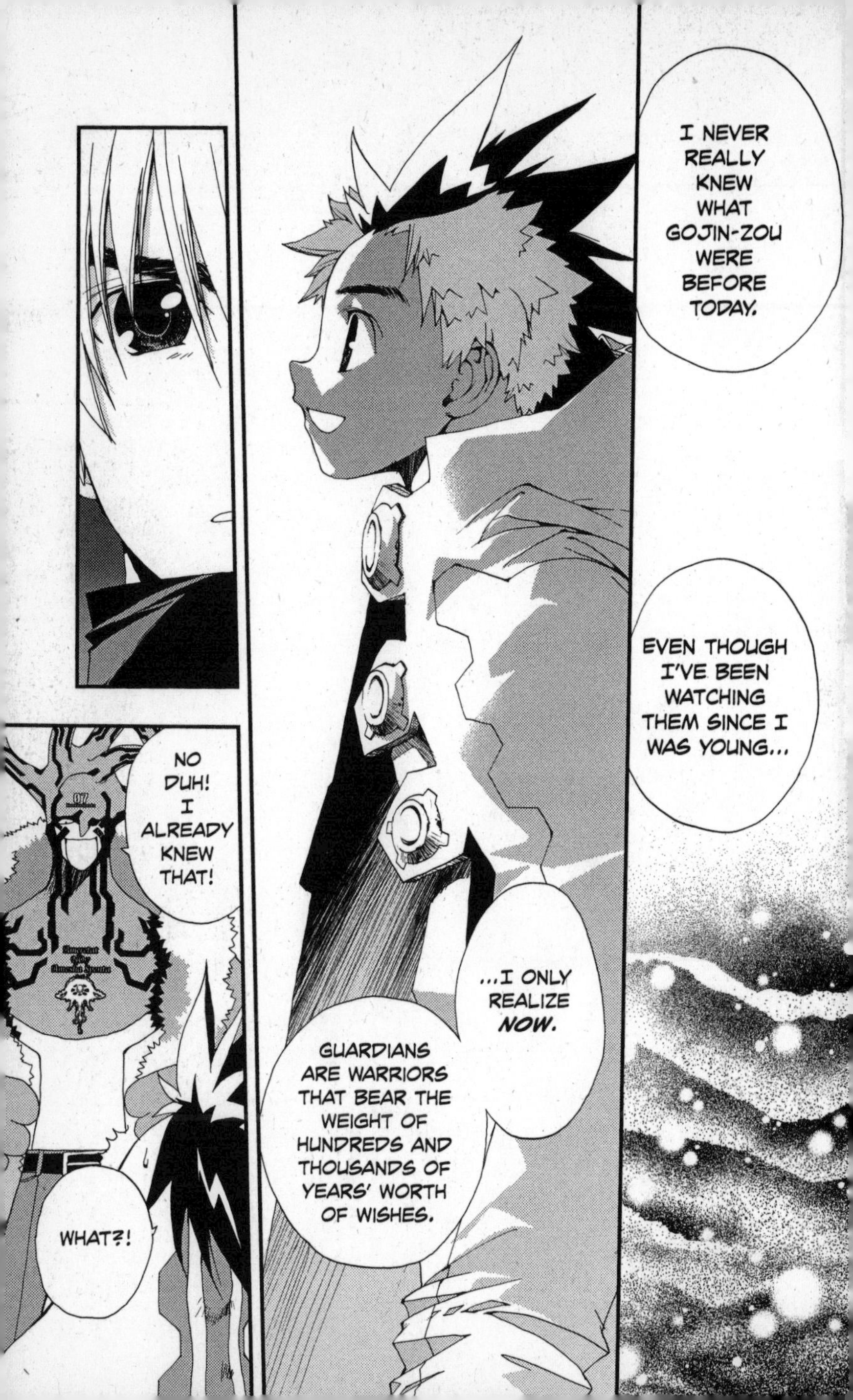
I NEVER REALLY KNEW WHAT GOJIN-ZOU WERE BEFORE TODAY.
EVEN THOUGH I'VE BEEN WATCHING THEM SINCE I WAS YOUNG...
...I ONLY REALIZE *NOW*.
GUARDIANS ARE WARRIORS THAT BEAR THE WEIGHT OF HUNDREDS AND THOUSANDS OF YEARS' WORTH OF WISHES.
NO DUH! I ALREADY KNEW THAT!
WHAT?!

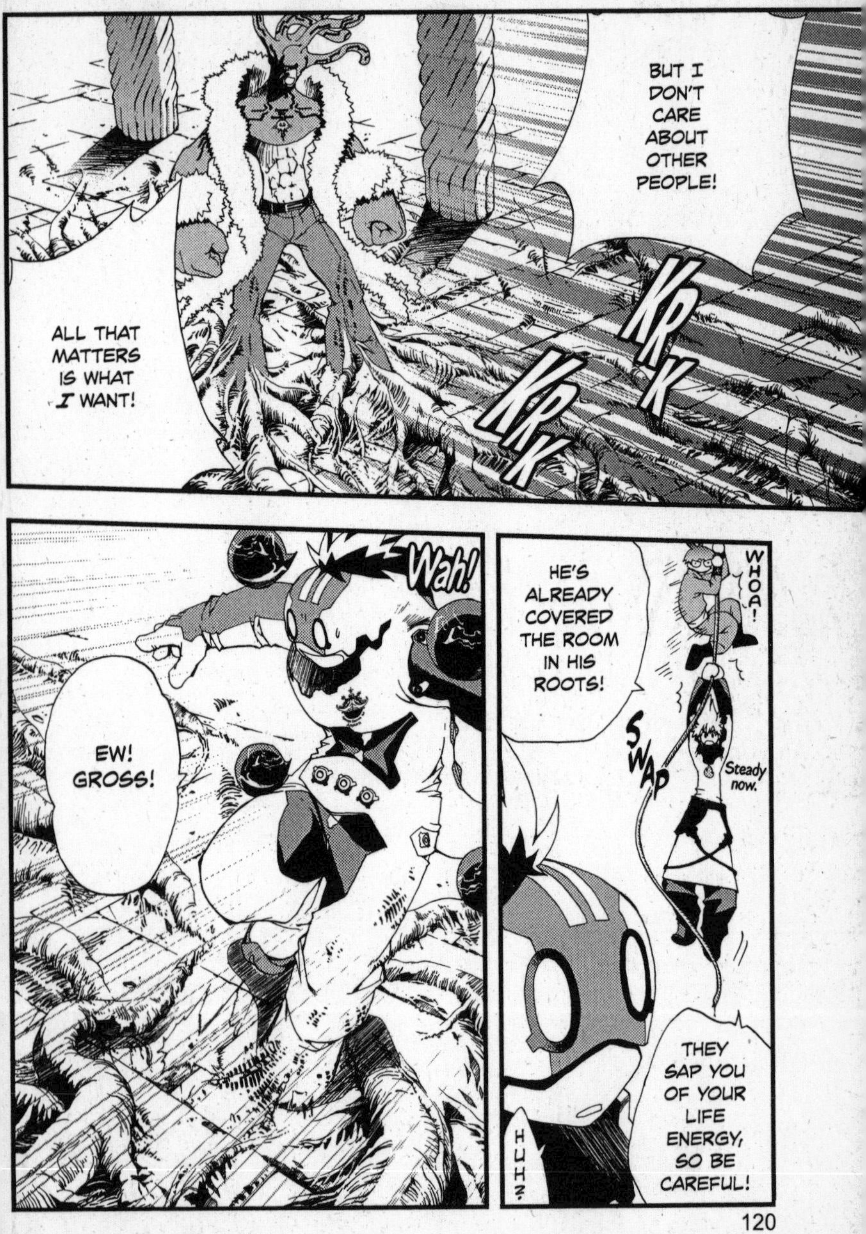
BUT I DON'T CARE ABOUT OTHER PEOPLE!
KRK
KRK
ALL THAT MATTERS IS WHAT I WANT!
WHOA!
HE'S ALREADY COVERED THE ROOM IN HIS ROOTS!
SWAP
Steady now.
THEY SAP YOU OF YOUR LIFE ENERGY, SO BE CAREFUL!
HUH?
Wah!
EW! GROSS!

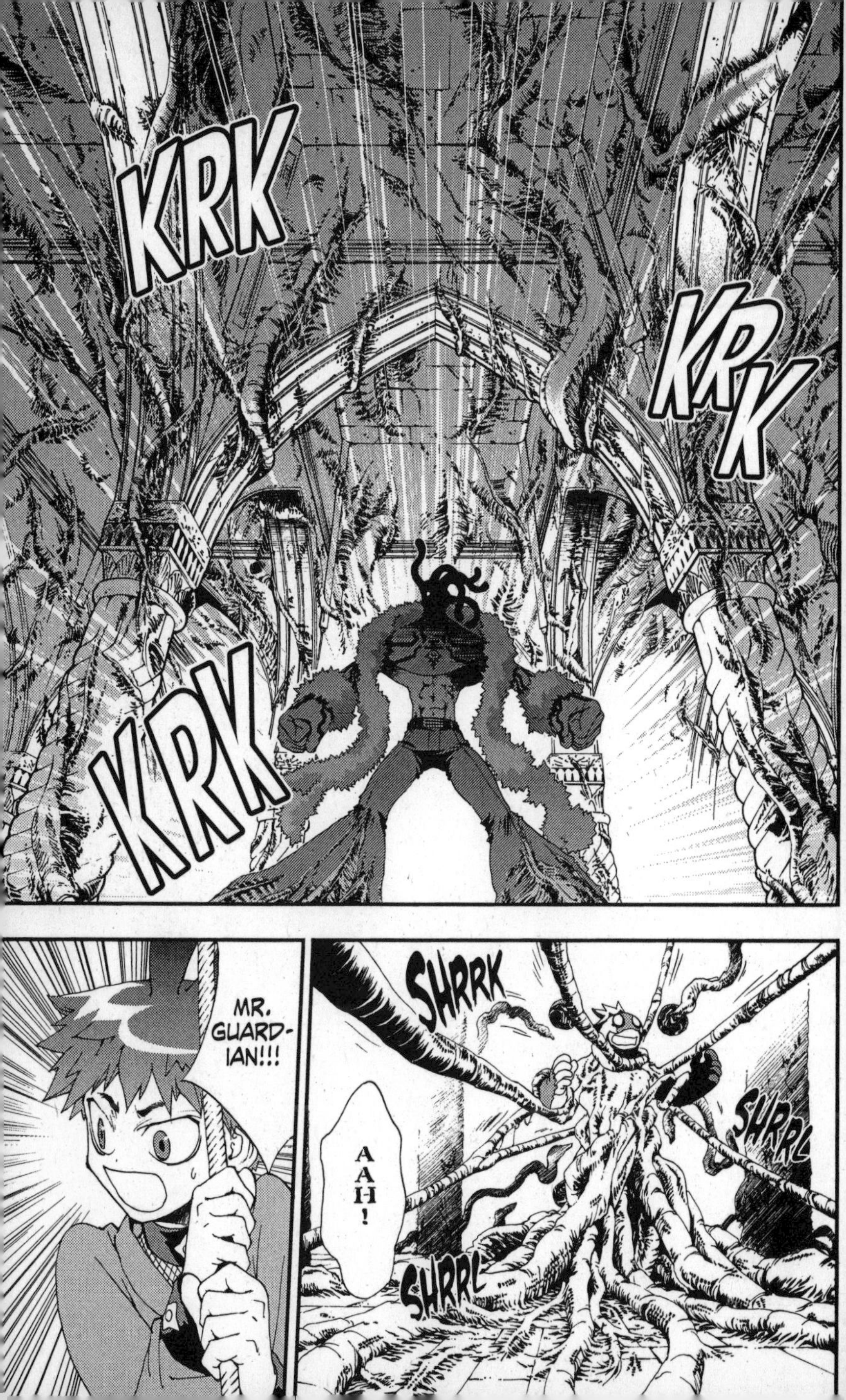
KRK
KRK
KRK
SHRRK
AAH!
SHRRL
SHRRL
MR. GUARDIAN!!!

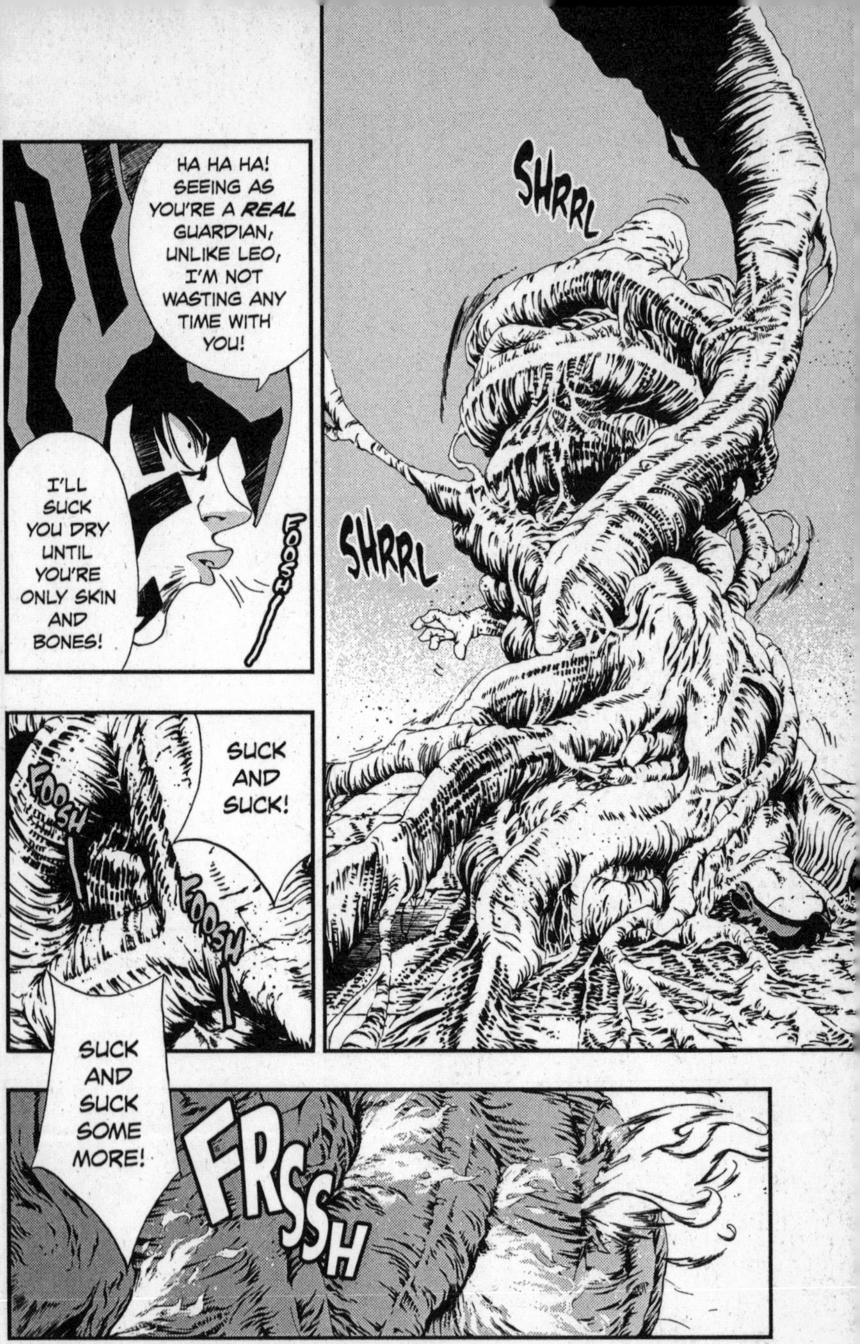
SHRRL
SHRRL
HA HA HA! SEEING AS YOU'RE A *REAL* GUARDIAN, UNLIKE LEO, I'M NOT WASTING ANY TIME WITH YOU!
I'LL SUCK YOU DRY UNTIL YOU'RE ONLY SKIN AND BONES!
FOOSH
SUCK AND SUCK!
FOOSH
FOOSH
SUCK AND SUCK SOME MORE!
FRSSH

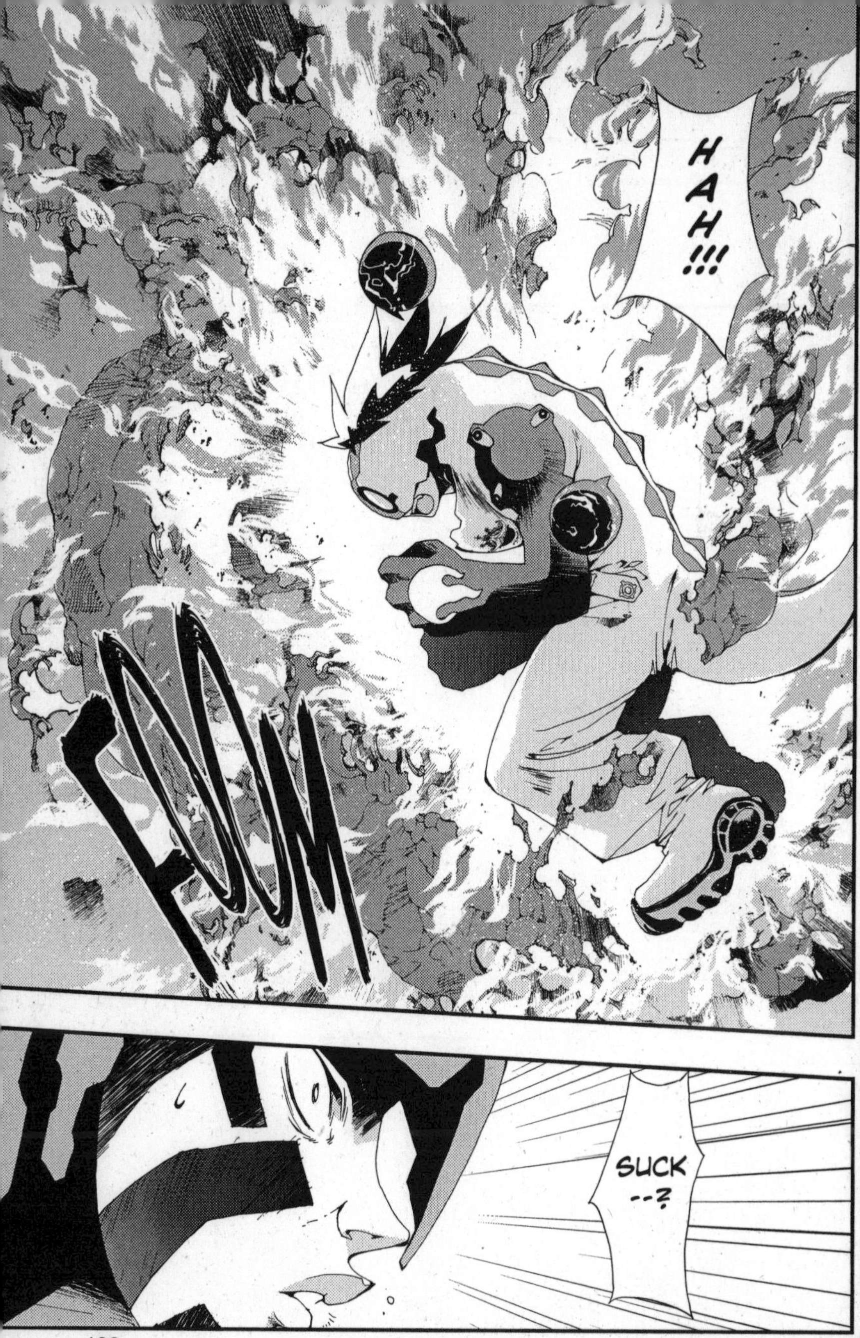
HAH!!!
FOOM
SUCK --?

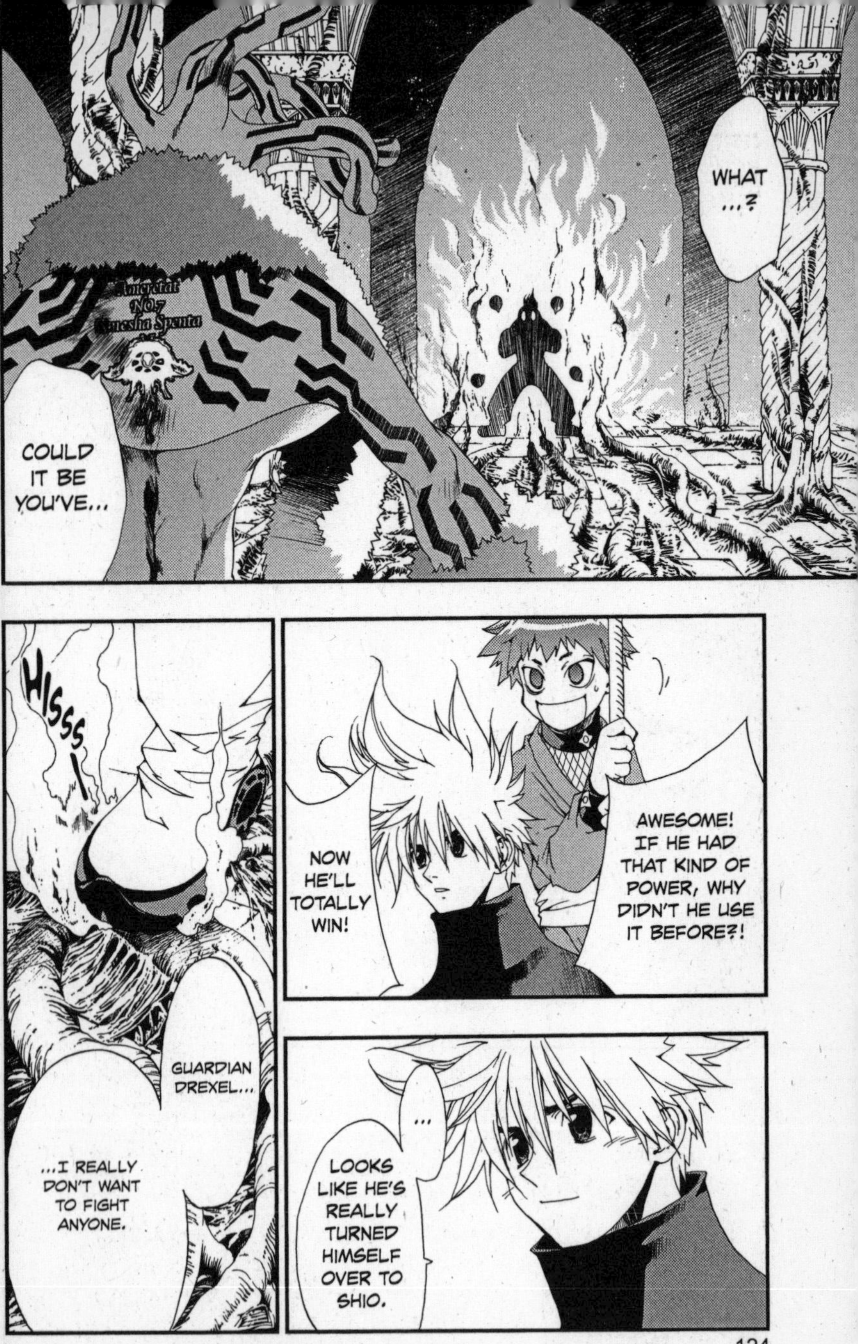
WHAT ...?
Ameretat
No.7
Spenta
COULD IT BE YOU'VE...
AWESOME! IF HE HAD THAT KIND OF POWER, WHY DIDN'T HE USE IT BEFORE?!
NOW HE'LL TOTALLY WIN!
...
LOOKS LIKE HE'S REALLY TURNED HIMSELF OVER TO SHIO.
HISSS!
GUARDIAN DREXEL...
...I REALLY DON'T WANT TO FIGHT ANYONE.

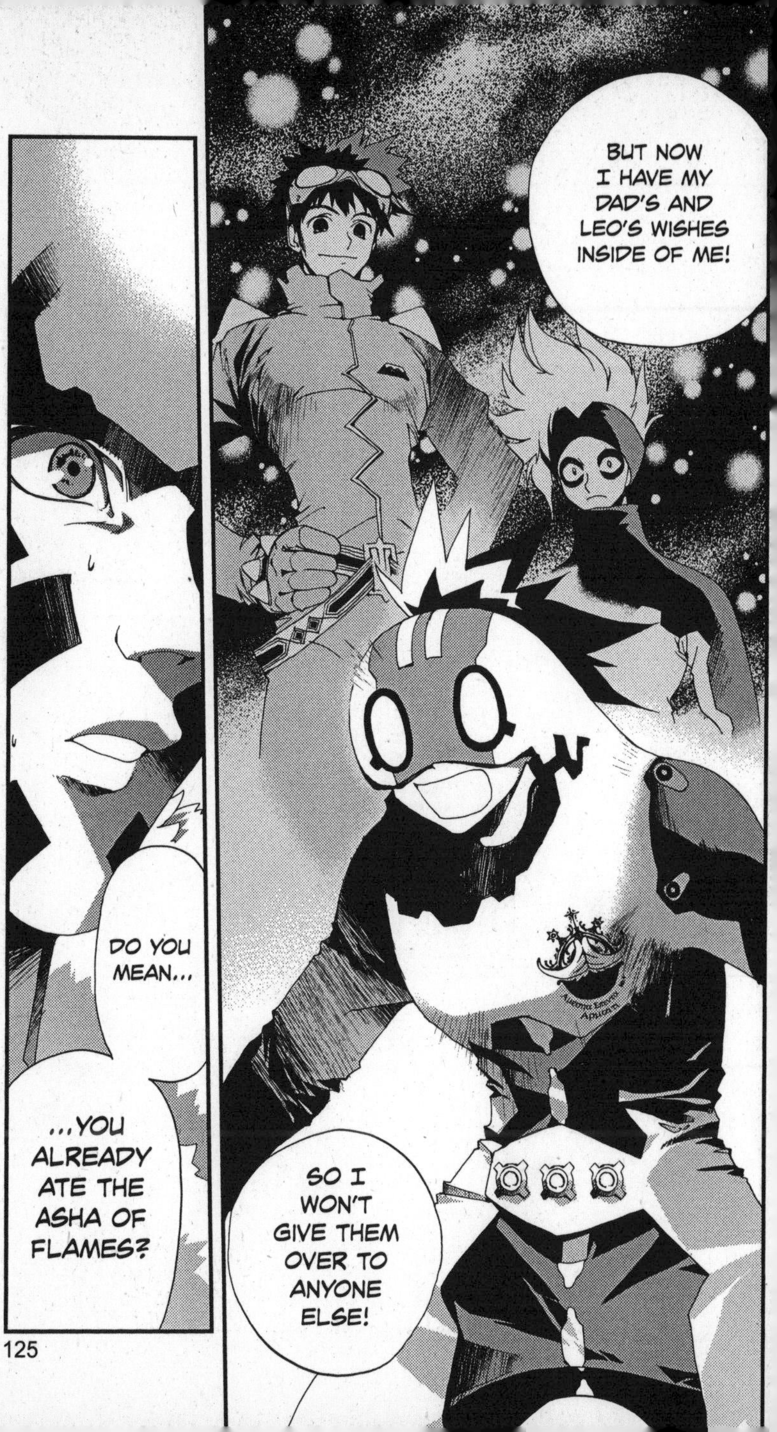
BUT NOW I HAVE MY DAD'S AND LEO'S WISHES INSIDE OF ME!
SO I WON'T GIVE THEM OVER TO ANYONE ELSE!
DO YOU MEAN...
...YOU ALREADY ATE THE ASHA OF FLAMES?

Wāq Wāq

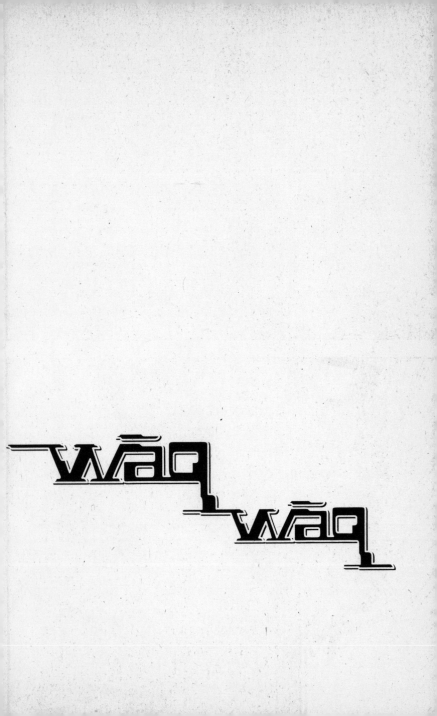

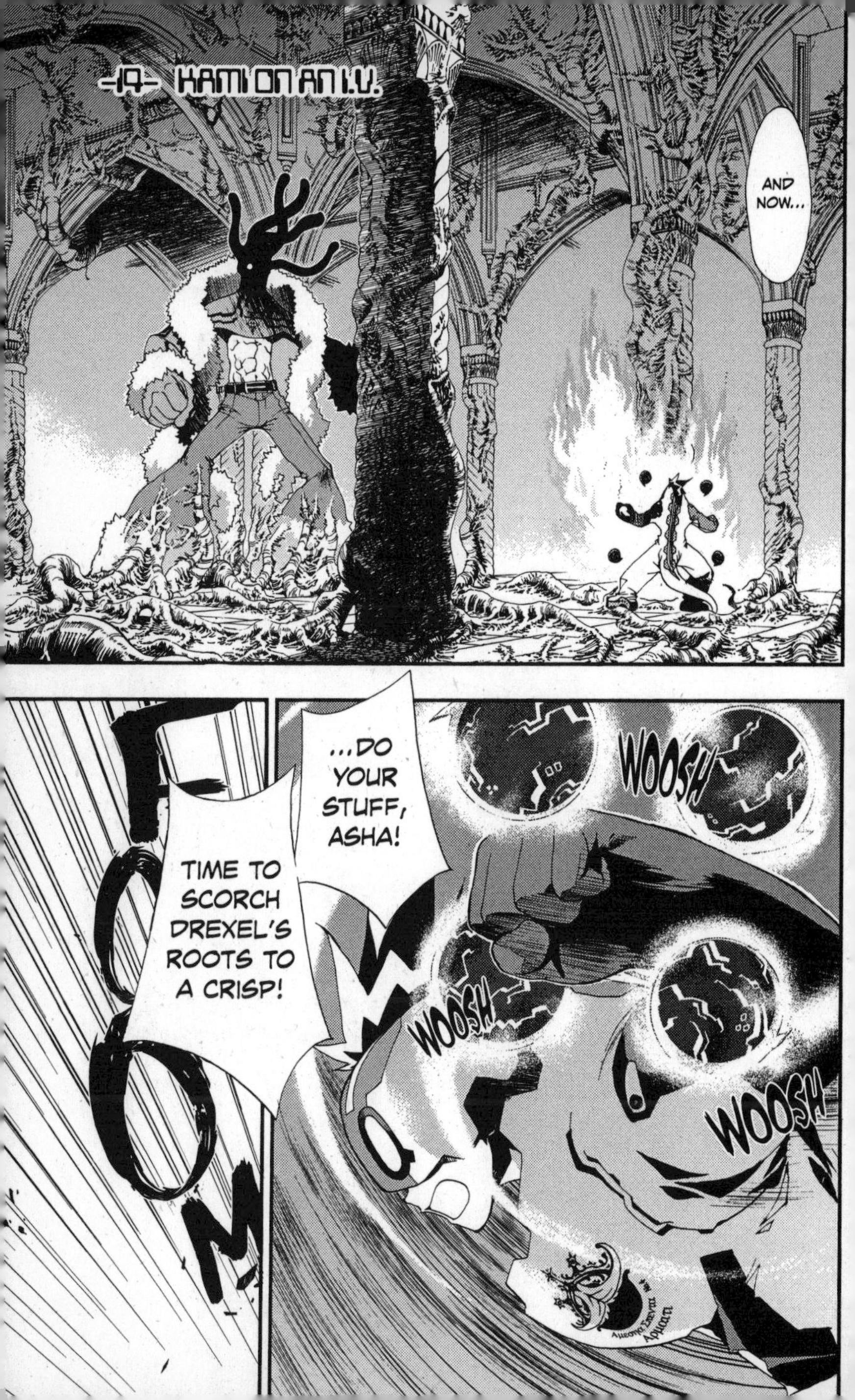
-19- KAMI ON AN I.V.
AND NOW...
...DO YOUR STUFF, ASHA!
TIME TO SCORCH DREXEL'S ROOTS TO A CRISP!
WOOSH
WOOSH
WOOSH
FOOM

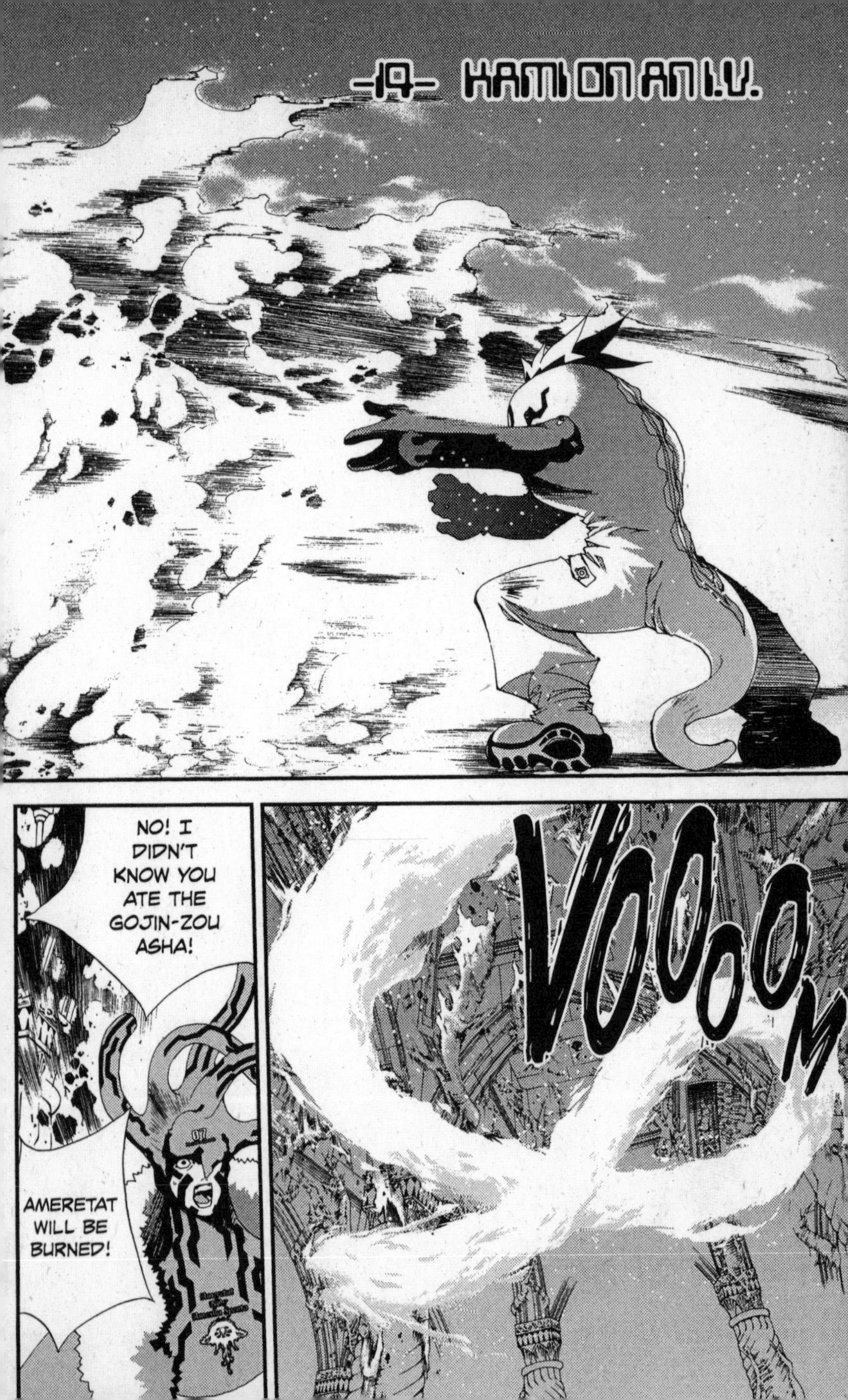
-19- KAMI ON AN I.V.
VOOOOM
NO! I DIDN'T KNOW YOU ATE THE GOJIN-ZOU ASHA!
AMERETAT WILL BE BURNED!

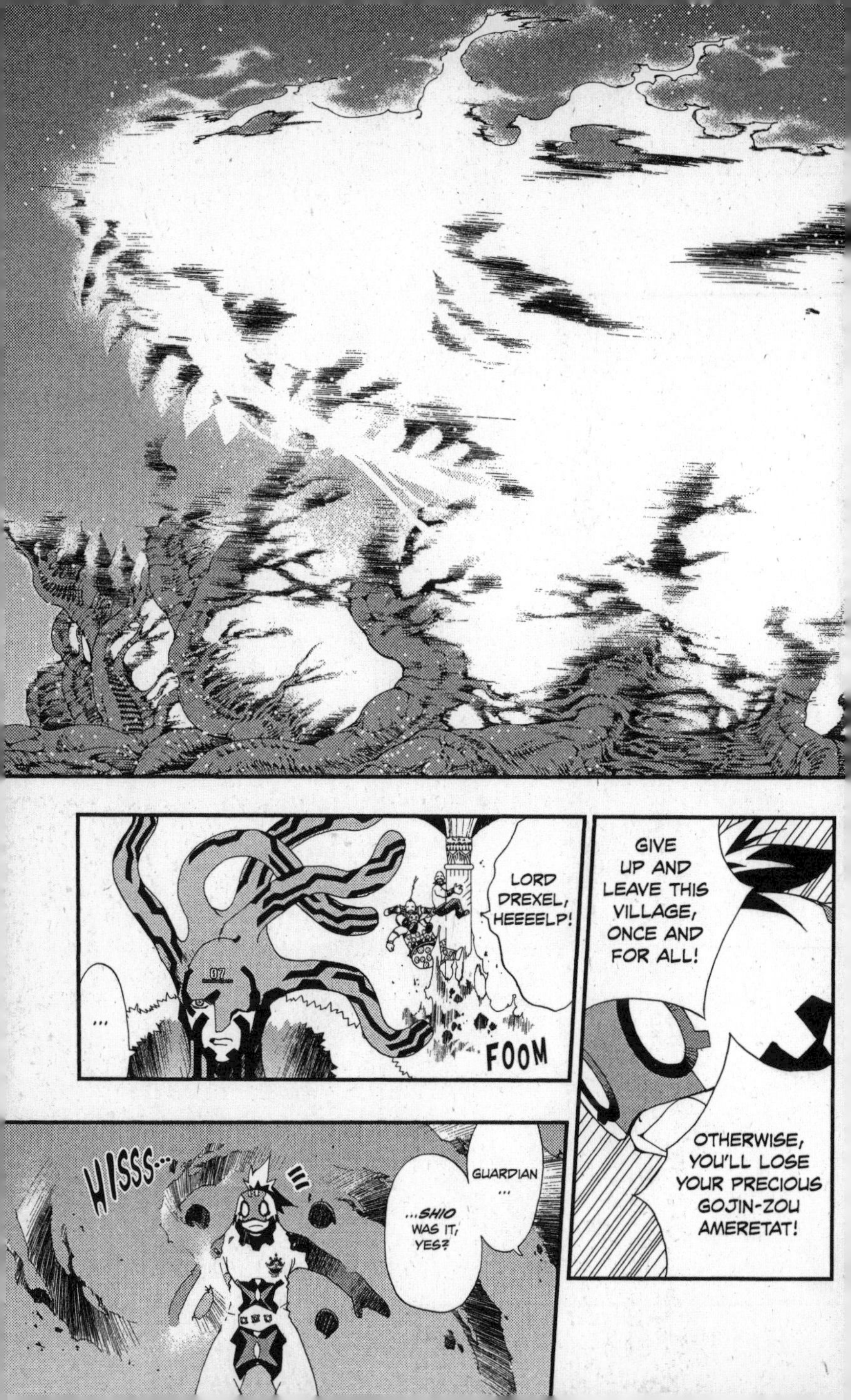
GIVE UP AND LEAVE THIS VILLAGE, ONCE AND FOR ALL!
OTHERWISE, YOU'LL LOSE YOUR PRECIOUS GOJIN-ZOU AMERETAT!
LORD DREXEL, HEEEELP!
...
FOOM
HISSS...
GUARDIAN ...
...SHIO WAS IT, YES?

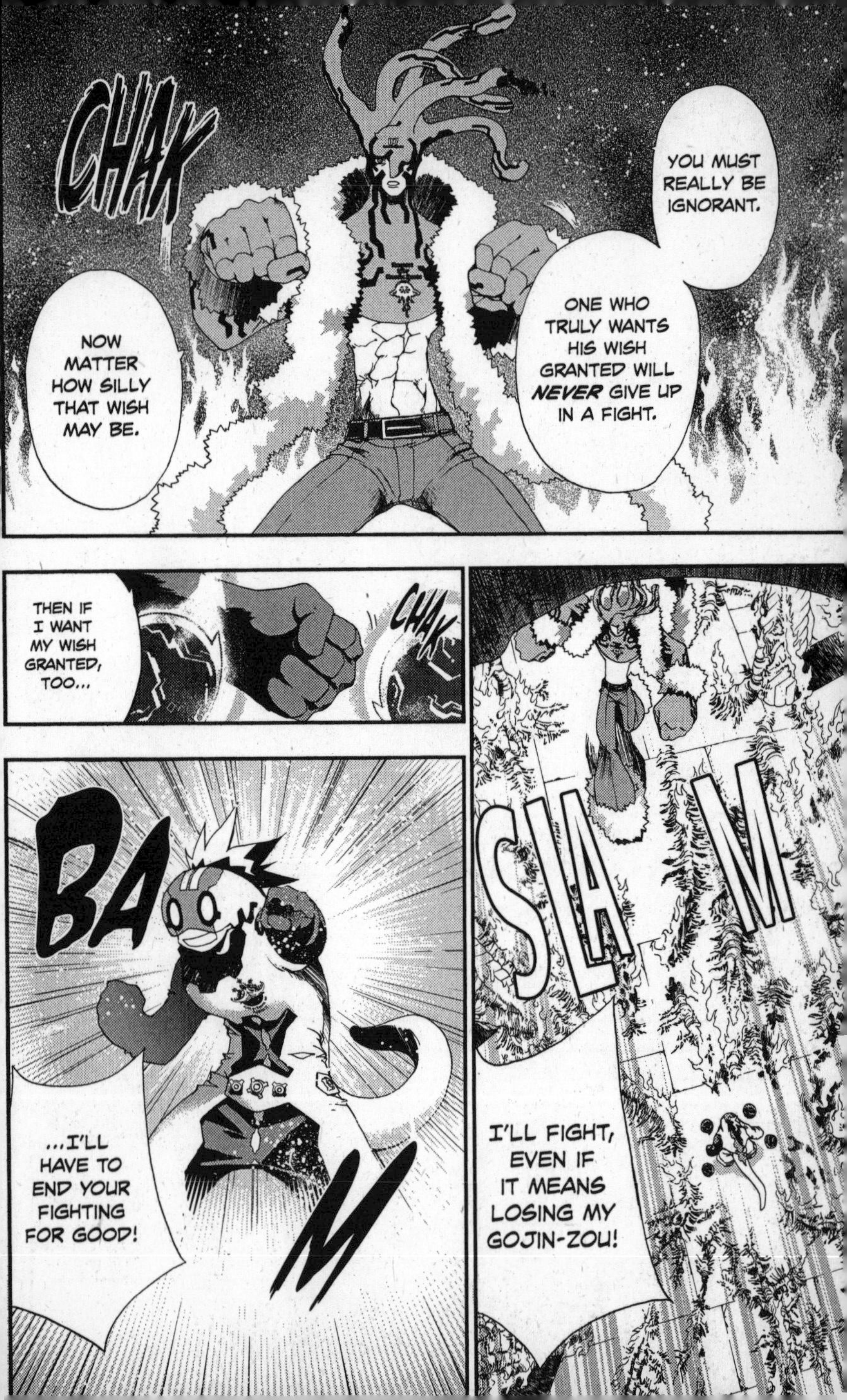
CHAK
YOU MUST REALLY BE IGNORANT.
ONE WHO TRULY WANTS HIS WISH GRANTED WILL ***NEVER*** GIVE UP IN A FIGHT.
NOW MATTER HOW SILLY THAT WISH MAY BE.
SLAM
I'LL FIGHT, EVEN IF IT MEANS LOSING MY GOJIN-ZOU!
THEN IF I WANT MY WISH GRANTED, TOO...
CHAK
BAM
...I'LL HAVE TO END YOUR FIGHTING FOR GOOD!

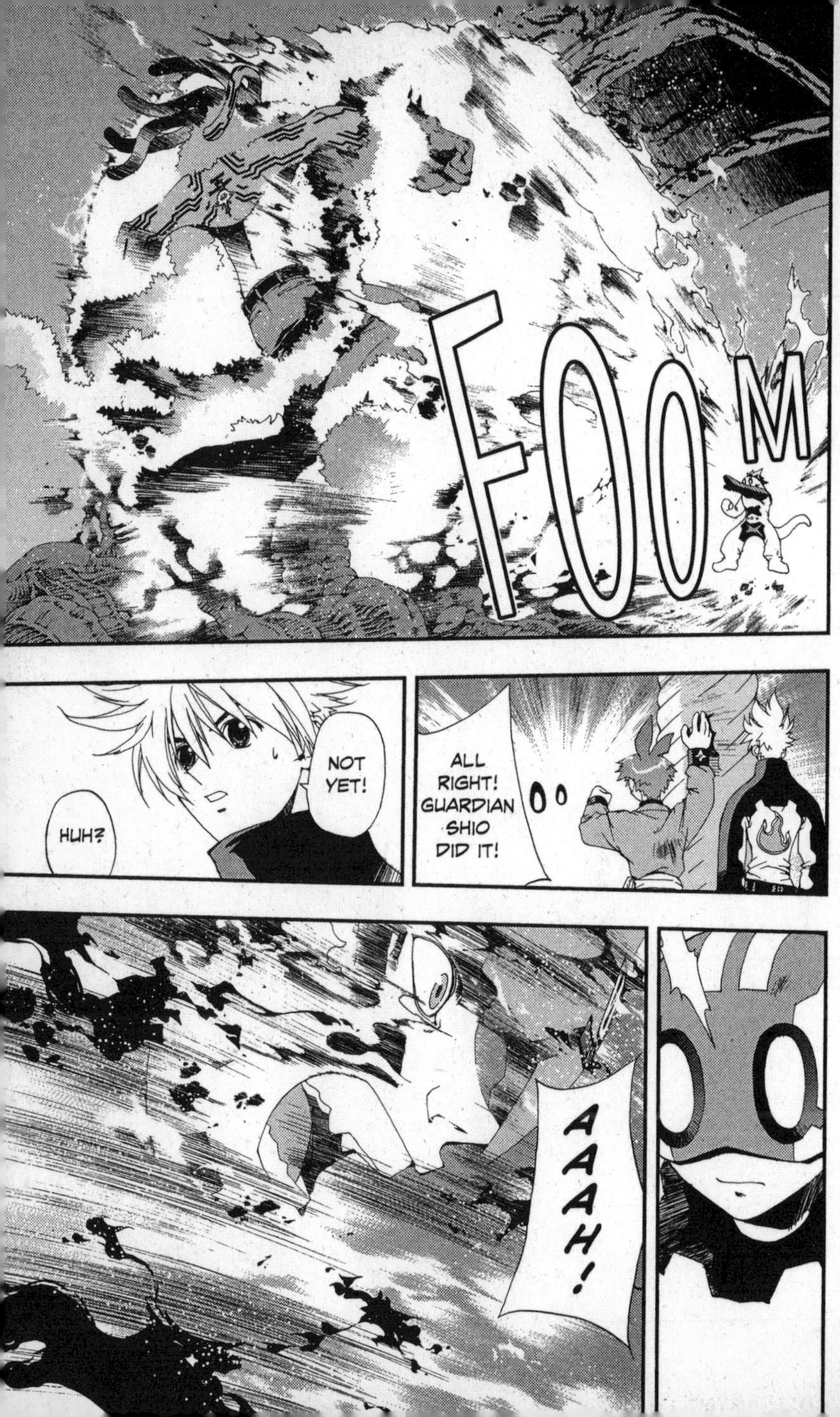
FOOM
ALL RIGHT! GUARDIAN SHIO DID IT!
O O
NOT YET!
HUH?
AAAAH!

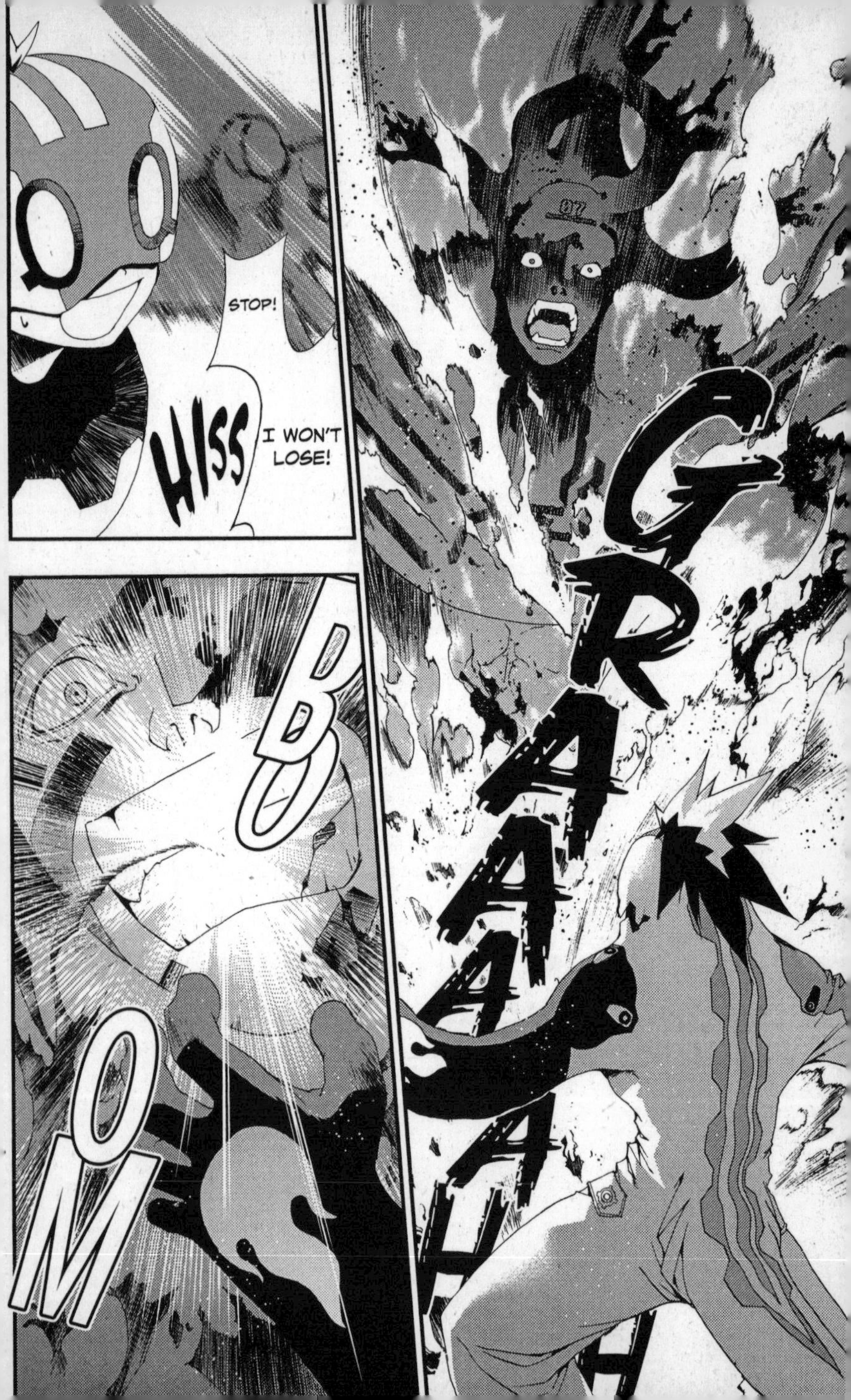
GRAAAAH
STOP!
HISS
I WON'T LOSE!
BOOM

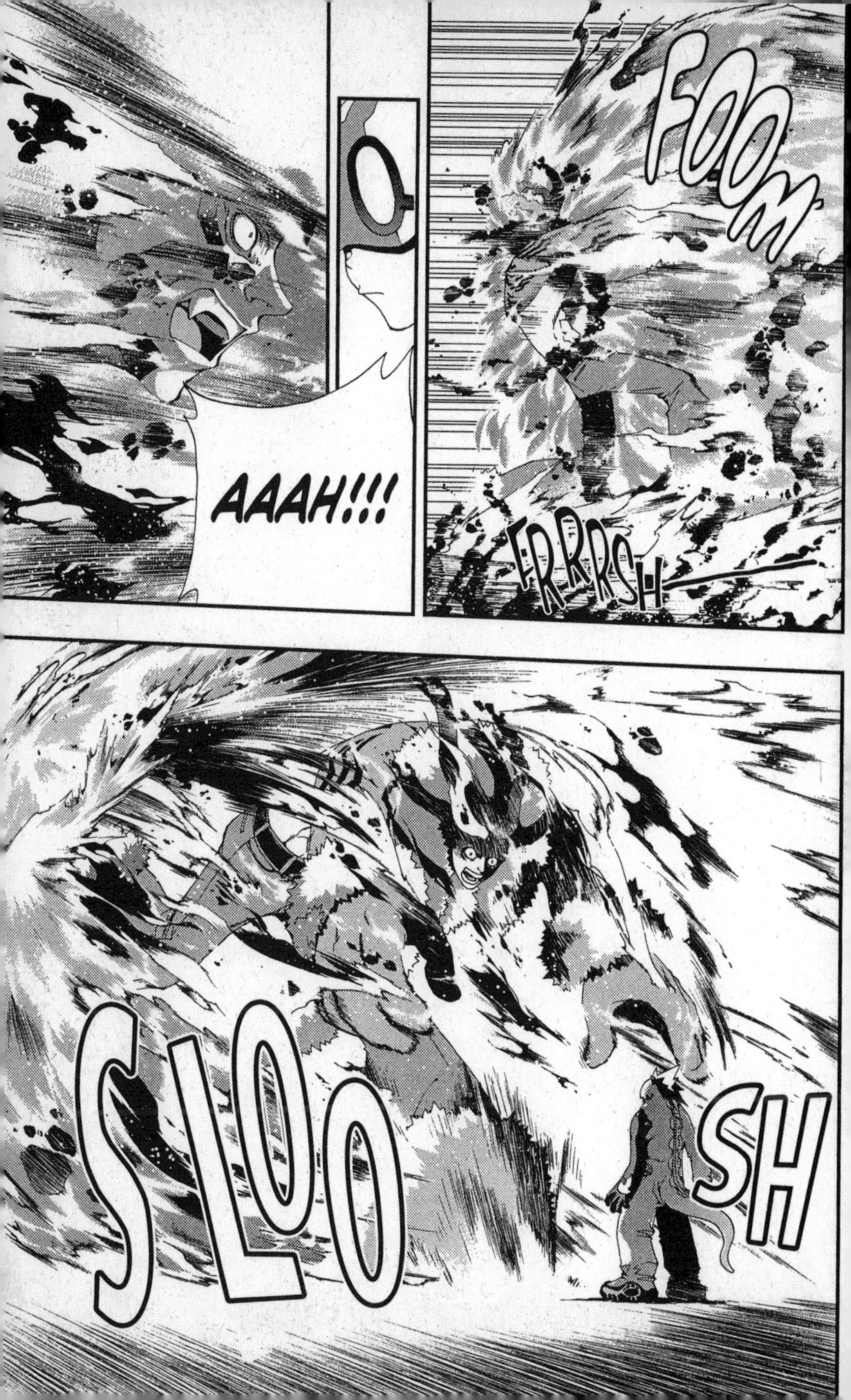
FOOM
FRRRSH
AAAH!!!
SLOOSH

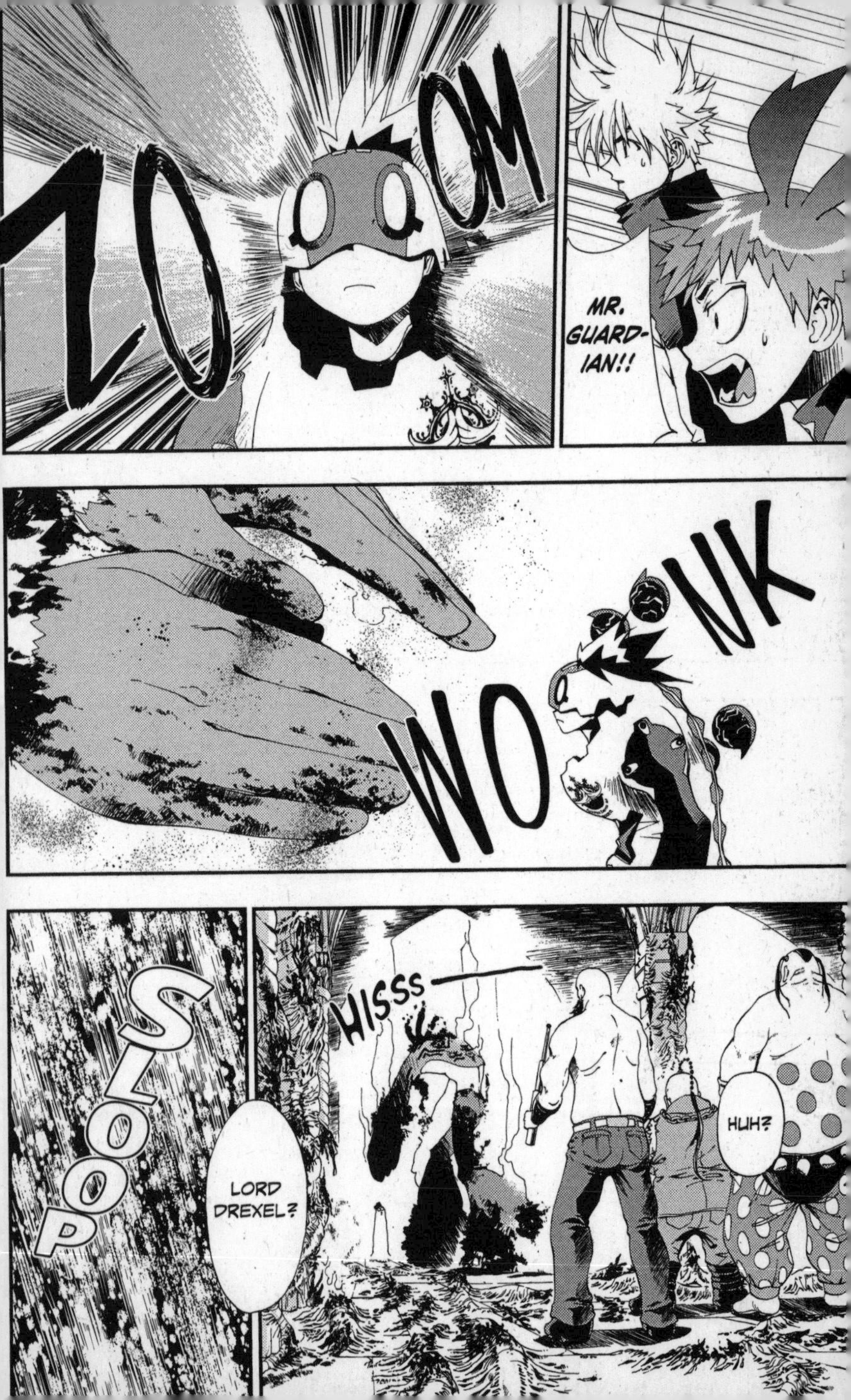

MR. GUARDIAN!!
ZOOOM
WOOONK
HUH?
HISSS—
LORD DREXEL?
SLOOP

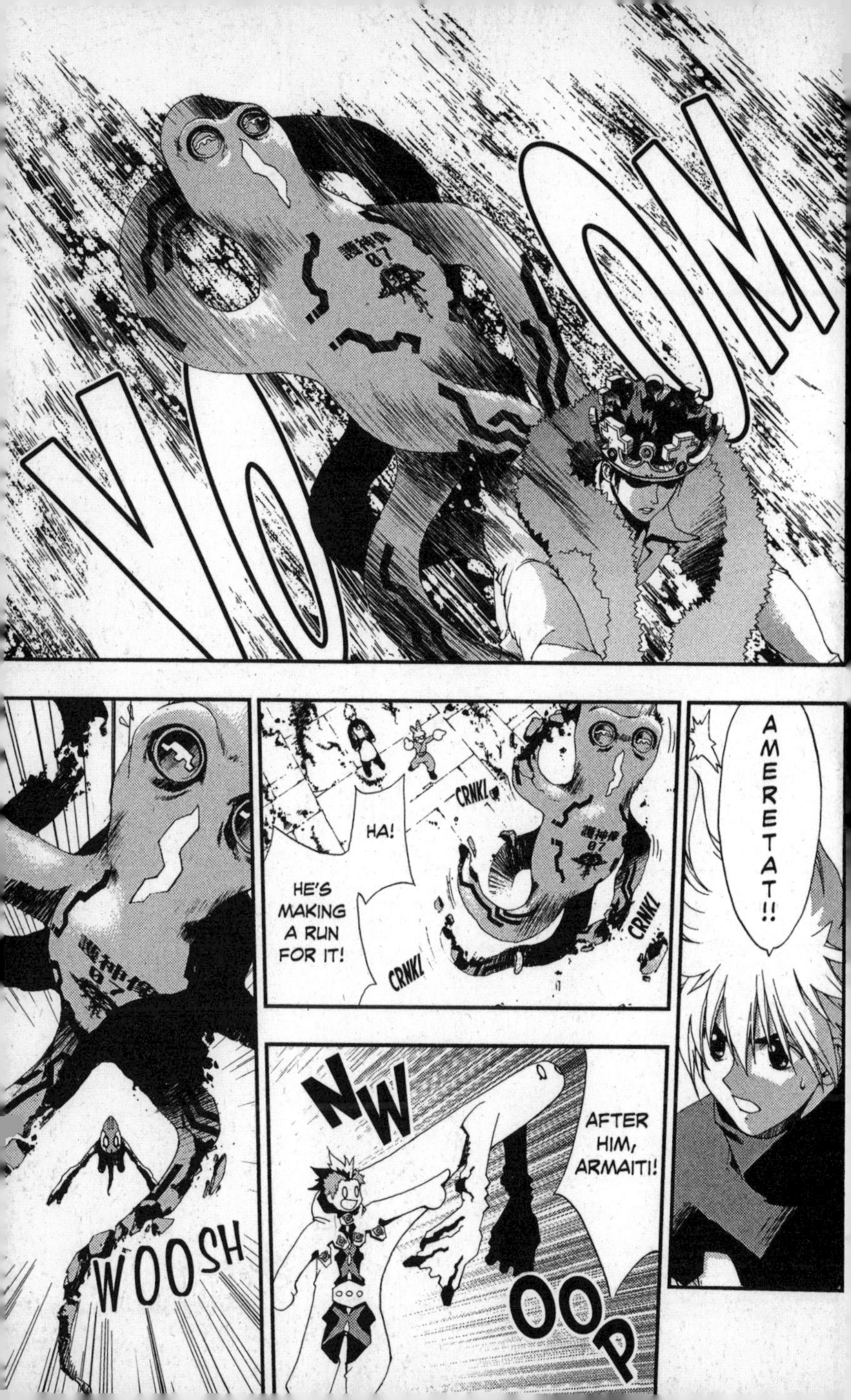
VOOOM
AMERETAT!!
HA!
HE'S MAKING A RUN FOR IT!
CRNKL
CRNKL
CRNKL
NW
OOP
AFTER HIM, ARMAITI!
WOOSH

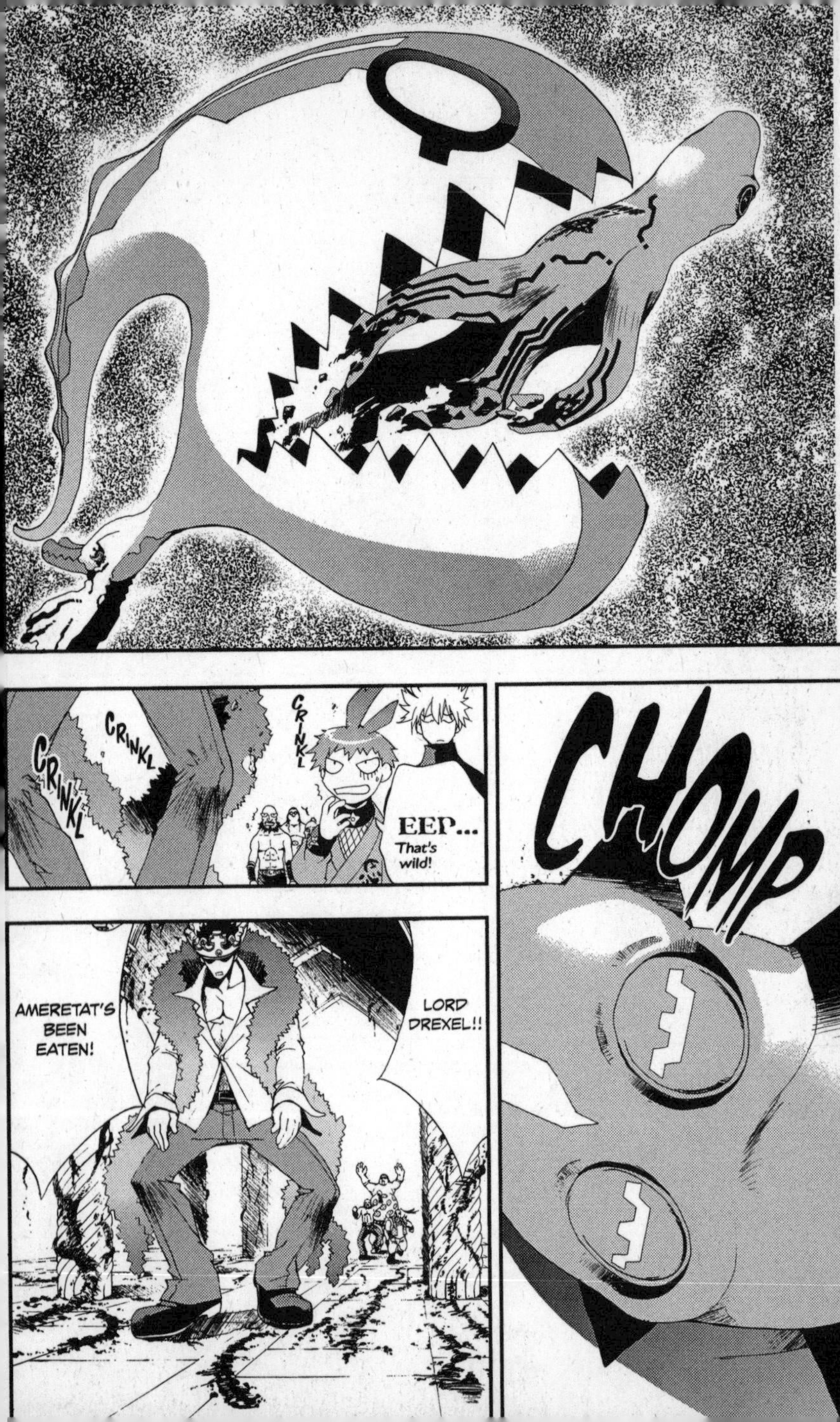
CHOMP
CRINKL
CRINKL
CRINKL
EEP... That's wild!
LORD DREXEL!!
AMERETAT'S BEEN EATEN!

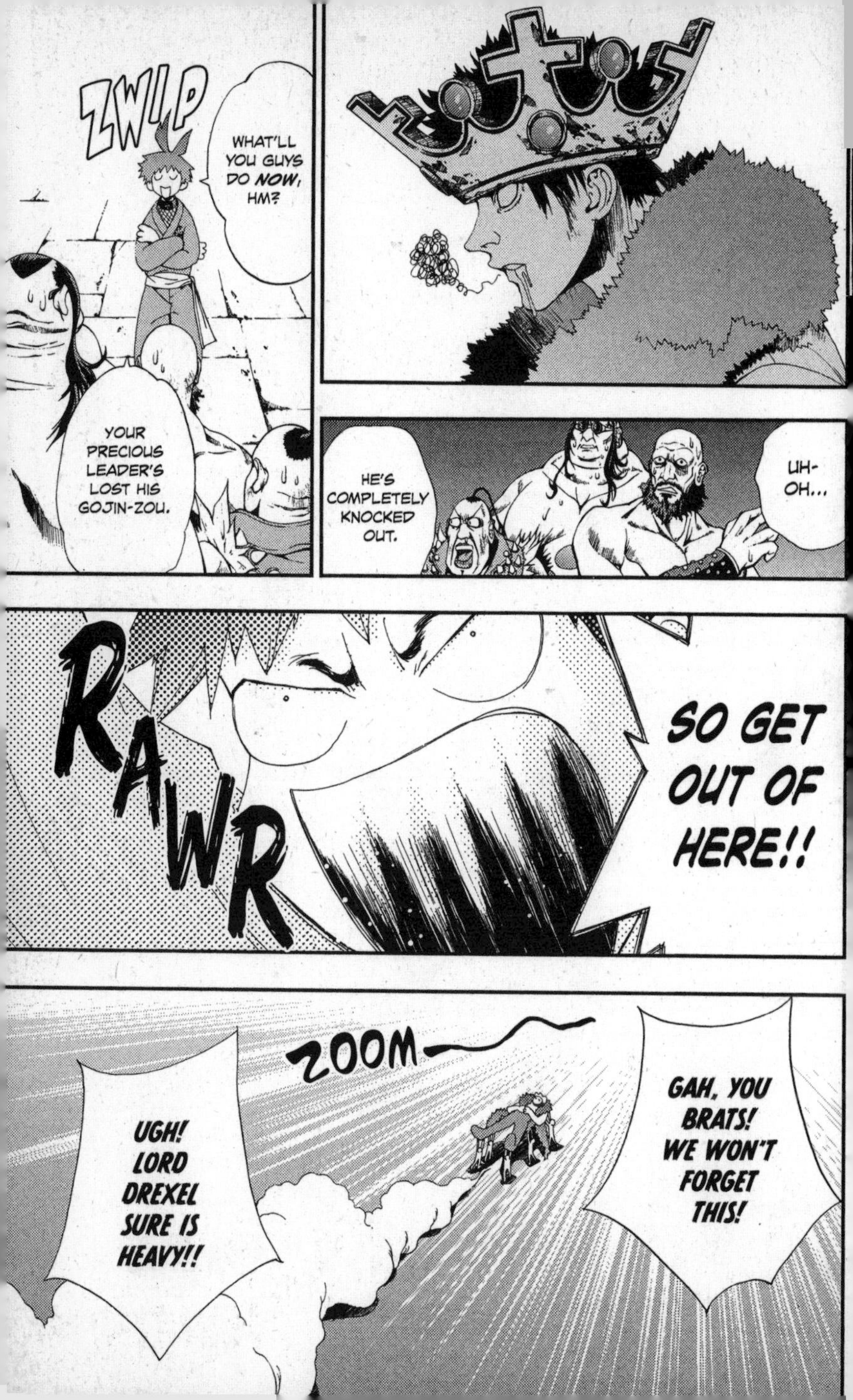
UH-OH...
HE'S COMPLETELY KNOCKED OUT.
ZWIP
WHAT'LL YOU GUYS DO *NOW*, HM?
YOUR PRECIOUS LEADER'S LOST HIS GOJIN-ZOU.
SO GET OUT OF HERE!!
RAWR
GAH, YOU BRATS! WE WON'T FORGET THIS!
ZOOM
UGH! LORD DREXEL SURE IS HEAVY!!

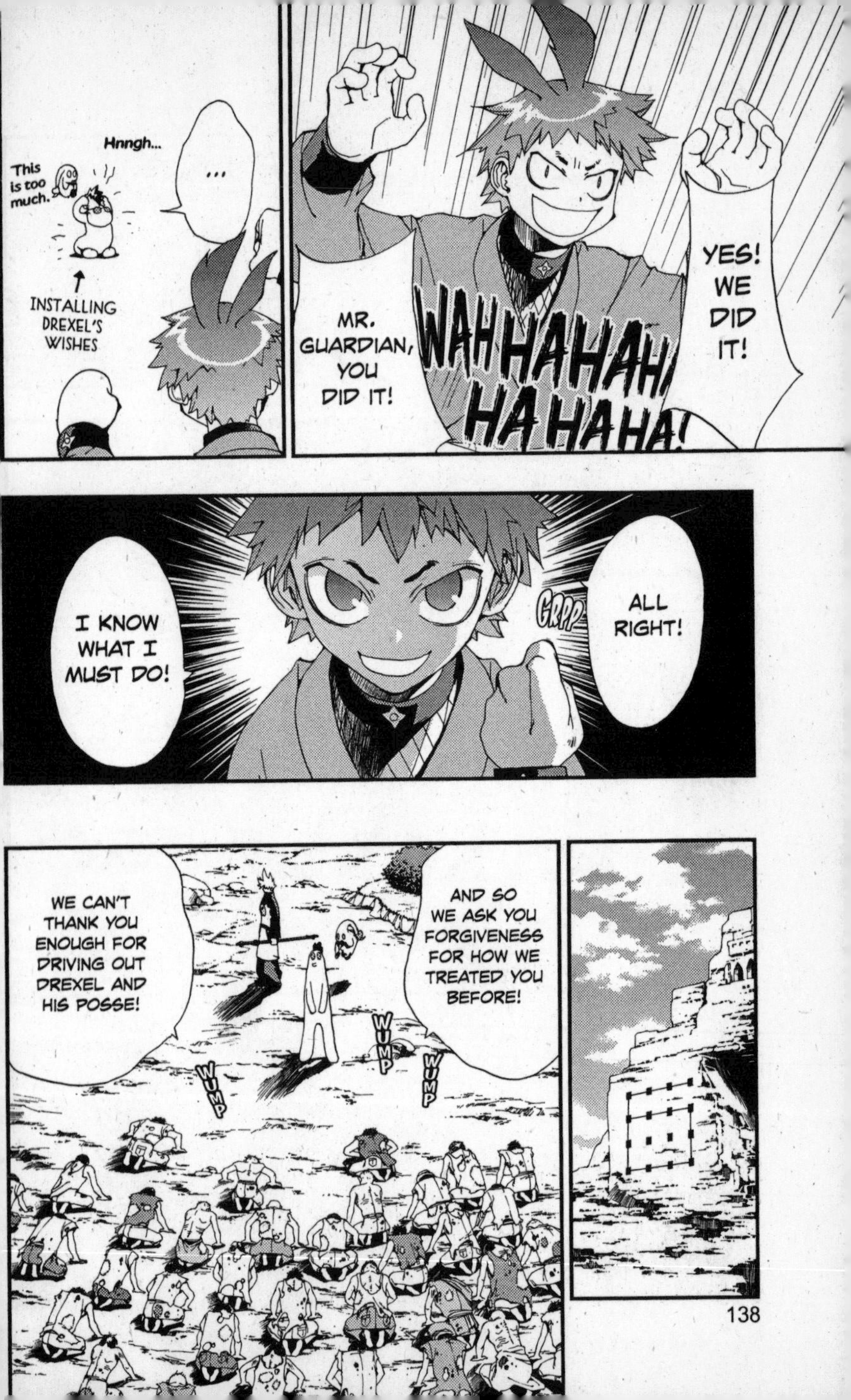
YES! WE DID IT!
WAHAHAHAHA HAHAHA!
MR. GUARDIAN, YOU DID IT!
...
Hnngh...
This is too much.
INSTALLING DREXEL'S WISHES
ALL RIGHT!
GRPP
I KNOW WHAT I MUST DO!
AND SO WE ASK YOU FORGIVENESS FOR HOW WE TREATED YOU BEFORE!
WE CAN'T THANK YOU ENOUGH FOR DRIVING OUT DREXEL AND HIS POSSE!
WUMP
WUMP
WUMP

READ THIS WAY

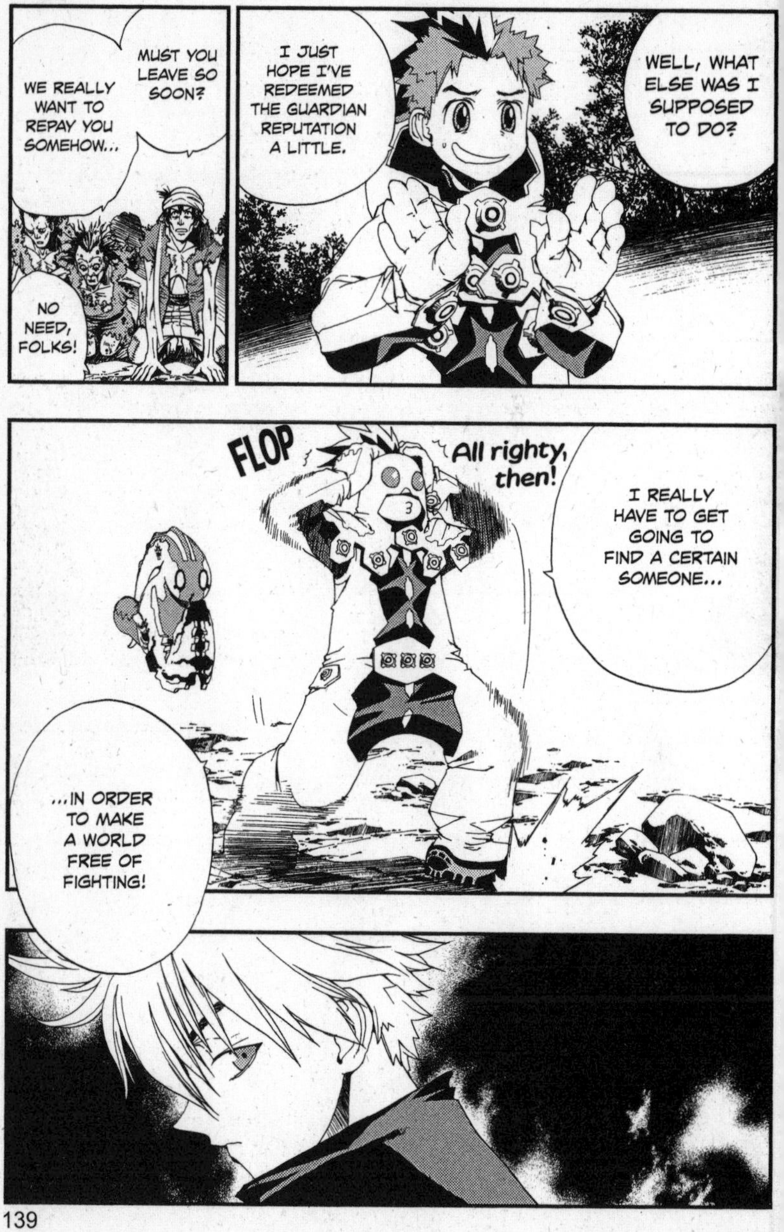
WELL, WHAT ELSE WAS I SUPPOSED TO DO?
I JUST HOPE I'VE REDEEMED THE GUARDIAN REPUTATION A LITTLE.
MUST YOU LEAVE SO SOON?
WE REALLY WANT TO REPAY YOU SOMEHOW...
NO NEED, FOLKS!
All righty, then!
FLOP
I REALLY HAVE TO GET GOING TO FIND A CERTAIN SOMEONE...
...IN ORDER TO MAKE A WORLD FREE OF FIGHTING!

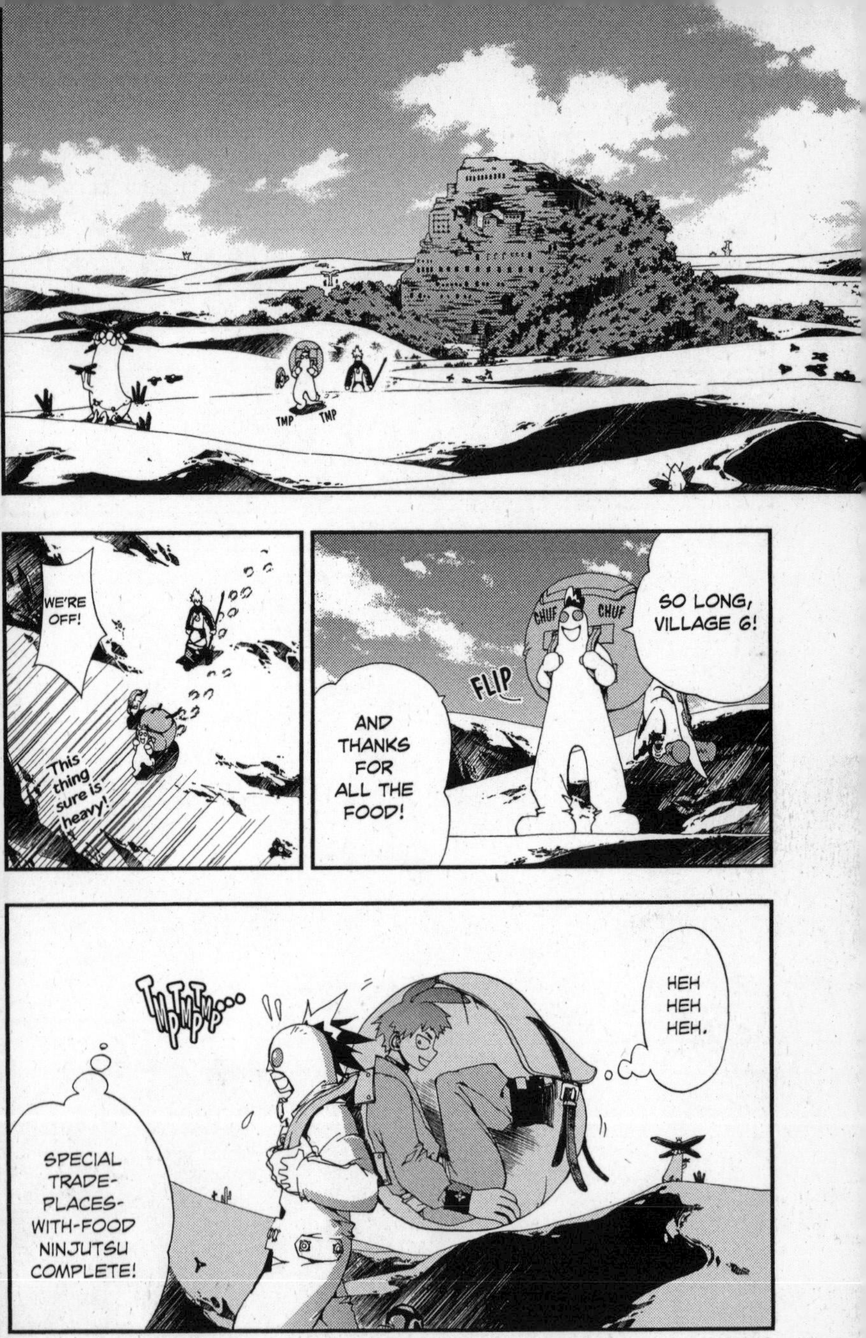
TMP
TMP
SO LONG, VILLAGE 6!
CHUF
CHUF
FLIP
AND THANKS FOR ALL THE FOOD!
WE'RE OFF!
This thing sure is heavy!
HEH HEH HEH.
TMPTMPTMPTMP...
SPECIAL TRADE-PLACES-WITH-FOOD NINJUTSU COMPLETE!

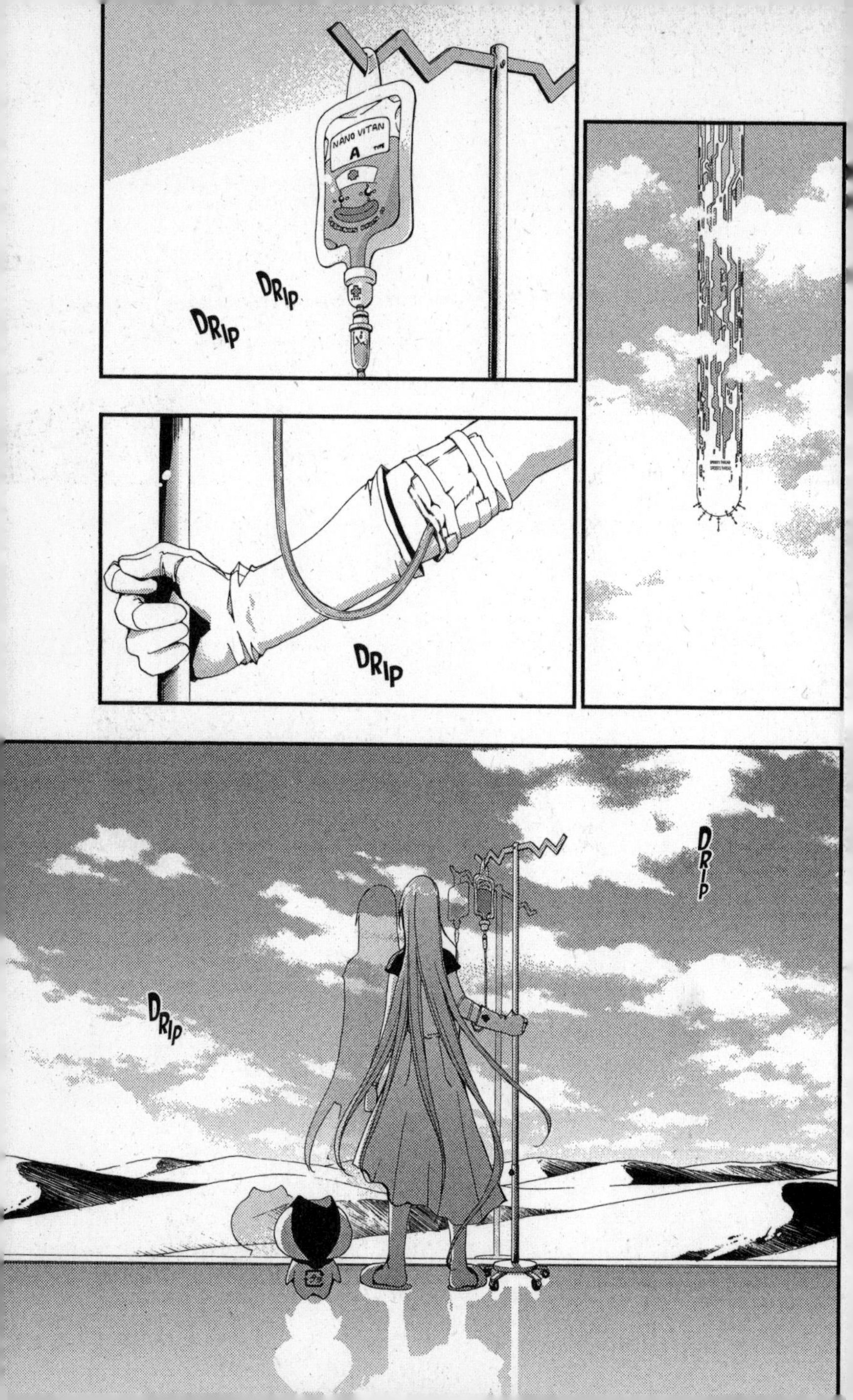
NANO VITAN
A
DRIP
DRIP
DRIP
DRIP
DRIP

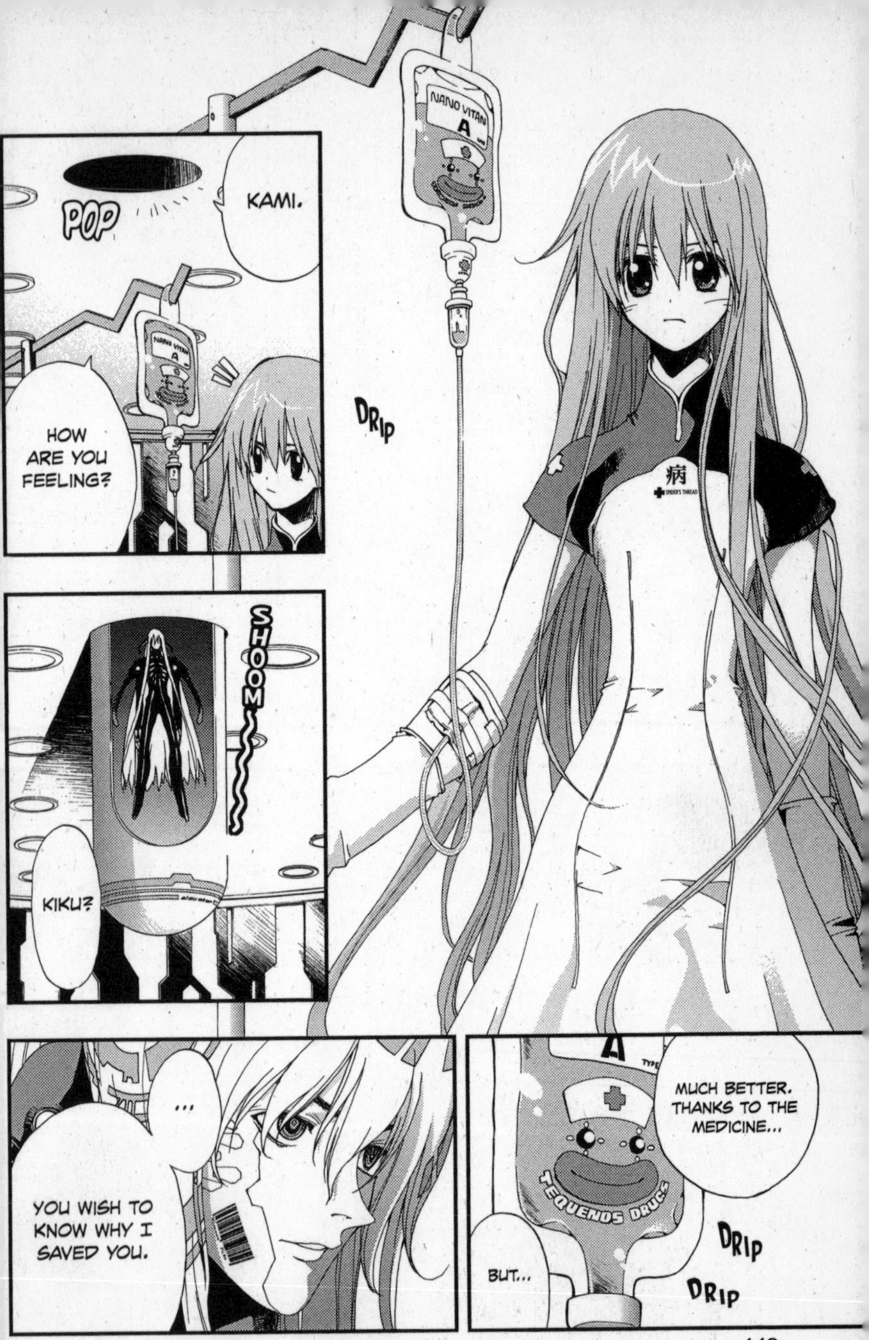
NANO VITAN
A
DRIP
病
SPIDER'S THREAD
KAMI.
POP
NANO VITAN
A
HOW ARE YOU FEELING?
SHOOM
KIKU?
A
TYPE
MUCH BETTER. THANKS TO THE MEDICINE...
TEQUENOS DRUGS
DRIP
DRIP
BUT...
...
YOU WISH TO KNOW WHY I SAVED YOU.

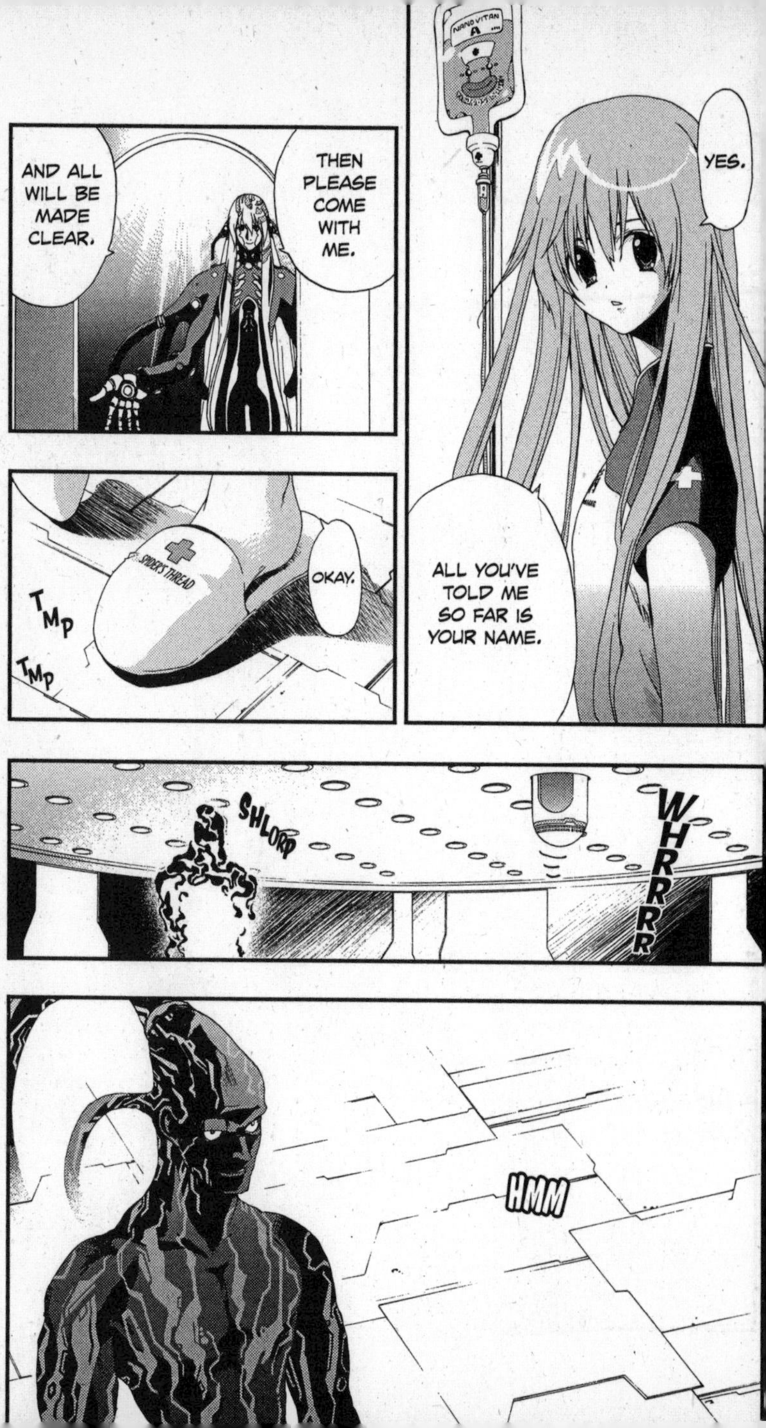
NANO VITAN
A
YES.
ALL YOU'VE TOLD ME SO FAR IS YOUR NAME.
THEN PLEASE COME WITH ME.
AND ALL WILL BE MADE CLEAR.
OKAY.
SPIDER'S THREAD
TMP
TMP
WHRRRR
SHLORP
HMM

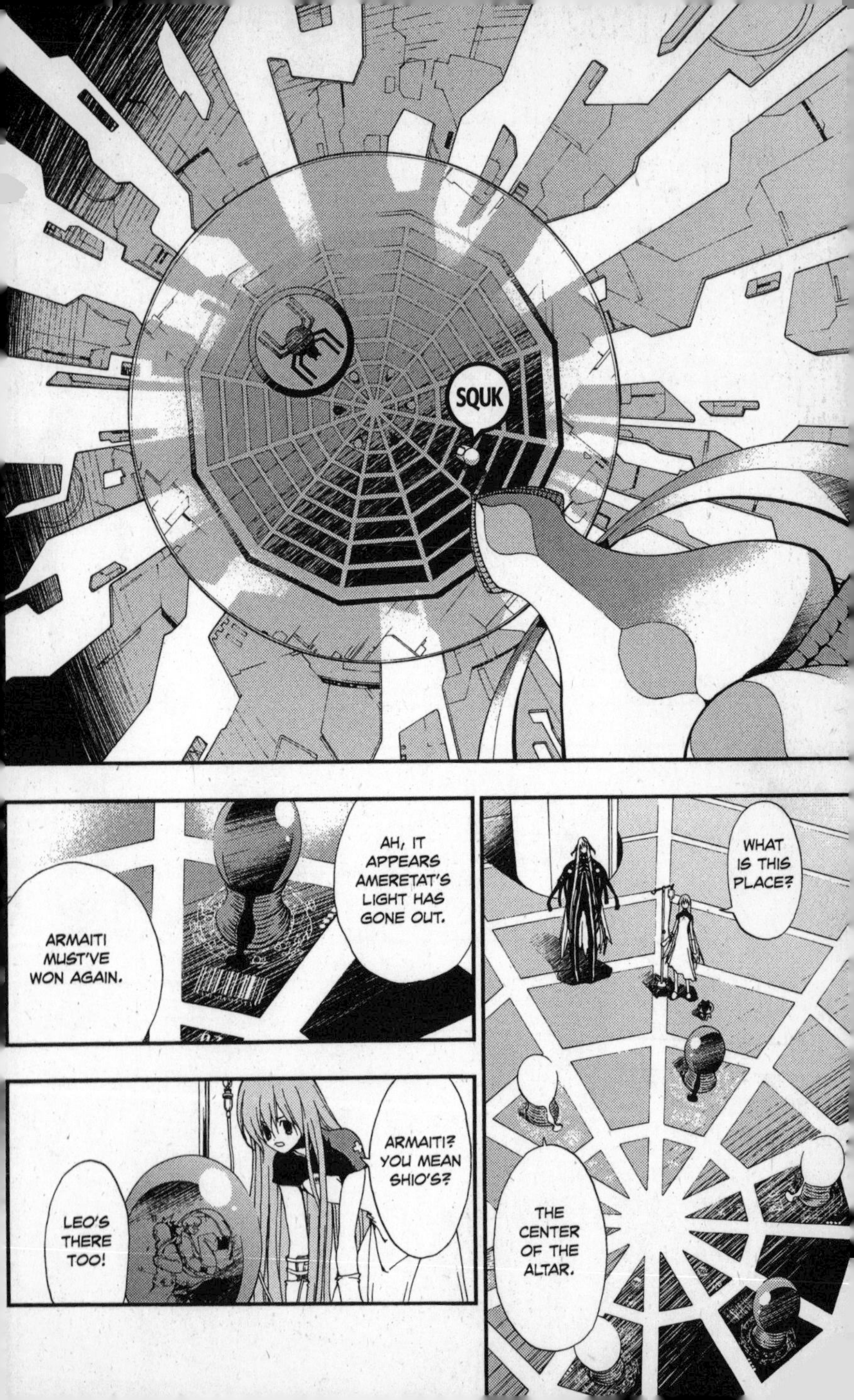
SQUK
WHAT IS THIS PLACE?
THE CENTER OF THE ALTAR.
AH, IT APPEARS AMERETAT'S LIGHT HAS GONE OUT.
ARMAITI MUST'VE WON AGAIN.
ARMAITI? YOU MEAN SHIO'S?
LEO'S THERE TOO!

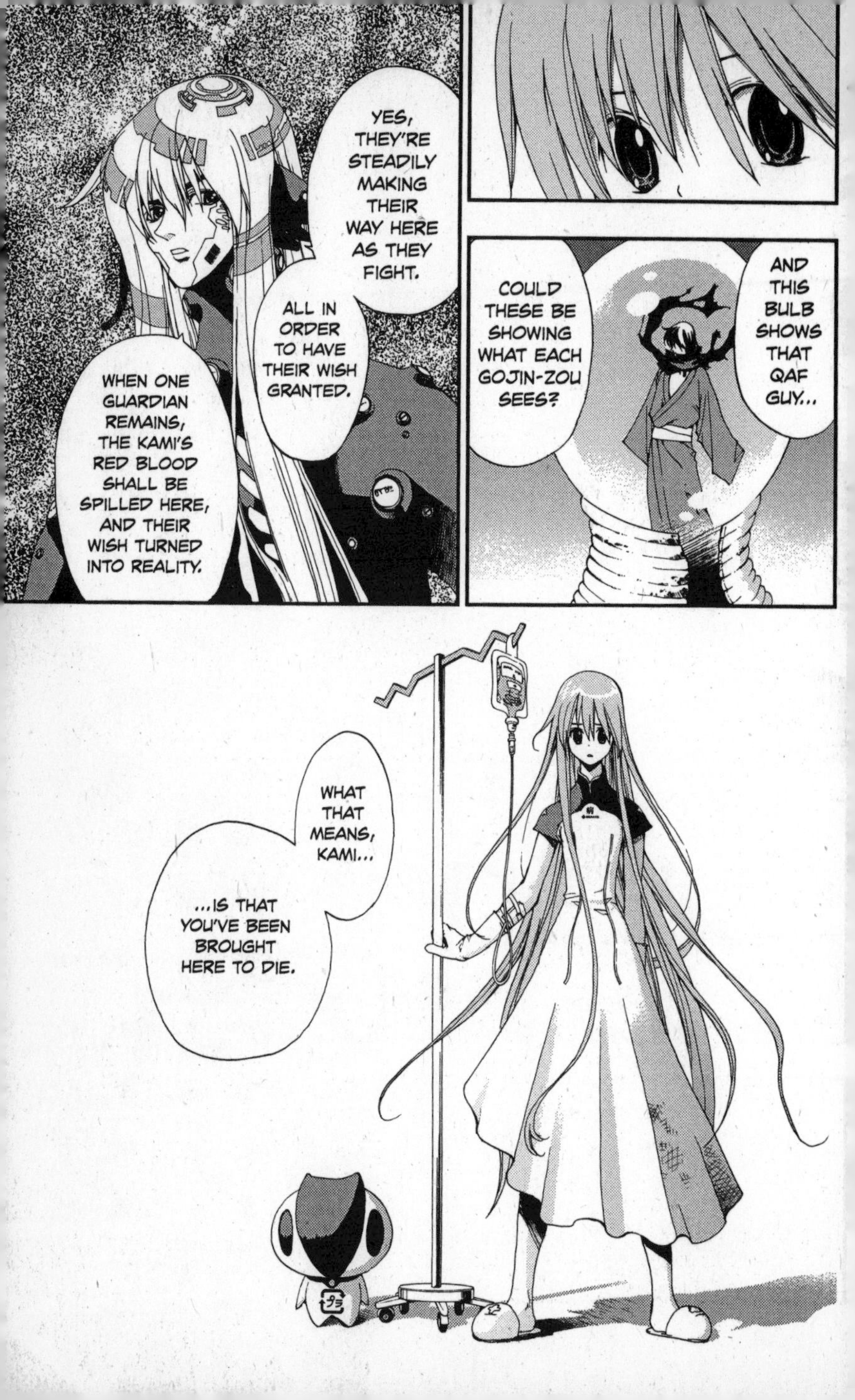
AND THIS BULB SHOWS THAT QAF GUY...
COULD THESE BE SHOWING WHAT EACH GOJIN-ZOU SEES?
YES, THEY'RE STEADILY MAKING THEIR WAY HERE AS THEY FIGHT.
ALL IN ORDER TO HAVE THEIR WISH GRANTED.
WHEN ONE GUARDIAN REMAINS, THE KAMI'S RED BLOOD SHALL BE SPILLED HERE, AND THEIR WISH TURNED INTO REALITY.
WHAT THAT MEANS, KAMI...
...IS THAT YOU'VE BEEN BROUGHT HERE TO DIE.

wāq wāq

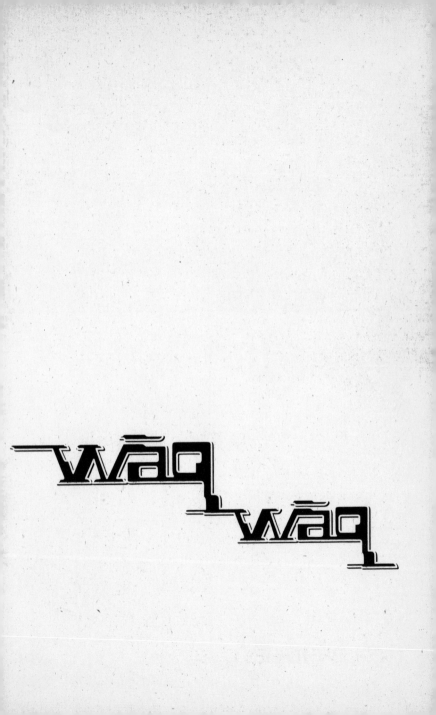

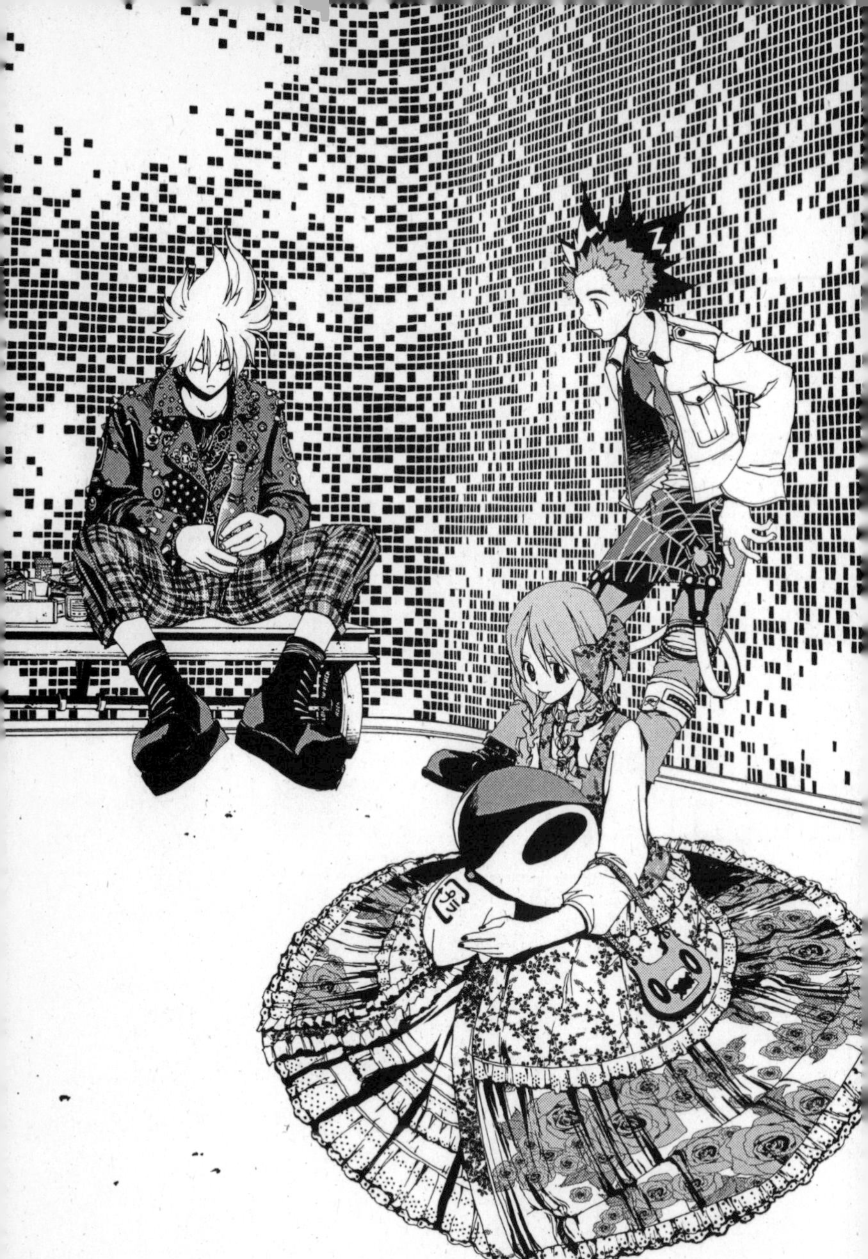

-15- OAF MAKES HIS MOVE

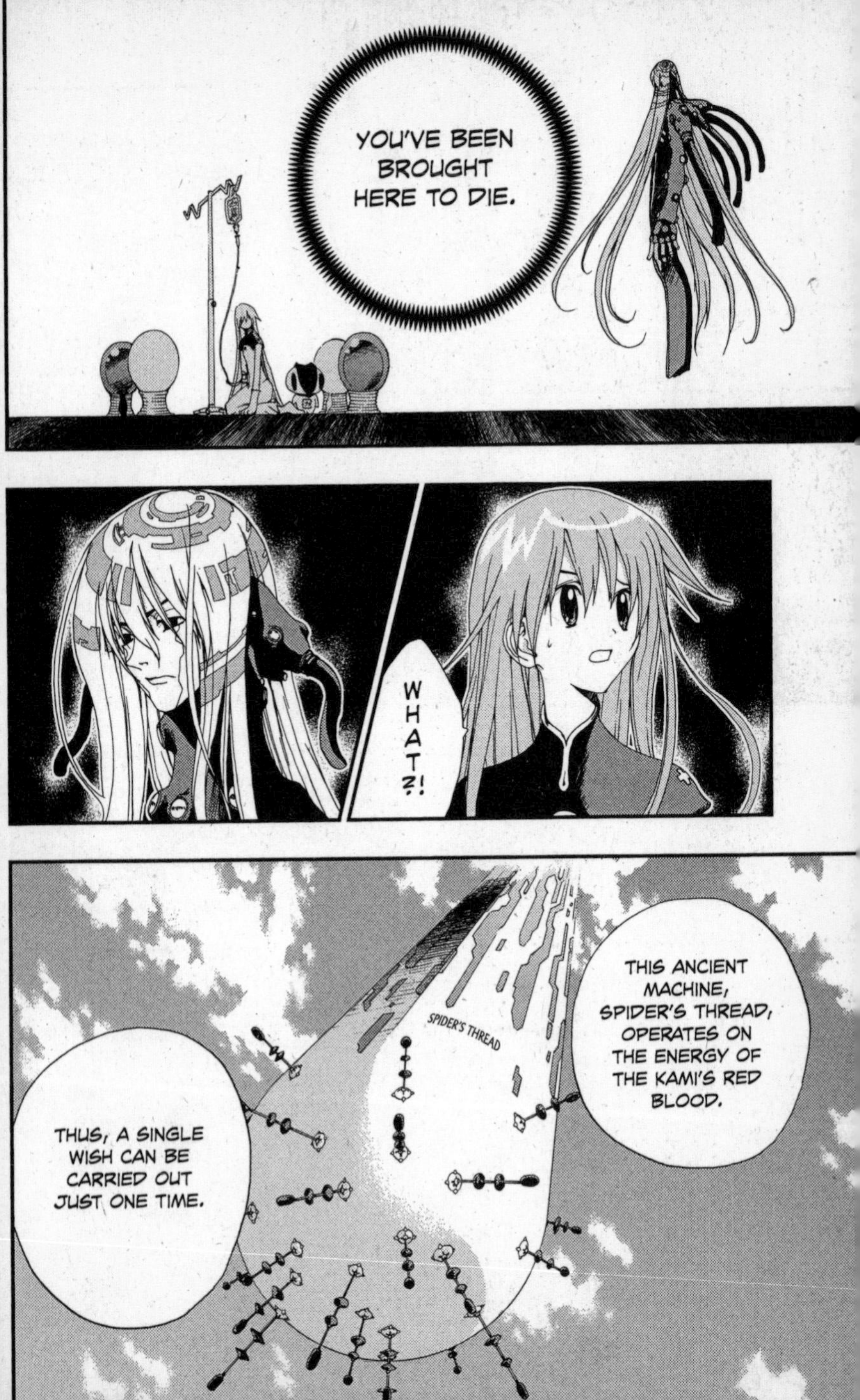
YOU'VE BEEN BROUGHT HERE TO DIE.
WHAT?!
THIS ANCIENT MACHINE, SPIDER'S THREAD, OPERATES ON THE ENERGY OF THE KAMI'S RED BLOOD.
SPIDER'S THREAD
THUS, A SINGLE WISH CAN BE CARRIED OUT JUST ONE TIME.

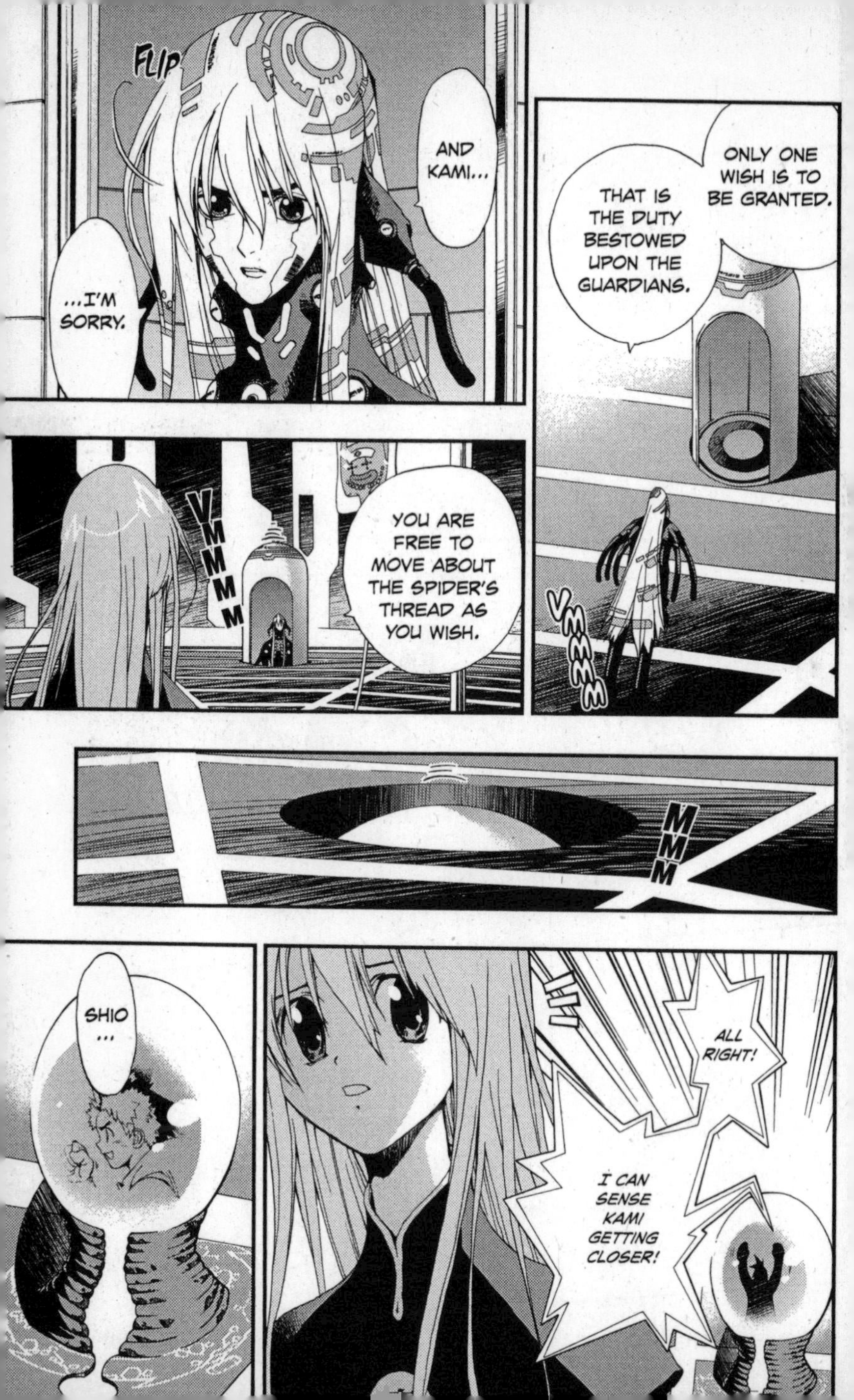
ONLY ONE WISH IS TO BE GRANTED.
THAT IS THE DUTY BESTOWED UPON THE GUARDIANS.
VMMMMM
FLIP
AND KAMI...
...I'M SORRY.
VMMMM
YOU ARE FREE TO MOVE ABOUT THE SPIDER'S THREAD AS YOU WISH.
MMM
ALL RIGHT!
I CAN SENSE KAMI GETTING CLOSER!
SHIO...

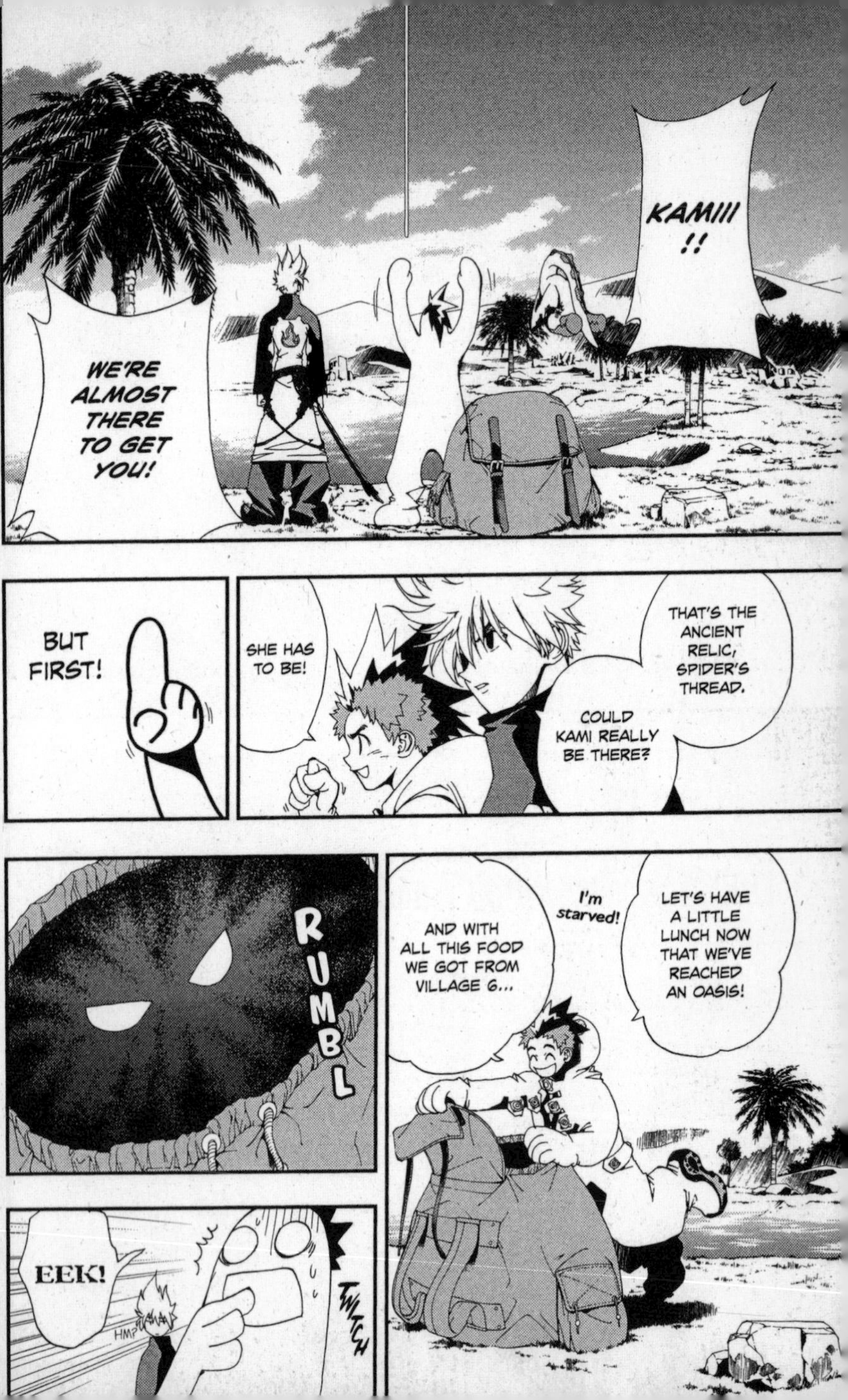
KAMIII !!
WE'RE ALMOST THERE TO GET YOU!
THAT'S THE ANCIENT RELIC, SPIDER'S THREAD.
COULD KAMI REALLY BE THERE?
SHE HAS TO BE!
BUT FIRST!
LET'S HAVE A LITTLE LUNCH NOW THAT WE'VE REACHED AN OASIS!
I'm starved!
AND WITH ALL THIS FOOD WE GOT FROM VILLAGE 6...
RUMBL
TWITCH
EEK!
HMP?

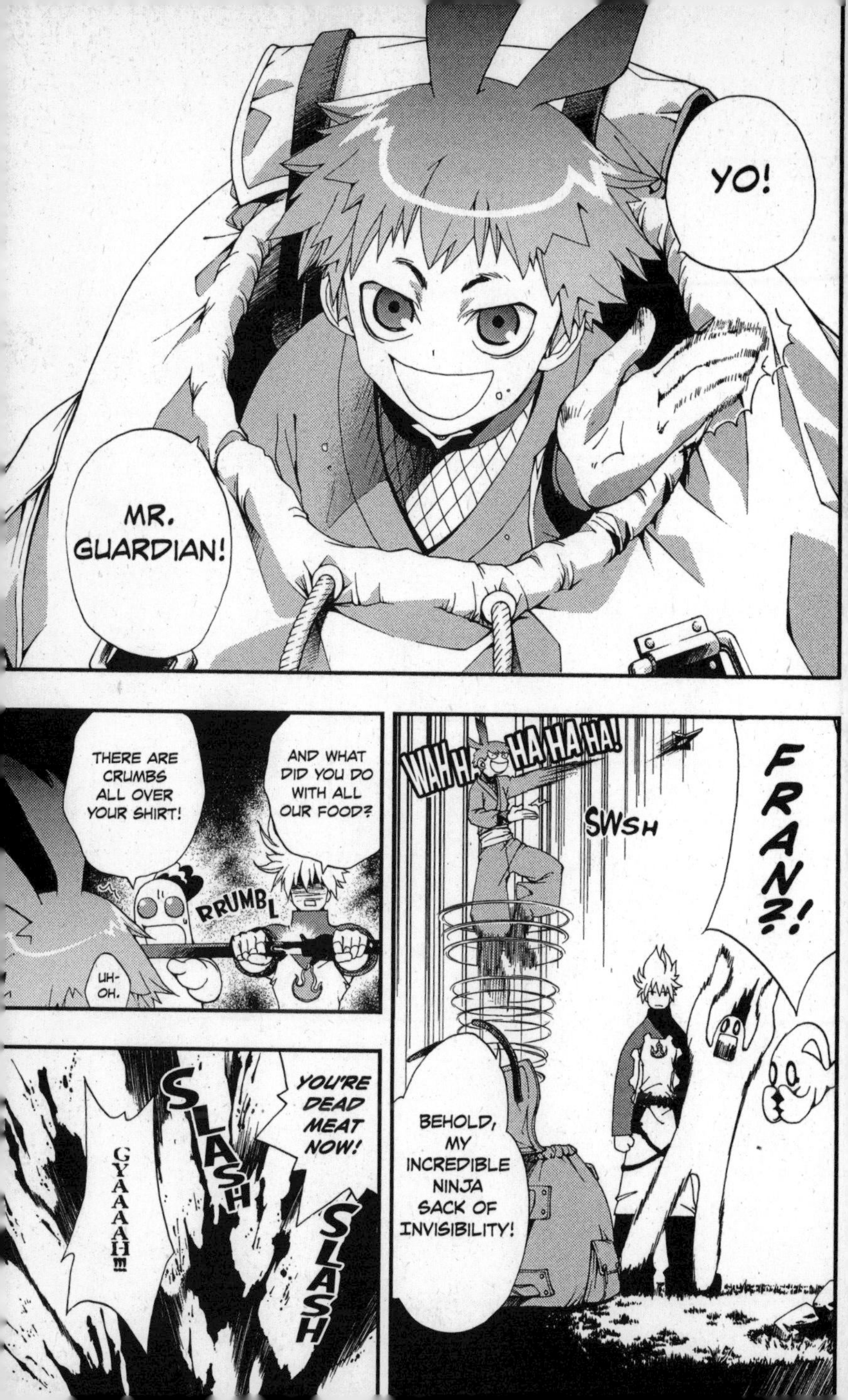
YO!
MR. GUARDIAN!
FRAN?!
WAH HA HA HA HA!
SWSH
BEHOLD, MY INCREDIBLE NINJA SACK OF INVISIBILITY!
AND WHAT DID YOU DO WITH ALL OUR FOOD?
THERE ARE CRUMBS ALL OVER YOUR SHIRT!
RRUMBL
UH-OH.
YOU'RE DEAD MEAT NOW!
SLASH
SLASH
GYAAAAAH!!!

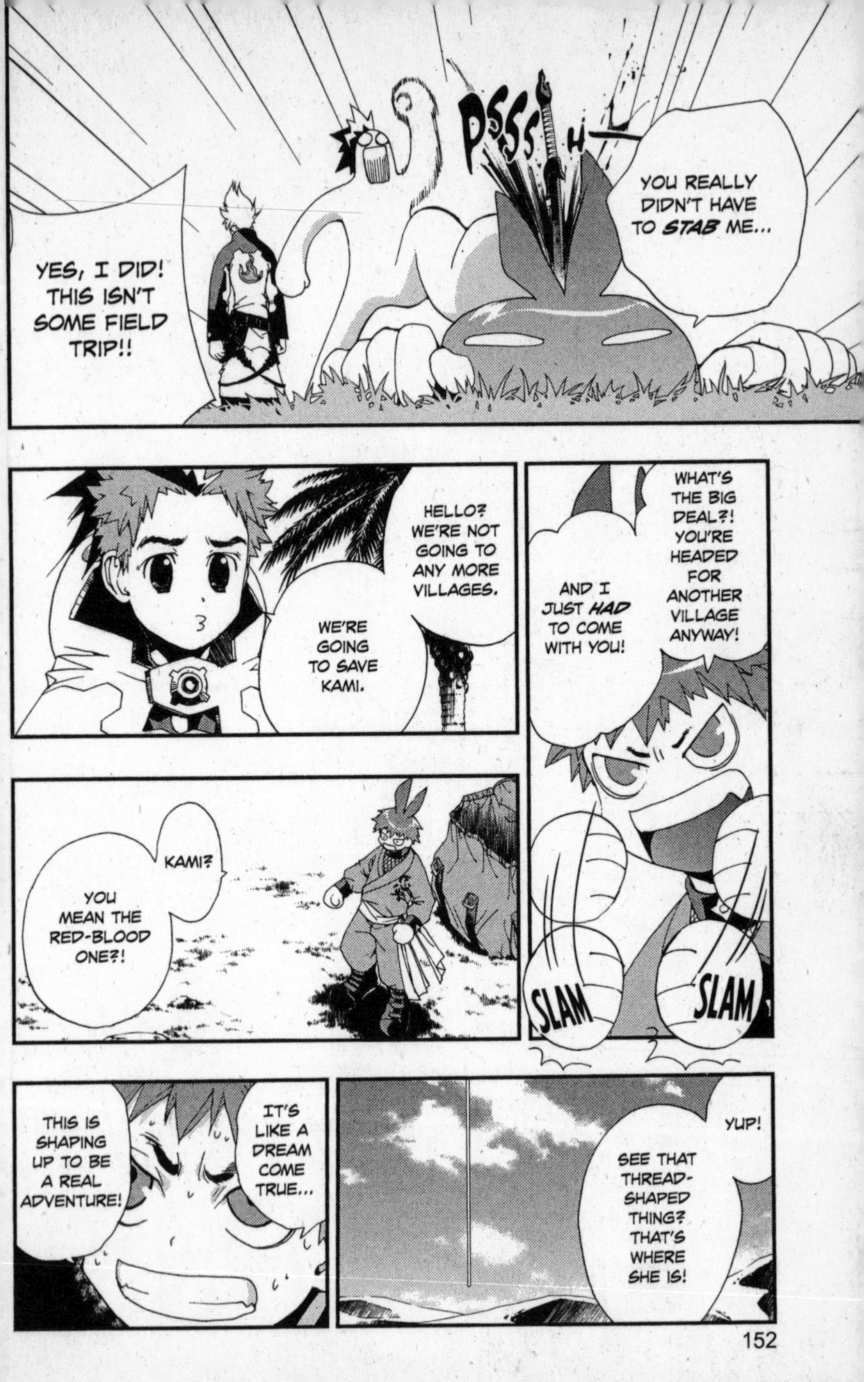
YOU REALLY DIDN'T HAVE TO *STAB* ME...
PSSSH
YES, I DID! THIS ISN'T SOME FIELD TRIP!!
WHAT'S THE BIG DEAL?! YOU'RE HEADED FOR ANOTHER VILLAGE ANYWAY!
AND I JUST *HAD* TO COME WITH YOU!
SLAM
SLAM
HELLO? WE'RE NOT GOING TO ANY MORE VILLAGES.
WE'RE GOING TO SAVE KAMI.
KAMI?
YOU MEAN THE RED-BLOOD ONE?!
YUP!
SEE THAT THREAD-SHAPED THING? THAT'S WHERE SHE IS!
IT'S LIKE A DREAM COME TRUE...
THIS IS SHAPING UP TO BE A REAL ADVENTURE!

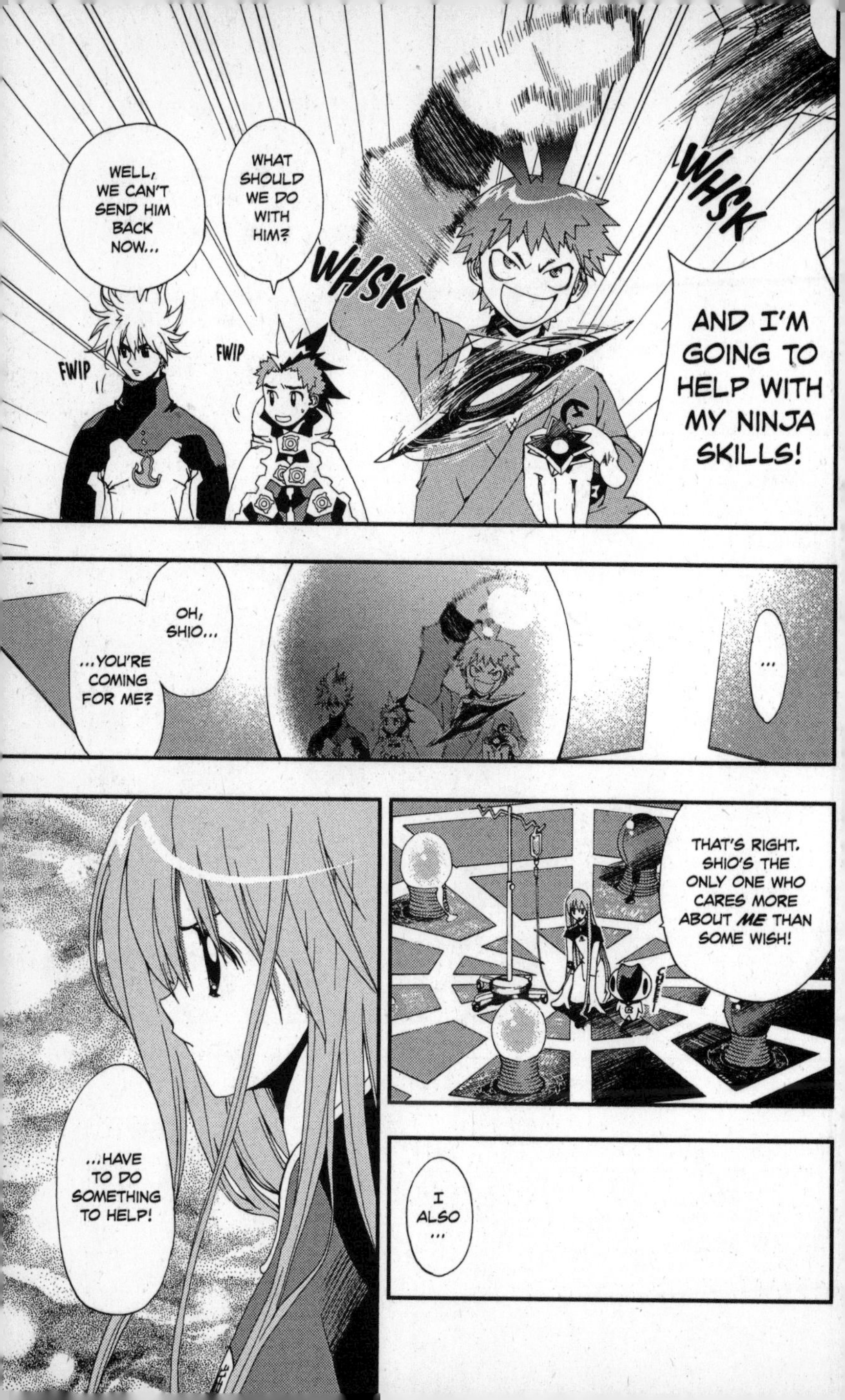

WHSK
AND I'M GOING TO HELP WITH MY NINJA SKILLS!
WHSK
WHAT SHOULD WE DO WITH HIM?
WELL, WE CAN'T SEND HIM BACK NOW...
FWIP
FWIP
...
OH, SHIO... ...YOU'RE COMING FOR ME?
THAT'S RIGHT. SHIO'S THE ONLY ONE WHO CARES MORE ABOUT *ME* THAN SOME WISH!
I ALSO ...
...HAVE TO DO SOMETHING TO HELP!

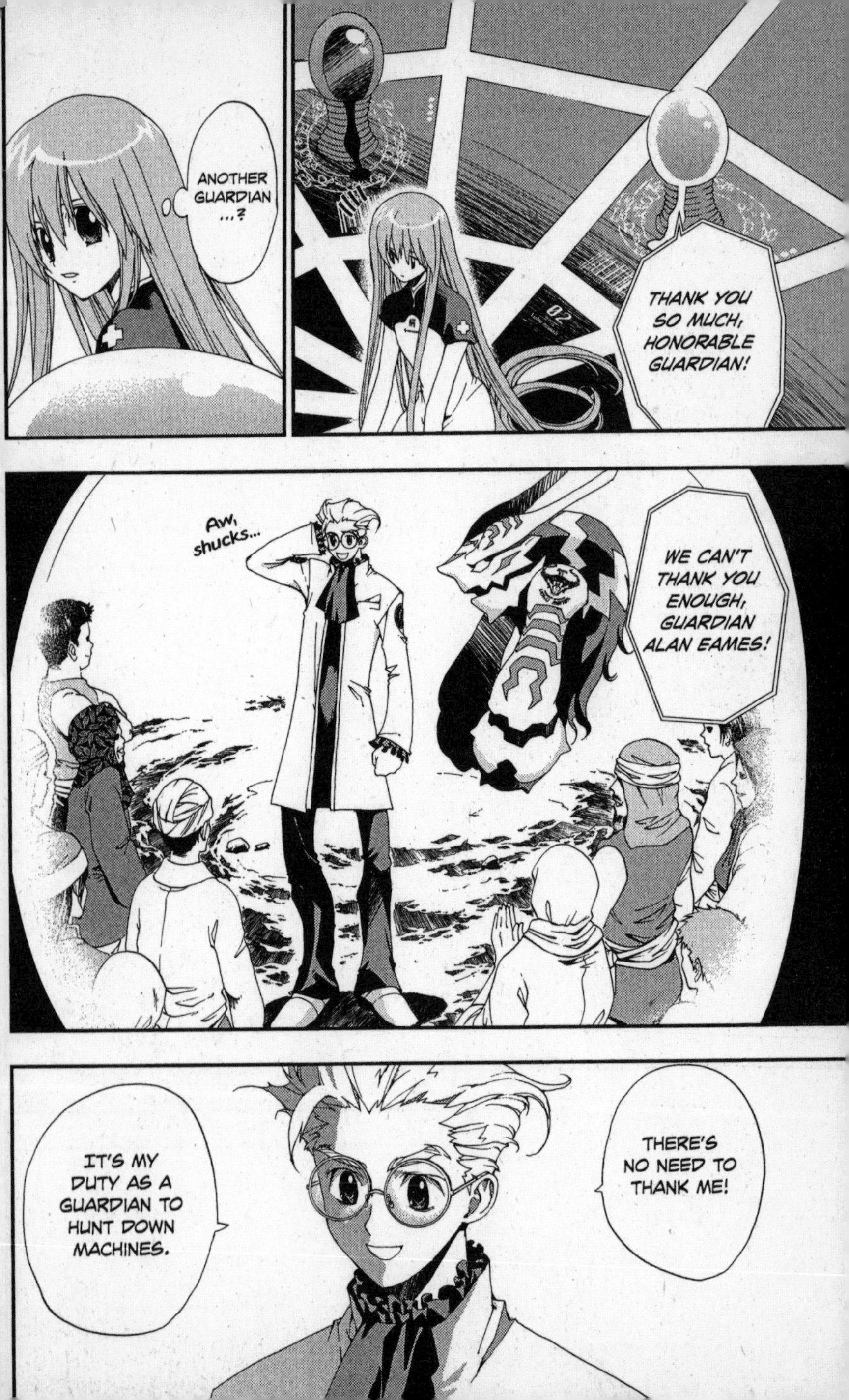
THANK YOU SO MUCH, HONORABLE GUARDIAN!
ANOTHER GUARDIAN ...?
WE CAN'T THANK YOU ENOUGH, GUARDIAN ALAN EAMES!
Aw, shucks...
THERE'S NO NEED TO THANK ME!
IT'S MY DUTY AS A GUARDIAN TO HUNT DOWN MACHINES.

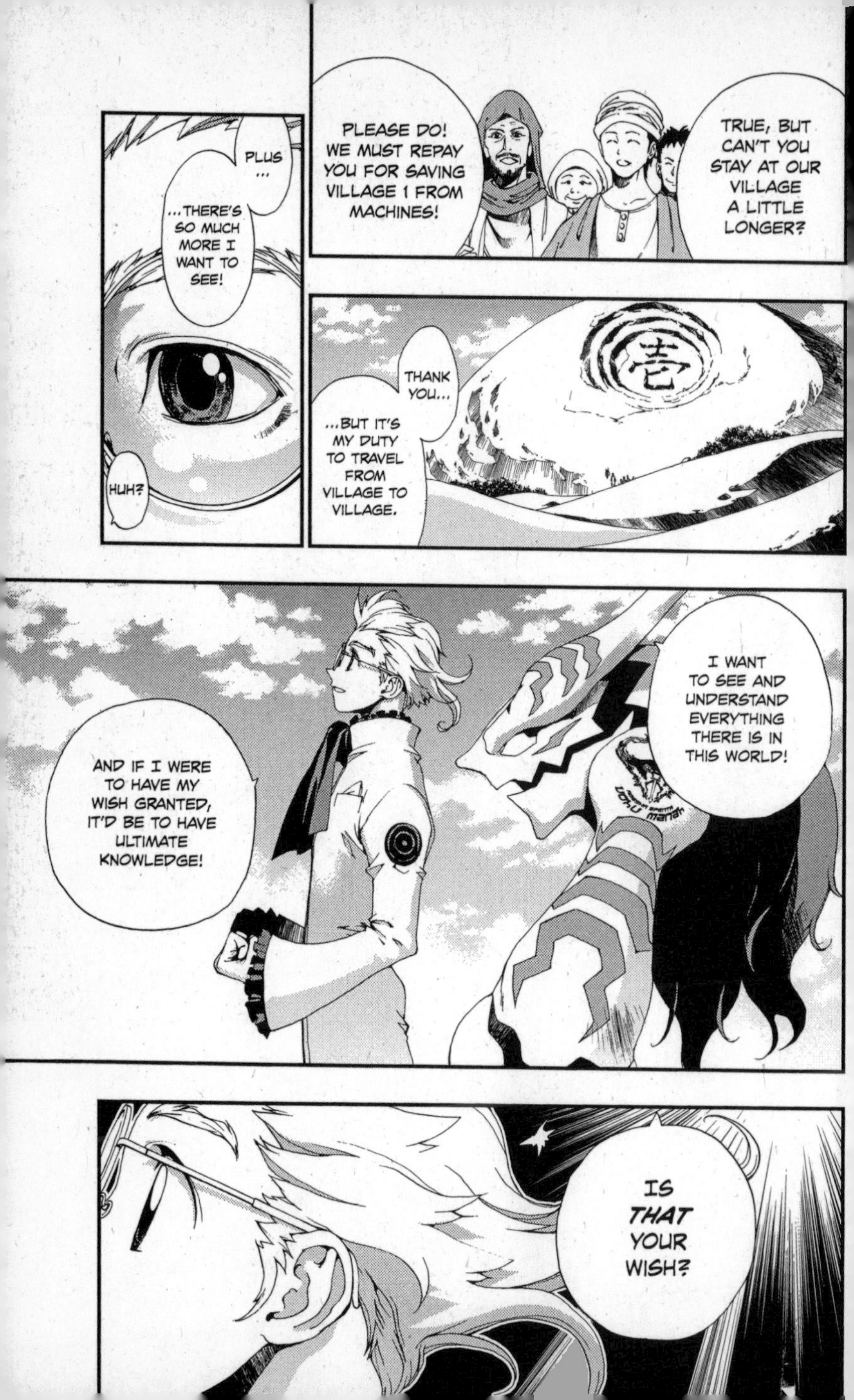
TRUE, BUT CAN'T YOU STAY AT OUR VILLAGE A LITTLE LONGER?
PLEASE DO! WE MUST REPAY YOU FOR SAVING VILLAGE 1 FROM MACHINES!
壱
THANK YOU...
...BUT IT'S MY DUTY TO TRAVEL FROM VILLAGE TO VILLAGE.
PLUS...
...THERE'S SO MUCH MORE I WANT TO SEE!
HUH?
I WANT TO SEE AND UNDERSTAND EVERYTHING THERE IS IN THIS WORLD!
AND IF I WERE TO HAVE MY WISH GRANTED, IT'D BE TO HAVE ULTIMATE KNOWLEDGE!
IS *THAT* YOUR WISH?

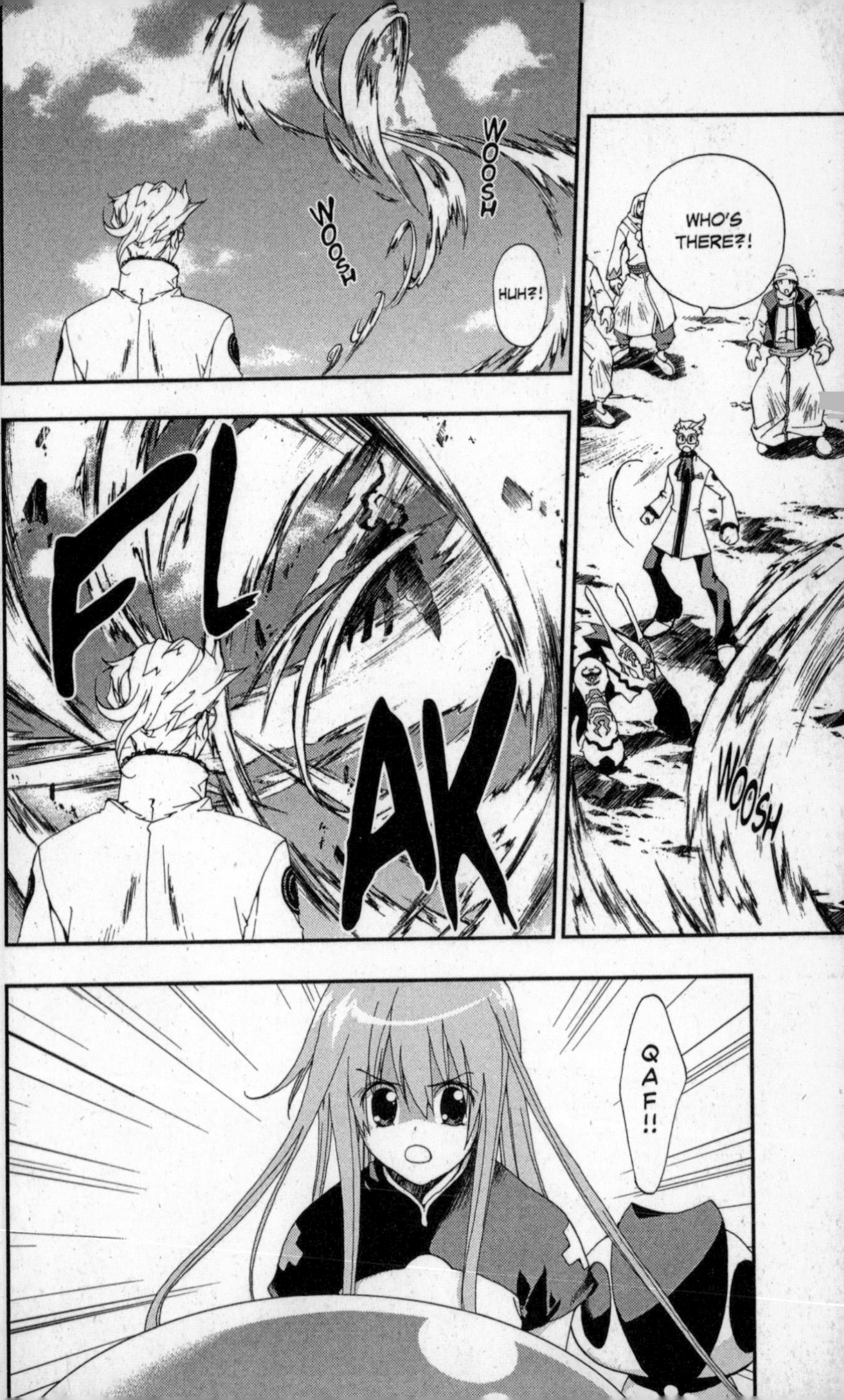

WHO'S THERE?!
WOOSH
WOOSH
HUH?!
WOOSH
FLAK
QAF!!

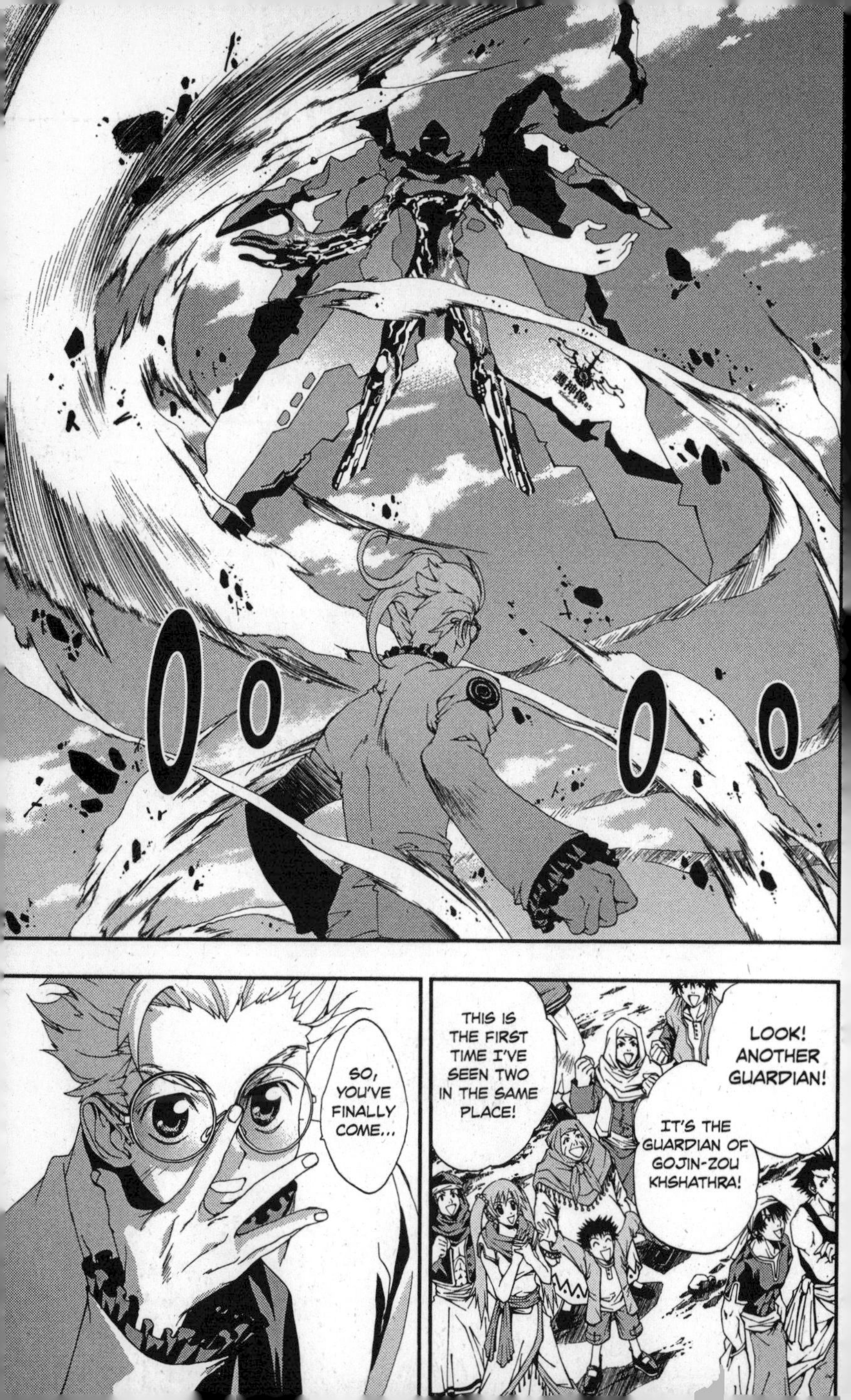
LOOK! ANOTHER GUARDIAN!
IT'S THE GUARDIAN OF GOJIN-ZOU KHSHATHRA!
THIS IS THE FIRST TIME I'VE SEEN TWO IN THE SAME PLACE!
SO, YOU'VE FINALLY COME...

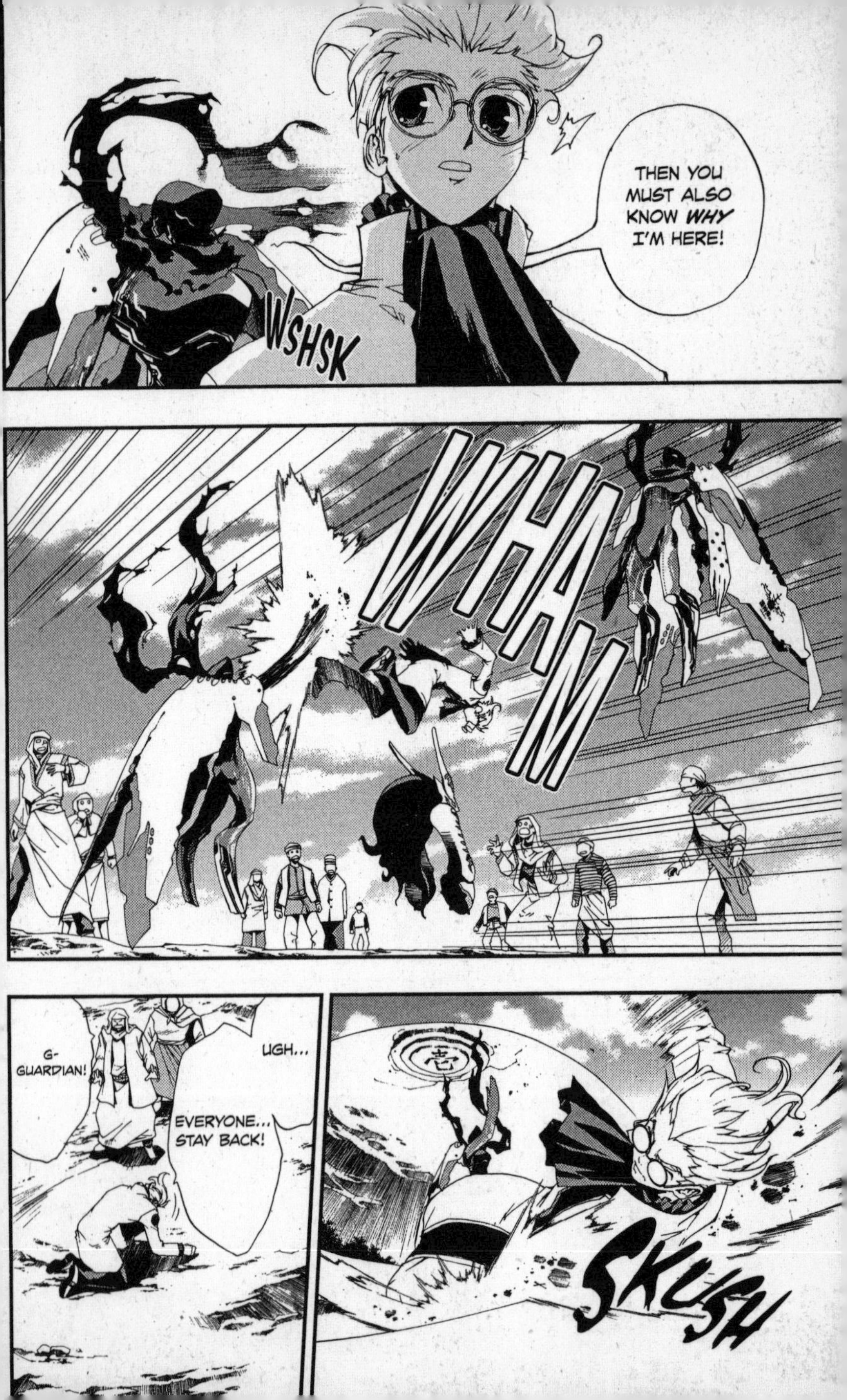
THEN YOU MUST ALSO KNOW WHY I'M HERE!
WSHSK
WHAM
SKUSH
UGH...
G-GUARDIAN!
EVERYONE... STAY BACK!

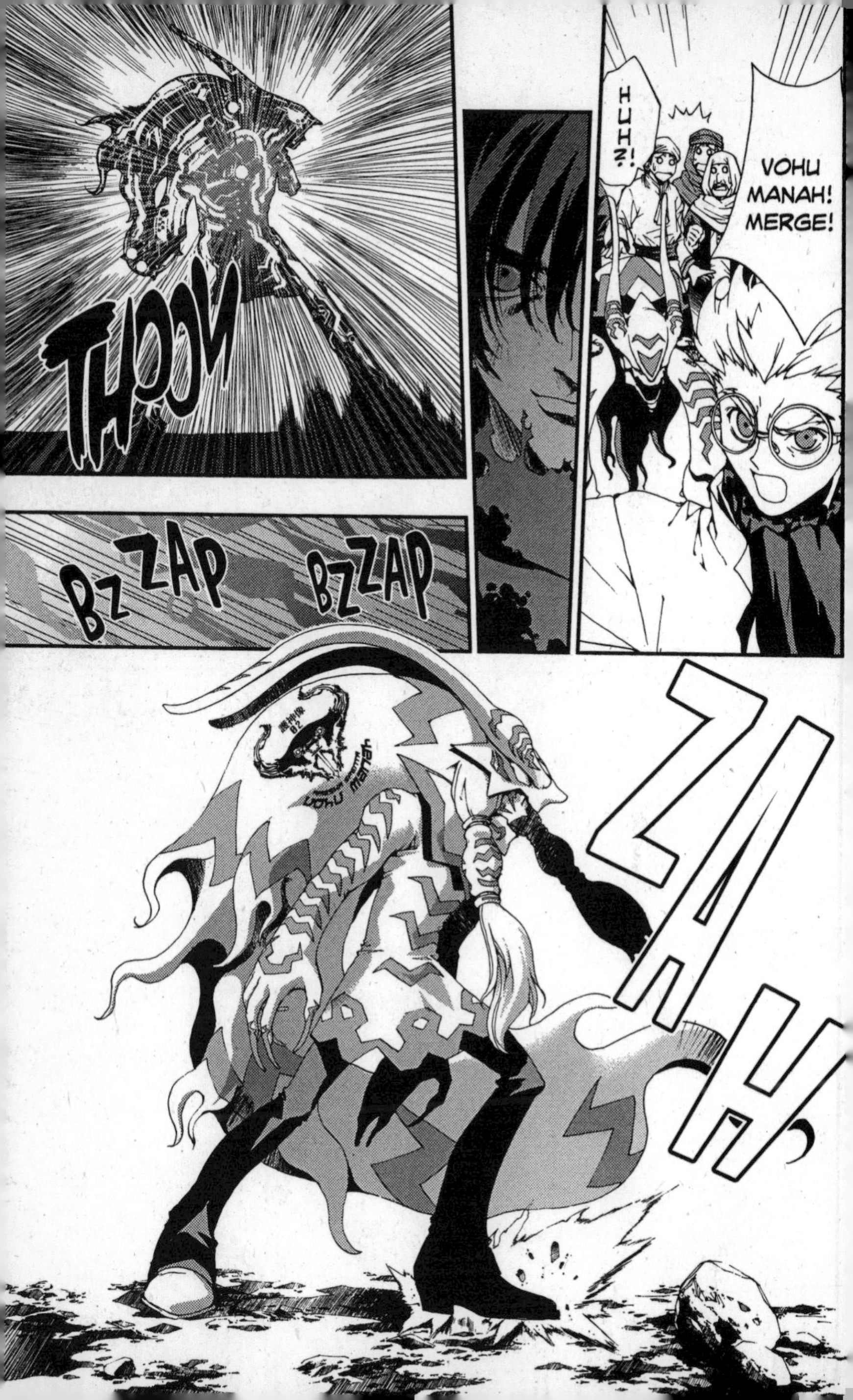
VOHU MANAH! MERGE!
HUH?!
THOOM
BZZAP
BZZAP
ZAH

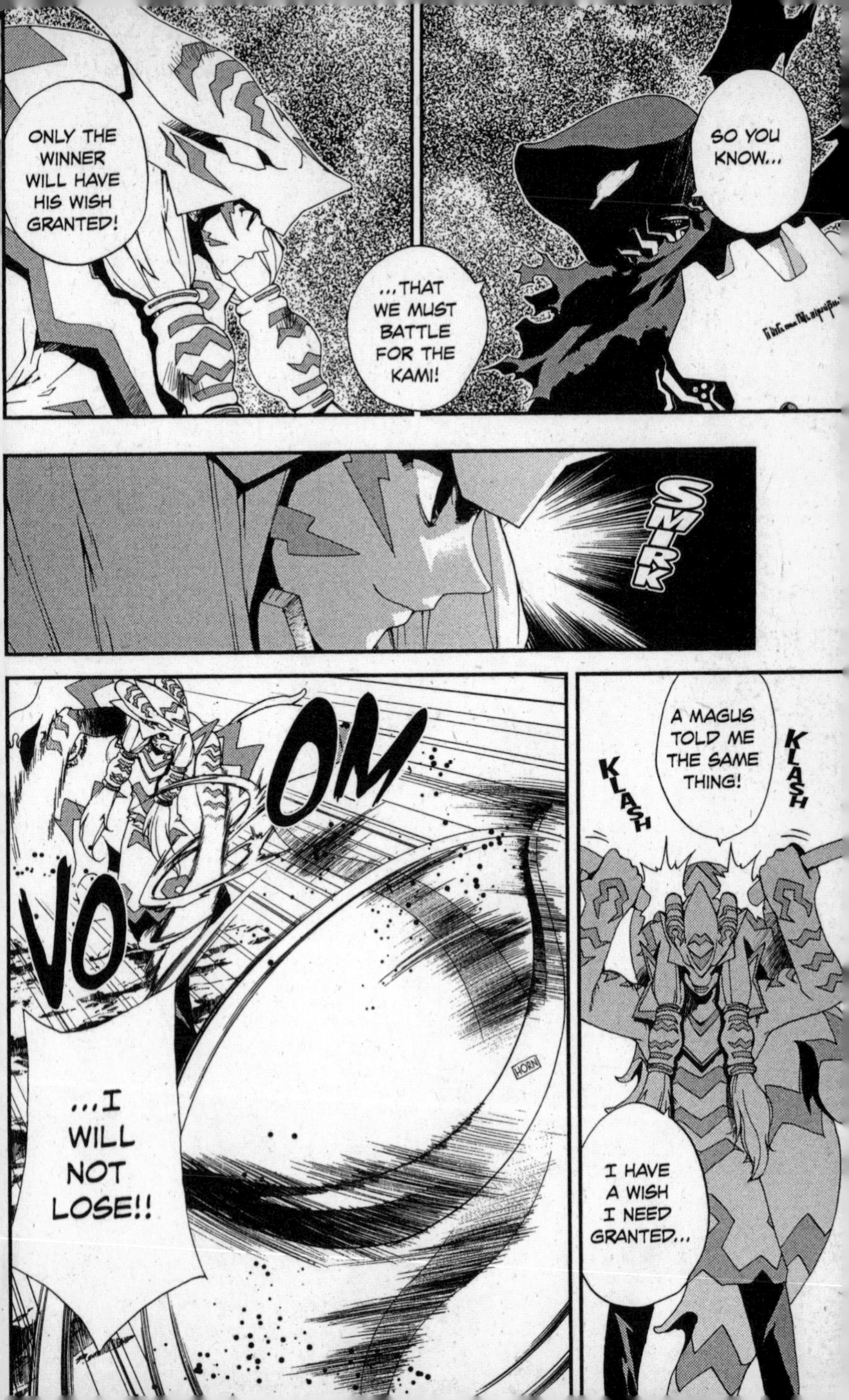
SO YOU KNOW...
...THAT WE MUST BATTLE FOR THE KAMI!
ONLY THE WINNER WILL HAVE HIS WISH GRANTED!
SMIRK
KLASH
A MAGUS TOLD ME THE SAME THING!
KLASH
I HAVE A WISH I NEED GRANTED...
VOOM
HORN
...I WILL NOT LOSE!!

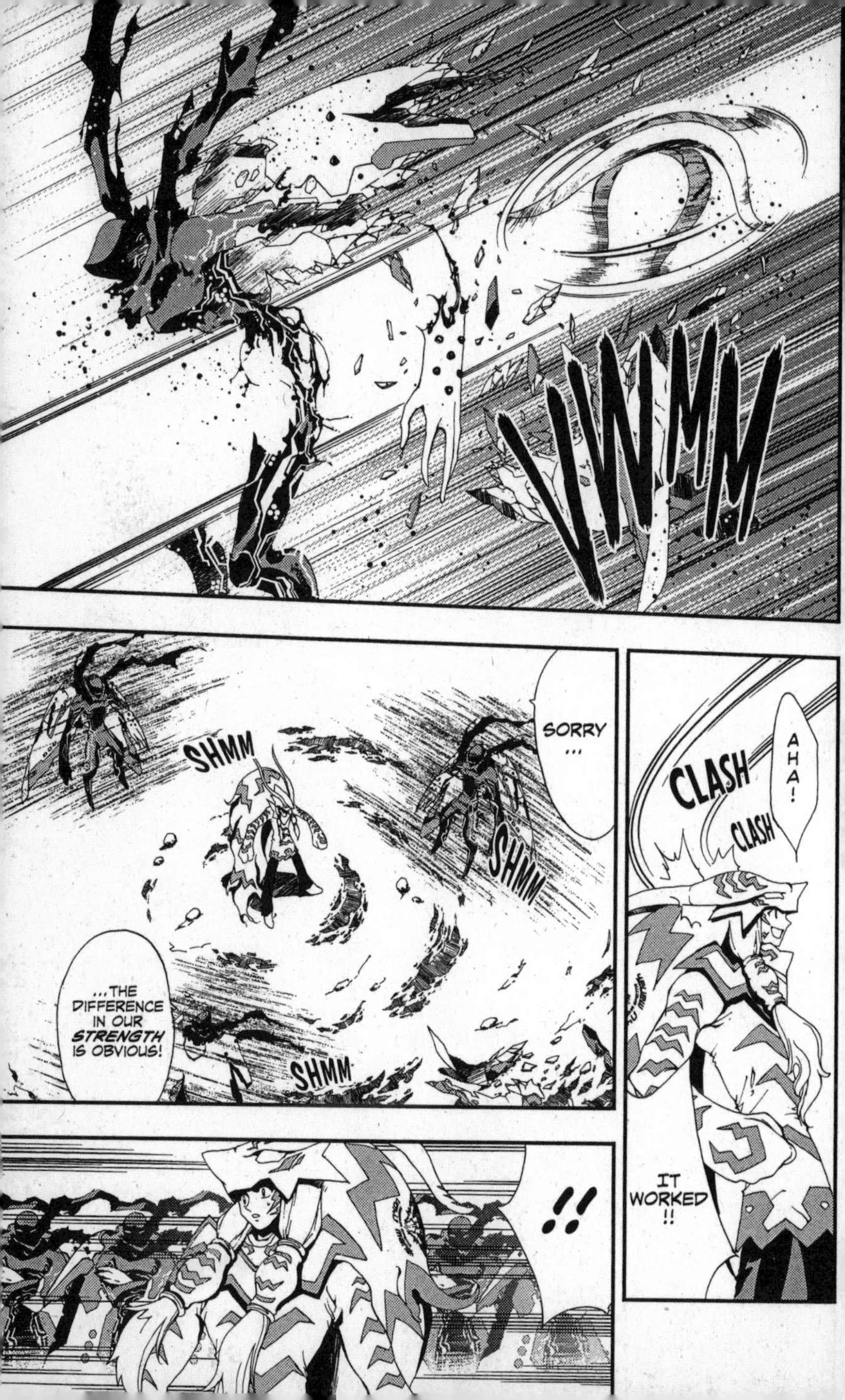
VWMM
AHA!
CLASH
CLASH
IT WORKED!!
SORRY...
SHMM
SHMM
...THE DIFFERENCE IN OUR *STRENGTH* IS OBVIOUS!
SHMM
!!

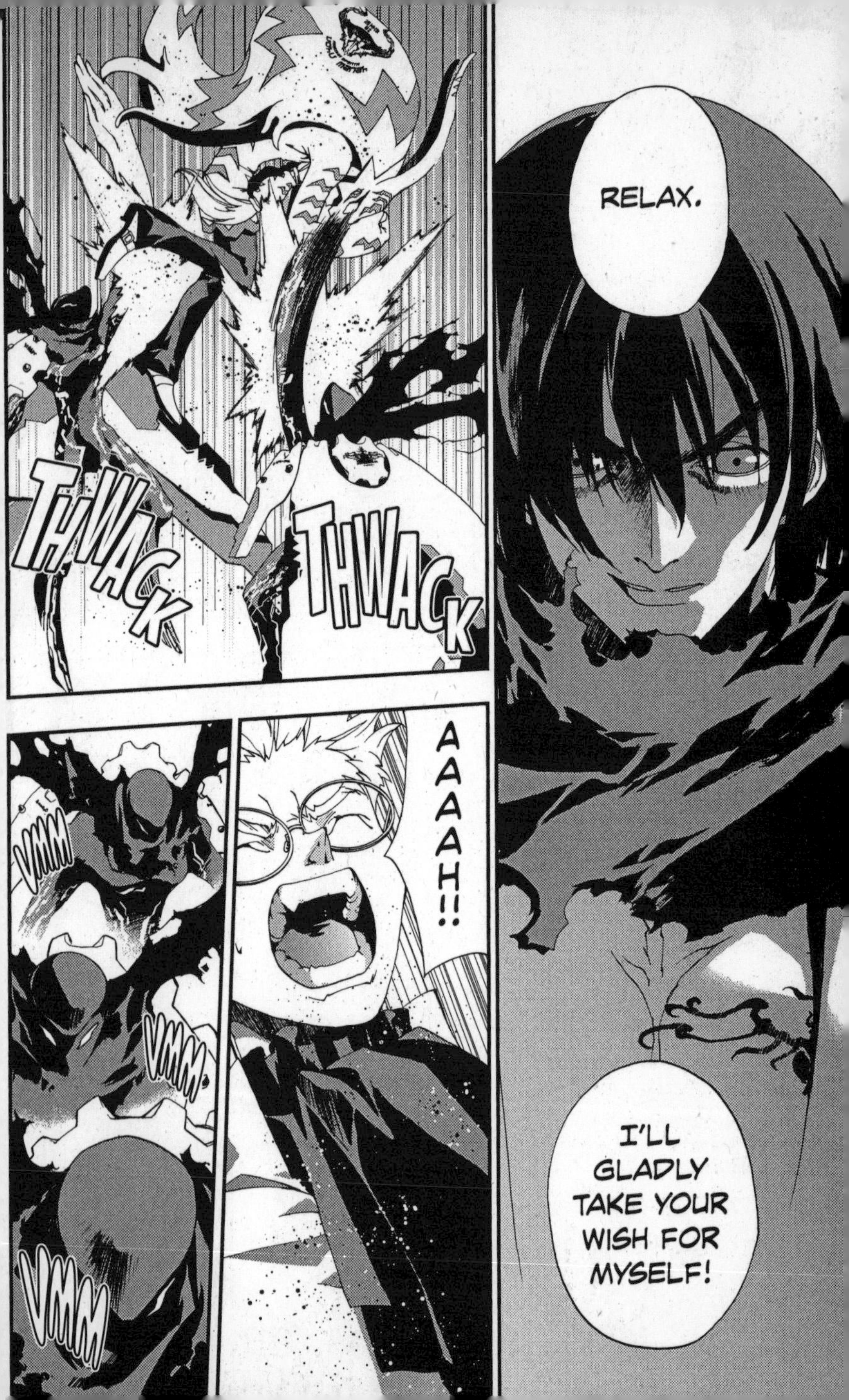
RELAX.
I'LL GLADLY TAKE YOUR WISH FOR MYSELF!
THWACK
THWACK
AAAAAH!!
VMM
VMM
VMM

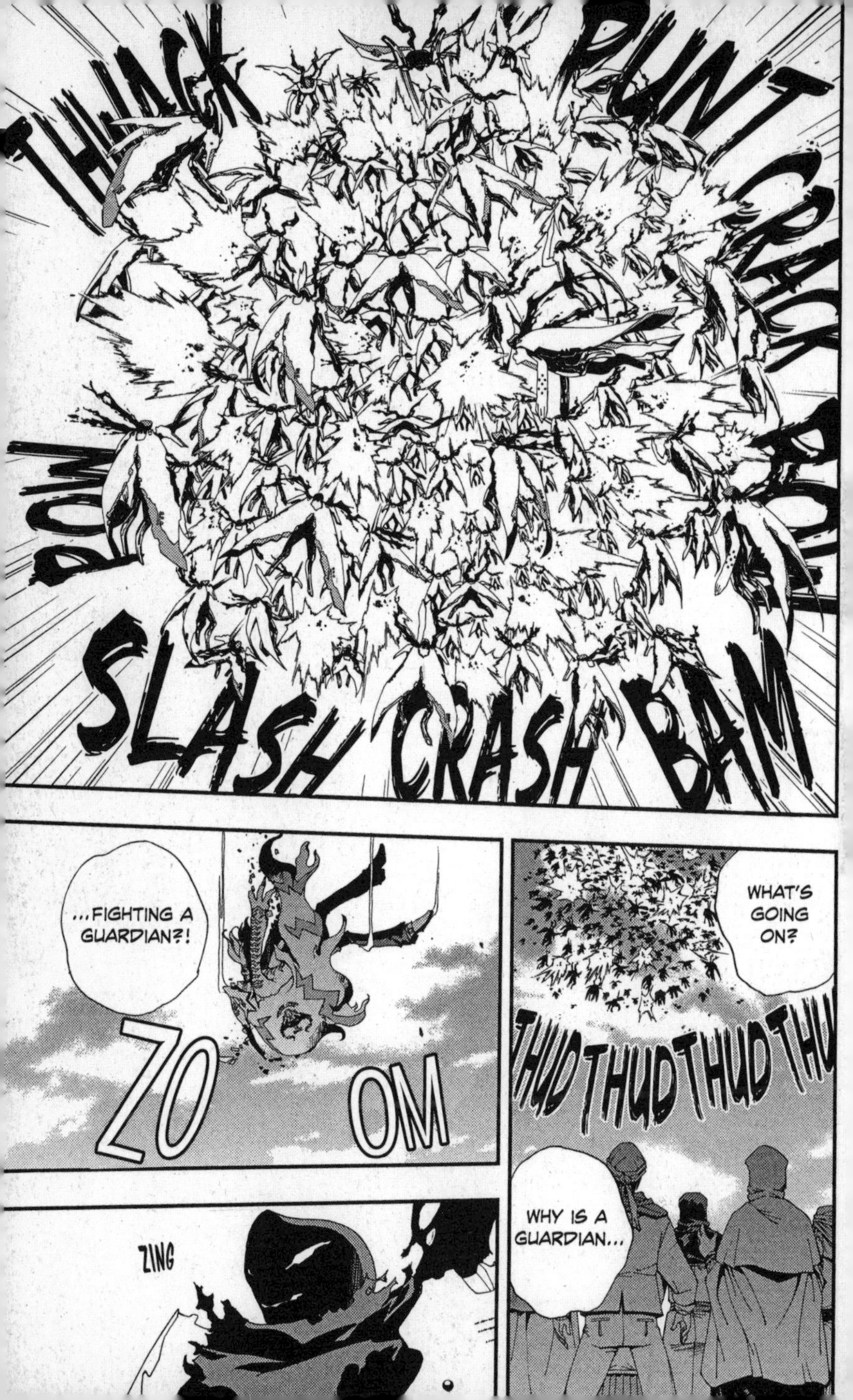
THWACK
PUNT
CRACK
SLASH
CRASH
BAM
WHAT'S GOING ON?
THUD THUD THU
...FIGHTING A GUARDIAN?!
ZOOM
WHY IS A GUARDIAN...
ZING

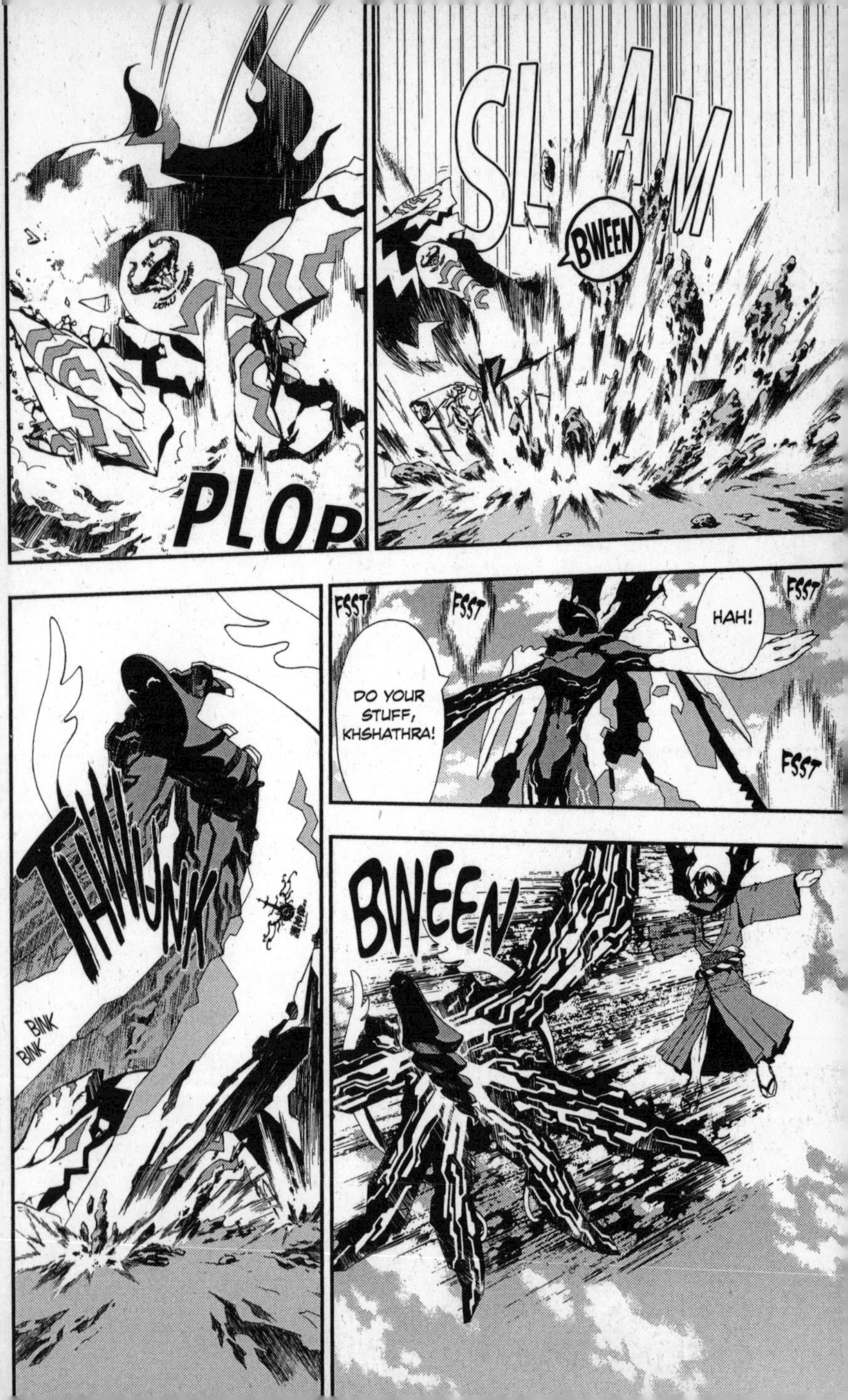
SLAM
BWEEN
PLOP
FSST
HAH!
FSST
FSST
DO YOUR STUFF, KHSHATHRA!
FSST
BWEEN
THWUNK
BINK BINK

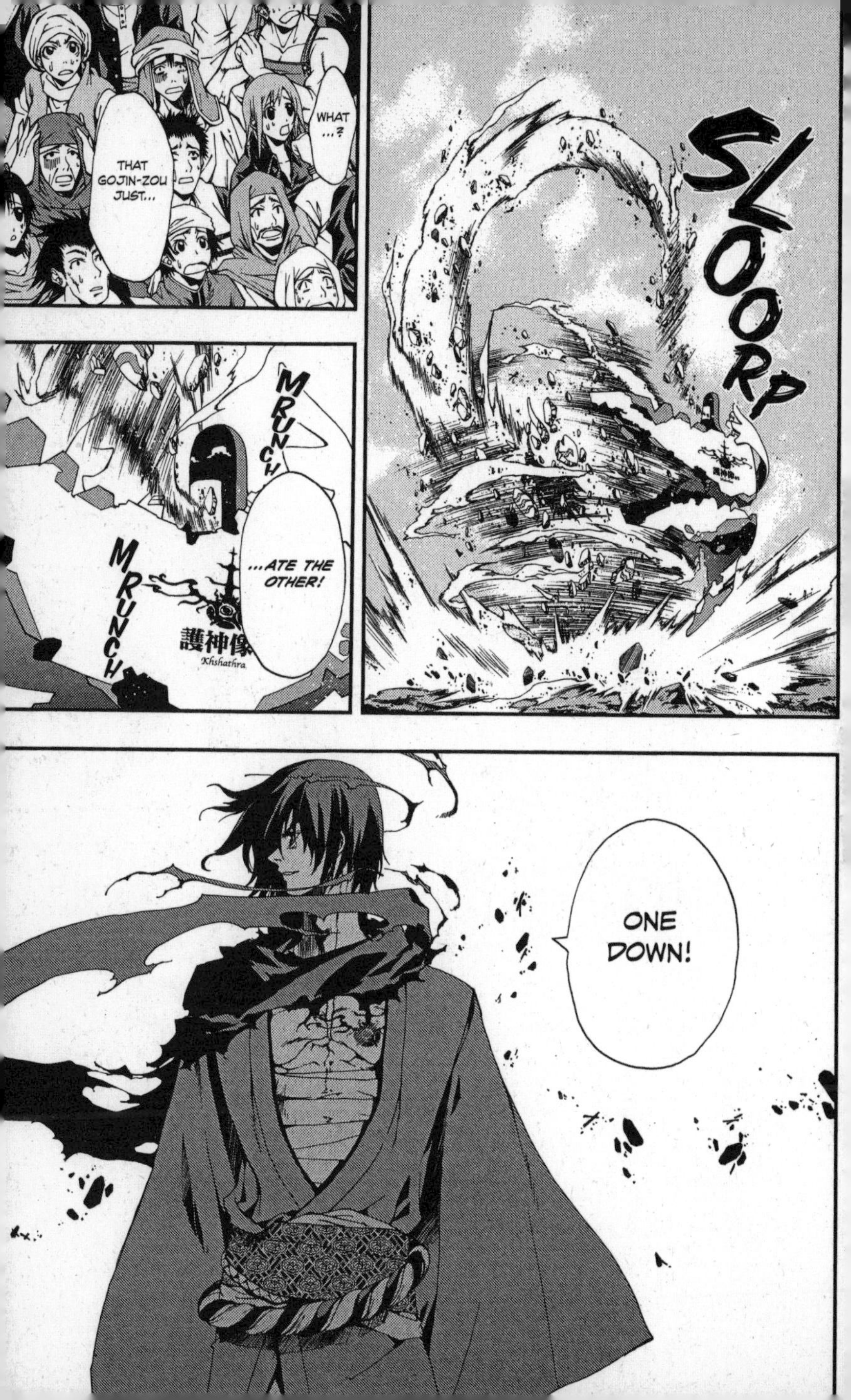
SLOORP
WHAT ...?
THAT GOJIN-ZOU JUST...
MRUNCH
...ATE THE OTHER!
MRUNCH
護神像
Khshathra
ONE DOWN!

Wāq Wāq

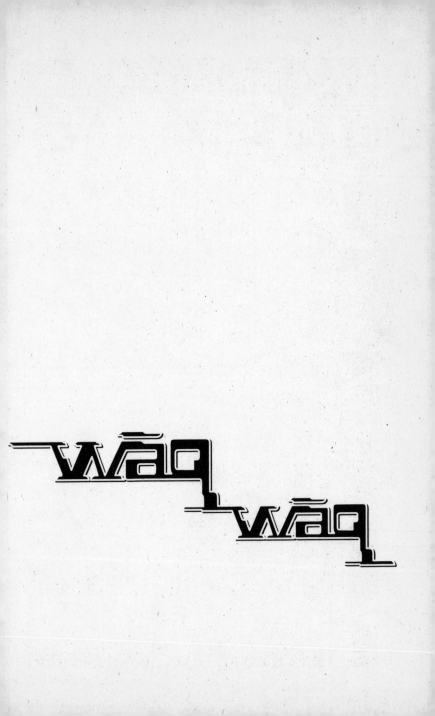

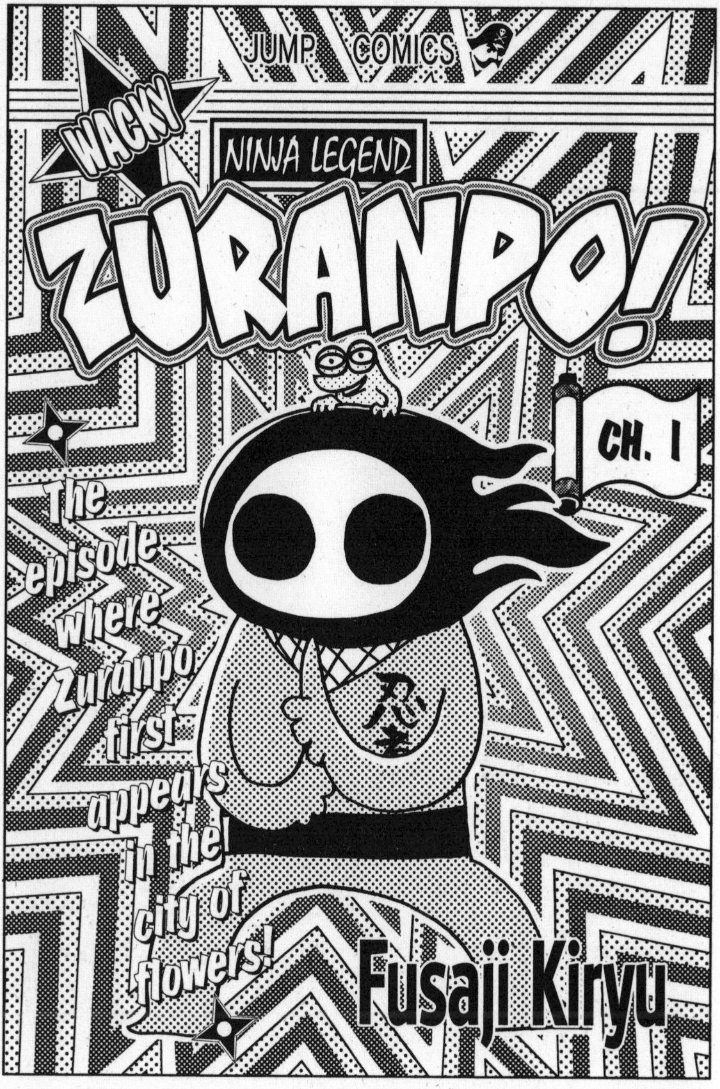
JUMP COMICS
WACKY
NINJA LEGEND
ZURANPO!
CH. 1
The episode where Zuranpo first appears in the city of flowers!
Fusaji Kiryu

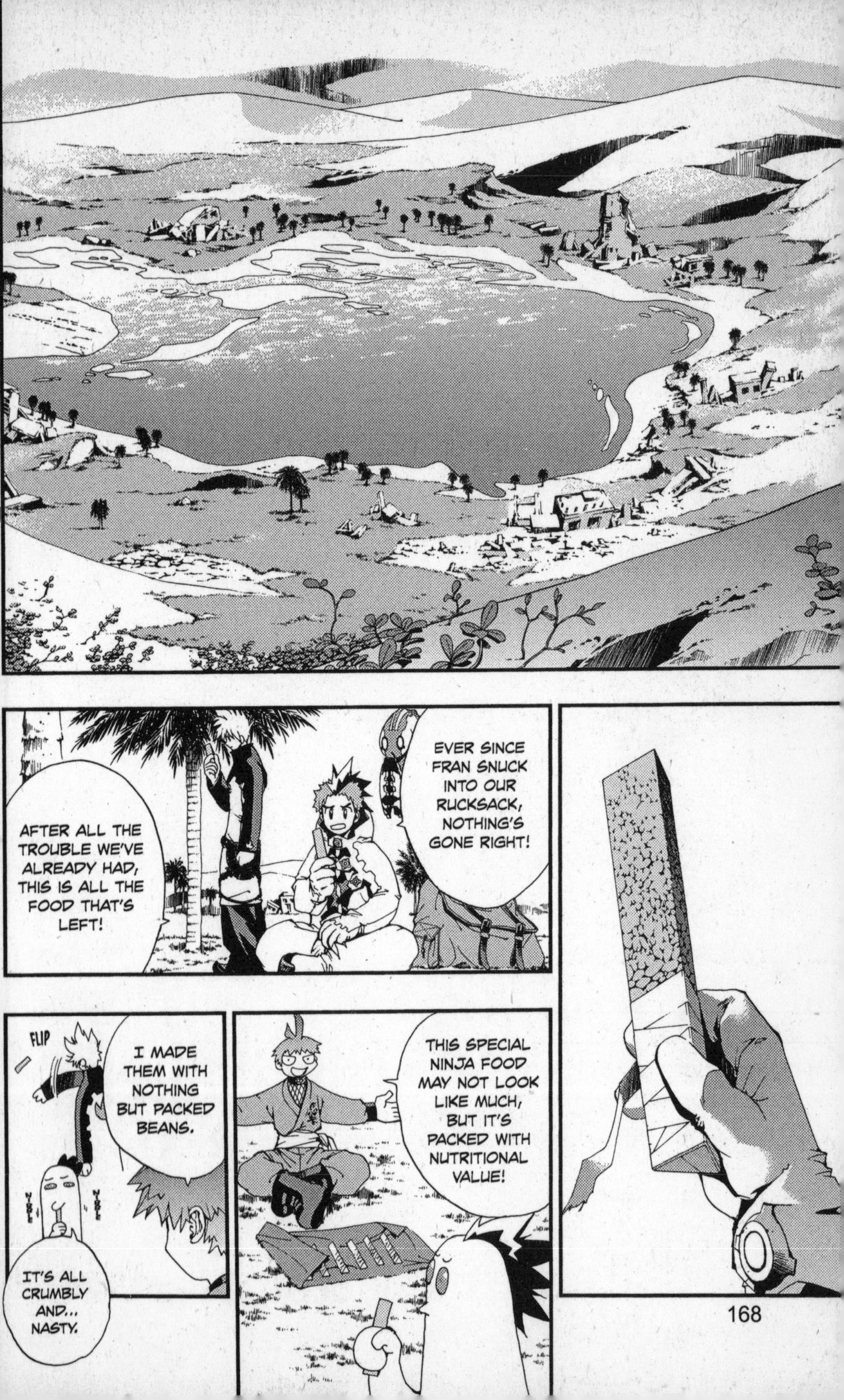
EVER SINCE FRAN SNUCK INTO OUR RUCKSACK, NOTHING'S GONE RIGHT!
AFTER ALL THE TROUBLE WE'VE ALREADY HAD, THIS IS ALL THE FOOD THAT'S LEFT!
THIS SPECIAL NINJA FOOD MAY NOT LOOK LIKE MUCH, BUT IT'S PACKED WITH NUTRITIONAL VALUE!
I MADE THEM WITH NOTHING BUT PACKED BEANS.
FLIP
NIBBLE NIBBLE
IT'S ALL CRUMBLY AND... NASTY.

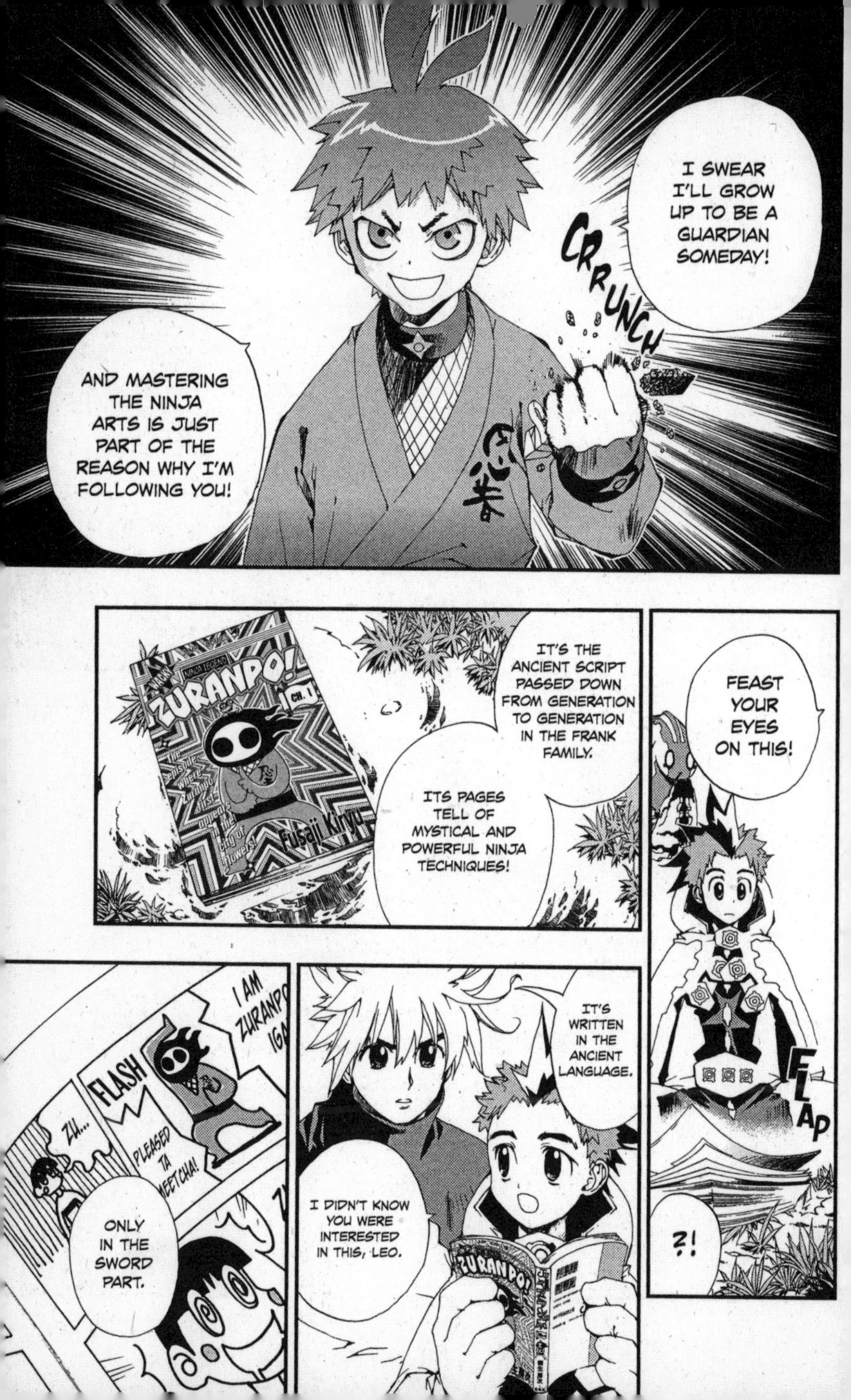
I SWEAR I'LL GROW UP TO BE A GUARDIAN SOMEDAY!
CRRUNCH
AND MASTERING THE NINJA ARTS IS JUST PART OF THE REASON WHY I'M FOLLOWING YOU!
FEAST YOUR EYES ON THIS!
FLAP
?!
IT'S THE ANCIENT SCRIPT PASSED DOWN FROM GENERATION TO GENERATION IN THE FRANK FAMILY.
ITS PAGES TELL OF MYSTICAL AND POWERFUL NINJA TECHNIQUES!
ZURANPO!
CH. 1
Fusaji Kiryu
IT'S WRITTEN IN THE ANCIENT LANGUAGE.
I DIDN'T KNOW YOU WERE INTERESTED IN THIS, LEO.
ZURANPO!
I AM ZURANPO
FLASH
ZU...
PLEASED TA MEETCHA!
ONLY IN THE SWORD PART.

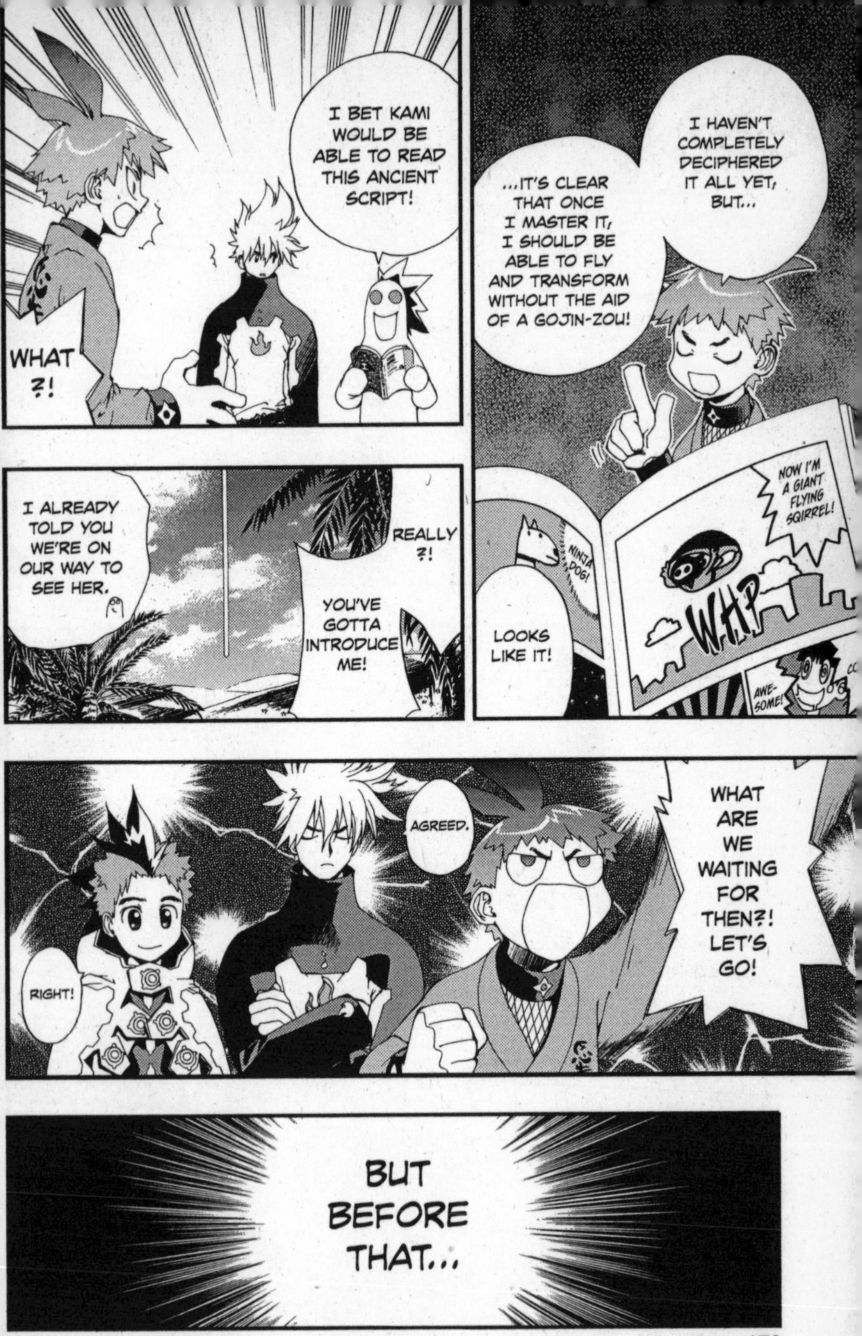
I HAVEN'T COMPLETELY DECIPHERED IT ALL YET, BUT...
...IT'S CLEAR THAT ONCE I MASTER IT, I SHOULD BE ABLE TO FLY AND TRANSFORM WITHOUT THE AID OF A GOJIN-ZOU!
NOW I'M A GIANT FLYING SQUIRREL!
NINJA DOG!
WHP
AWE-SOME!
LOOKS LIKE IT!
I BET KAMI WOULD BE ABLE TO READ THIS ANCIENT SCRIPT!
WHAT?!
REALLY?!
YOU'VE GOTTA INTRODUCE ME!
I ALREADY TOLD YOU WE'RE ON OUR WAY TO SEE HER.
WHAT ARE WE WAITING FOR THEN?! LET'S GO!
AGREED.
RIGHT!
BUT BEFORE THAT...

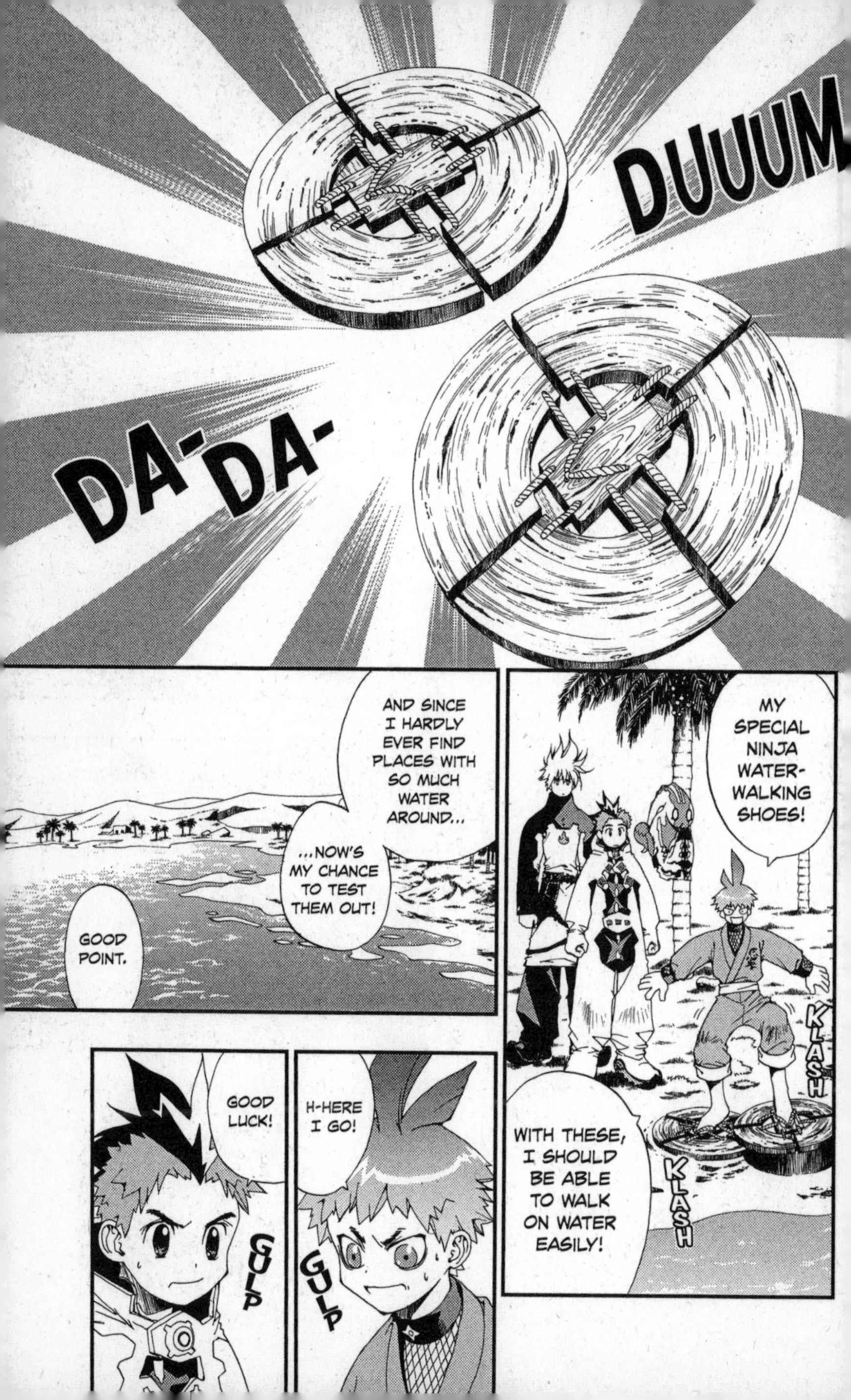
DUUUM
DA-DA-
MY SPECIAL NINJA WATER-WALKING SHOES!
KLASH
KLASH
WITH THESE, I SHOULD BE ABLE TO WALK ON WATER EASILY!
AND SINCE I HARDLY EVER FIND PLACES WITH SO MUCH WATER AROUND...
...NOW'S MY CHANCE TO TEST THEM OUT!
GOOD POINT.
H-HERE I GO!
GULP
GOOD LUCK!
GULP

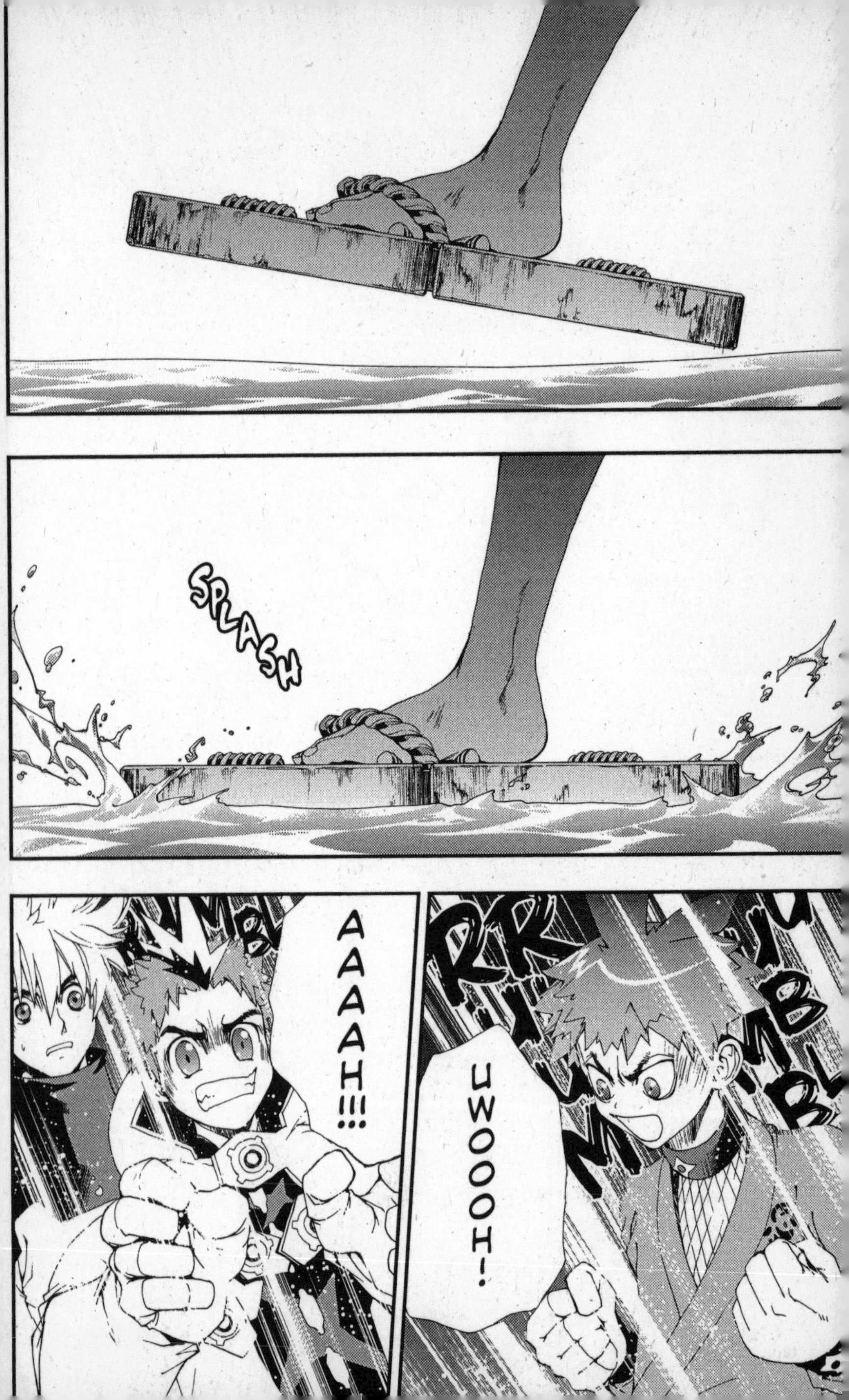
SPLASH
UWOOOOH!
AAAAAH!!!

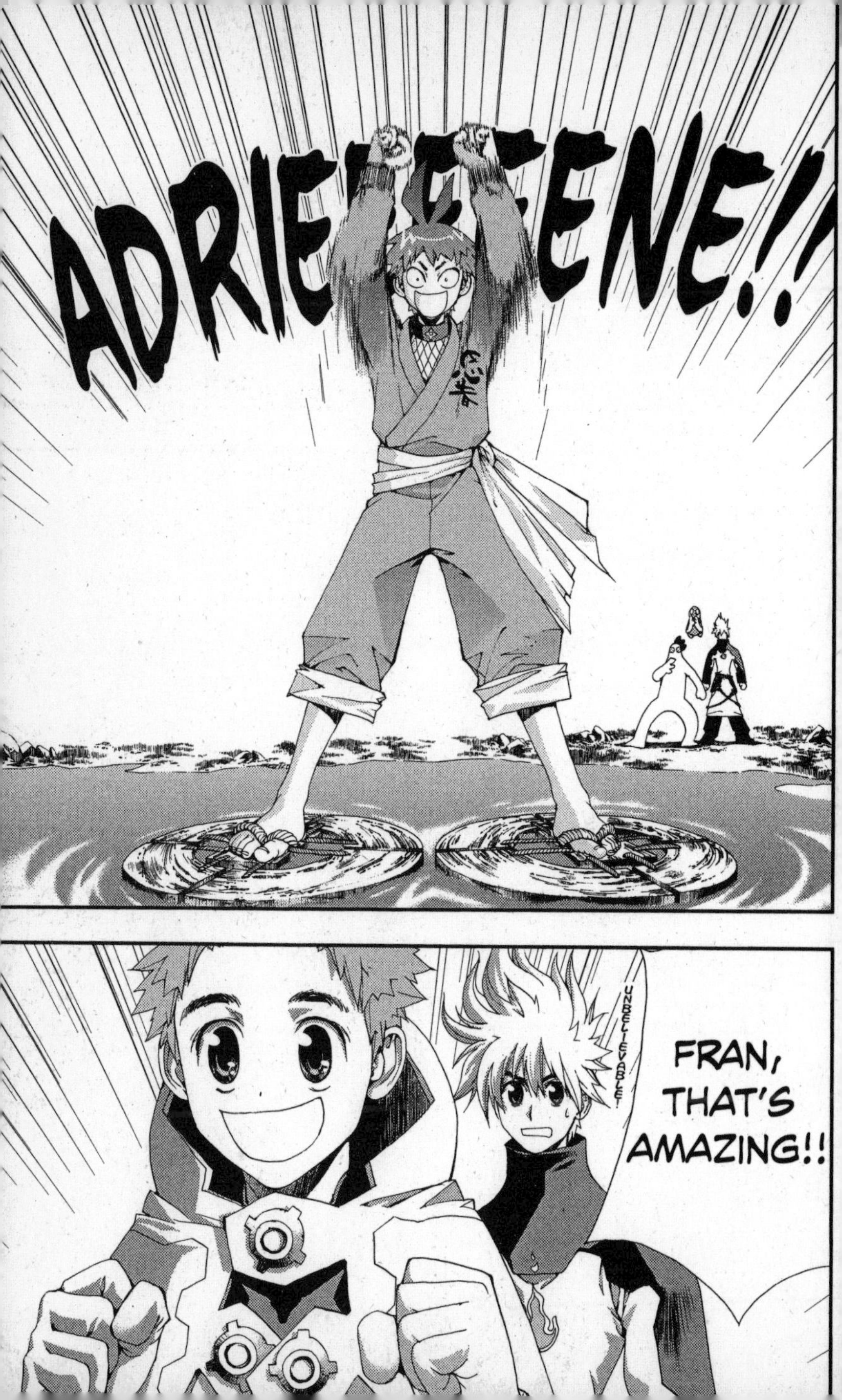
ADRIE ENE!!
FRAN, THAT'S AMAZING!!
UNBELIEVABLE!

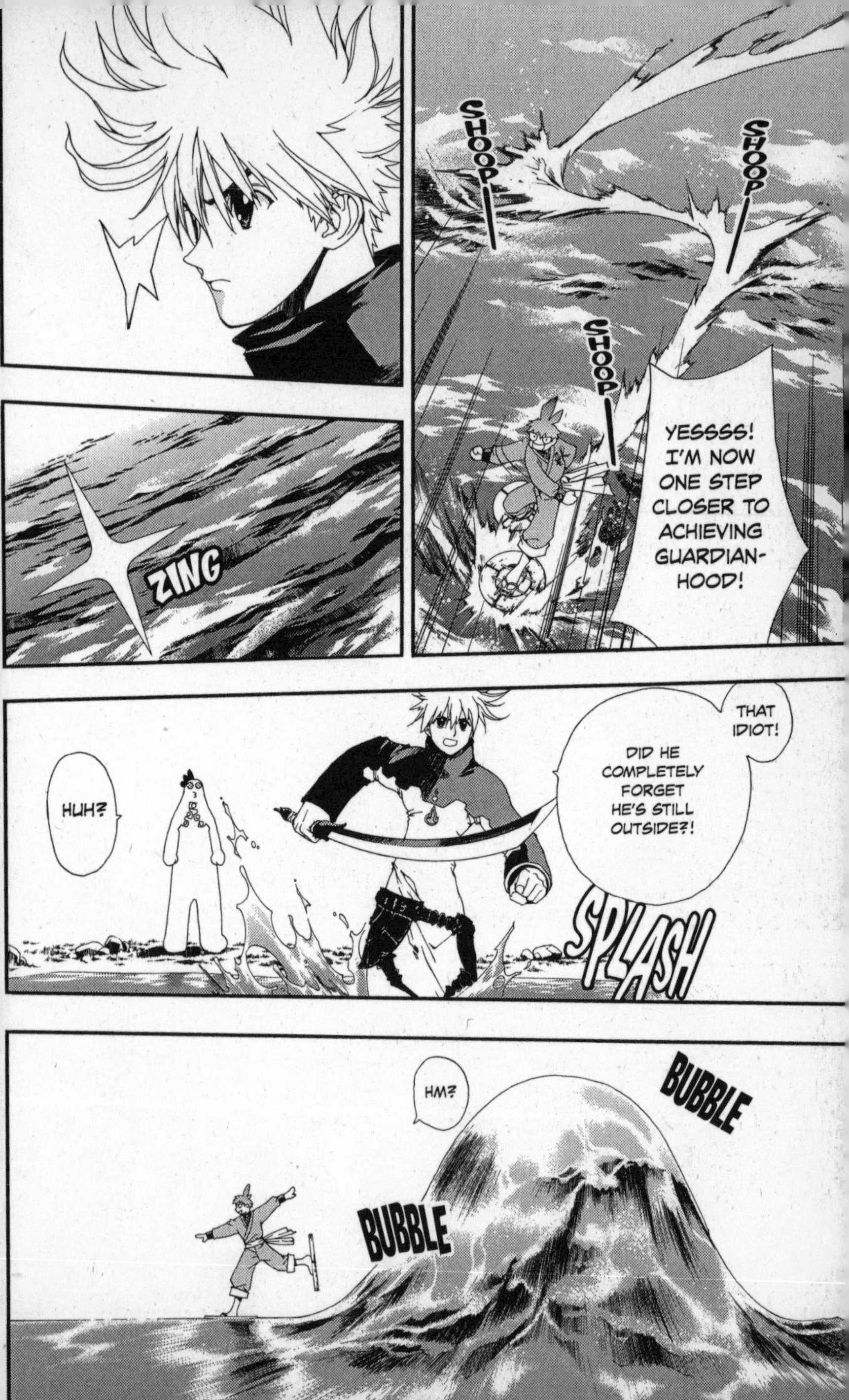
SHOOP
SHOOP
SHOOP
YESSSS! I'M NOW ONE STEP CLOSER TO ACHIEVING GUARDIAN-HOOD!
ZING
THAT IDIOT!
DID HE COMPLETELY FORGET HE'S STILL OUTSIDE?!
HUH?
SPLASH
BUBBLE
HM?
BUBBLE

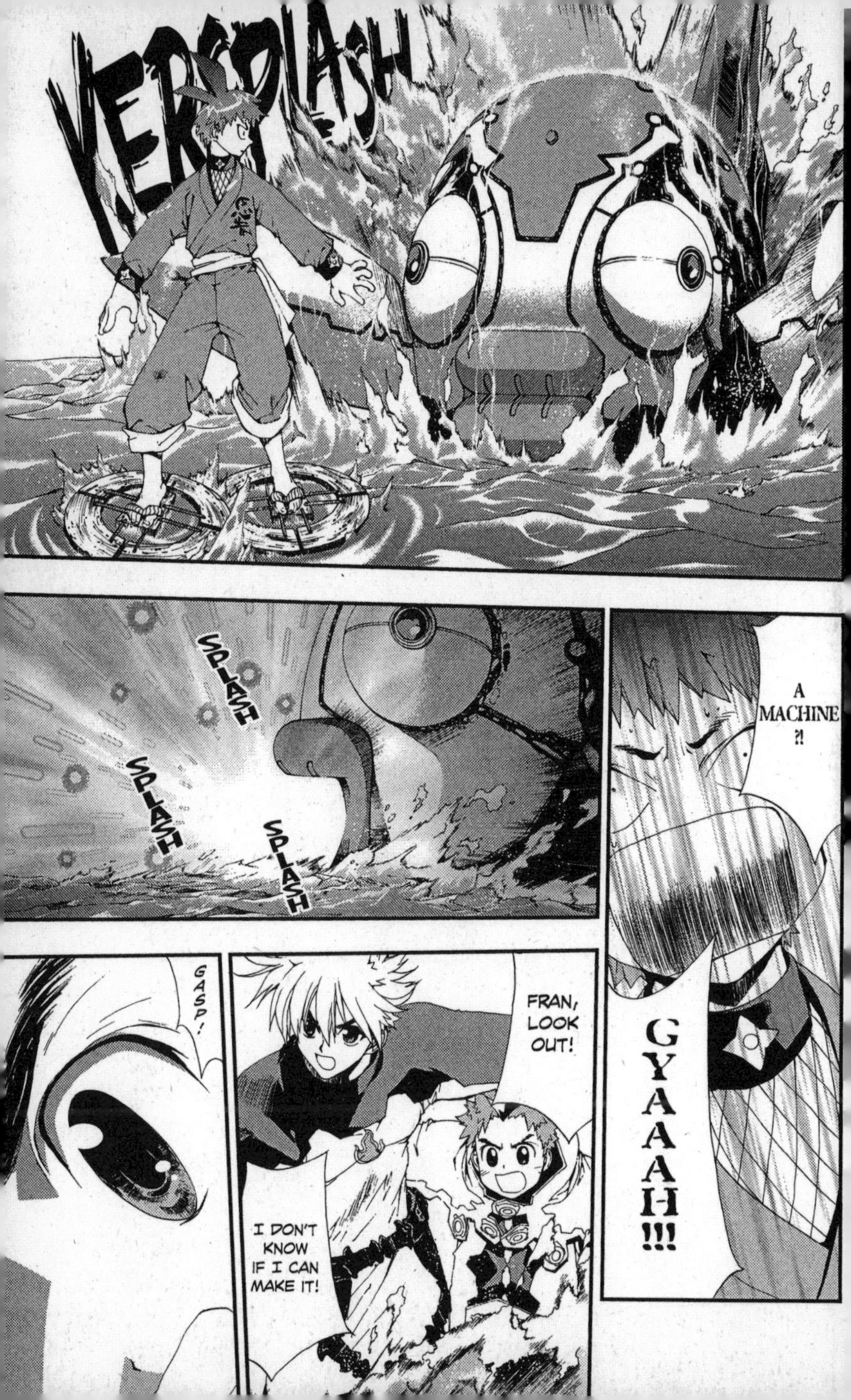
KERSPLASH
A MACHINE ?!
SPLASH
SPLASH
SPLASH
GYAAAAH!!!
FRAN, LOOK OUT!
I DON'T KNOW IF I CAN MAKE IT!
GASP!

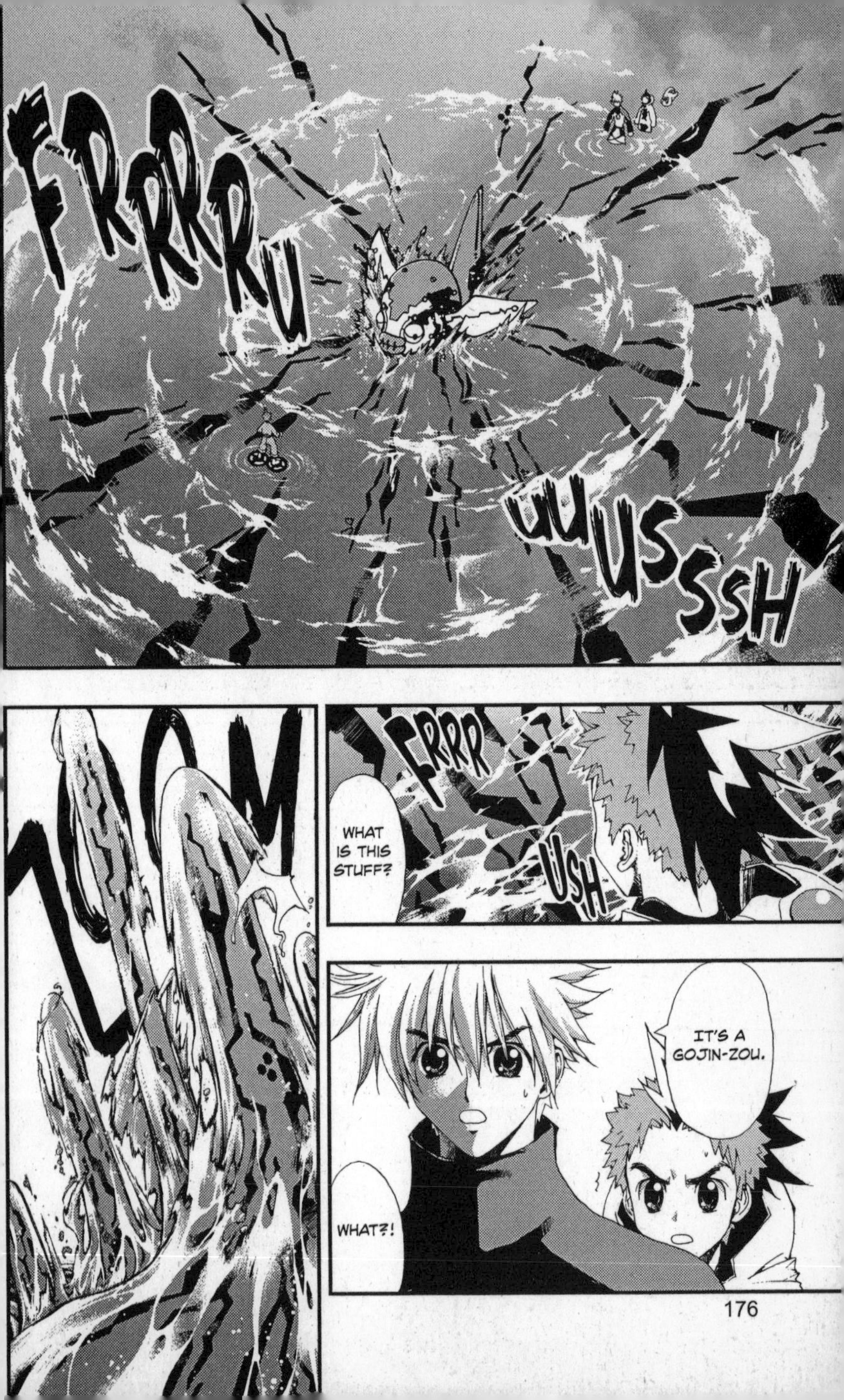
FRRRRU
UUUSSSH
FRRR
WHAT IS THIS STUFF?
USH
IT'S A GOJIN-ZOU.
WHAT?!
ZOOM

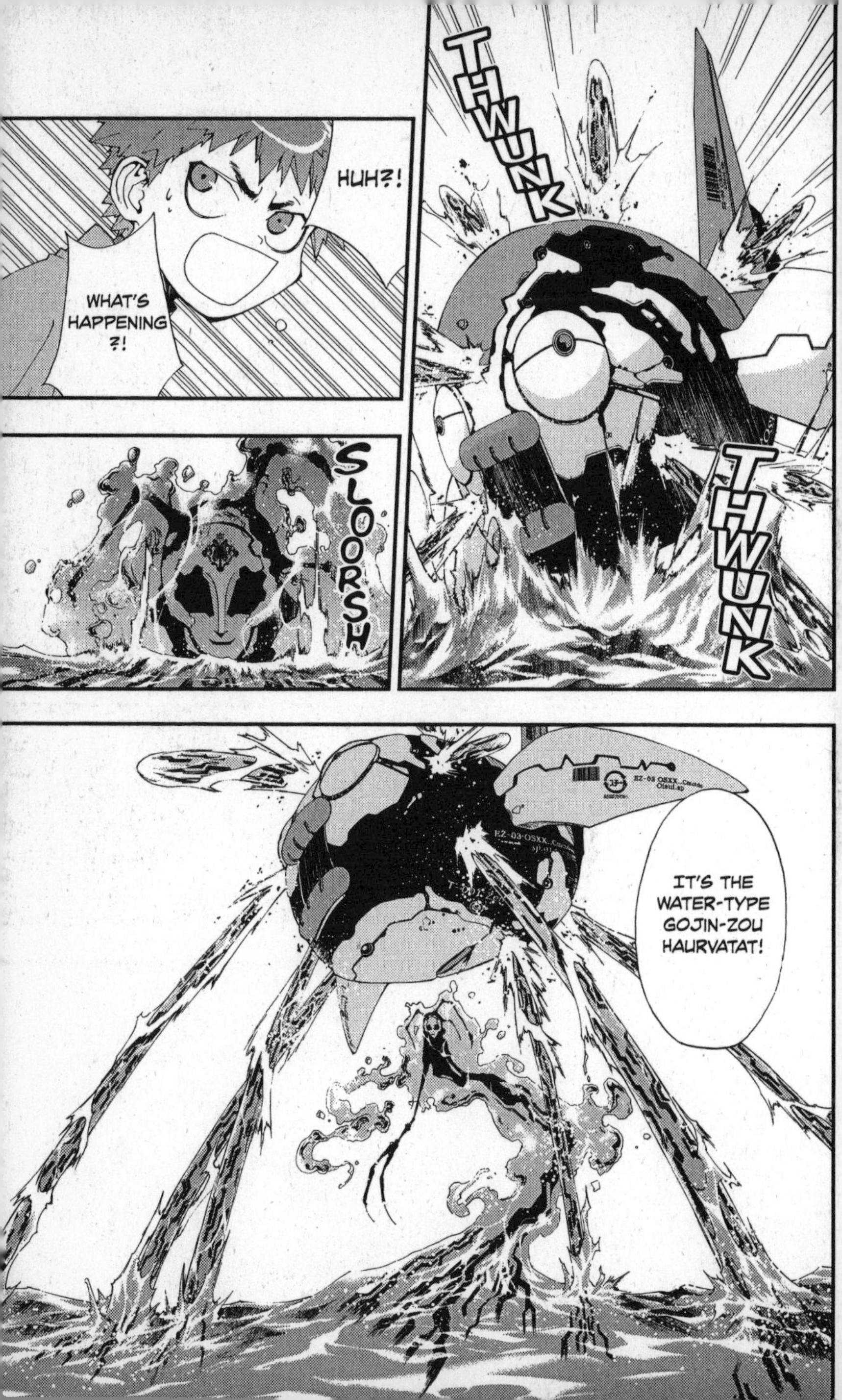
THWUNK
THWUNK
HUH?!
WHAT'S HAPPENING?!
SLOORSH
IT'S THE WATER-TYPE GOJIN-ZOU HAURVATAT!

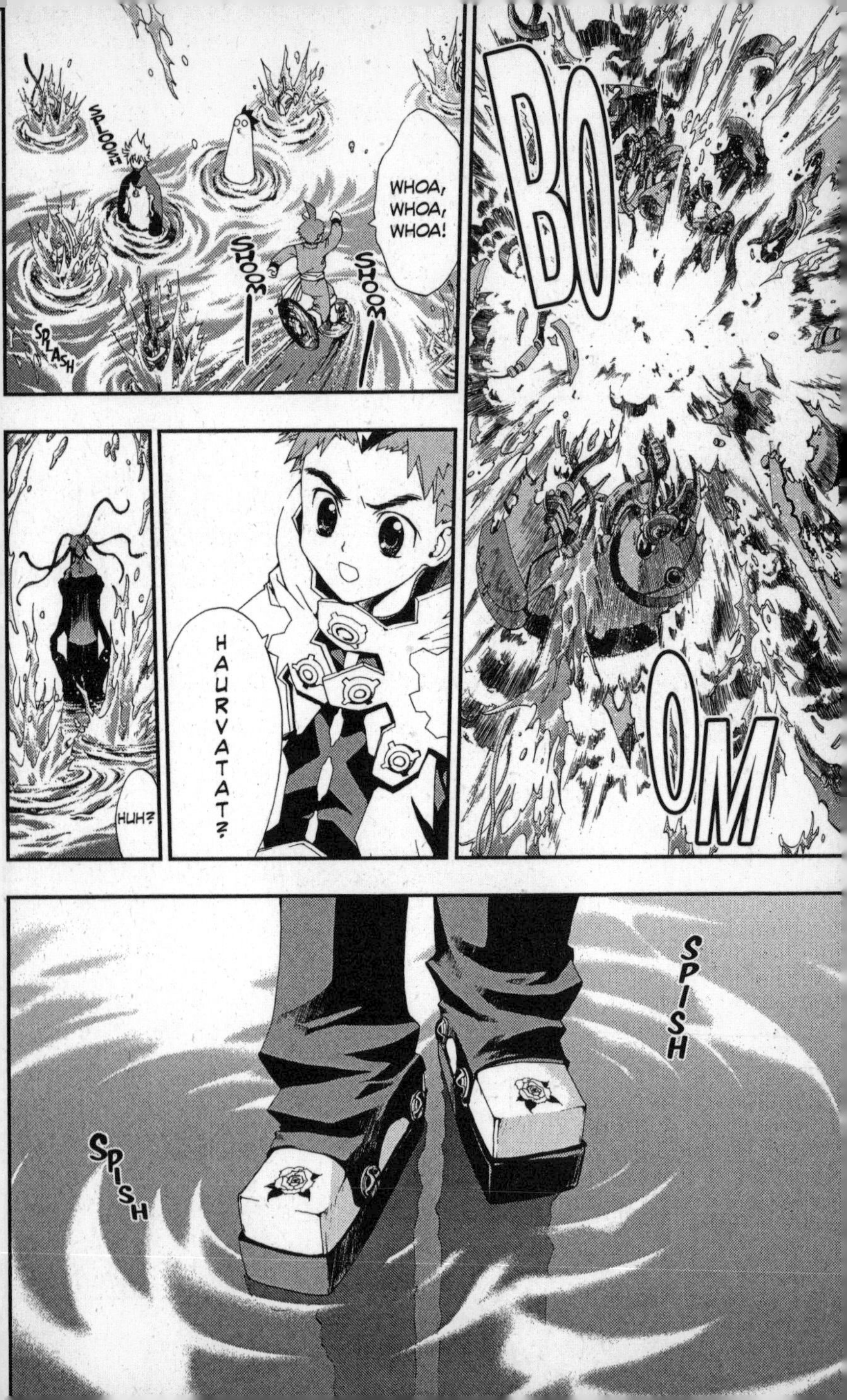
BOOM
WHOA, WHOA, WHOA!
SHOOM
SHOOM
SPLOOSH
SPLASH
HAURVATATZ?
HUH?
SPISH
SPISH

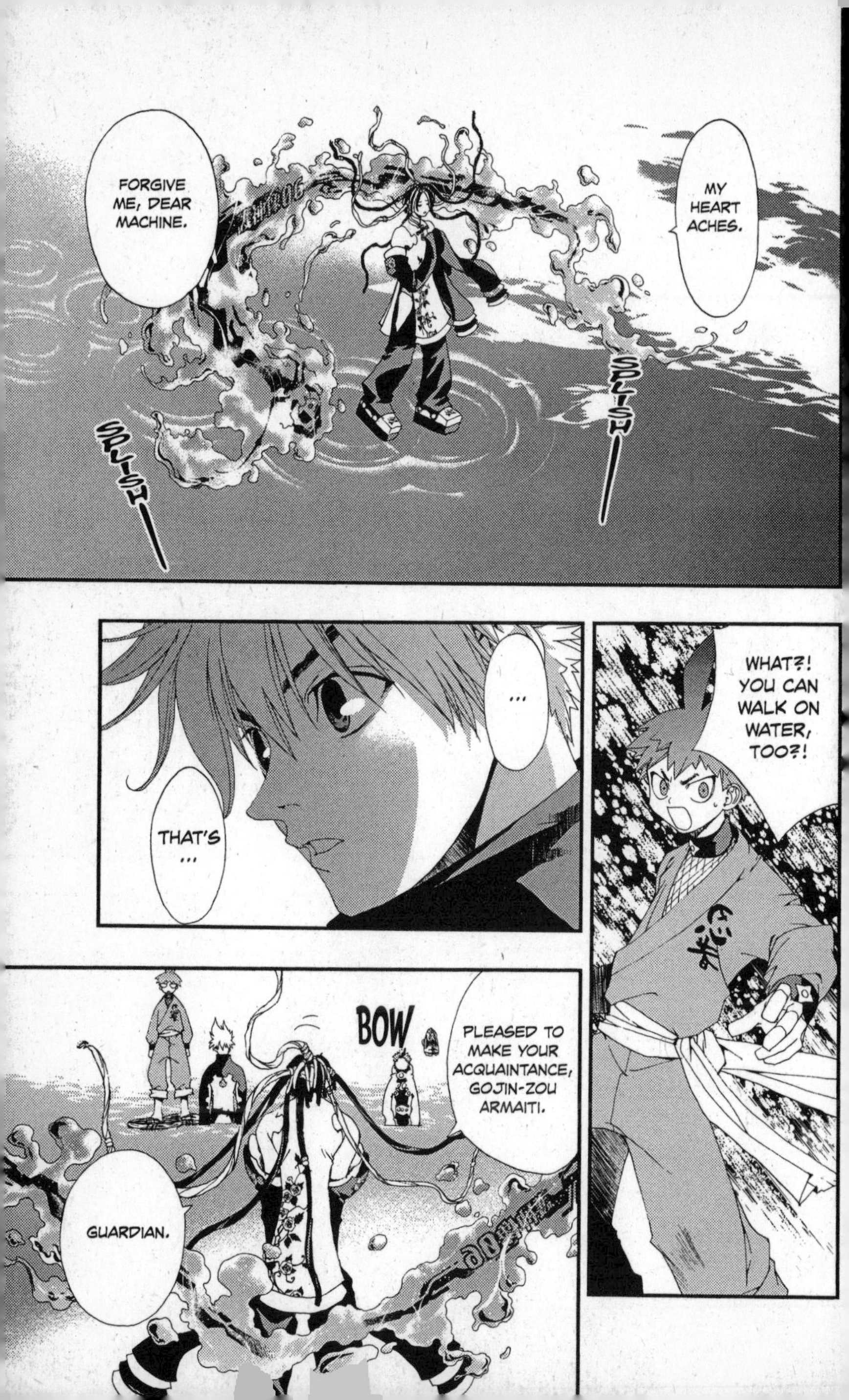
MY HEART ACHES.
SPLISH
FORGIVE ME, DEAR MACHINE.
SPLISH
WHAT?! YOU CAN WALK ON WATER, TOO?!
...
THAT'S ...
PLEASED TO MAKE YOUR ACQUAINTANCE, GOJIN-ZOU ARMAITI.
BOW
GUARDIAN.

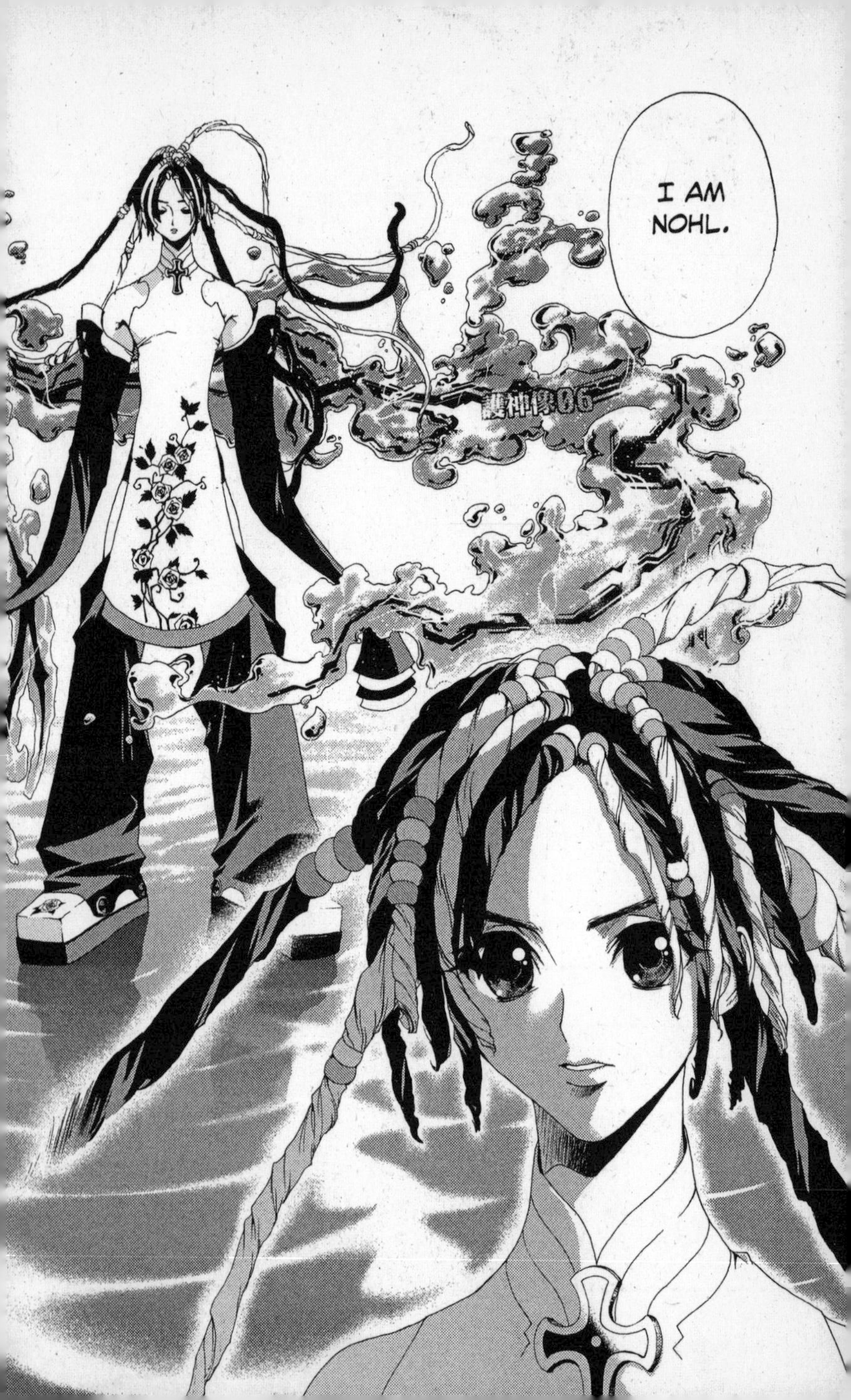
I AM NOHL.
護神像06

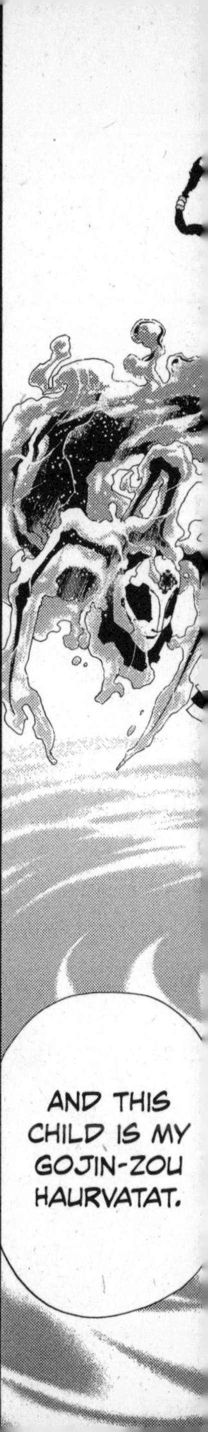
AND THIS CHILD IS MY GOJIN-ZOU HAURVATAT.

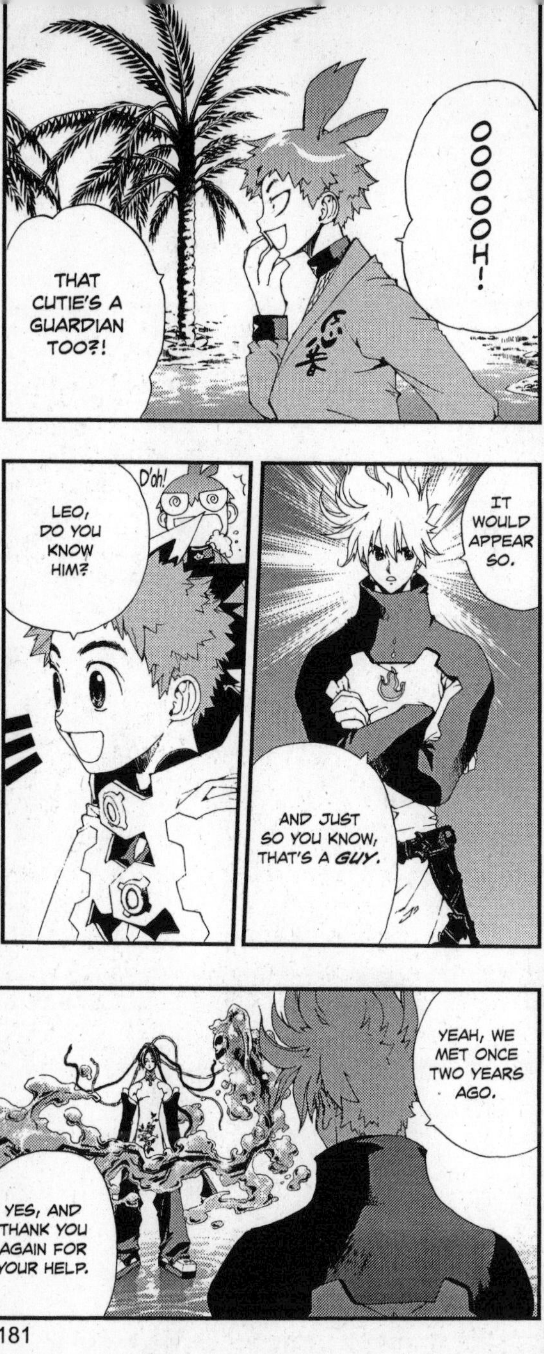
OOOOOOH!
THAT CUTIE'S A GUARDIAN TOO?!
IT WOULD APPEAR SO.
AND JUST SO YOU KNOW, THAT'S A *GUY*.
D'oh!
LEO, DO YOU KNOW HIM?
YEAH, WE MET ONCE TWO YEARS AGO.
YES, AND THANK YOU AGAIN FOR YOUR HELP.

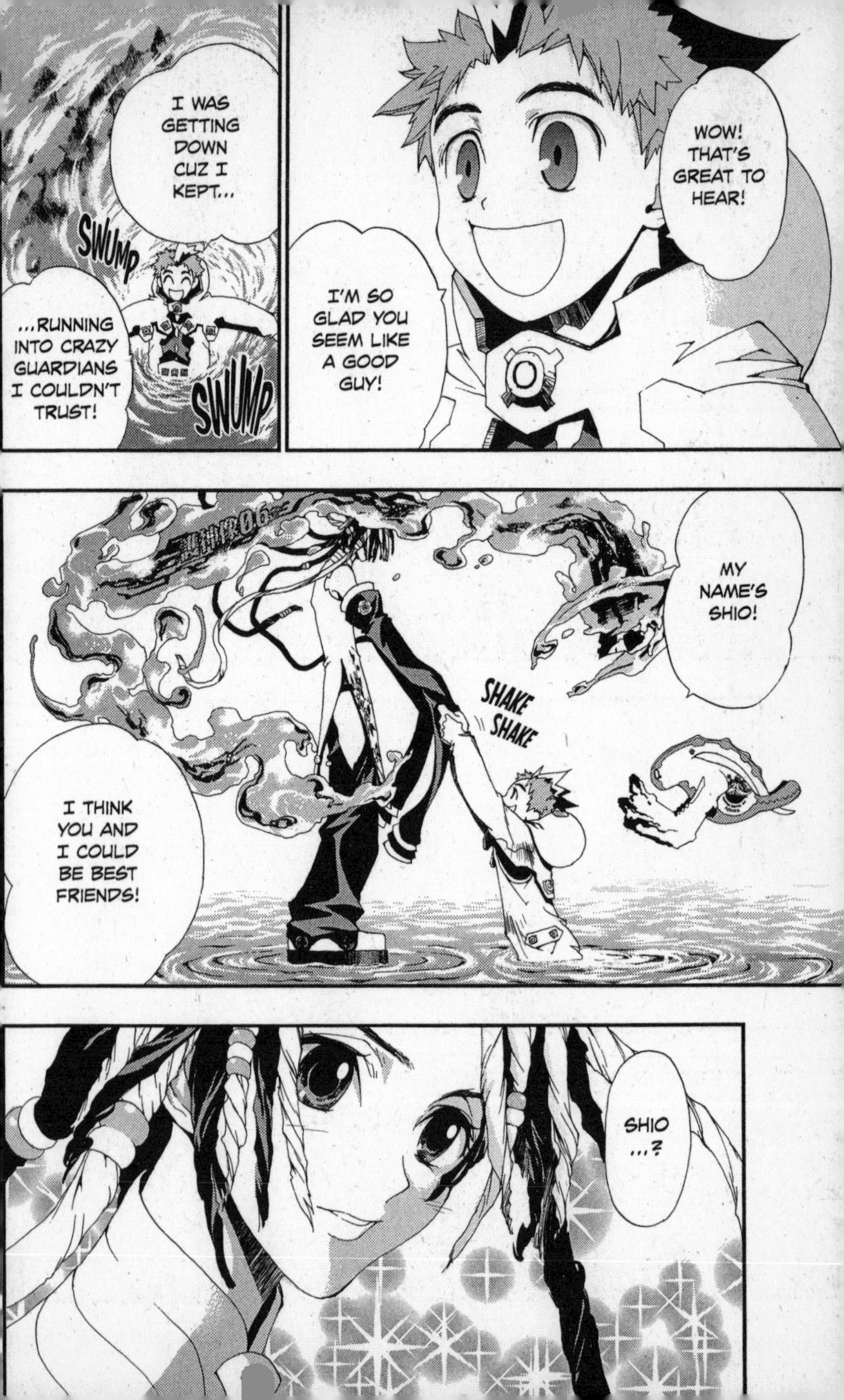
WOW! THAT'S GREAT TO HEAR!
I'M SO GLAD YOU SEEM LIKE A GOOD GUY!
I WAS GETTING DOWN CUZ I KEPT...
SWUMP
...RUNNING INTO CRAZY GUARDIANS I COULDN'T TRUST!
SWUMP
MY NAME'S SHIO!
SHAKE SHAKE
I THINK YOU AND I COULD BE BEST FRIENDS!
SHIO ...?

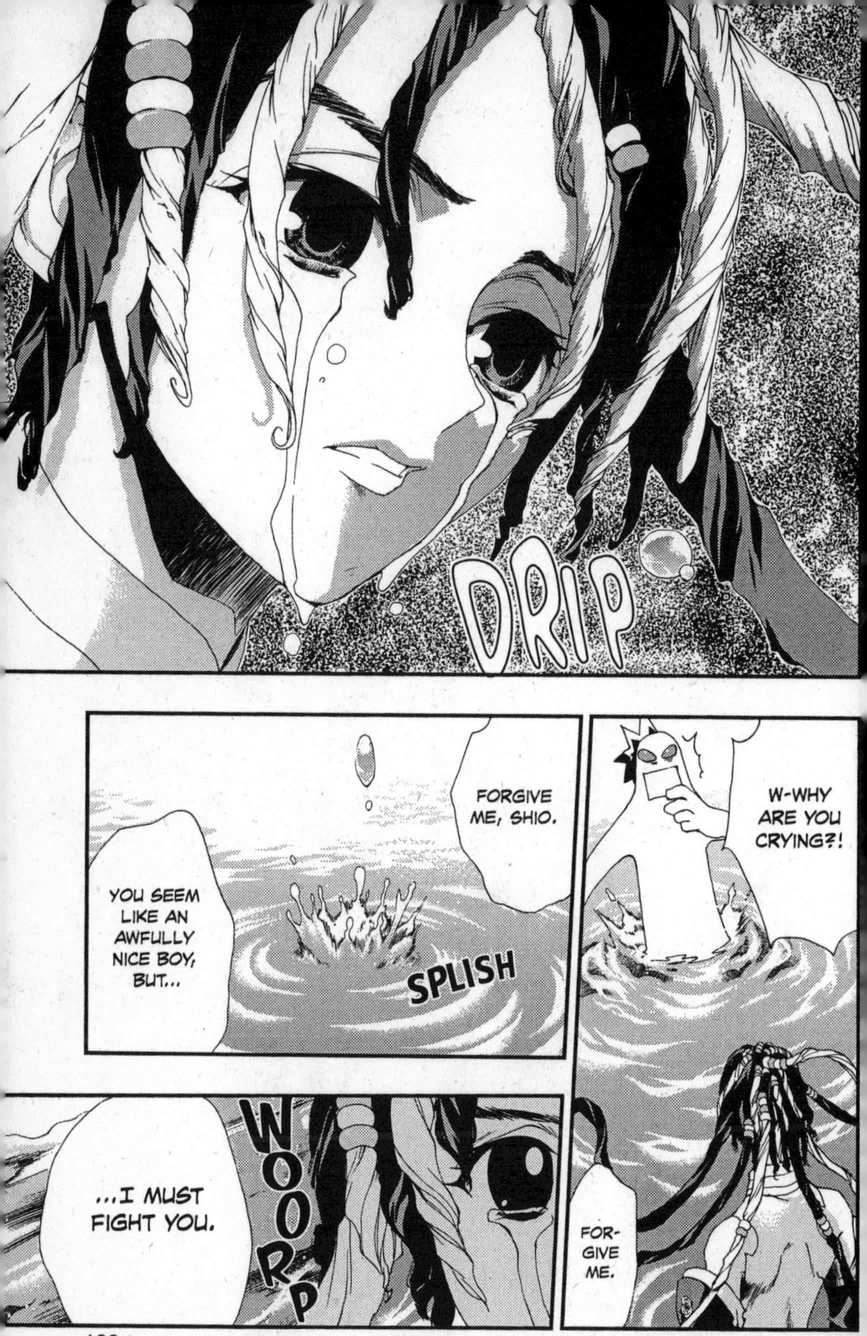
DRIP
W-WHY ARE YOU CRYING?!
FOR-GIVE ME.
FORGIVE ME, SHIO.
YOU SEEM LIKE AN AWFULLY NICE BOY, BUT...
SPLISH
WOORP
...I MUST FIGHT YOU.

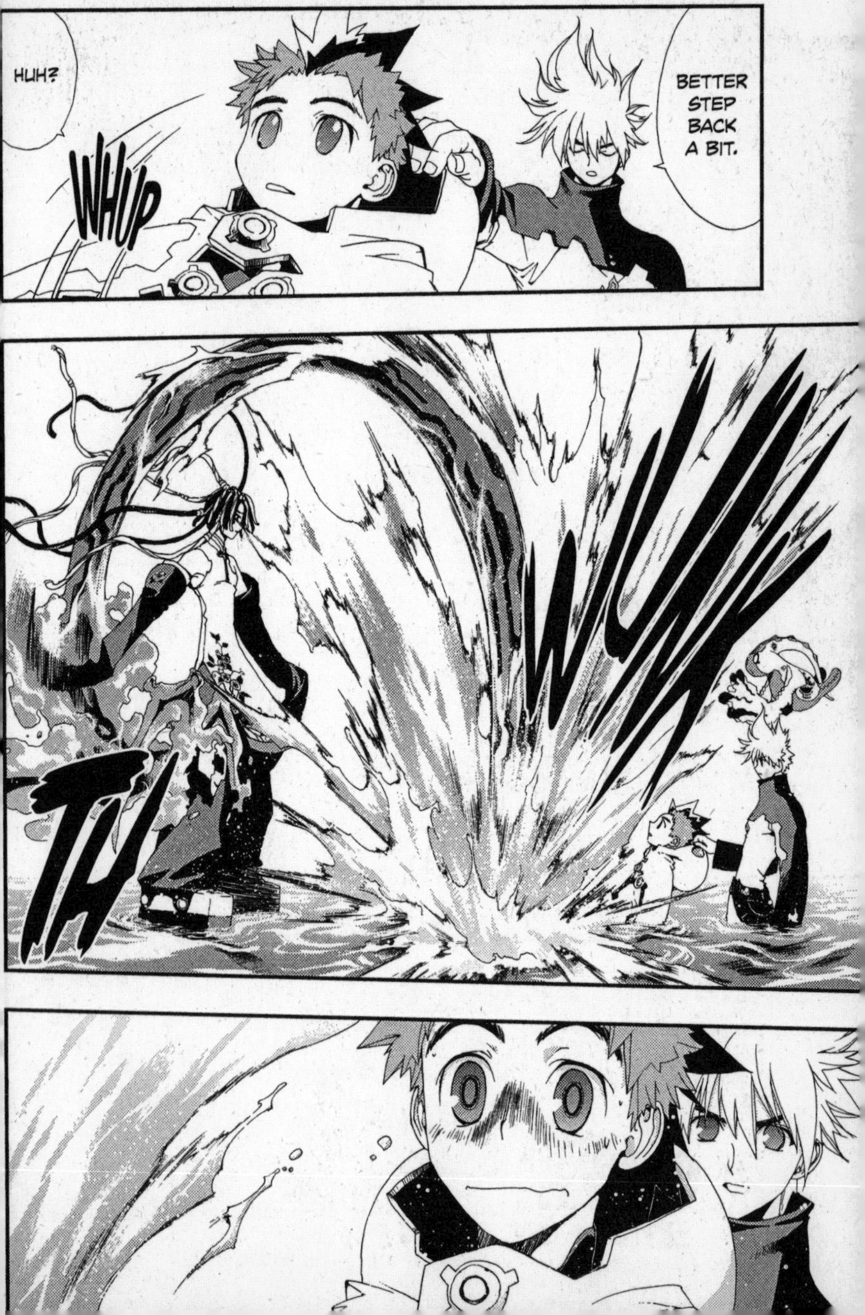
BETTER STEP BACK A BIT.
HUH?
WHUP
TH

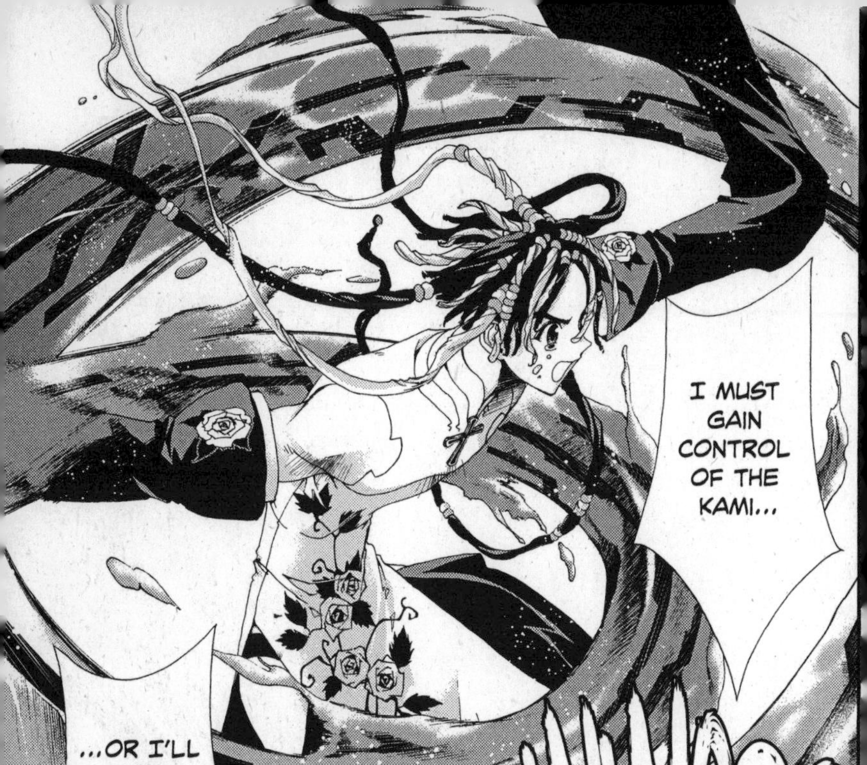
I MUST GAIN CONTROL OF THE KAMI...
...OR I'LL LOSE THE ONE MOST PRECIOUS TO ME!
ZWWORP

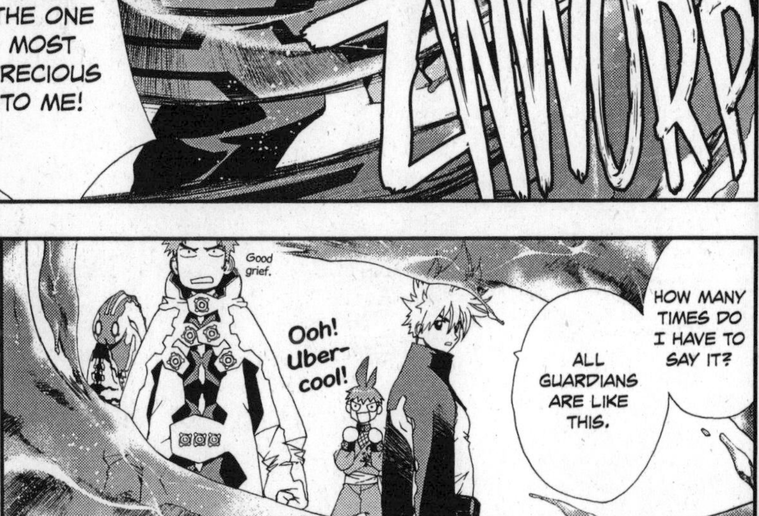
HOW MANY TIMES DO I HAVE TO SAY IT?
ALL GUARDIANS ARE LIKE THIS.
Ooh! Uber-cool!
Good grief.

Coming Next Volume

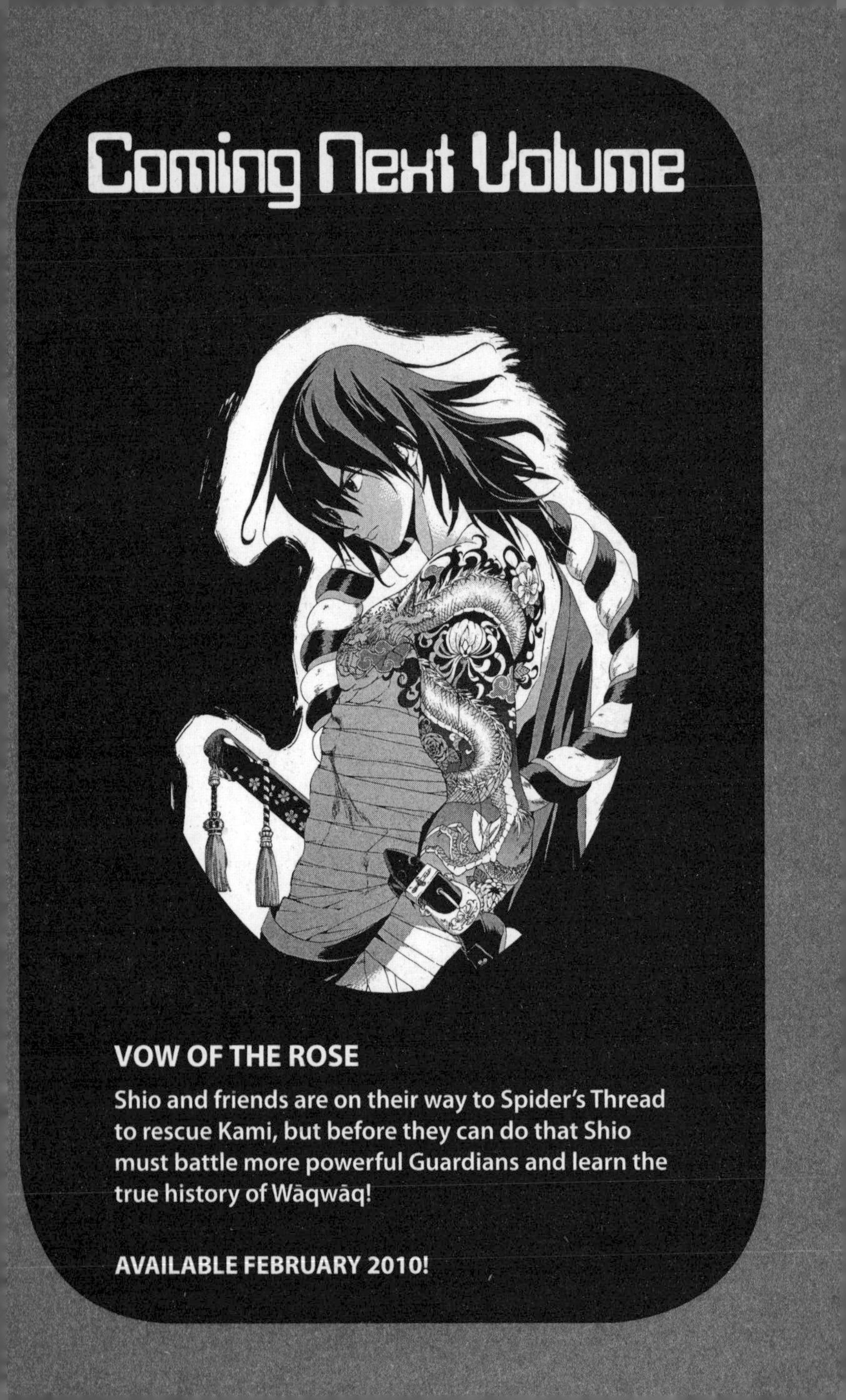

VOW OF THE ROSE

Shio and friends are on their way to Spider's Thread to rescue Kami, but before they can do that Shio must battle more powerful Guardians and learn the true history of Wāqwāq!

AVAILABLE FEBRUARY 2010!

VIZ MEDIA

ANIME ON hulu

Watch Your Favorites. Anytime. For Free.

www.hulu.com

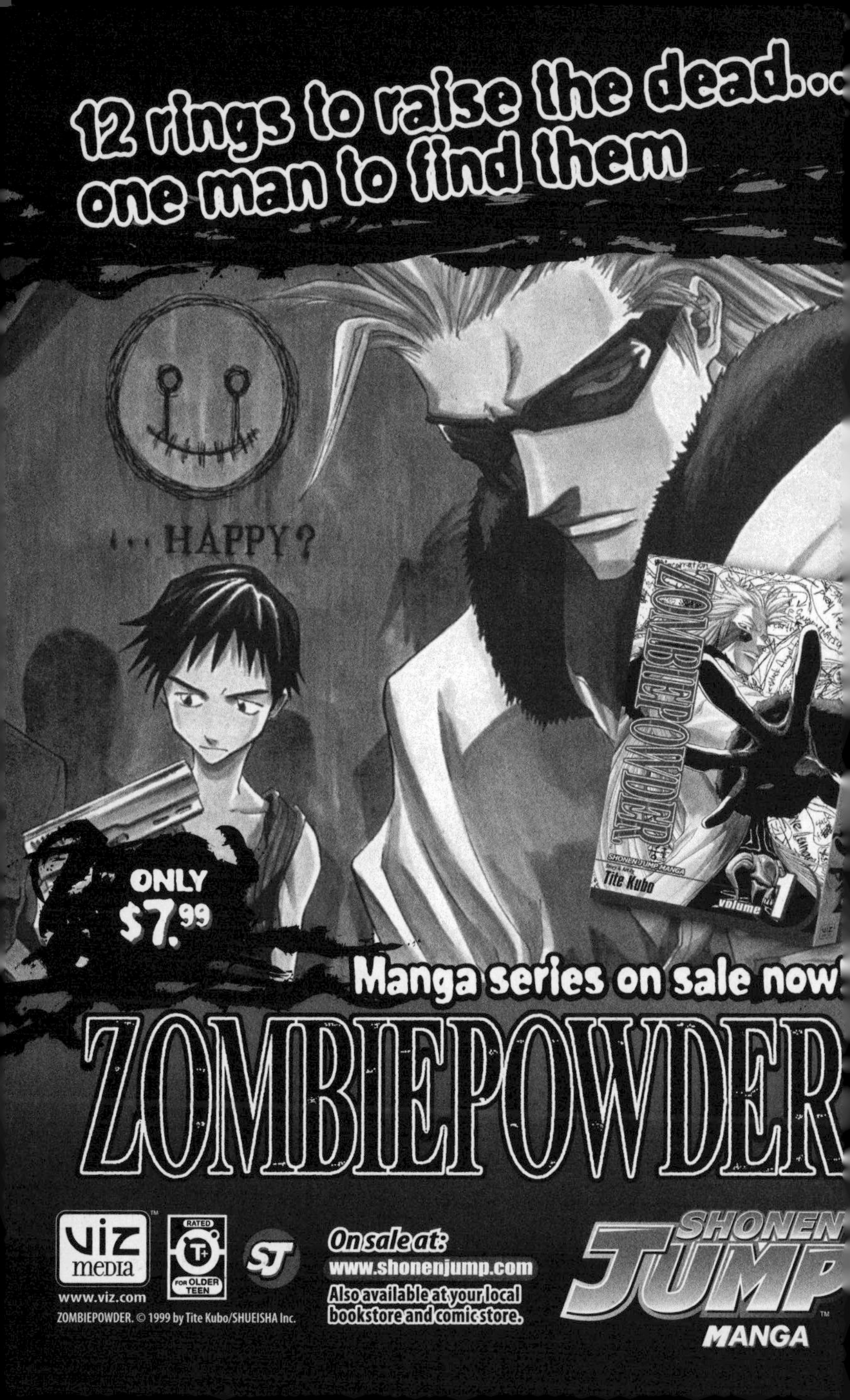

12 rings to raise the dead...
one man to find them
...HAPPY?
ZOMBIEPOWDER
SHONEN JUMP MANGA
Tite Kubo
volume 1
ONLY $7.99
Manga series on sale now!
ZOMBIEPOWDER
viz media
www.viz.com
RATED T+ FOR OLDER TEEN
SJ
On sale at:
www.shonenjump.com
Also available at your local bookstore and comic store.
SHONEN JUMP MANGA
ZOMBIEPOWDER. © 1999 by Tite Kubo/SHUEISHA Inc.